Served in HM Forces for 22 years as pharmacy technician and medical supply officer. Served in Hong Kong, Singapore, Malaysia, Nepal, Cyprus, Germany, London, Aldershot, Southampton. Retired as warrant officer in 1986. Married to Mo for 50 years and has two sons, Jason and Justin. Travelled worldwide with Mo. Lives in Stourbridge, West Midlands. Widowed in 2016. Main employment after leaving the RAMC was as transport manager for a paper recycling company. Retired from work in 2012. Plays golf (badly) and bridge. Currently does voluntary work at a Covid vaccination centre.

Dedicated to lovely wife Mo during our 50-year marriage and who accompanied me for 20 years in our travels around the world with the army, never complaining about yet another posting to foreign climes.

To our two fine sons, Dr Jason Mansell and Justin Mansell, who reminded me when my memory was somewhat vague.

To our daughters-in-law, Dr Lynne Armstrong and Kate Mansell.

To our four grandchildren: Oscar, Stella, Ben and Alex, all of whom joy and laughter into our lives.

Trevor Mansell

21 HOUSES

AUSTIN MACAULEY PUBLISHERS™

LONDON • CAMBRIDGE • NEW YORK • SHARJAH

A CIP catalogue record for this title is available from the British Library.

ISBN 9781035836468 (Paperback)
ISBN 9781035836475 (ePub e-book)

www.austinmacauley.com

First Published 2024
Austin Macauley Publishers Ltd®
1 Canada Square
Canary Wharf
London
E14 5AA

Grateful thanks to ex-military friends who provided me with information regarding names and dates of various people and places.

Table of Contents

Foreword

This is the story of fifty-five years of my life with the love of my life, Maureen, and the numerous places around the world in which we lived during our married life.

I was still a schoolboy of 15 at Central Grammar School in Birmingham when I met Maureen. My father had died young a year before, and I was living with my mother in College Road in Alum Rock, Birmingham.

Although Maureen (known as Mo) and I didn't know each other at the time, we had a mutual friend in Eileen Thomas. She lived in Mount Pleasant in Small Heath, the same small council estate as my cousins with whom I used to stay during school holidays as both my parents worked. As youngsters we all used to play around the streets and parks in the area. Mo lived near in Arthur Street nearby and went to school with Eileen.

Eileen's father was a man of many talents, he kept an allotment where he grew vegetables for the family table, he made fishing rods out of old tank aerials and he was an accomplished bag piper. He practiced in the bathroom and many a time led the local children around the estate while he played on the pipes.

I was 15 years old when Eileen arranged a day trip to Southend-on-Sea on a Saturday in early August and asked if I would like to go. Most of the teenagers in Mount Pleasant, including my cousin Tony, would be on the trip and I said that I would join the gang on the coach to the sea side. I didn't know that Eileen had also invited her friend, Mo, to come as well.

We joined the coach to Southend in the early hours and began the long drive to the coast. These were the days before motorways and the trip was long and hot. The company was good natured as we were all friends and the usual teenage banter flowed freely. We finally arrived in Southend about an hour before lunchtime.

The tide was well out and a crowd of ten or twelve of us wandered around the attractions on the sea front with its arcades and shops selling souvenirs, candy floss and sea side rock. After an hour or so, it was Eileen who suggested that it was time for lunch. Four of us broke away from the group to find a restaurant, Eileen, myself, my cousin Tony and a tall, slim, beautiful brunette, Maureen McCluskey, who I had had my eye on for some time. Tony also had the same idea and was chatting animatedly with her. I would bide my time until an opportunity arose to make a move.

We found a nearby fish and chip shop, had lunch, and then took a leisurely stroll along the nearly one-and-a-half-mile pier to finally find the sea. From there, it was the fun fair!

Fun fairs in the 60s were not like the giant amusement parks of today. For a couple of pounds, there was a great deal of fun to be had. The games were simple and gave us a lot of laughs. The rifle range, 'hook a duck,' bingo, hoopla and the merry-go-round. The highlight of the fair was the Big Dipper, but I hated them, they scared me. I then spotted Tony, Eileen and Mo heading towards it, and, swallowing my fear, hurried after them.

I managed to elbow Tony out of the way as he was about to take his seat next to Mo and plonked myself down next to her; a few seconds later, the car started to move off. The ride terrified me, plunging down the first drop and hurtling around the corners. I hung on grimly to the rail with one hand, the other gripping Mo's hand tightly. Finally, the ride was over and taking a deep sigh of relief, apologised to Mo hoping that I hadn't hurt her hand. She was laughing and said that I was as white as a sheet and that her hand was alright. We left the Big Dipper arm in arm and made our way back to the coach. It would be 25 years before I ventured on to a Big Dipper again.

We sat together on the coach home, at first chatting together about ourselves. Mo's dad, Ted, was from Ireland and had served before and during the war in the Royal Navy and the Merchant Fleet. Spending some time on the Arctic Convoys in 1942–43, after which Ted retired from the service. Mo's mum was a Scot and met and married Ted in Ayr, Mo was born in August 1943, and Ted and Bessie moved to Birmingham a few weeks later that year. Ted to work as a millwright in an engineering company and Bessie worked riveting the wings on Spitfires at a factory in Castle Bromwich. When we met, Mo, who was now 17, was working in the offices on the same site, Fisher and Ludlow, where the Mini was being built. That same factory is today Jaguar/Land Rover.

We finally arrived back in Mount Pleasant later that night. Mo and I said our goodbyes, kissed and arranged to meet up later the following week. We met two or three times a week. By this time, Mo had moved with her family from the back-to-back house in Small Heath to a brand-new four-bedroom council house in Kingshurst on the outskirts of Birmingham. Mo had 4 siblings—Ann, her younger sister, and brothers Alex, Douglas and Andrew.

Our entertainment in the evenings being the cinemas or dances to a live band at the Locarno in Birmingham City centre. We also enjoyed live theatre, especially English farces like Charlie's Aunt, Lady Windermere's Fan and the Importance of Being Earnest. One of the most memorable shows we went to was 'A Fast-Moving Beat Show' at Birmingham Hippodrome. This featured Gene Vincent and Eddie Cochran with Joe Brown ending the first half. His set was a showstopper and the audience were on their feet shouting for more.

Eddie Cochran was killed in a car accident just a few short weeks after his UK tour ended. He and Gene Vincent, who was injured in the crash, were on their way to London Airport when the taxi they were in went out of control. Eddie was thrown from the vehicle and died in hospital in Bath a few hours later. Gene Vincent broke his leg and would walk with a limp for the rest of his life.

I finally left school and started work. I became a laboratory assistant in brass foundries in Birmingham, the first being in the area recently made infamous on television as one of the places haunted by the Peaky Blinders. The Garrison Tavern was just across the road from one of the foundries.

It was obvious that the company for which I worked was struggling and I started looking for another job. I was on day release from work and went to Aston Technical college to study for an ONC in chemistry. By pure coincidence, Mo's eldest brother Alex was in the same class. It was on the course that I learnt of a job going at another local, larger foundry, United Non-Ferrous Metals, a subsidiary of GKN. I wrote to the chief chemist and asked for an interview. I received a prompt reply, went for the interview, and was offered the job there and then. Not only better money, but a bright and airy chemistry laboratory, and with a friendly group of people, willing to help me through the work. My first job in the new place was to analyse the percentage copper in the brass produced by the furnaces, a task that was to stand me in good stead three years later.

On the days and evenings when Mo and I were not seeing each other, we both pursued our own interests. I spent some of my time with friends, doing what teenagers at the time did, mostly hanging around a coffee bar, making one cup of coffee last an entire evening, and playing the pin ball machine until the owner invited us to leave. Saturday afternoons saw me playing rugby. After leaving school, I played for Erdington at scrum half for a season. I then went on to play for Guest, Keen and Nettlefolds (GKN), the parent company for UNFM. Most of my Saturday and Sunday mornings were spent on Kingsbury ranges, honing my skills with my .303 Lee Enfield rifle. I eventually went on to Bisley in 1963, our team of 4 winning all the Army Cadet trophies, and I topped the Cadet Hundred.

It was around this time that I became estranged from my mother. Although I did not realise it at the time, she had become menopausal and the symptoms manifested themselves as paranoia and depression. I was unable to cope with her mood swings and moved out of the family home and into a bed and breakfast nearby.

I was now over 18 years old and deeply in love with Mo and had asked her to marry me. She accepted, but in the position in which I now found myself, could see no way of being able to afford to get married. I had to find a way of saving money, although I enjoyed the job I was doing, I had to find a solution to my dwindling finances.

We had visited a number of jewellers and looked at engagement rings. Many of those that Mo liked were well outside what I could afford. Later, chatting to my shooting coach, he mentioned that he had a friend who was a diamond cutter in the Jewellery Quarter in Birmingham and that he may be able to help us out. Mo and I were introduced to Mike who produced a selection of diamonds and Mo picked out a half carat, brilliant cut stone, with a princely price tag of just £26.00. I also had a school friend, John Taylor, who worked as a jewellery designer, and he produced a design for a beautiful solitaire engagement ring in platinum and gold. Mo and I were both delighted with the design and a week later, he called me and told me it was ready. All told, I paid a little under £100.00 for an engagement ring that would later have an insurance value of about £2000.00. John later produced Mo's wedding ring, along with silver bracelets for Eileen and Mo's sister Ann, who were bridesmaids at our wedding.

We became engaged on Valentine's Day, 1964. We had arranged to meet at our favourite Chinese restaurant in what was then the Bull Ring in Birmingham. I had managed to purchase a single red rose on my way to the restaurant and, during a break in the meal, I passed the rose in its box to Mo. I had attached the ring to the rose and it glittered in the candlelight. As I had hoped, Mo was delighted both with the ring and the rose. We finished our meal and went to the theatre in town.

Later in the year, during a break in my studies at the college, I ventured into Birmingham town centre. I found myself in Great Charles Street and across the road was the army recruitment office. I had spent 5 years in the Army Cadet Force and was now in the TAVR. I enjoyed time with them along with the friendship and discipline, the annual camps and, of course, the rifle shooting.

I crossed the road and entered the office and was welcomed by the recruiting sergeant. We sat and chatted while he took notes, asking me my interests, educational qualifications, and suggested a number of options that would be of interest to me in the Regular Army. I told him I had no interest in joining the infantry and that I would want to learn a trade, laboratory work being my forte. He gave me a book about the Royal Army Medical Corps, suggested that I read it, and return later and discuss matters further.

I saw Mo that evening and told her that I had been to look at the possibilities of joining the army. She said that it might be a good idea and that we should explore all the possibilities. There were two potential trades listed amongst the many in book I had been given—laboratory technician and dispenser. Both had some appeal and they were both well paid on qualification. Mo and I went together back to the recruiting office having decided that we would get some more information, particularly the situation regarding a woman married to a soldier.

After much discussion, during which we were extolled with all the great benefits of being in the military, and in particular how wonderful a life of an army wife would be (much of which we took with a large pinch of salt), we left the office agreeing that army life had a certain appeal. We spent a great deal of time talking about the possibilities of army life and eventually mutually agreed to take a leap of faith and see where it would lead.

I returned to the recruiting office on 24 April 1964, and said that I wished to join the Royal Army Medical Corps. I had to undergo a medical at the office to make sure I was fit to become a soldier. I was surprised to find that I was colour blind and that this would preclude me training as a laboratory technician, but sufficient to train as a dispenser once I had completed basic training at the RAMC depot at Keogh Barracks, near Aldershot. I told the recruiting sergeant that I was obliged to give my employer a month's notice and I was advised that this was acceptable as I would be given a month's unpaid leave, and that my official enlistment date would be today, once I had signed the enlistment papers and taken the Oath of Allegiance. I signed on and was given a rail warrant and told to report to Keogh Barracks on 2nd May. I gave my notice to the Chief Chemist at UNFM the following Monday.

The same day as I signed on, I noticed that a friend of mine had also signed up for the military. Pete had joined the Royal Engineers and was due to join them in a few days. I had a letter from him telling me that he was in basic training in Cove, near Farnborough, not far from where I would be in a couple of weeks' time. He told me in his letter that once he had been issued with his kit, he had to make a parcel of his civvies and send them back home. He would get them back once his training was complete after 16 weeks. My first day in the army was somewhat different—a little surreal.

Mo and I had spent as much time as possible together over the three weeks before I was due to leave for Keogh Barracks. I had told her that it could be up to four months before we could see one another again.

The days came and went and it was soon time for me to get the train to Ash Vale to begin my basic training. We said our tearful goodbyes at New Street Station in Birmingham with me leaning out of the carriage window and waving until the train disappeared into a tunnel. After a change to Waterloo, I continued my journey to Ash Vale. I arrived late in the afternoon and made my way to the barracks and asked at the Guard Room for the for the Orderly Sergeant. He duly arrived after a few minutes and ticked off my name on his list of others who had previously arrived. He bade me follow him to find a bed space in a barrack room. After a short walk, we arrived at the main building, and, following the Sergeant up a flight of stairs, we entered a long room in which there were several other young men about the same age as myself. These were to be my close companions in squad 64/11 over the next few weeks.

I found a bed space and a locker. The Sergeant then told me that the Quartermaster Stores were now closed until Monday, so I would be free to do what I wanted until then. I thanked him and as a parting shot as he walked towards the door, he suggested I might take the time to get my bloody hair cut!

I spoke to one or two of the guys who had been issued with kit and I found out that we were allowed to keep our civvies. They were also free for the weekend and a few of them would be going to sample the delights of Aldershot. This was not for me; I had a girl back home who I was not expected to see for a good while. I repacked a few things into a small suitcase, borrowed from one of my new roommates, made up my bed and headed back to the station.

I took the train back to Waterloo and from there travelled on the Underground to Watford Junction. From there, I hitch hiked to the M1 Motorway. This would be the first of many hitchhiking travels over the next four years. From the slip road of the motorway, I got a lift quite quickly by a motorist heading for Rugby, he agreed to take me as far as the Blue Boar Services at Watford Gap. From here, I could get another ride along the M45 and the A45 and towards Birmingham. These were the days before motorway speed limits and I made the trip in good time. I asked my latest motorist to drop me off at Stonebridge, a junction on the A45 between Coventry and Birmingham. From here, I hoped to get a lift along the A452 to Kingshurst and Mo.

I was dropped off a short walk from Mo's house in Kingshurst. I knocked on the door and was greeted by an astonished Mo, staring at me in disbelief. It had only been a little over twelve hours since we had said our farewells at New Street Station. I explained that I couldn't get any kit until Monday morning, when I had to be back in barracks at Ash Vale. Apart from getting a haircut on Saturday morning, we spent every waking hour that weekend until I had to leave after lunch on Sunday.

After saying farewell to Mo for a second time in 48 hours, I thumbed my way back the way I had come. With three or four lifts, the last driver dropped me off in Central London. I took the train from Waterloo to Ash Vale and made my way to Keogh and my barrack room. After a quick wash and change, I found the NAAFI and met up with some of my squad mates.

On Monday morning, we were up at 6 o'clock and after a hurried breakfast, we were marched across to the clothing store where we were issued with our kit. And so began 16 weeks of basic training: bulled boots, blancoed webbing, hours on the drill square, barrack room inspections and early morning parades. My time in the Army Cadet Force made most of the training relatively easy, and along with the comradeship of my fellow squaddies, I enjoyed the time at Keogh.

Apart from the occasional weekend guard duty, most of the weekends were free and I travelled up to see Mo. Hitchhiking was easier now that I could travel in uniform. Quite a lot of drivers were sympathetic to a serviceman in those days. If I got a weekend duty at short notice, I could let Mo know via telegram. Thus, I had the best of both worlds, enjoying my weekdays training to be a soldier, and at weekends being in the company of the woman I was so in love with.

Training over I was now a medical assistant Grade 3 and it was the day of our squad's passing out parade. Mo came down to watch the parade, which had the accompaniment of the RAMC Band. Afterwards we retired to the NAAFI to celebrate the end of our training with a few drinks. I introduced Mo to my squad mates who were taken with her friendliness and her beauty. It was time to leave on a weekend pass and went to the station at Ash Vale and took the train back home.

Just after the passing out parade and waiting for a posting, I twisted my knee during a bit of horseplay in the barrack room. I went sick the next day, my knee having swollen and making it difficult to walk. The medical officer took one look at my knee and immediately sent me to the Cambridge Military Hospital for admission and physiotherapy.

I spent five days having intensive physiotherapy, trying to do squat thrusts, pedalling a stationary bike, along with other exercises to get my knee back into shape. I was seen by a surgeon at the end of the week who came along and poked me in the knee. As I yelped in pain, he said, "Well, that was a waste of time, you've obviously torn a cartilage. I'll have you in theatre on Monday."

Knee surgery then meant going under the knife, and not the keyhole method that is the norm these days. I was prepared for surgery on Monday morning, ready for the ministrations of the civilian resident orthopaedic surgeon, Paddy Irwin.

The anaesthetist gave me an intravenous injection off Sodium Pentothal and asked me to count backwards from ten. I remember getting as far as 7; the next thing I recall was waking up in a ward with the physiotherapist standing by my bed. I was still woozy from the effects of the anaesthetic, but the physio insisted I tried to raise my leg. I struggled to get it a few inches off the bed, grunting with pain.

The next few days were torture. The physiotherapist came every morning, getting me to raise my leg into the air. He also added a sand bag on my foot, gradually increasing the weight each day, and telling me to continue the exercise during the day. The object was to build up the strength in my quadriceps, although the enforced bed-rest was seriously boring. At least, I had a visit from Mo, who was kindly bought down to Aldershot by her friends from work.

I had a visit from a member of the Army Scripture Readers who saw my bed card, apart from showing my name, rank and number, listed my religion as agnostic. This was enough for him, as he made a beeline for my bed every day. I begged the nurses to tell him I was asleep every time he entered the ward, but he was convinced he could convert me. At least, I could escape the ward after a week when I was allowed out of bed and get off the ward in a wheel chair.

After three of four days in the physiotherapy department, the staff were pleased with the strength in my quadriceps, the operation scar had healed and the stitches came out after a week. I was pronounced fit enough to be discharged and given a week's leave, which I would spend with Mo and her family in Kingshurst. By the end of the week, my leg had strengthened to the point where I no longer need the aid of a walking stick and I was able to walk without a limp, and it was time to return to Ash Vale.

On my return to Keogh, I found that I was posted to 19 Company at Saighton Camp in Chester, a Medical Reception station (MRS). I left for Chester the following day, arriving at the camp in the afternoon. I got my directions to the HQ, which was housed in a couple of old 'spider' units. The building also contained a medical centre and a small ward of about 10 beds. I was marched in to see the CO, Major Tubby RAMC, who after a brief introduction passed me over to a corporal who took me over to another 'spider' to find by bed space I had a single room with a desk. A change from the barrack room at Keogh which I had shared with about 20 others. At least, I had managed to contact Mo and let her know where I was and that I would be home at the weekend, hitchhiking down the A41 to Birmingham.

I lasted about 4–5 weeks in Chester. I was not impressed with the unit. The buildings were old and dilapidated, food in the canteen was poor and most of my time was spent cleaning the barrack block and the MRS. After a falling out with the barracks corporal, I ended up in front of the CO on a charge of insubordination. The hearing lasted about 10 minutes after which I was given a week's restriction of privileges, and an immediate posting to the Medical Reception Station at Gamecock Barracks, home of the Junior Leaders Regiment of the Royal Artillery at Bramcote, near Nuneaton. I was told by the corporal whom I had offended that Bramcote was a so-called 'punishment posting'.

I was on the train on my way to Nuneaton less than 90 minutes after being wheeled into the CO's office. I was met at Nuneaton by a Sergeant who took me to my new unit and showed me to a room in a barrack block, not far from the MRS. Having dropped off my kit the Sergeant took me to the MRS to meet with the CO. He was a retired Colonel in the RAMC and had a somewhat intimidating look. I stood to attention at his desk while he delivered a 10-minute dressing down to me. I was severely shaken, never having received such a diatribe.

Once this was over, his demeanour changed and he invited me to sit and asked if I had eaten. I said that I had arrived after lunch in the canteen was over, whereupon he summed the MRS cook and instructed him to prepare a meal for me. I was to discover that the warnings of Bramcote being a punishment posting was widely exaggerated and over the 9 months I spent there were most enjoyable. I learnt a lot from the Colonel, Sergeant, and the rest of the staff of the MRS both civilian and military.

Bramcote was just over 20 miles from Kingshurst and Mo, and I spent most of my free time heading along the A47 towards the love of my life. One Friday morning while waiting for a lift I spotted the Colonel arriving for work, I saluted him as he passed me in his Triumph Vitesse 6 Convertible. A few minutes later his car reappeared and stopped alongside me. It was driven by the MRS Sergeant who told me the Colonel had told him to drop me off on the main road to Birmingham.

One my most memorable and frightening experiences happened to me in Bramcote. I had a free afternoon and along with the MRS chef, went out for a walk in the summer sunshine. We made our way along a canal towpath to a nearby caravan park where the chef had a friend. We arrived at his friend's caravan and knocking on the door, got no reply from inside. The occupant of the caravan next door came out and told us that his friend had gone out for the day and that she did not know when he would be back. We left the caravan site and headed to a pub where we had a cooling drink and the made our way back to barracks.

We had been away for a couple of hours and as we entered the barrack gates we were arrested by the regimental police and marched into the guard room. No explanation was forthcoming as we were locked in separate cells and our shoes and belts removed.

After about an hour sitting and wondering what was going on, my cell door was opened and I was ushered into a room and confronted by a gentleman who produced a warrant card indicating that he was a detective sergeant from the local police. I was asked to relate my movements, times, and give the names of people to whom I had spoken. I knew the approximate times but I wasn't aware of any names. I told him of our visit to the caravan park, the next-door neighbour of the chef's friend, and the pub where we had stopped for a drink.

The detective took down my statement, and, after I had signed it, I was escorted back to my cell where I sat and sweated for another hour. Suddenly our cell doors were opened and our shoes and belts returned. The detective reappeared and told us we were free to go. We both breathed a sigh of relief before asking our arrest was all about. It appeared that two young men answering to our description, even down to the clothes we were wearing, were seen burgling, and running from a house close to where we had been that afternoon. We were fortunate in that our statements corroborated our movements, along with the times and people who had seen us, and footprints left in a flower bed did not match our foot wear. We never heard whether the original thieves had been caught along with the property they had stolen.

After about nine months at Bramcote, I was called into the Colonel's office and was told that my application to train as a dispenser had been accepted and I was to travel to The Army School of Pharmacy at the military hospital in Colchester in June 1965. I had a month before I was due to join the course and I spent as much time with Mo as possible during this time.

I travelled to Colchester by train and was met at the station and taken to the hospital ready to start the course. I was allocated a bed in a barrack room with 6 of my classmates. The following morning after doing the usual administration requirements, I joined the course at the school. There were about 40 of us to start with, including 6 soldiers from the Sierra Leone Military. We were introduced to the staff of the school. The head of the school was 'Pop' Pirnie and below him were two other lecturers, "Felix" Berman and Mr Edwards. There was also a secretary who I believe was Mrs Evans.

The first month was taken up with Maths, Physics, Chemistry and English. Following the test results on these subject about half a dozen of the class were failed and left the course. Those of us left started the course proper. There were several subjects to get grips with, including pharmacology, forensic pharmacy, chemistry both theory and practical, and anatomy and physiology, which I found the hardest subject. We made up medicines in dispensing practical using the recipes from the British Pharmacopoeia and Codex.

Most of the lectures were dictated accompanied by handouts. Practical chemistry work was relatively easy for me, especially as I had spent two and a half years working in industrial laboratories and I was able to help others who were finding the work difficult. Equally some of my fellow students helped my understanding of anatomy. A good part of the evenings was taken up transcribing notes taken during lectures into hard back exercise books. By the time, the course had finished I had amassed a dozen or more books of notes.

During our free time a few of us had taken up horse riding. The Royal Horse Artillery had stables across from the hospital, and for the princely sum of a £1.00 a week we were taught to ride and eventually, when we were considered competent, we were able to take out a horse unsupervised. The only proviso was that we were required to muck out the stables once a week. I rode two or three times a week, usually in the early mornings. My first mount was a retired cavalry horse called Winston; he was a chestnut gelding of about 15 hands. He was a good ride but tended to take off at a full gallop when I least expected it. I swapped him for Caesar, a grey, 17 hands, and also retired from the Household Cavalry where he was a drum horse.

All the time I was in Colchester I travelled up to see Maureen most weekends. Hitchhiking my way via Braintree and Bishops Stortford to pick up the M1. One of my fellow students had a car and he often drove me as far as Marks Tay to the east of Colchester. I was lucky with lifts and frequently made the journey in under 5 hours. There was no speed limit on the motorway at that time.

Mo came down to Colchester a couple of times. We once stayed with Mike Holmes and his wife Midge, they were married and lived in Brightlingsea, so Mike travelled into Colchester every day on his trusty moped. Mike and Midge were to become our good friends and we worked together in several places around the world over our respective careers in the army.

In November of 1965, we finalised the arrangements for our wedding, I had asked permission from the CO of the hospital to get married, as was the requirement those days. The date was set for 22nd January 1966 which would be once the first part of the Dispensers Course would be over, and also the day after my 21st Birthday, timed to coincide with the various marriage allowances that were available at the time.

The examinations for the first section of the course were in the second week of December, the pass marks were high and set at 50% with an overall average of 60%, 13 examinations in all. We got the results the following week, and to my delight I had passed and I was now a dispenser, Grade 3. With our wedding imminent, I wrote a letter to the company officer to be allowed to remain at the hospital in Colchester, as the second part of the course was a year working under supervision in a hospital pharmacy.

With the course and exams finished and our wedding arrangements finalised, I took the time looking for somewhere to live in or near Colchester after Mo and

I were married. I found a flat on Mersea Island, which was about ten miles from Colchester, and had a bus service into the city. The flat on Mersea was to be the first of our 21 houses and flats where we would spend our married life.

Our wedding took place at St Barnabas Church in Kingshurst on 1966 on a snowy January afternoon, Mo looking beautiful as she walked down the aisle on the arm of her father. We held the reception at a local pub, danced to a live band and toasted each other with Asti Spumante. A work colleague of Mo's took the wedding photographs and later presented us with a beautiful album as a wedding present.

Festivities over we changed our wedding clothes and headed off to London for a short honeymoon. We went to the theatre and to the cinema and saw the latest Bond movie, *Thunderball*. We were also invited into a BBC studio for an audience review of various programmes the BBC were intending to show over the next year, one of which was the pilot of 'Bewitched,' starring Elizabeth Montgomery and Dick York.

With the honeymoon over, we boarded a train to Colchester and on to our flat on Mersea Island.

Chapter 1
Sea View Avenue, West Mersea, Essex

I opened the door to our first home, a furnished upstairs flat a few hundred yards from the beach at West Mersea. A friend in Birmingham had helped us move some of our belongings, engagement and wedding presents, a couple of weeks before we actually moved in, so we had enough essentials to tide us over for a couple of days.

Mersea Island lies in the River Blackwater Estuary and is connected to the mainland by a short causeway, known as the Strood, the first being built by the Saxons in the 7th century. The Strood is covered by the tide twice a day, although the water is rarely deep enough to prevent the buses from crossing. The island is also a major site of oyster fishing and had been so since Roman times. Oysters from Mersea are shipped around the world and is a main source of income for the island.

Most weekends we took the bus into Colchester for shopping. There was a Sainsbury's in the town, very much unlike the super market of today. Essentially just another high street shop. One Saturday as we carried our shopping from the bus station in Mersea a 1930s chauffeur driven Rolls Royce, complete with chintz curtains, pulled up beside us, and a dear old lady in the rear wound down her window and asked us if we would care for a lift. Naturally being loaded down with our shopping, we accepted gratefully, the chauffeur opened the passenger door for us and we settled into the rear seats for the two-mile journey to our flat.

I had become friendly with John, a fellow dispenser who had been on the course a year before me and was now working in the pharmacy at the hospital. He was married to Carol and they also lived on Mersea Island, just half and hour's walk from us. Most weekends we alternated at each others' houses for an evening meal. One evening as we walked home along the esplanade around midnight, we were stopped by a young policeman demanding to know what we were doing out so late at night. Mo was incensed, and holding her hand out and showing him her wedding ring told him in no uncertain terms "I'll have you know, I'm a married woman!" The policeman, non-plussed, stuttered his apologies, wished us goodnight, and went on his way. We carried on home, me almost paralysed with laughter, I had to sit on the stairs when we got home, unable to climb up to our flat until I had stopped laughing.

Within a few weeks of settling into our flat, Mo got a job in Colchester at Vent-Axia, a company making extractor fans. She travelled into work every day on the bus, while I bought a moped to get to the hospital, as the bus timetable didn't get me into Colchester in time for work. The moped was fine except when the tide covered to Strood, but at least I could telephone and advise my boss that I might be a bit late. I kept an eye on the tide tables and usually set off early, sometimes arriving well before anyone else.

As winter turned to spring our life together was idyllic. We both enjoyed our jobs and West Mersea was a great place to live, we had good friends in John and Carol. However, all was to change when a posting order arrived moving us to Chester. It was not a posting I was looking forward to in the least, given my previous experience at Saighton Camp.

We had a couple of weeks' notice, so packing up our few belongings and arranging for removals would be easy. Mo was aware that I would have to go up to Chester and look for somewhere to live, leaving her behind to finalise packing up our flat, ready to move at short notice. I organised a removal company, letting them know when we would require their services for the move to Chester. I took the train to Chester where I was met at the station and taken to the unit.

After going through the usual admin procedure, I was introduced to my new boss at the medical supply and dispensary departments in the 'Spider' unit opposite the HQ. The staff consisted of Brian, a staff sergeant and Don, a corporal who between them managed the medical stores together (Don was shortly after posted to the Trucial Oman Scouts, and later left the army to train as a pharmacist); and Joe, a retired RAMC Major who ran the dispensary. Joe was to be my mentor over the remains of the year until I started the final phase of my dispenser training.

I managed to get a couple of days off to look for somewhere to live in Chester, and after viewing a couple of places took over a flat that was to be our second home together.

Chapter 2
Flat 6, 2 Abbots Grange, Chester

Our new flat was in a listed building about 10 minutes' walk into Chester City centre. The house was a typical late Georgian building with high ceilings, two bedrooms along with a kitchen and bathroom, a bit on the expensive side at six guineas a week. As soon as I had the keys in my hand, I contacted Mo with the address and for her to get in touch with the removal company, and to let me know the details of when our belongings would arrive in Chester. I arranged a railway warrant for Mo to travel up to me once I had time and date for our things to arrive in Chester.

Mo organised everything, transferred our bank account, paid the removal company, and let me know when everything was due to happen. I had four days to get the flat ready, so my evenings and other free time was taken up with food shopping, tidying the flat, and general housekeeping. I was so looking forward to having my lovely lady with me again. We had only been apart for a couple of weeks, but I was missing her very much.

Mo arrived at Chester station the day before the removal van was due to deliver our belongings. After giving her a big hug, we grabbed a taxi and headed off to our new home. Mo was quite taken with the flat as I showed her around. The main bedroom was quite large and the bed was comfortable. The kitchen was a little on the small side, but adequate for our needs. I kept the wonders of the bathroom until last.

Over the bath was an enormous copper geyser. To light it up to provide hot water, there was a pilot light on the end of a pivoted tube. The gas to the pilot was turned on and lit with a match, then the water supply to the geyser was turned on followed by the gas supply and the pilot swung in to light the burners. With a whoosh, the gas fired up and, in a few seconds, hot water cascaded into the bath. Mo was somewhat wary of the Heath-Robinson geyser, so I was summoned to fire it up when Mo wanted a bath. Such a system would be illegal these days as there was no forced ventilation in the bathroom, so a window had to be open even in the coldest weather to drive out the steam and potential flue gases from the geyser.

Chester was founded in AD79 as the Roman city Deva Victrix. A lovely city, with its Cathedral, black and white fronted shops, particularly those in the Rows on Forgate Street. It is the best-preserved walled city in Britain, the walls which are Grade 1 listed extend, with only a short break of 100 yards, for nearly 2 miles. Many of the streets are named for the original gates for entry into the old city— Eastgate, Westgate, Bridgegate, and Forgate. We regularly walked along the walls, stopping to take in the views over the city and the river Dee. Chester Racecourse was easily visible from the wall to the west along the stretch from Watergate. From there, we could watch the horse racing for free.

The highlight of the walk, was the bridge over Forgate Street, with its ornate clock. Here we could descend from the walls and take a lunch stop at one of the many cafes on Forgate Street.

Of the many and varied shops on Forgate Street was our favourite—British Home Stores—this would become BHS and eventually disappear from our high streets many years later. The store had a food department and it was here that we discovered fruit flavoured yoghurt and Norwegian Jarlsberg Cheese. We also spent a fair bit of our disturbance allowance to stock up on bedlinen, towels, and kitchen utensils.

During our short stay in West Mersea we had hired a television set from a company called DER (Domestic Electrical Rentals). When we were due to move, we contacted them and asked them to take the TV back, explaining that we were moving to Chester. The company was understanding and gave us the address of their branch in Chester. Once we had settled into Abbot's grange, we again arranged a rental TV from the company. It was cheaper to hire in those days as a new TV could cost anything up to £100, which was well outside our budget and the rental charge was very cheap in relation to the full cost of a new set.

Mo landed a job at Western Command Headquarters at Capital House across the river Dee. She was taken on as a trainee comptometer operator. A comptometer was a mechanical calculator which a few years later became the link between mechanical and electronic calculators and would eventually become obsolete. She was required to go to London for a few days on a training course, and was happy at the prospect of travelling on her own. I was pleased for her to get a job, not only would it add to our income, and she would be able to meet other people outside of our military acquaintances. She passed the course easily and made a few friends along the way. Passing the course also had the added bonus of a pay rise.

Chester had a superb Philharmonic Orchestra which staged regular classical music concerts at the town hall which was just a few minutes' walk from our flat. The very first concert we attended featured two pieces, The Overture to Ruslan and Lyudmila by the Russian compose Glinka, followed by Beethoven's third Symphony 'Eroica'. Today I cannot hear those pieces of music without being immediately transported back to our very first concert in Chester. We also heard the great Alan Civil play Mozart's 4th horn concerto, and Peter and the Wolf but I can't recall the name of the narrator.

In early October, I was contacted by the housing officer on Saighton Camp to tell me that they had accepted a flat as a hiring in Hoole, a district of Chester, and would we be interested. We were certainly interested, as taking it would mean a £2.00 drop in weekly rent. We went together to have a look at what was on offer, and notified the housing officer that it would suit us fine. So began our move to our third residence in less than a year after getting married.

Chapter 3
Hoole Lane, Chester

We went to have a look at our prospective new flat. It was in an old gloomy house at of what was then the bottom of Hoole Lane. We rang the doorbell an met our prospective landlady, a Mrs Kay. This was not her proper name as we found out shortly after moving into the flat and she was married to a Pakistani gentleman (although we didn't know it at the time of our meeting), and had shortened her surname to make things easier for her. The inside of the house belied its exterior. The house was bright and well decorated. She invited us into her sitting room and made us a cup of tea before we went up to see the flat. We caught a fleeting glimpse of her husband and she told us that that was Mr Kay who was on his way to work a night shift.

The flat was self-contained with its own front door. It was small but totally adequate for our needs. It had a sitting room, dining room, kitchen with a refrigerator, bathroom and one double bedroom. It was clean and the furniture, though a little dated was perfectly suitable for us. Mrs Kay told us that she would provide new nets and curtains for all the windows and there was a little decorating to be completed which would be done by the time we moved in. This would be in a couple of weeks' time as we had to give notice to our present landlady.

On our way home, Mo turned to me and said that she thought Mr Kay must be a coal man as he had appeared to be quite dark. We later learnt that he was a Pakistani and worked at Chester Zoo as the elephant keeper. He was a really pleasant and cheerful chap once we got to know him and would happily fix things around the flat if there was anything we needed doing.

A couple of weeks after seeing the flat, we packed up our belongings and with the help of an army 4 tonne truck moved the short way to Hoole Lane. After unloading our boxes and taking them into our flat, along with our DER TV set, we had a wander around the local area. There were a few shops just along the lane and in the surrounding streets, a green grocer, bakery, a small electrical shop, and a laundrette (we had yet to splash out on a washing machine). Most of the area has now been redeveloped and the house and our flat no longer exist. At the top of the lane was the main A56 where we could both get buses, Mo across the river to Western Command, and myself to Saighton Camp.

On 21st October 1966, shortly after we moved into Hoole Lane, a major disaster struck Aberfan, South Wales. A coal tip collapsed and engulfed the local school. 144 people including 116 children were killed. 60 soldiers from the Beachley Apprentice School in Chepstow went to assist the rescue, essentially removing bodies from the wreckage of the school.

By now, it was late October 1966, and I was due to start the final stage of my training towards becoming a dispenser Grade 1 in January 1967. I would spend the first month of 1967 at the Defence Medical Equipment Depot (DMED) in Ludgershall near Andover in Hampshire. From there, I would return to the School of Dispensing for 5 months. My main concern was leaving Mo on her own in Chester for the time I would be away. She was unperturbed at the prospect, saying that she would be perfectly safe in our flat, particularly as Mr and Mrs Kay, with whom she got on well, would be at home most evenings, and she also had the companionship of her workmates at Western Command HQ. I also assured her that I would make every effort to get home to Chester at every opportunity.

In early January 1967, armed with a railway warrant and some of my military kit, I made my way from Chester to Ludgershall and DMED. Here I met up with the eight of my fellow students who had all passed the first phase of the dispensers course (John H, Jim D, Jim A, Mike, Chris, Oscar, Wally, and John T), who had successfully passed the first part of the course. The students from Sierra Leone and Nigeria did not return for the rest of the course. We arrived on the 3rd January; the following day Donald Campbell met his tragic death on Coniston Water while trying to break the world water speed record in Bluebird. Again, weekends were free and I made my way up to Chester a couple of times during my month in Ludgershall. One of the weekends coincided with my birthday and our first wedding anniversary. I had sent a card and managed to get a bunch of roses in celebration of our first year together. I can't remember how I got home; I know that I hitch hiked my way north, but it was probably via Gloucester and Shrewsbury.

Our month at DMED consisted of working in the various departments and learning of all aspects of medical supply and accounting. We learnt the correct storage and safe keeping of controlled drugs, storage of flammable products and gases. Identification of surgical instruments, and obtaining supplies from DMED in order to keep the medical supply departments of the units in which we would eventually be working efficiently stocked.

DMED was an enormous site, with its own railway sidings and a forest of steel racking containing everything from safety pins to operating tables. It held mobilisation stores—complete hospitals contained in boxes, ready to be shipped out to the far corners of the world if and when the military was deployed in a conflict or a disaster zone. We were introduced to the officers who were responsible for sourcing all the stock for their various sections held in the depot. One of the most important people to whom I was introduced (although I did not realise it at the time) was the chief pharmacist. He was Mungo Maloch, a Scotsman with a cheerful disposition. He would be a great help to me in my later service career when I moved out of hospital pharmacies to head up a hospital medical supply department.

DMED was tasked to supply all three services worldwide with their medical requirements—from the smallest RAF station to the large service hospitals. Many of the workforce on the floor of the warehouse were civilians, mostly from Ludgershall and the surrounding area. Many were related to one another and had worked there for a few years. One of the ladies in the drug section was Cora who supervised her team in a pick and pack operation. It was later in the remaining days of my army career to meet and work with Cora, who was married to Tom, the warehouse foreman.

Jim D had a car, a Saab 90, and one weekend Mo had written to tell me she was going to Birmingham to visit her family. Jim suggested that we sample the delights of the New Forest as we were only about 45 minutes from the area. After a quick change into civvies, four of us set off towards Fritham in the heart of the New Forest, Jim diving carefully down the dark roads of the forest, particularly as the forest ponies roamed freely across the roads. We ended up at The Royal Oak, a small thatched roofed pub in Fritham, and made our way into the bar. We made our drinks last, sat and chatted and put the world to rights before setting off back to Ludgershall.

The final week of our time at DMED came to an end and we were due to return to the school in Colchester in a few days. One or two of the guys, Jim included, went directly on to Colchester, Jim kindly offering to take most of my kit in his car, allowing me to travel lightly to Chester. I took some leave, and, armed with a railway warrant headed back to our flat where I arrived a few minutes after Mo had come home from work. I had not seen Mo for two weeks, the longest period of time we had been separated since we were married.

My few days leave was over too quickly and I returned to Colchester and the School of Dispensing. I promised Mo that I would return home as soon as I could get away. There was no telephone in the house in Chester and correspondence was by letter or telegram, the latter being used if I was stuck in Colchester for a weekend duty.

My fellow student and I were billeted in a room above the NAAFI, 6 of us sharing the reasonably spacious room, and the bathroom. We also had a quiet room where could revise in the evenings after our day at the school. Mike had been promoted to Sergeant and he and Jim A were in the Sergeants' Mess opposite.

We soon settled into the routine of lectures, practical work in chemistry and dispensing. I found the subject of organic chemistry hard, more so than the anatomy and physiology of the first part of the course the previous year but our revision sessions in the evenings help my understanding and I gradually got to grips with the subject. Practical chemistry, given my industrial experience was a gift, and I was able to assist those who were struggling.

As a break from our studies some of us took up various pastimes in our free time, we became reacquainted with our horses, and I rode my old friend Caesar a couple of early mornings a week before breakfast. There was also a gym and swimming pool a short walk from the hospital where we either played two on two basketball or cooled off in the summer months in the pool. We also had a table tennis table in one of the rooms above the NAAFI, and this is where I met Grafton, a heavyset black soldier, an infantryman on secondment from the Kings African Rifles. For his six feet four inches size, he was surprisingly quick on his feet which made him a formidable table tennis player. He also had the most amazing Oxford accent. We also formed a scratch rugby fifteen and managed to recruit Grafton into the side as a prop forward. The team was probably the worst team ever. We had a great short season, playing nine games and managed to lose all of them! There was beer in the bar after the game and the banter on the coach in the way back to Colchester made up for the losses.

Time on the course passed quickly, and before we knew it the examinations were upon us. All the hard work and revision was now going to be put to the test. The previous exam criteria were the same as before, each paper to be passed at 50% with an overall pass mark of 60%. Seven written papers and practical dispensing and practical chemistry. The latter was heaven sent. We were presented with a crystal of copper sulphate and we were required to determine the percentage copper in it. The process to perform this was exactly the same as that which had been part of my work in industry and I had finished the analysis in about 20 minutes. I knew from experience that my result was within a couple of decimal points of the true figure. That was in the days of what was known as 'wet chemical analysis.' These days the process would take a couple of minutes using modern equipment.

A couple of days later the exam results were in. We had all passed the course and were now Dispensers Grade 1 and returned to our units. Nine of us went our separate ways, and only one of those crossed my path again over the next 20 years. Just four of us completed a career in the RAMC, Mike, Chris, Jim A and myself. Oscar now lives in Sri Lanka, but four (John T, John H, Wally and Jim) have disappeared without trace.

I returned to Chester and Mo at the end of June 1967, Brian and Joe were still in the medical stores and dispensary and I was pleased to be working with them again. I received congratulations from them and from the CO on passing the course and I was looking forward to learning more of the practical side of my trade.

The medical stores and dispensary were responsible for supplying the many outlying medical centres dotted all over Western Command, in all of Wales and the Counties of Cumberland, Westmorland, Lancashire, Staffordshire, Shropshire, Herefordshire, Cheshire. Brian was required to visit 'our customers' on a regular basis, essentially to trouble shoot and advise.

In the dispensary, we put together all their pharmaceutical supplies, tablets, creams and ointments. We made up 2 litre bottles of cough mixtures and indigestion remedies. At the school, we made up small quantities of these, but here in Chester we were producing bulk supplies. Our production was put together with those items picked from the medical stores—surgical instruments, bandages, plasters—and packed up for despatch either by road or rail. One or two of the local units sent their own transport to collect their stock.

Chapter 4
6, Blacon Hall Road, Chester

One evening at home, our doorbell rang. It was Mr and Mrs Kay who had come to tell us that they were thinking of moving and putting the house on the market, not immediately, but they thought it would be better for us to look for somewhere else to live. I approached the housing officer the next day and told him we would probably need to find another house or flat. He said he would look into it and as soon as he had anything, he would contact me. True to his word, I received a telephone call from him to let me know he had just taken on a bungalow in Blacon. It would take a few days to sort out the paperwork and inventory with the owner, but we would be able to take a trip over to have a look at the place he had in mind.

The bungalow was detached and had a large garden, and an overgrown hawthorn hedge which ran the entire length of the garden and growing out on to the footpath. The owners were still in residence but due to leave within the coming week to their new house in Chester. We were invited in and found the place to be clean and tidy, two decent size bedrooms, living room, bathroom and a well-appointed kitchen. A great improvement on our place in Hoole. There was also a garage which certainly come in useful as I was now the proud owner of a BSA Bantam motor bike, the moped having given up the ghost a few months previously. The bike had a problem with its third gear, which was why I got it free from a soldier who was posted abroad and didn't have the time or money to get it fixed. I managed to drive the bike over to a local mechanic, who for the princely sum of £30 repaired the gearing and serviced the two-stroke engine. I used the Bantam until early the next year when I sold it on for the original £30 when we were posted.

We were happy to take the bungalow and informed the housing officer we would move in as soon has the present owners had moved out. Working in the dispensary and medical stores gave me access to a good supply of cardboard boxes quite a few of which were 'borrowed' for packing up our possessions prior to moving to Blacon. Packing up was relatively easy as we did not have anything in way of furniture apart from a coffee table and our treasured Ferguson radiogram. We spent our evenings packing ready to move, leaving out one or two essentials to keep us going until we moved. The housing officer got us a unit van when it was time to go, we said our farewell and thanks to Mr and Mrs Kay and headed off to our new place in Blacon.

We loved the bungalow in Blacon, we had good neighbours and the house itself was nicely decorated. Shortly after moving in, we invited Brian, my boss in Saighton, and his wife Anita, over for dinner. They would be the first of many visitors to our house. The BSA Bantam was a godsend as far as travel to work the bus service took 40 minutes and I had to change in Chester. It took me just 20 minutes on the bike. At least, Mo could get a bus direct to her job at Western Command.

One evening in mid-August a passer-by knocked on our door and complained about the overgrown hawthorn hedge which had encroached outwards and now restricted access along the pavement. I explained that we were not the owner of the house but I would speak the him with a view to getting the hedge cut down to a reasonable size. I contacted the owner who agreed that he had been intending to trim the hedge, but time had been against him due to him moving out of the house. I suggested that I would do it for him and we negotiated a small fee for my time and effort.

I set to work on the hedge in the summer evenings and at the weekends. It was a hard job and eventually, after three weeks, I had the hedge cut back and reduced in height to about 5 feet. A few passers-by commented on the great improvement, especially now that it was no longer necessary for them to step into the road to avoid the overhanging bushes. Getting rid of the cuttings was no problem as I burnt small amounts and the smoke arose it did not to annoy the neighbours, most of the smoke from the fire being driven by the wind over the railway embankment next to the bungalow. I managed to keep the garden reasonably under control, mainly by keeping the grass cut with the mower left behind by the owner.

In October 1967, there was a serious outbreak of foot and mouth disease in the United Kingdom which spread rapidly, particularly to North Wales and Shropshire. The military in Western Command were tasked with helping to fumigate farm buildings in order to destroy the virus causing the disease. From DMED, we ordered huge quantities of Formaldehyde solution and potassium permanganate used to generate the Formaldehyde vapour for the fumigation process. The outbreak was finally brought under control after 6 months, by which time we had left Chester for foreign climes.

Winter came and with it, Christmas and the New Year, we were happy in the bungalow, but I was becoming somewhat disenchanted with work in the dispensary. There was not enough variety in the work to keep me occupied and I was keen to get into a main stream hospital pharmacy. Shortly after we had celebrated our second anniversary, the unit chief clerk told me he was visiting the RAMC Records office and was there anything I wanted. I told him I would dearly love a posting to a hospital—anywhere worldwide. He returned a couple of days later and mentioned that there was a remote possibility that a position may come available in the British Military Hospital in Kluang, Malaysia.

I believed my chances of getting the posting to be impossible, particularly as the post description was for a sergeant and I was disappointed with the news. I was still a private soldier and the likelihood of getting even an acting promotion would be out of the question. I learnt a few days later that fellow dispenser, Dave Y, who I knew of but never met, went to Kluang. We would meet a couple of years later.

I put my disappointment at not getting the posting to Kluang behind me in the belief that something would turn up. Sure enough, at the end of February the chief clerk called me with some news. I rushed over to his office and was told I was to be posted to Hong Kong in late April. I couldn't wait to get home and tell Mo the good news. I was wary as to how she would take being on the other side of the world and away from her family. I should not have worried, she was as happy as I was, looking upon the posting as a great adventure. Among the places in the world, she had always dreamt of seeing, Hong Kong was very near the top of the list, along with the Taj Mahal and Mount Everest. I told her I had been advised that I would have to look for somewhere for us to live as I did not have enough points to qualify for a quarter. I would travel out on my own and as soon as I had got a flat for us, she would be sent for and fly out to me. She would have to do nothing by way of arrangements as all that would be handled by the military.

We had a couple of months grace before I was due to fly out to Hong Kong. I was measured up for tropical kit—olive-green shorts, shirts and socks—and these arrived at the unit clothing store a few days later. They went straight into my army issue suitcase along with kit I wasn't using. Mo suggested she leave Chester in late April and go to stay with her family in Birmingham until she was due to join me. She handed in a month's notice to Western Command in mid-March, and then we started packing up in earnest. We were issued with plywood boxes from the Military Forwarding Operation (MFO), along with instructions on what could and could not be included in the packing.

Chapter 5
First Flight

Our three large boxes where filled, nailed down and addressed. They were picked up a couple of days before we were due to leave. I had sold the Bantam to another soldier at Saighton Camp, had a final look around the house, left the keys with our next-door neighbour and headed off with Mo to Chester Station. I spent a couple of days with Mo and her family before I was ready to leave for RAF Brize Norton in Oxfordshire.

I had a degree of apprehension about the journey I was to embark upon. Travelling half way across the world had no worries for me, apart from a school trip to Paris eight years previously, I had never been out of the country. It was flying that worried me—I had never flown before and I did not know what to expect. I cannot remember how I got to Brize Norton, probably by train to Oxford where I was met and taken on to the RAF Station. After an overnight stay, we were bussed to RAF Lyneham from where we due to fly out early the next morning.

Next day, after the formalities of documentation and checking in baggage, and given a boarding card, we were taken to our aircraft, an RAF VC10, for our flight to the Far East.

The first that struck me as I climbed the steps and entered the aircraft was that the seats faced the rear of the cabin. A much safer system in an accident, but one which commercial airlines have never bothered to implement. I found my seat near the back, and sat next to a couple of men on their way to Singapore. Soon the doors were shut and the plane began its taxi towards the runway. The RAF cabin crew toured the aisles checking seat belts and seats. We were given the safety procedures as we taxied, almost identical to commercial flights today.

Soon we reached the end of the runway, and without stopping the engines powered up to a roar and the VC10 raced down the runway. The nose lifted and we seemed to take off almost vertically. One of the guys next to me said that we had 45 seconds to beat the record as he opened a newspaper which showed the wreckage of an aircraft which had crashed 44 seconds after take-off. The very thought did nothing to assuage my nervousness. Soon enough, we reached our cruising height, and the aircraft seemed to fall back as it settled into its cruising attitude. Seat belt signs and no smoking signs went out and we settled in for a long flight. There was nothing by way of entertainment apart from a few old copies of Country Life and Punch magazines. Drinks consisted of coffee, tea or orange juice, and no alcohol. A far cry from commercial air travel these days. Lunch came around about three hours after take-off, I can't remember what we had, all I can say is that now in 21st century economy class, meals bear a remarkable similarity to the meals served in 1968 as we flew high over the eastern Mediterranean.

Soon we were beginning the descent to our first stop. The captain announced that we were shortly to arrive in Abu Dhabi in the Persian Gulf. Apart from a little turbulence as we flew over the mountains of Europe, the flight had been uneventful and my worries about flying had all but disappeared. I was still concerned about how Mo would fare, travelling on her own for the her first ever flight.

We touched down in Abu Dhabi and taxied to the terminal. When I say terminal, I mean a mud brick, two story building about the size of a small semi-detached house at home. The VC10 came to a stop and the cabin doors were opened. Within seconds, the desert heat overcame the air-conditioning. A dry heat I had never experienced, it had to have been in the forties Celsius, and this was in the late afternoon.

At least, the terminal had some facilities including a wash room and a shop, a far cry from the ultra-modern airport of today. After a wash and shave, sandwiches, and an ice-cold beer we waited around for an hour or so until we were boarding ready to continue our journey east. Although it was still light as we took off, the sky gradually became dark. The cabin lights were dimmed and I tried to sleep. There were some around me who were fast asleep, those who could drop off anywhere. Unfortunately, I was not one of them, I dozed, waking at the slightest noise. The flight seemed interminable, but after a while the sky started to brighten and the dawn light illuminated the wings of the plane. The tone of the engines changed as we started our descent. All I could see from my window was blue sea, but as we were making a gradual turn and a small island came into view, it appeared to be a strip of concrete, running from one end of the island to the other.

"Down below us is the Island of Gan" came the captain's voice over the speaker, "I'm going to attempt to land on it." We continued our descent and eventually passed over the runway, at the end of which waves were breaking. We disembarked at the terminal and I had my first view of palm trees thick with coconuts and enormous black fruit bats. We were on an atoll in the southern Maldives, a group of islands in the Indian Ocean on the equator. It was hot and humid, but not unpleasant. The icing on the cake would have been a quick dip in the inviting waters surrounding the island, as this was not to be, I settled for a quick refreshing cool shower. We were soon back on the aircraft and continuing our journey eastward.

Our next stop was RAF Changi in Singapore with a flight time of about five hours. A meal was served after a couple of hours which helped to pass the time. Soon enough we began our descent into Singapore which, from the air, the island looked lush and green. We touched down smoothly and, when we reached the end of the runway, made a turn, and stopped. A Land Rover with a sign on the rear stating, "FOLLOW ME" in large red letters. We taxied behind the Land Rover until we reached the terminal buildings.

The cabin doors opened allowing the warm tropical air to permeate the aircraft. We made our way down the steps to a bus which took us to the terminal. After the heat and humidity of our first experience of Singapore, the air-conditioning was a very welcome respite. There were few facilities, after all this was a military base. I found the gents toilets where I could have a wash and shave, before returning to the transit area and waiting until we were called back to the plane.

We left Changi for Hong Kong on what was to be the shortest leg of our long flight, a mere four and a half hours. Another meal, probably lunch, I had by now lost track of time. We had certainly lost a day somewhere along the way. Soon enough, the captain announced our descent into Kai Tak Airport and we were to be making our approach over the city. We headed north over Stonecutters Island and shortly after turned south over Unicorn Ridge. Continuing our bumpy ride another announcement from the captain that we were making a turn and it would be a little noisy. The turning point was a hill, the summit of which had been levelled and painted in red and white squares. This was Checkerboard Hill and as we passed over it the air brakes lifted on the wings and the VC10 dropped like a stone. We flew low over the buildings of Kowloon City, people waving from their rooftops as we passed by. The height of the blocks of houses got lower and lower as we neared the airport. Finally, we passed over the perimeter fence and touched down smoothly on the single runway, number 13, a finger of tarmac built out into Hong Kong harbour. I learnt much later in life that Kai Tak Airport is one of the most difficult places in in the world in which to land.

After over 24 hours travelling, all I needed was a place to lie down and sleep. I collected my luggage and made my way through immigration and out of the arrivals area.

Waiting for me were a group of people who had ideas other than sleep. They were laboratory technicians from the hospital, Harry C, Paddy A and Des R, the latter being a civilian scientific officer. Des relieved me of my luggage and took it to his car, while the three of us went upstairs to find a bar. We ended up in the observation lounge, Harry telling me it was traditional for new arrivals to have a drink or two while we waited to watch my aircraft start on its return journey home. I ventured out on to the balcony and looked out over the apron and runway of the airport. Night had fallen and there was a gentle breeze coming off the harbour, carrying with it the smell of the sea and jet fuel. To this day the smell of jet fuel immediately takes me back to my first night in Hong Kong and the lights of buildings in the distance, reflected in the calm waters of the harbour.

The next two days passed in the stupor of Jet lag; sleep eluded me as I woke at unearthly hours of the morning. Fortunately, I had arrived on a Wednesday and I was given a tour of the hospital the next day. I was introduced to the RSM and company officer, and then taken up to the pharmacy and medical supply department. Here I met my boss, S/Sgt Charlie P, along with Paddy D and Sgt Ray Beacher both medical storemen. There was also Frankie So, a Chinese Clerk. In the pharmacy, across from the office were two Chinese pharmacists with whom I would be working. Mr Pho and Mr Ng who had both qualified in Canada.

The hospital was built on a hill in Wylie Road in an area of Kings Park, and opposite the civilian hospital, The Queen Elizabeth. It was opened in June 1967 and replaced the Bowen Road military hospital on Hong Kong Island. It consisted of two towers, a 15-storey block, being the hospital building, the other block was a 12 stories accommodation tower containing administration, canteen, barber shop and other facilities. My room was on the eighth floor with views over Kowloon peninsula.

Hong Kong was amazing and I made full use of my spare time, either with friends or exploring on my own. There had been some unrest recently but this had subsided before I arrived. I felt completely safe in my wanderings around Kowloon Peninsula or Hong Kong Island. However, my main preoccupation was to find a suitable place so that Mo could come out to join me. I looked at several places in Kowloon, but they were either too expensive, too small or in need of a good clean.

Eventually, after about six weeks of house hunting, I found a flat in Argyle Gardens in Kowloon. It was on the ground floor, well within my budget and I could move in immediately. On my return to the hospital, I advised the administration that I had found a flat and asked permission to live out. This was granted and they began the process of bringing Mo out to Hong Kong, I was told that this could take up to a fortnight before she would be with me. I wrote immediately to tell her the good news, and that she should expect to contacted soon with details of travel arrangements.

Chapter 6
Argyle Gardens, Kowloon, Hong Kong

The flat was a perfect size with two bedrooms, bathroom, and kitchen. It was light and airy, nicely furnished. It was also secure as it had a strong, open-work steel door which closed and locked against the main entrance door. I only had to provide some bed linen and towels, which I obtained from a huge Chinese Emporium on Nathan Road. I was sure Mo would like the flat and looked forward to seeing her within the coming weeks.

Our boxes had arrived a few weeks before and they were bought to the flat where I started to unpack. I had moved our belongings into the flat three or four days before Mo was due to arrive. I had a few callers within minutes of opening the flat—mainly 'look-see' boys wanting to sell me paintings, jewellery, watches, and souvenirs. I sent these away, preferring not to buy at the door. I had a few days off and the day before Mo's arrival I answered a knock on my flat door to find a young Chinese boy, asking me if I wanted a store-boy. He was from a local grocery shop and said he could take a grocery order in the morning and deliver it the same day. He also mentioned that he knew my wife was arriving shortly. How he knew that I had no idea. He gave me a notebook to write down my orders which I used to make out a list for basic groceries which would be sufficient for a few days. He left with a promise to be back the following morning. My grocery order arrived, as promised, in the morning. I checked it off and paid the bill, along with a tip for the service.

Mo's flight was due to touch down in the afternoon in late May, and after tidying up the flat, I made my way to Kai Tak to wait nervously for my lovely lady to arrive. I went up to the bar and observation balcony and watched for the aircraft coming in from the seaward direction, at least Mo would have a smoother landing than I had experienced.

At last, the RAF VC10 appeared on the horizon and within a few minutes touched down at the end of the runway, turned onto the taxiway and parked on the apron below me. I watched as the passengers came down the steps and boarded a bus to take them to the terminal. I looked for Mo but could not make her out in the distant crowd.

I made my way down to the arrivals area, my heart thumping in anticipation of seeing Mo again after ten weeks. And there she was, looking completely unruffled as if she had just stepped off a 10-minute bus ride. I rushed to her and took her in my arms in a bear hug, giving her a big kiss. Once she had disentangled herself from me, she stood back looking a little embarrassed, particularly as quite a few of her fellow passengers were looking at us with smiles on their faces.

I took her luggage and we made our way out of the airport, flagged down a taxi and told the driver to take us to our flat in Argyle Gardens. We were only about 15 minutes from our flat and Mo sat and marvelled at the sights and sounds of Hong Kong. I had a thousand questions for her, but these could wait until we were home in our flat. Once inside I showed Mo around the place and she seemed quite happy with it. I suggested food, but all she wanted was a drink and a sandwich, after which she was going to take a bath and get some sleep. Her eyes were drooping as she drank her tea and ate her sandwich, meanwhile I ran her bath ready for her. I left her to get ready for bed, tided away the remains of sandwiches and tea, and looking into the bedroom I saw she was fast asleep.

Over breakfast the next morning I asked Mo how she had fared on her long flight to Hong Kong. She told me she had managed to sleep on and off which was the reason she was not as jet-lagged as I had been when I arrived. She had made friends with another army wife and her baby who was also meeting her husband after a longer period than Mo and I. When they landed at Singapore, Mo had taken the baby while her mother managed to get a shower and freshen up. Mo was just about to get in the shower herself when the flight was called for boarding.

We decided to take a walk around the local area so Mo could get her bearings when the time came for me to go back to work. I was not due back at the hospital until Monday so we had a couple of days together. As we walked to the end of the road to the T Junction at Argyle Street, Mo spotted the local police station, the entrance of which was protected by sandbags and barbed wire. Seeing she was a little worried by this, I assured her that it was a hangover from the recent troubles in Hong Kong but that this was now over and the colony was now safe and peaceful. We continued our walk along Argyle Street to the junction with Waterloo Road. Mo was surprised to see old London double decker buses. The bus to Kings Park and the hospital stopped here so we waited a short while before one arrived. Even though the rush hour was over the bus was packed, there must have been some thirty people standing as we joined the crush. The fare was just a few cents and we were at Kings Park in 10 minutes.

I took Mo up to the hospital and introduced her to my colleagues in the pharmacy and medical stores. We took the stairs to the Pathology Lab where we met Harry and the rest of the staff. Harry was kind enough to invite us to his house on Saturday evening. We asked if we should bring anything and he suggested a few beers. With that, we left the hospital and made our way back to Argyle Gardens.

As it was Friday night, I suggested we went out for a meal in the evening. We got ready and made the walk along to Argyle Street to find a restaurant. Opposite the bowling alley there was a brightly lit Chinese place with the menu posted on the door. We entered and was shown to a table for two. Inside the restaurant was clean with flowers on the tables.

We made our choices, sharing the platters as they were placed on the table. The meal was excellent, and for sweet we chose Toffee Apple, not realising how this dessert would come. It arrived with slices of apple floating in a sea of toffee. I picked out a slice of apple with my chopsticks and was about to place it in my mouth when the waiter came and stopped me. He had also put a bowl of iced water on the table, "Very hot, sir," he said and taking my chopstick with the apple slice from my hand, dropped it into the bowl. Immediately the toffee solidified and became crisp and crunchy. That was the technique, take a slice, drop it into the icy water and eat—delicious. Had the waiter not stopped me I would have seriously burnt my mouth.

We sat back from the table, full to bursting having tasted our very first authentic Chinese dinner. After coffee, I called for the bill, which, when it arrived, considering the excellent meal we had enjoyed, I thought it to be very reasonable. I took out my wallet—to my horror discovering I had confused the Hong Kong dollars—I was short of the bill by five dollars, at the time about 40 pence. I had visions of ending up washing dishes in the kitchen or being chased down the street by irate Chinese waving cleavers.

I called a waiter over and asked to speak to the manager. He came over and after I had thanked him for a most excellent meal, explained that I was short of his bill by five dollars. He assured me that it was no problem and accepted all the cash that I had on me. The staff in the restaurant thought the entire matter to be most amusing and were laughing as we left. A few days later Mo went back to the restaurant, asked for the manager, and handed over the five dollars along with a ten-dollar tip. At first, he refused to accept, but Mo insisted, again to much mirth among the waiters.

On Saturday evening, we took a 5-minute taxi ride to Harry's quarter in Perth Street. Here we met Harry's wife, Pauline who was about five months pregnant and could balance a glass of beer on her swollen belly. Both Harry and Pauline were good fun to be with and we remained friends with them until we left Hong Kong.

We spent our leisure time exploring Hong Kong, walking the length of Nathan Road with its multitude of shops and bars. One of the bars I had been introduced to while on my own was the Kings Lodge in Chatham Road, off Nathan Road. Its main advantage was that it did not have 'Bar Girls' who touted for the customers to buy drinks at grossly inflated prices. In the lounge downstairs was a resident pianist, Ponchin Garcia, who played a grand piano at which guests could sit and drink while Ponchin played their requests. The bar was popular with many of the staff of the hospital, and American servicemen on 'R & R' from Vietnam. Another 'local' for hospital staff was Jordan's Bar which was handy to drop in for a drink after a trip to the cinema.

We also took advantage of the swimming pools at Gun Club, Backdown Barracks and, particularly, the pool on Stonecutters Island, which was also the site of the military prison. There was regular ferry boat to the island and we made full use of it.

Although our store-boy continued to collect and deliver our grocery orders, Mo liked to shop in a local market, known by the Brits as 'Stinky's,' essentially because it did. I went with Mo one morning and as we walked around a sudden shadow threw the area into darkness, a Boeing 707 passed low over the buildings on its way to landing at Kai Tak. I instinctively ducked but Mo was unphased saying that it happens all the time and there would probably be another along shortly.

We were not destined to stay in Argyle Gardens for long. Around the end of August I was offered a flat in army quarters in Boundary Street. This was a low-rise construction of eight floors, not far from Argyle Gardens. Mo had made friends with quite a few army wives, some of whom lived in the quarters and one or two of them were not over-complimentary about the place. However, we decided that we would look at the flat we were being offered. The quarter was on the eighth floor with a balcony looking out towards Argyle Street. The flat was clean and tidy, recently well decorated; with two bedrooms, bathroom, a decent sized kitchen, and a large living room furnished with a rattan three-piece suite. We decided to take it.

Chapter 7
Flat 8, Boundary Street,
Kowloon, Hong Kong

We moved into Boundary Street in September, and unpacked ready to make the flat our home for the next couple of years. Meanwhile, I had recently been promoted to Lance Corporal which, along with an increase in pay, and not paying rent for the flat in Argyle Street, gave me a little more in the way of disposable income.

In the courtyard below the block was a shoe mender, and there was usually a taxi waiting to take residents to work, shopping or to one of the local swimming pools. The problems associated with a few of the flats were mainly confined to the bottom three floors where there were infestations of cockroaches in some of the flats.

Shortly after moving in one of Mo's friends asked us to babysit. Just before they left for their evening out, they showed us where coffee and refreshments were in the kitchen, and told us not to put the lights out in this room. Unfortunately, after making a cup of coffee, I left the kitchen and by force of habit, switched off the lights. When I returned about an hour later and switching on the light, immediately understood why I was not supposed to leave the room in darkness. Every surface was covered with tiny cockroaches. I blasted the insects with a can of insecticide and swept up the dead and dying and dumped them in the waste bin. We were never troubled by beasties, which was fortunate as I absolutely hate cockroaches.

I volunteered to go on a 5-day mountain rescue course organised by the RAF. The first day took me and a dozen others out to the New Territories with an instructor. He pointed across to the horizon to a peak in the distance. "That's Tai Mo Shan," he said, "the highest peak at a bit over 3000 feet. Anyone who thinks they cannot make it, they can leave now." A couple of guys left and the rest of us set out on the 10-kilometre hike to the mountain. It must have taken at least four hours of steady trekking up over several ridges until we reached Tai Mo Shan. The view from the top out towards Tai Po was worth it. We finally made our way to Clearwater Bay Road, after climbing up a ridge aptly named 'One Rise More,' where, thankfully, transport waited to take us back to base. The rest of the course was spent in a quarry next to the Amoy soy sauce factory. We climbed and abseiled down the walls of the quarry taking 'casualties' harnessed onto our backs down the sheer walls of the quarry. It was exhausting, but enjoyable.

I took up several sporting activities in Hong Kong. The hospital was the minor units water polo champions, and, as I was a reasonable swimmer, I joined the team for the coming season. We played once a week; our home pool was Gun Club. Water polo is a brutal sport, I got both my eyebrows split and in need of stiches. We had a good season, but came second in the league losing to the military police.

I took part in the annual cross harbour swim, a kilometre across one of the busiest harbours in the world. Among the 2000 plus swimmers was Ronnie Wong Man Chu, Hong Kong's Olympic hopeful, who represented the colony in the '68 and '72 summer Olympics. The race started from the jetty at Tsim Sha Tsui on Kowloon side, and terminated at HMS Tamar on the island. Ronnie did the crossing in under 30 minutes, swimming between two police launches. I think I was just under an hour. A wife of one of the hospital staff took to the water in a white swim suit, when she emerged at Tamar, her suit was a dark shade of grey. I was stung by a jelly fish, which became infected and I ended up on a week of antibiotics. The race was eventually suspended for 33 years in 1970 due to pollution problems. The swim continues today.

Shortly before Mo's birthday I managed to get on a Scuba diving course at Blackdown barracks. The course was over five days the first of which was spent in the classroom learning about the physiology and dangers of diving, along with a swimming test. The next two days we were taught the basics of snorkel diving, and the last day was an open water test. This took place in the harbour opposite Sham Shui Po and included a twenty-foot snorkel dive. One diver with an aqua-lung descended to twenty feet and one by one we duck-dived down to find him. It was difficult as the visibility in the water of the harbour was minimal. The only way to find the diver was to swim down his trail of bubbles. I managed to find him on the third attempt. We were also given lectures and training in the use of

Scuba equipment, eventually culminating in open water diving off the coast of Hong Kong. We dived off Bluff Island and off the Nine Pins group of Islands in the South China Sea. We dived from a landing craft, ideal as we could drop into the water from off the lowered ramp. The latter was the deepest I had dived at 70 feet where I spotted a giant Manta Ray in the crystal-clear water, and caught a crayfish.

One funny incident occurred on the Bluff Island dive. Des, the civilian scientific officer in the hospital laboratory, had bought a set of his own air tanks. These were a twin set, shorter and a little bulbous than the cylinders we were all using. He referred to them as his 'Tadpoles.' He reckoned that they would float. So, saying this he dropped them off the ramp of the landing craft, whereupon they immediately sank into ninety feet of water. One of the instructors had to dive down and retrieve them from the bottom of the sea and presented them back to a red-faced Des.

Half way through the course it was Mo's birthday and I had my diving log book signed off as a qualified snorkel diver. To celebrate these events and unknown to Mo I had booked a table at a restaurant in a hotel in Wanchai on Hong Kong Island and we took the Star Ferry across the harbour. The hotel I had booked was the Luk Kwok, mentioned in a Dennis Wheatly novel. In those days of political freedom in Hong Kong, the Luk Kwok was overtly Nationalist Chinese. There was a bust of Chiang Kai-shek, who at the time was President of Taiwan and Director General of the Kuomintang. He died in 1975 a year before Mao died in China. The hotel today is known as the Gloucester Luk Kwok.

Mo and I enjoyed our meal and a floor show, and over a final cup of coffee, Mo leaned over to me and whispered in my ear that she was pregnant. My coffee almost ended up in my lap as I jumped up from the table, grinning broadly at the news and walked around and gave Mo a big kiss and a bear hug. What the other diners in the restaurant must have thought I had no idea, and I didn't care either. We left the hotel arm in arm and with a spring in my step and made our way to the ferry terminal and home. There will be a couple of other memorable evenings at the hotel but I will never forget that first night at the Luk Kwok.

My last two qualifying dives were in Clear Water Bay on 20 August 1968. No great depth—30 to 35 feet—but the current had increased and the visibility underwater was deteriorating. As we came ashore and were taking all our kit off the dive boat, the boat owner, a Chinese gentleman looked towards the horizon and pointed to a line of cloud. "Typhoon coming," he said to the dive marshal.

Sure enough, when we got back to base at Blackdown barracks we found that typhoon warning 5 had been hoisted.

The Hong Kong Observatory had a system of typhoon warnings which were hoisted around the island depending on where the radar showed the typhoon's position and predicted direction. Typhoon warning number 1 was hoisted when the storm was about 350 miles to the east of the colony. Typhon warning 5 meant that the storm was still a few hundred miles away but heading in our direction. Swimming pools were vacated, windows were taped up to prevent flying glass should the window be shattered, and in general, people stayed indoors. By the time I got home, the warning had increased to typhoon 5 and we were likely to be hit by Typhoon Shirley as it was known. All units in Hong Kong had a 'Typhoon Squad,' a group of personnel nominated for duty during a storm to assist with the safety of staff and patients and the hospital building. Unfortunately for me, I was one of those listed for the week, just in time for Typhoon Shirley and I had to report to the hospital immediately.

I left Mo in our flat and headed for the hospital and reported in for duty. Myself and a couple of others were given the task of fitting storm shutters to the window of the wards. This meant being out on the balconies on step ladders while the wind speeds gradually increased along with heavy rain. I must admit to being a little wary by the time we had reached the top few floors. When we finished that particular job, we were sent into the accommodation block to make sure that all windows were shut. Access to the rooms was via a corridor which faced the outside of the hospital and had louvre windows. All of them were not completely shut and the wind drove the rain against them, giving the impression that the corridor was like a car wash with water and spray filling it. I managed to get the windows closed and got soaked into the bargain.

We were stood down temporarily and given a change of clothes. I managed to find a spare bed upstairs in the accommodation wing. When I awoke the next morning, the storm had increased and typhoon warning 7 had been raised, Shirley was now just 150 miles to the south east of Hong Kong. Typhoon 9 came up in the early afternoon and, two hours later we were at Typhoon 10. At 7 o'clock that evening, the eye of the storm was centred over the Peak on Hong Kong Island, wind speeds dropped from 75mph to almost zero and an eerie quiet fell for several minutes. Rain continued to fall in torrents and gradually wind speed picked up as the storm moved inland into China.

Overnight into the 22nd August the storm warnings were lowered and by the time I awoke and returned to duty we were down to warning 3. Myself and a few others were tasked with taking down the shutters from the windows in the wards. This was a lot easier as the winds had died down making the job of climbing the step ladders a lot less daunting. From the upper floors of the hospital, we could see some of the damage the storm had wrought, trees were uprooted and many neon signs were lying in the road, having been ripped off their fixings. Fortunately, there no fatalities and only four people suffered minor injuries. With all the shutters down and stored away, we were stood down and allowed to go home, leaving the last few remnants of the typhoon squad to clean and tidy up.

Naturally I was keen to get back home to Mo, having been quite concerned about her, alone and pregnant in a top storey flat in a ferocious typhoon. I arrived to find Mo pleased to have me back, but unconcerned over the events of the past couple of days. It turned out that one of the neighbours had looked in to make sure she was alright and invited her into her flat for a coffee.

Over the next few months Mo's bump started to show. She had regular check-ups at the hospital and her pregnancy was progressing normally. It turned out that Harry had performed her pregnancy test in the laboratory and knew about it before I did. We carried on exploring Kowloon and the island, spending time in the swimming pools and shopping on Nathan Road. Mo also came with me on my diving trips.

One of members of our diving club, a Colonel at the hospital, was also on the committee of the sailing club at Shelter Cove. During the typhoon a number of boats had come adrift from their moorings and the Colonel had suggested to the committee that our divers could go down in the cove and retrieve the moorings and bring them up to the surface for repair. The committee agreed and for the princely sum of 50 Hong Kong dollars for every mooring found and we went to work at weekends diving in Shelter Cove.

The area we searched was not very large and the water shallow, less than 30 feet. However, the visibility once we submerged was zero and akin to being in an old London smog. The only way to find the mooring chains was to swim along with our hands thrust deep into the mud, and being frequently startled when a fish or a crab leapt out of the mud as we disturbed it. Altogether I made 10 dives and retrieved half a dozen mooring chains, and along with my companions we found and bought to the surface 20 chains. The diving club funds were richer by 1000 dollars. My last dive in Hong Kong was again in Shelter Cove in March

1969 inspecting the moorings after the winter. It would be 5 years until I clipped on diving gear once more.

We had some more good news when I heard that our friends from Colchester, Mike and Midge, and their two children, were posted out to the hospital in Hong Kong. Mike was to take over the medical supply department and would effectively become my boss. I was enjoying my work in the hospital pharmacy, my colleagues, both military and civilian were good to work with. Mo and I particularly enjoyed going out occasionally for departmental dinners at local Chinese restaurants. Our Chinese staff always arrived at least a couple of hours before we did and played Mah Jong while they waited for us to arrive.

The water polo club also organised dinners at the Luk Kwok Hotel. I went to a couple of these which were quite lengthy male affairs. With 14 at the table, we were served with 15 courses over the evening. We took a break or two from the eating and drinking to take in the floor shows. The drinks were cheap as we had an arrangement with the management of the hotel which allowed us to take in our own supply of beer with a small charge for corkage. This entailed carting 3 or 4 crates of locally brewed San Miguel beer over to the island on the Star Ferry. Not being a drinker, two bottles was enough for me during the evening.

On the evening of the first dinner at the Luk Kwok, when it was time for us to leave, one of the diners suggested that it would be a good idea to steal the life belt that adorned the Commander in Chief's security gate. We made our way up Bowen Road to do the dirty deed only to find that that the life belt was well rivetted onto the gate. Meanwhile one of our number spotted the road sign for Bowen Road was screwed to the wall. Taking out his Swiss army knife he managed to unscrew it from the wall.

Bowen Road had a certain significance for us medics as that was the site of the original military hospital. The sign was quite heavy and while carrying it down to the harbour it was dropped and skittered down the steps of Ladder Street. 2 o'clock in the morning was not a good idea to be sending a steel road sign clattering down the street. One or two lights in nearby houses went on, the road sign was hastily retrieved and we quickly made out way to the harbour. Star Ferry ceased operating at midnight so the only way across to Kowloon was by private 'Wallah-Wallah' rowing boat, infinitely more expensive that the ferry at a dollar instead of 30 cents.

The road sign eventually found its way to the hospital where it was cleaned and repainted. It was later displayed above the bar in the Sergeants Mess, along with that of the Mount Kellet road sign (Mount Kellet used to be the site of the Naval Hospital on the island), which was also relieved of its mounting after another water polo dinner at the Luk Kwok. Some months later, members of the Hong Kong Police Force were invited to the Sgts Mess for a social evening. One of the senior British Police Officers eyed the road signs over his pint, and, turning to the RSM said, "We thought it was you buggers who pinched those signs!"

I had a run-in with the local police force one evening in early January just after New Year 1969. Mo and I went to the cinema in Jordan Road to see Jane Fonda in *Barbarella*. We enjoyed to movie and returned home in a taxi. When I went to pay for the cab, I could not find my wallet, fortunately Mo had enough cash and she paid the taxi driver.

Losing my wallet in Hong Kong was a major problem—my British army identity card was in it, and the loss of this item could be a serious matter. My only option was to go to the police station on Argyle Street and report the loss. Leaving Mo at the flat I walked the short distance to the police station. When I arrived there, it was getting on for 11 o'clock and the place was packed with Chinese. I climbed the steps and the crowd of Chinese parted like the Red Sea and I found myself at the front desk which was manned by a British police sergeant. I explained to him that I had lost my wallet which contained my ID card. On hearing this, the policeman told me to come with him and we ended up in a Police Land Rover hurtling over to the cinema, blue lights flashing and the siren blaring. The cinema was closed. We headed back to the station where I made a report and was advised to tell the company officer at the hospital what had happened. I did that the next day, sat through a diatribe from the officer on the ramifications of losing my ID card, and went to work.

I received a telephone call at around 10 o'clock from the police to give me the good news that my wallet had been found by the night watchman at the cinema and handed in. My ID card was intact but there was no money in the wallet. I replied that I had only about 10 or 20 dollars in it anyway, and I was relieved that my wallet had been found. The voice on the other end asked if I wanted to press charges against the night watchman. I said, "Of course not, if he's had the cash, he can keep it as a reward." I collected the wallet from Argyle Street at lunchtime, went back to work and told the company officer the good news. His reply was that I should be more careful in future.

Mo and I loved Hong Kong, more so after Mike and Midge arrived. Mike was a very good photographer and I had recently bought a camera and I was keen to learn from him. We spent most lunchtimes exploring in and around Kowloon taking photographs of people and places. I learnt how to develop and print my black and white film using the bathroom as a darkroom. I also took a lot of transparencies, but these were processed commercially.

One Saturday morning Mike and I took a bus ride along the west coast of the peninsula almost to the Chinese border. From there, we went to Kam Tin Walled Village, the ancestral home of the Tang Clan for over 500 years. We were wandering along the main street taking photographs when we were shouted at by a group of women. They were not too pleased at being photographed and proceeded to chase us out of the village brandishing brooms.

Getting another bus, we travelled east parallel with the border with China we fetched up at Clearwater Bay Road. From there, we arrived back in Kowloon and made our way home. In all the trip had cost us about 20 dollars in bus fares. We could have made the same excursion in the luxury of a Rolls Royce for around 500 dollars, curtesy of the Peninsula Hotel, however this was a little outside our budget, although they did provide a complimentary picnic with champagne.

On one of our lunchtime excursions around Kowloon, we came across a street vendor selling oil paintings. His wares were displayed on a fence around a building site on Nathan Road. I was taken with a picture of Ladder Street on the island and, after a little haggling, bought the picture. Mike quite liked the picture and asked the vendor if he could get him one similar to it. The man said it would be difficult but if Mike came back in a couple of weeks, he might be able to get one. We duly returned in a fortnight, the picture seller recognised us and enthusiastically greeted Mike telling him that after much searching, he had located the picture for him. He went behind the fence to get it, and we peered through a gap in the fence, seeing him energetically levering the top off a crate containing at least a dozen of the very same picture. Mike and I still have the pictures 50 years on.

October 31st came around and with it a fancy-dress Halloween Party in the hospital NAAFI. Mike was dressed as a corpse, along with fake blood stains and a livid scar around his throat. Midge was a bride of Frankenstein and I was a Werewolf with furry hands and face, Mo was a very pregnant witch.

With the party in full swing, somebody mentioned that there was no one from the pathology laboratory there. Just then the doors opened and four laboratory technicians all dressed as Count Dracula, complete with flowing capes and protruding fake incisors, courtesy of the dental department. They were carrying a coffin which they carefully placed on the dance floor. Gradually the coffin lid creaked open, and one of the nurses slowly rose up and snarled at the surrounding partygoers. She was dressed as a bride of Dracula, with a flowing white dress and pale white-faced make-up. A set of Dracula teeth completed the effect. The assembled crowd was suitably impressed and applauded the scene.

All too soon the party was over and we left for home. We waited on a corner outside the hospital and tried to flag down a taxi; about three slowed to pick us up, but on surveying the four of us, waiting under a street lamp in our finery at 2 o'clock in the morning, accelerated away into the night leaving us standing. Despite having to walk home in the early hours, we all agreed that it had been an excellent party.

Our time in Hong Kong passed quickly, Mo's pregnancy progressing well with no complications. She had regular check-ups with the gynaecologist and midwives at the hospital, and soon the day arrived when I got home from work and found that Mo was in labour. We picked up her ready packed bag and took a taxi to the hospital. Heading up to the maternity ward. Mo was seen by the midwife and told that she could expect little to happen within the next 24 hours. I stayed with her for a few hours, until the ward sister told me I had to leave Mo for her to try and get some sleep. There was a radio room in the hospital basement which had a bed. Making sure it was not likely to be need that night, I got permission from the duty officer to use it, explaining that my wife was in labour and due to deliver our first child probably next day. The room had a telephone and I used it to tell the ward sister where I was, and settled down for the night.

I was awakened by the shrill ringing of the telephone. Looking at my watch I had been asleep for about 15 minutes. The maternity ward sister was calling me to come up to the ward immediately as Mo was about to deliver our first child. So much for nothing likely to happen for 24 hours. I had left Mo only a couple of hours ago. I rushed up the stairs to the ward and quickly found my way into the delivery room. Mo had a pair of midwives with her, one of them British the other Nepali, both of them officers in the Queen Alexander Royal Army Nursing Corps. They gently assisted Mo as she delivered our first born. Jason was finally born a few minutes before midnight on Sunday 26th March 1969, and at 10 pounds, was the biggest baby born in the hospital at the time. I was delighted and in tears as I kissed Mo and stroked her sweat soaked hair. One of the midwives ushered me out of the delivery room telling me I could return in an hour or so after mother and baby had been checked and bathed.

I returned to the ward an hour or so later. Mo was sitting up in bed looking a little tired but seemingly none the worse for having given birth not long ago. She told me that one thing that had taken her mind off the pain of childbirth was the view from the delivery room out across to the lights of Hong Kong harbour and to the island. She said it must have the best view of any delivery room in the world. Giving birth had not dulled her sense of humour. I left Mo to rest and sleep and went to find my son in the nursery; he was sleeping and although I wanted to hold him there and then, I let him sleep on, I would see him in the morning.

Over the next couple of days, I visited Mo and Jason as often as the ward sisters would allow me on to the ward. On the Tuesday, I saw Mo sitting beside her bed with Jason in her arms, they both looked wonderful. One of the nurses joined us saying that it was Jason's bath time and held her arms to take our baby from Mo and left the ward with him. When Mo didn't follow the nurse, I must have looked a little quizzical. Mo told me that Jason got two or three baths a day. Because he was such a big baby the Ghurkha wives on the maternity ward used him for bathing practice, supervised by one of the midwives. Jason must have been the cleanest baby in Hong Kong.

I returned to work on the Wednesday, and as soon as walked into the office my boss told me I was wanted in the company office. I made my way over to the company officer and knocked on his door. I entered and saluted the him and he congratulated me on the birth of my son and asked if mother and baby were doing well. I thanked him and told him that both of them were fine. He said that he had some good news for me. There had been an establishment inspection and it was noted that I was surplus to the hospital requirements and that therefore I was to be posted to Singapore. I was quite pleased in some respects as there was a promotion to full Corporal included. The bad news was that I was supposed to fly out that coming Saturday!

I was panicked by this news—I would not be able to pack the flat up in time and I certainly couldn't expect Mo with a week-old baby to be ready to come with me in time—she wouldn't be allowed to fly anyway. I rushed up to the ward and told Mo what was happening. She immediately burst into tears at the thought of leaving Hong Kong at such short notice. Once Mo had stopped crying, I told her that I would try and get matters sorted out and get some more information on what was to happen to her and Jason. I left the ward and went back to the medical stores office where I told the quartermaster about the posting. He was as stunned as I was at the news.

Matters took a turn for the better sooner that I had expected. Shortly after I had left the maternity ward, the commanding officer's wife had called in to see the mothers and babies. Seeing Mo sitting and looking a little glum she asked if everything was alright. Mo told her the news that I was posted and supposed to fly on Saturday. The CO's wife told Mo not to worry and that she would have a word with her husband.

Later that day as I was just leaving work, the telephone rang in the pharmacy. I picked up the receiver to hear the RSM telling me to report to the CO's office immediately. I rushed over to the office and knocked on the door and entered. Standing at the CO's desk I saluted and was told to stand at ease.

The CO was a softly spoken man and at first congratulated me on the birth of our first child and then said he had some news for me. A signal had been sent to the records office in the UK outlining the difficulty with my posting. The reply from UK was that the posting and promotion still stood but, but under the circumstances, there was to be an eight-week delay in its implementation. This was a great relief to me and I could not wait to tell Mo the good news. I thanked the CO profusely and rushed up to the maternity ward to let Mo know that matters had taken a turn for the better. She was delighted that there would be a delay but a little worried about flying off to a new country with an eight-week-old baby. I told her that all would be well as we would get a 'Sky cot' for Jason and he would even get his own baggage allowance.

Mo and Jason were discharged from the hospital the next day and along with gifts and flowers we took a taxi back to Boundary Street. We had quite a few visitors over the next couple of days—neighbours and work colleagues. One of our neighbours kindly gave us a baby carriage which doubled up as a carry cot and would later convert into a push-chair. There would also be a number of things to sort out, not least of which was to get Jason registered with the British Consulate in Hong Kong in order that he would be recognised as a British Citizen. The eight-week delay would be enough for us to get organised, there would be plenty of time to get the flat packed up ready to for us to move.

Over the next couple of weeks MFO boxes were delivered, assembled, and packing up started in earnest. We had not bought a lot of things apart from clothes for Mo and Jason, some souvenirs, and a few pictures, so the three boxes we bought to Hong Kong, along with one additional box were sufficient for us to get all our possessions packed and ready to go. Our boxes were collected within a week or two of our departure and the flat was nearly empty. Now we could relax, knowing everything was ready for us to move out of Hong Kong and fly off to Singapore.

We were having a cup of coffee on our balcony one afternoon when we heard the sound of a jet engine closer than usual. We could hear and see aircraft on their approach to Kai Tak coming from behind our flat, but the sound of this one came from the front. Then we saw it, a Cathay Pacific Boeing 707, we were looking down on it, and appeared to be following the white line down the middle of Argyle Street. It was off course by a few miles, and given the angle of Argyle Street and the runway at the airport I thought the pilot would never land his plane. I was wrong, at the perimeter of Kai Tak the aircraft made what appeared to be an impossible turn and touched down safely on the runway. Breathing a sigh of relief, I turned to Mo and said that I was glad I wasn't on that flight!

The time for us to leave Hong Kong arrived, we were sad to be leaving the vibrant city and many of our friends behind, although we were looking forward to our new posting, knowing that we had quite a few friends in Singapore, including Mike and Midge who had also been short-toured and had flown out two or three weeks beforehand. I had said my farewells to my colleagues at the hospital the day before, particularly the Chinese staff of the pharmacy, with whom I had enjoyed working. We were picked up from Boundary Street in the unit minibus and driven to Kai Tak. Shortly after checking in our luggage, the flight to Singapore was called and we boarded the bus to the aircraft, another RAF VC 10. Jason was being a little fractious, which was hardly surprising, the hustle and bustle of the travel and the noise in the airport must have been very confusing for him.

The cabin staff helped Mo with Jason, giving her a seat belt extension so she could hold our baby during take-off. The stewardess told Mo Jason would almost certainly cry when we took off, due to the noise and the change in air pressure would make his ears pop. She said it would be better to let him cry as this would clear his ears. Sure enough, he howled until we reached cruising altitude, when he suddenly stopped and dropped off to sleep. Once the seat belt lights went off, I helped Mo take off her seat belt, took Jason from her and placed him in a sky cot in the vacant seats across the aisle from us. He slept almost all the way to Singapore only to wake up when the descent gave him some discomfort in his ears.

Chapter 8
The Savoy Hostel,
Ayer Rajah Road, Singapore

We were advised before we left Hong Kong that there were no quarters available for us and we would spend a short time in the Savoy Hostel for a few weeks until a quarter became available. Our accommodation was essentially a chalet with one bedroom and a shower. It was quite comfortable and clean. Meals were served in a communal dining room and the food was very good and variable. The hostel was surrounded by lawns tended by a local gardener and all in all was quite pleasant. There was a local bus service which took me to the hospital which was a ten-minute ride from the Savoy.

On my first day at the Alexandra Military Hospital, I reported to the administration office to complete the usual documentation. I was told that it would be about 4 weeks before a quarter would turn up. The mother and baby clinic was also fairly close to the Savoy and Mo used to walk along the Ayer Rajah Road with Jason in his buggy. She also took him to Dover Road swimming pool about 20 minutes from the hostel. Jason really enjoyed splashing about in the warm water of the pool.

Meanwhile we were becoming concerned about Jason as he didn't seem to be putting on any weight. He was being bottle-fed as Mo's milk had stopped mainly as a result of the upheaval of moving to Singapore. He was sick after every feed and didn't seem to tolerate any of the formulae we tried with him. The clinic did not share Mo's concern until one of the SSAFA nurses said Jason was a good weight at a little over eight pounds, but when Mo said that he was ten pounds at birth, alarm bells started to ring. Mo explained that he was vomiting after every feed and that we had tried a lot of different formulae. The nurse gave Mo a voucher to be used at the local NAAFI for the good old standby National

Dried Milk, the only one we had not tried. The results were amazing, no more sickness after a feed and within a short time Jason was putting on weight.

I had taken over from John and Carol who we knew in Colchester. Unfortunately, we didn't get to meet them as they had left for the UK shortly before we arrived, essentially due to the delay in our posting. I worked in the pharmacy with Terry, a warrant officer 1st class, and a Malayan other rank Sergeant Salim, we also had a Chinese lady who kept the place clean and tidy. The medical supply department was directly across the corridor and was run by WO2 John C along with a sergeant and a private soldier both medical storemen. I was by now wearing my full Corporal stripes on my olive-green shirts, although I wore a white coat in the pharmacy.

At the far end of the hospital corridor, an extension to the outpatient's department was nearing completion and incorporated a satellite pharmacy. Once this building work was complete the satellite would become my domain. The present pharmacy would remain to service the needs of the hospital wards and the outlying medical centres around the island of Singapore.

Mike, had also been caught up in the establishment changes, was also in Singapore and had arrived a couple of weeks before Mo and I. He was working at the Singapore Medical Equipment Depot (SMED), in Tanjong Berlayer, the main supply depot for the hospital in Singapore and those in the Malaya Peninsula—Terendak, Kluang, Taiping, and the military maternity hospital in Penang. We met up most lunch times and went for a meal in one of the many restaurants or food stalls around the area. We always had our cameras with us and looked for opportunities for photographs. By now, I had a Petri single lens reflex camera and I used both monochrome and transparency film. Mike used a Mamiya twin lens reflex and was an excellent photographer.

Our main hunting ground for photo opportunities were in the hundreds of Kampongs in Singapore. These were villages where small populations lived, each village usually having its own ethnic population—Chinese, Tamil, Hindu, Muslim, or Malay. Mike and I wandered around the Kampongs with our cameras very much visible, but not taking any photographs. We were usually surrounded by children all crying out. "Orang putih!" meaning white man and this brought us to the attention of the adults in the village. Now we could point to our cameras and using the polite phrase in Malay: "Boleh saya ambil gambar?" which is translated as "May I take a picture?" This was usually met with a nod of agreement and we continued around the kampong mainly photographing the villagers and their children. Later in the evening, the film would be developed and the best of the pictures printed on postcard size. A few days later, we would return to the kampong and hand out the photographs we had taken. After that, we could roam around the place at will and take as many pictures as we liked.

One lunchtime, we found a Tamil kampong and as we wandered around as usual, Mike noticed we were being followed by a large, heavyset Tamil man sporting a vicious-looking parang (knife) in his belt. Believing discretion was the better part of valour Mike suggested we made a sharp exit from the village. We found ourselves back on the road and, having walked a few paces, came face to face with our follower who stepped out of the bushes standing with his hands on his hips. We cautiously approached him, and as we got within a few steps, he asked in perfect English, "Why do you not take any pictures?" We followed him back into the village and did the usual, shot a roll of film and went back a couple of days later, found our friend and gave him an envelope of postcard prints. He was very happy and invited us back into his house for a cup of tea.

The kampong all over Singapore were soon to be demolished and the population relocated into high rise flats elsewhere on the island. Mike and I both agreed it would be a sad loss of the culture of Singapore, but all was done in the name of progress.

Five weeks into our stay at the Savoy Hostel, Jason was now thriving and Mo was enjoying life in Singapore, we were offered a quarter in the town. I went to visit to see what it was like, only to find that it was a flat on the fourth floor and there was no lift. With Jason still in his stroller, Mo would have great difficulty getting him up four flights of stairs. I had no option but to turn it down and hope for something more suitable to come up. What I didn't realise was that by refusing a quarter we immediately went to the bottom of the waiting list. I was not aware of this until the chief clerk at the hospital told me a few days later. Then shortly after this the Manager of the Savoy informed us that stays at the hostel were time limited and under normal circumstances, we should be out in six weeks. However, at the time there were no other families scheduled to arrive, there were a couple of chalets vacant and we could stay until the last moment.

With the possibility of being evicted from the Savoy, I started house hunting in earnest. I got information on places to rent mainly by word of mouth, fellow members of the hospital staff letting me know that a house or flat may be coming available in the area where they lived. Many had gone by the time I got to them, one was not even completely built, and some were too far out from work and the city.

After a couple of weeks, John, a staff sergeant in the Pathology Lab, dropped by the pharmacy to let me know that a house opposite him had become vacant. He had approached the landlord and asked him to hold it for me to consider taking it. I contacted the landlord and made an appointment to see the house in Pasir Panjang, not far from the Savoy.

We went to see the house the next day. It was perfect, and recently built. An end of terrace house with a garden on three sides. Mo loved it. The rent was also reasonable. The landlord and I shook hands and I took possession of the keys.

Chapter 9
36, Taman Mas Merah,
Pasir Panjang Estate, Singapore

The name in English means Red Gold Park. We packed up our few belongings from the Savoy and took a taxi to our new house. It had three bedrooms, bathroom and shower, and a large kitchen. It was newly furnished throughout with a comfortable rattan three-piece suite in the spacious living room, and the landlord had provided a cot and a playpen for Jason. As a landlord he was most accommodating, any problem, no matter how small was quickly rectified. He was also able to recommend an amah to help Mo around the house. The rent for the house was reasonable but after 5 months I managed to have it taken over as an army hiring. This was beneficial to both myself and the landlord. The latter guaranteed a regular rental income and tenant, while I gained a considerable reduction in the rent I paid.

There was a local bus stop at the top of the road, the hospital was just a ten-minute trip along the Ayer Rajah Road. I usually bought a fruit drink and a slice of fruit from the pedlar who had a stall next to the homeward bound bus stop. Quite a few Brits were horrified at Mike and I patronising local food stalls, particularly the open fronted shops in Chinatown or a village stall where a Coca Cola was usually served with a glass of ice and a bottle of warm coke. A favourite was Cha Sui Fan (red cooked pork shoulder with rice), from a hawker stall on Ruma Bomba Circus, a traffic island down the road from the hospital and close to the local fire station. In the 18 months we spent in Singapore, neither Mo nor I ever got an upset stomach.

The street was a cosmopolitan mix of people, although there was a fair number of military families living there. John, who found the house for us lived directly opposite, another John from the Royal Engineers lived a couple of doors up from us with his wife and three lovely young daughters, along with a small menagerie including a gibbon and a small deer. My immediate neighbour was Japanese with his wife and daughter.

Shortly after we moved in one of our neighbours dropped round to see Mo and to ask if she needed an ahma to help around the house. Mo said she decided to wait and see if she could cope with Jason and running the house in the heat of Singapore.

She lasted a fortnight! Within a few days we had taken on a Malaysian ahma for three days a week. She would clean around the house and do our laundry. Her name was Aminah and she lived in a kampong about 15 minutes' walk from our house. She would also babysit in the evening or at weekends for an extra payment. On most weeks, she usually worked 3 full days on Monday, Wednesday, and Friday. If we wanted to go into Singapore on Saturday morning, we would give her the Friday afternoon off and she would come in to watch over Jason on Saturday. Often when we returned from shopping, we would find Jason in his playpen along with our furniture out on the front lawn while Aminah mopped the living room floor which was mosaic tiled. She was very good, especially with Jason.

Due to the heat and humidity of Singapore, a clean uniform every day was a necessity, sometimes twice a day. I had sufficient olive-green shirts and shorts which Aminah would launder and starch on the days she came into work for us. Mo saw to Jason's nappies and her own smalls. It was an indication of Aminah's honesty that I frequently returned home to find Singapore dollar notes which I had forgotten to remove from my pockets, hanging on the washing line to dry along with my shirts, or small change left on my bedside table when I had left coins in my uniform pockets. My uniforms were always beautifully starched and pressed and hung in my wardrobe.

Within walking distance of our house was a night market every Tuesday evening on Pasir Panjang Island. Mike and Midge frequently visited and we went off to the market together to look around and haggle with the stall holders. It was a great place for buying material lengths for dresses for the ladies and shirts for the men. There was also a local Malay man who made satay on an improvised barbeque. Satay is a local dish of small pieces of meat—beef or chicken—marinated and grilled on a skewer and served with a spicy sauce of ground peanuts. Each stick of satay cost 10 cents and was accompanied with a handful of sticky rice wrapped in a banana leaf, and a salad of lettuce and onion. We usually purchased 60 sticks for the four of us, the satay man delighted as we bought most of his stock of raw material for the evening.

Mike and Midge bought a car, a Humber Hawk—a limousine with enough room for half a dozen or more. It also was air-conditioned in that cool air rose up from the holes in the floor as we drove along. We went with them into Malaysia, picnicking by the waterfalls in Kota Tinggi. A lovely spot for cooling off in the pools of the river, and for keeping a bottle of wine or a couple of beers well chilled. We also went to the Malaysian coast on the South China Sea, in the state of Johore on a beach at an aptly named place called Jason's Bay.

The bay had a soft sandy beach and the sea was shallow for hundreds of yards. Mike's two sons kept Jason entertained, all three of them plastered with sunscreen cream and sand as they played on the beach. There was an 'Ais Kacang' hawker stall nearby where we sat under a billowing parachute canopy. Ais Kacang was nothing more than shaved iced with a variety of fruit salad and jellies added, and finally a pouring of Carnation milk over it. At 50 cents a bowl, it was a tasty bargain. We all enjoyed. "Ikan Bilis," fried white anchovies, another tasty snack, we could buy them in a paper cone from one of the wayside stalls for a few cents, and eat them as we drove along in Mike's car.

Local food in Singapore was tasty and cheap. There were plenty of hawker stalls and mid-priced restaurants all over the island. Directly opposite the hospital there were two cafes, one was the Highland Bar and the other, accessed via the paper shop was a place affectionately known as 'The Shacks.' The Highland Bar was essentially two restaurants, Indian food at the front, Chinese in the rear, with chairs and tables on the pavement outside. The Shacks was just that. A tin roof attached to the railway cutting fence, air-conditioning supplied by the draught from passing trains.

The sole dish any day was paratha and curry, any variety depending on what was available at the time. The parathas were cooked while we waited, by a chap sat on the earth floor with a cast iron plate over a gas ring. There was also no cutlery, so we ate with our fingers. When we were not out at lunchtime with our cameras, we usually ate in one or other of these two fine dining establishments. We occasionally ate lunch in the pharmacy, our cleaning lady would go across the road to the Highland Bar and bring back a curry wrapped in a banana leaf.

A few of the guys from the hospital who also ate at the Shacks, pushed the boat out one night and went for a meal at the Singapore Hilton. After dinner, they managed to 'liberate' a couple of menus. These were leather-bound with gold embossed tooling on the cover and gold tassels. These were later presented to the owner of the Shacks, but the Hilton menu inside had been replaced with a single sheet of paper on which was written 'Dish of the Day—Paratha and Curry.' The menus were still in the Shacks when we left Singapore a year later.

One of the more salubrious restaurants was the Singapore Lady a three-decked riverboat brought over from Hong Kong in 1968 to serve as a floating restaurant and tourist attraction. Diners were ferried to and from the vessel, which was moored in Singapore Harbour opposite Clifford Pier. Housed within the vessel's first two decks were bars, lounges and a Polynesian-themed restaurant that could accommodate up to 250 people. On top was a sun deck where guest could gather to view the sights of Singapore and to take photographs of the occasion.

We went to the Singapore Lady with Mike and Midge to celebrate their wedding anniversary. We started off in the lounge bar and had a cocktail before dinner. The cocktails were listed in the bar menu and were not any that I recognised. A couple I remember were 'Vicious Virgin' and 'Missionary's Downfall,' whatever their names, they were very alcoholic and tasty, but one was certainly enough.

We splashed out on dinner, Lobster Thermidor times four; we also had a German glass wine dispenser at the table. This held about two regular bottle of wine and when your glass was empty you held the glass against a spring tap and refilled your glass. The meal was excellent, and afterwards we retired to the sun deck to take some photographs and to admire the brightly lit view across the river. We took the ferry back to Clifford Pier where there was a taxi waiting to take us home. After paying the restaurant bill, we scraped just enough change between us to pay the taxi driver when we got back to our flat. I was saddened to hear in 1972 the Singapore Lady closed down, despite the great food and atmosphere we had enjoyed back in 1969.

Most people can remember where they were or what they were doing when a momentous world event took place. I had just opened up the forward dispensary at the hospital and switched on my portable radio to listen to the news on the BBC World Service. It was 8 o'clock in the morning on Monday 21 July 1969. The headline was that Apollo 11 had landed safely on the moon some 4 hours before.

I worked in the forward dispensary for about three months. In this short time, it was evident that the system wasn't working—the room was too small to keep a reasonable amount of stock and I could not meet every prescription written by the doctors in the outpatient's department. For every patient's prescription, I dispensed, I had to send two up on the long walk to the main dispensary in the hospital. Eventually it was decided to close my little domain as it was just too inefficient for what was its original purpose. It was a good idea was to have a dispensary close to where patients would have their prescriptions filled quickly, but not well thought out due to the limited space in the room built to house it.

I moved back up to the main pharmacy and worked with a new staff Sgt dispenser, Ken H. I got the distinct feeling after a short time that he was not happy working in the pharmacy, and I found him aggressive to work with. Eventually an ideal solution to the problem was found. Ken preferred working in medical supply and suggested to Mike that they exchange places. This move was accepted and as they were both the same rank, they swapped and Mike came up to the hospital and worked alongside me. The move was good for both Mike and I as our lunchtime excursions out into Singapore were made easier.

Mike and I joined a photographic club where I learnt quite a lot about technique. After a few weeks, we managed to get on the committee, Mike as chairman and myself as competitions secretary. We held a competition once a month, and invited various photographers from other clubs to demonstrate various aspects of photography, for example portrait and landscape work, lighting, and retouching.

I was impressed by the results Mike was getting from his Mamiya twin lens camera. It had the advantage of using a larger film size and as a result better definition in the final photographs. I decided to get one for myself and scoured the classified advertisements in the Straits Times. Eventually I found what I was looking for and contacted the seller. We met in the Highland Bar across the road from the hospital and, over a cup of coffee, haggled over the price. After much toing and froing, I decided he was asking too much, thanked him for his time and walked away. He followed me and finally agreed my price. We were standing in the middle of the road and shook hands on the deal, exchanging money and camera while cars hooted their horns at us to get out of their way.

One evening we were taken on a tour of the Chinese quarter by a reporter from the local newspaper, the Straits Times. He was very knowledgeable and told us all about the various businesses and traditions of the Chinese people. We were lucky in that there was a 'Wayang,' a Chinese opera, being performed in one of the streets. Mike and I went up the rear steps and found ourselves in the actors' dressing room where we took some excellent photographs of the various actors in their traditional dress. When we went to leave, we took a wrong turn and ended up on stage, much to the amusement of the audience.

During my time in Singapore, I was shooting at least three rolls of Kodak Ektachrome 35-millimetre film every week. I had them processed by Kodak via a local camera shop and viewed the results on a light box in the shop, discarding any that were not good enough or duplicated. I usually kept probably 10 from each set of 36. I still managed to bring over 2000 transparencies from Singapore.

Apart from our weekly lunch time photographic trip we often went out at weekends, usually early to get the best of the morning light. One memorable trip was into the market in China Town, where we watched and photographed a butcher slaughtering several large monitor lizards for the pot, using just basic tools. He also despatched a soft-shelled turtle which kept drawing its head inside its shell as the butcher attempted to lop off its head. There was blood all around him in the street.

We also joined the Thaipusam gathering. This is an annual event brought to Malaysia and Singapore in the 1800s, when Indian immigrants started to work on the Malaysian rubber estates and in the government offices. Thaipusam is a time for Hindus of all castes and cultures to say thank you and show their appreciation to one of their gods, Lord Murugan, a son of Shiva. With the crowds of several thousand people joining in or witnessing the procession around the streets until it reaches Sri Thendayuthapani Temple where milk is poured over the statues of Lord Marugan as offerings and worship.

The whole festival can get quite hypnotic with the music and drumming. Many in the crowds were overcome with the emotion of the event. Particularly those carrying wooden kavadi decorated with flowers and peacock feathers balanced on their shoulders. Other devotees carry spiked kavadis that require elaborate preparation and dig into the flesh on their back and chests. We managed to get into the temple which was packed with devotees, the noise of the chanting and drumming was deafening, the air heavy with clouds of incense; we took many photographs and eased our way out of the crowd and into the fresh air outside the temple.

I had hoped to continue diving when we got to Singapore, but I was dismayed to find that the nearest club was in Changi about 20 miles away and I did not drive. I also discovered that they often spent weekends away on one or two of the islands. I decided that would be unfair to Mo, leaving her with Jason and looked for something local where we could spend our free time together.

Shortly after abandoning the idea of diving a notice came on company orders regarding a sailing course. I made a few enquiries and found that the Royal Singapore Yacht Club, where the course was to be held, was just a few minutes taxi ride from where we lived, and the hospital Pathologist, Colonel Van Reenen, was a member and a keen sailor. I applied for the course and was accepted. The course entailed a five-day intensive training session, after which, providing I passed, I would be awarded a 'C' helm. This would allow me to take out a small sailing dinghy either alone or with a crewman. We were to be taught in a 14-foot dinghy, a GP14 which was used for all levels of sailing, from training beginners through club racing to competing at regional, national and world events. It is relatively stable boat and ideal platform in which to learn to sail.

Close to the area of the club was the main shipping lane for the oil terminal at Jurong. Massive oil tankers, some bearing thousands of tonnes of crude oil plied their way to the terminal. Power is required to give way to sail under normal circumstances, but a large notice in the sailing club advised members not to expect a half million tonnes of oil taker to take avoiding action to avoid a 14-foot dinghy.

On day two, we went out as crew with an experienced sailor. It was a warm day with a gentle breeze, ideal sailing weather for a beginner. We were out for an hour or two where I learnt the commands from the skipper and how to steer the dinghy against the wind, and how to tack and jibe the boat. I was allowed to take the helm for a short period, taking instructions from my teacher. I loved it, especially when the wind got up and we were speeding along.

All to soon it was time to head back to the club, and my first taste of sailing was at an end. Over the next 3 days I became more confident in handling the dinghy, although I admit to capsizing a couple of times, managing to get the boat upright, bailed out and sailing again. On the penultimate day, we sailed single-handedly in a Firefly dinghy, shorter than the GP14 at 12 feet long. It was certainly lively as the wind rose, but great fun even with just the mainsail hoisted.

On the last day, we had a competition, sailed a race over a figure of eight course. I started out as helm and we were quite well placed among the ten boats in the race. My crew was a Captain in the Royal Engineers who was keen to get away early for his daughter's birthday party so I gave him the helm to finish the race. We did quite well, finishing in the top four and headed back to the club jetty having dropped the mainsail and sailed in on the jib. We were travelling fast with an on-shore wind and a rising tide.

As we approached the jetty, I said I would step off the dinghy and pull the boat in as we got close. In the event, as I stepped off, I slipped and fell on my back, missing the boat which sailed on up the river. The captain managed to turn the boat but was unable to sail it back on just the jib due to the wind and rising tide. I swam out to him and helped to raise the mainsail and we made our way back to the jetty and moored up. By now, the captain was running late so I told him to go while I tidied up the dinghy. I saw him later in the month and he told me he made the party by the skin of his teeth.

The sailing club was a heaven sent, being just a mile and a half from our house. Mo could take Jason there in his buggy when I was out sailing. There would be quite a few people in the club house where Mo could sit and have a drink and chat with other members and their wives.

Mo did not always come to the club with me. She often took a Taxi to Tanglin and took Jason in his buggy to the Botanical Gardens to see the macaques. She would also walk the length of Orchard Road stopping of at Dairy Lane for an ice cream and real milk imported from Australia. Jason, who was now getting bigger and sitting up was a source of curiosity among the local Chinese and Malay children with his blonde hair. Mo went out on most days with Jason, often to the pool at Dover Road, she also went to the SSAFA clinic to get Jason checked out at Sandes on the Wessex Estate, about 15 minutes by taxi from home. There was also a good swimming pool on the site along with a cafe where one could get a cup of coffee and a sticky bun.

She and Midge frequently met up at her house on Chip Bee Estate in Holland Village. Midge knew an excellent Chinese dress maker who would arrive with an armful of ladies' fashion magazines. She could expertly reproduce any dress featured in the magazines at a fraction of the cost of the original. One of those she made for Mo was a Vogue original, a white top with a full-length dark navy skirt. Mo looked beautiful in it.

With his milk sorted out Jason was now doing well and thriving. He said his first word one evening while I was holding him on the balcony outside one of the bedrooms. It was not Mummy or Daddy, but pointing up at the night sky, he said, "Moon." Where that came from, I have no idea. He slept through the night only keeping us up one evening when he was cutting some back teeth.

He had regular check-ups at the clinic and by the time he was 11 months old he made his first steps. After that, there was no stopping him, he used to run around through the house and into the garden, even in the rain. We had a high chair for him and as he got older, he ate more or less what we did, although we used to blend his food in the Kenwood mixer we had recently bought from and electrical retailer behind the Highland Bar. When he made a mess, Mo used to take him out into the back yard and hose him and his high chair down with lukewarm water. He was a real water baby and loved splashing about in the blow-up pool we got for him. He was also completely at home in the swimming pools to which Mo used to take him. He bought much joy to our lives.

I sailed as often as possible in my GP14, and soon became competent enough to be invited by Colonel Van Reenan to join the racing team. As a team of four we competed against other teams from clubs around the island. Dinghy racing was quite tactical and cut throat. The rules of the race were that competitors swapped boats with the opposition after the first race. The winner taking the boat of the of the losing dinghy of his opposing team member. Frequently the colonel ended up in the slowest boat, but it was to his credit as a sailor that he often won in it.

The hi-lite of the sailing year was the Round the Island Yacht Race. It was open to all types of boats, from the single-handers to the 4 masted yacht "Brigand of Changi." The first leg of the race was the Seletar Passage race, from our club to the jetty at RAF Seletar. We sailed out from the club heading for the Straits of Johore with a strong on-shore wind. The boat was going well, speeding along, and bouncing off the wave tops and we were driving it hard.

My crew and I were leaning out to keep the dinghy as upright as possible on a broad reach, when there was a load crack as the mast broke away from its housing in the bottom of the boat. The wire shroud on the starboard side holding the mast from the top, parted company and whipped between us into the decking, chopping out a sizeable chunk of the woodwork on which we were sat. Seconds later we were swimming as the boat went over. Luckily, we quickly managed to get the dinghy upright and bailed out. The mast and sail were still tethered to the port shroud and floating beside us, we hauled it onboard and removed the sail. The dinghy was unmanageable with only the jib sail, so we dropped it and got the paddles out. Our problem was soon spotted by the safety boat which made its way over to us, hitched a rope to the bow and towed into the yacht club at

Seletar. Our round the island race was over, as repairs to the dinghy and its later return to our yacht club would take at least a week.

We had a crisis in the pharmacy and medical supply department at the hospital. It happened that an eagle-eyed medic had spotted some children's antibiotic medicines for sale on a stall in Johor Bahru. He bought a sample and later requested information from DMED in Ludgershall. It turned out that the batch number was identical to that supplied by DMED to us in Singapore.

An investigation was carefully instigated and it eventually turned out that our Malay Sergeant who, with help from an orderly on the children's ward was secretly adding more of the antibiotic than was originally ordered for the ward's daily requirements. The orderly was secreting the excess stock in his locker until they could safely remove it and take it into Johor for sale on the black market. The Malay Sergeant was Court Marshalled and dismissed from the service, the orderly prosecuted and fired.

I approached the administration officer to apply to spend some time at SMED in Tanjong Berlayer with a view to obtaining the qualification of medical storeman, class two. I had already spoken to one of the officers at Tanjong Berlayer who said he would look favourably on my application. My month at DMED at the start of my dispenser class one course gave me the qualification of medical storeman class three. My application was successful and I swapped with Ken for 4 weeks in order to obtain the qualification.

When I wasn't being instructed in the finer arts of the responsibilities of a medical storeman, I worked as the dispenser. I had an office in the ante room of the cold storage refrigerator where temperature sensitive pharmaceuticals were kept. I fulfilled the pharmaceutical requirements of the hospital including controlled drugs, the keys to the security cabinets containing these sensitive items remained in my possession at all times.

Working in the cold room for any length of time, where the temperature was set at 4 degrees Celsius, I wore a heavy wool jumper. There was a lot of harmless banter between me and the medical storemen on the site, and they frequently nipped into the ante room when I was in the cold room and switched the lights off. After this happened a couple of times, I took the precaution of keeping a torch handy so I find my way out of the spacious refrigerator.

We had a rest room at SMED which had an ancient dentist chair in one corner which was used by a local barber who came once a week to keep those of us who needed keeping their hair neat and tidy. He was also very good with a cut throat razor, and, following a haircut and shave applied hot towels and gave a quick massage. All this for the princely sum of five Singapore dollars, about £1.00.

After my month at SMED, I took the written and practical exams for the medical storeman class 2. I then returned to the hospital to await the results, swapping back with Ken. A few days later I got the news from the hospital chief clerk that I had passed.

The military in Singapore were allowed a duty-free ration of beer. This amounted to 30 cans of beer each month. We were issued with a ration card which was initialled by the NAAFI manager every time we bought all or part of our duty-free beer. I very rarely used all my ration and frequently gave part of my allowance to those who got through their ration before the end of the month.

As the Christmas season approached, we were allowed to draw the ration for November, December, and January. 90 cans of Tiger altogether. One of the medical storemen at SMED discovered that a careful application of bleach on a cotton bud erased the signature on the card and he was able to draw an extra ration of 90 cans by bleaching out the signature. He did this several times until he made a hole in his ration card. However, by the time this happened he had enough duty-free beer to last him for the remainder of his time in Singapore.

I decided that it was about time I learnt to drive, and asking around found a recommended driving instructor. I took a taxi to the driving school office which was in the grounds of a large house in the city, and there I met my instructor, a Chinese gentleman by the name of Mr Chan. We spent the first half of the lesson filling in forms and learning the rudiments of the Singapore Highway Code. We then went out to the car in which I was to be taught how to drive. I was a little dismayed to find it was a Morris Minor, probably a mid-60s version. I was expecting something a little more modern. Mr Chan opened the passenger door for me and we left the driving school and headed out to Singapore city. It was just before 5 o'clock in the evening and the Singapore rush hour was in full swing, although the traffic was not as heavy then as it is today.

We came to a stop halfway along the main Singapore thoroughfare of Orchard Road where Mr Chan got out of the car and invited me to sit in the driver's seat. He got in beside me and pointed out the car's controls. He then told me to start the car and drive off! I had never sat behind the steering wheel of a car in my life, the only motorised vehicle I had ever driven was my trusty BSA Bantam, but at least that experience had made me aware of traffic. After a couple of kangaroo starts, I got the hang of the clutch and accelerator and we moved off into the stream of cars and lorries along Orchard Road. Within half an hour, we were back at the driving school having driven there with no serious incidents, it was a help that in Singapore one drove on the 'proper' side of the road, namely on the left, a hangover from Britain's colonial past in Singapore and Malaysia.

Mr Chan used to pick me up from the hospital on the evenings when I had booked a lesson and I had about 20 sessions before Mr Chan felt I was ready for a driving test. Before this, I had to take a theory exam, introduced in Singapore years before a similar system was started in the UK. Passing this meant I could arrive at the test centre without an appointment and hope to get a test.

Getting a test in Singapore was essentially a lottery. The head of the test centre announced to the waiting crowd of around 150 people that on this day they would be conducting 50 driving tests. One the staff went round and collected the licences of public sector workers—medical staff, police, firemen and those of the armed forces, both local and British. On my day, there were 10 of these who would definitely get a test that day. The remaining 140 had their licences collected, placed in a large bag and 40 were picked out as in a raffle. These 40 would get a test. The remaining unsuccessful 100 would have to come back another day.

I managed to pass the test first time and was awarded my Singapore diving licence by the head of the centre. Not only would I be able to drive in Singapore and Malaysia, I would be legally allowed to drive in the UK for 3 months after arriving back home. The first thing I did after getting my licence was to hire a Mini and drive around for an hour with no one else in the vehicle.

We continued to enjoy our time in Singapore, weekends sometimes meant going into the city to see a movie. We went to see MASH at one of the cinemas in town and judging by the raucous laughter at the banter and the jokes there were quite a few medics in the audience.

The Hygiene and Malaria Control Unit on the Ayer Rajah Road had a social club called the Anophele Inn (after the anopheles mosquito which carried the malarial parasite), where films were shown a couple of time a month. They did a great line in curry puffs as well.

We had our first taste of pizza at Gino's, a newly opened Italian restaurant in Tanglin. The menu claimed that all the ingredients in his dishes, apart from eggs, came from Italy. The pizzas certainly were delicious, as was the bottle of Chianti we had with them.

We frequently went out with Mike and Midge, usually to a club—the Pink Pussy cat was a favourite—which had the latest entertainment, a discotheque. One or two of the nightspots we visited were a little more formal than others, in that gentlemen were required to wear a tie. The rules changed from week to week, so the ladies, ever resourceful, always carried a tie in their handbags. Jackets were usually optional, except in the more upmarket establishments, which we couldn't afford anyway.

Penang is an island in the Andaman Sea two or three miles off the north west coast of Malaysia and about 500 miles from Singapore. Towards the end of our time in Singapore I was asked to go up to Penang to cover the dispenser at the British Military Maternity Hospital so he could go on leave. It would be for a couple of weeks and I suggested that I went with Mo and Jason. We would stay at Sandes Soldiers Home, a short distance from the hospital. I was given a railway warrant for myself but would pay for Mo and Jason to travel. Our rail journey was on the overnight Golden Arrow express from Singapore, with a change of trains at Kuala Lumpur, and on to Butterworth in northern Malaysia for the ferry across to Penang.

We had a minor crisis at home on the evening before we went to Penang. I had bought some Malaysian Currency (Ringgits) a few days previously and went to our bedroom to put them with the rest of our documents ready for the next day. I could not find them where I thought I'd put them. Mo and I searched high and low for them and knowing that it was possible that Aminah had found them and put them somewhere safe.

I went off to her kampong to ask her if she had moved them. She said she hadn't but she came up to the house with her son to help us with the search. It was a hot night and the ceiling fan in the bedroom was on full blast. All my clothes were laid out on the bed and the pockets search for the missing money, which, as they turned up empty were replaced in the wardrobe. Aminah's son picked up the last jacket and as he did so, he shook it vigorously. Suddenly the Malaysian ringgits were flying through the air like confetti with the breeze from the fan. When I had put the notes into what I thought was the inside pocket of the jacket, I had managed to stuff them into the sleeve instead, and the lad's shaking the jacket had dislodged them. With the panic over, I took Aminah and her son back to her kampong, giving her 50 dollars for her trouble.

Later the next day we made our way to Singapore's main railway station on Kepple Road to board our train to Kuala Lumpur. In 1970, it was possible to travel direct from Singapore into Malaysia and onwards north through the country. Nowadays it is necessary to change trains in Johor Bahru across the straits from Singapore island. We found our berths for the night and got Jason settled for the long journey north to Kuala Lumpur. It would take almost ten hours to cover the 230 miles, stopping at most stations on the way. I slept fitfully in my bed, but Jason woke only a couple of times, given a drink and a change of nappy, and went back to sleep.

We finally arrived at Kuala Lumpur at around 6 o'clock on Friday morning so we had about an hour and a half before our connection to Butterworth. I took a walk outside the station to find a place where we could get something to eat. There were a few places open and a breakfast of Char Kway Teow, noodles and vegetables, went down very well. The outside of the station across the road was a hangover from British colonial days, it was reminiscent of an Indian Mogul Palace, quite an imposing building for a railway station. Returning to the station we had a few minutes to wait before our connecting train arrived.

We had good seats on the train, which travelled slowly along the single track, and stopped frequently. One of the stations I remember was Slim River which was the site of a battle between the invading Japanese military, and Indian, Australian, and British forces in January 1942. The battle was lost to the Japanese which effectively ended the British defence of Malaya.

We arrived in Butterworth in the early afternoon and made our way to the ferry to cross to Penang. The crossing took a little over 20 minutes and from the jetty we took a taxi to Sandes. We had the weekend before I had to start work, but first we needed to get something to eat and recover from the long journey. Our accommodation was a chalet bungalow in the grounds of the home. There was a play area for the children along with a swimming pool. Meals were served in a communal dining room. It was reminiscent of a holiday camp in the UK. There was a message in reception from the chap I was relieving on Monday. He would come and collect me in the morning and take me over to see where I would be working and to meet various people at the hospital.

John S, the dispenser, arrived to take me to the hospital the next morning. The British Military Maternity Hospital was not far from Sandes. It was quite small relative to the hospital in Singapore. I met some of the staff including the commanding officer who was quite friendly and welcomed me to Penang. The dispensary was a reasonable size and well laid out. After going through the routine of running the dispensary and introducing me to the local staff who would be working with me, John accompanied me back to Sandes. I wished him a good break on leave and waved him goodbye for the two weeks he would be away.

I got back to Sandes to find that Mo had already made friends with a Navy wife whose husband was on a training course in Penang. She had a daughter the same age as Jason and they were busy chasing one another around the lawns. At least, Mo and Jason would have some company while I was away working. We would have the weekends and Wednesday afternoons to explore Penang together. On the first Wednesday afternoon, Mo and her friend had decided to go into Georgetown, the capital of Penang, to do some shopping, and were taking the children with them. In some respects, I was pleased that Mo was not going to be bored staying in Sandes while I was working.

I hired a bike and armed with a map rode over to find the Reclining Buddha at the Chayamangkalaram Buddhist Temple. The Buddha was imposing and enormous, some 110 feet from head to toe. One of the largest reclining statues of Buddha in the world. It also contains a Columbarium where the ashes of those devotees cremated are stored. Outside at the entrance to the temple are several brightly coloured statues of Yaksha and other mythical creatures. I spent a couple of hours exploring this temple and a Burmese Buddhist temple a few minutes cycle ride away, taking photographs and examining the statues and artworks in the temples, before cycling the seven miles back to Sandes.

We explored Penang over the weekends, and fell in love with the island, vowing to return when we could, although it would be almost 30 years before we returned. Georgetown, the capital, was a delight, low-rise and full of open fronted shops and hawkers selling street food. There were many buildings in the colonial fashion, a hangover from the days of the British involvement in Malaysia. There was Little India and the Chinese quarter neither of which have changed little over the years. The population was mixed, with Chinese, Indian and Malay. Various religions, Moslem, Christian, Buddhist all co-existed, it was not unusual to see a Buddhist temple across the road from a mosque. There were also several Victorian style Christian churches dotted around the island.

There was a good beach at Batu Ferringhi in the north of the island, an area which would later become a major tourist area with many excellent hotels. There were none during our time and the beach was deserted. We travelled to the top of Penang Hill on the funicular railway, then the longest in the world. The view from the top was superb. Penang was destined to become a UNESCO-designated world heritage site in 2008, a well-deserved accolade.

All too soon our time in Penang came to an end. I handed the dispensary keys back to the commanding officer who thanked me for my short time at the hospital. We packed our bags and said goodbye to the staff at Sandes and made our way back to the ferry across to Butterworth to get the train back to Singapore.

By now, it was mid-August and I knew that we would certainly receive a posting order within the next few weeks. Sure enough, at the end of the month the chief clerk called asking me to come to the company office. I was hoping for somewhere exotic, but this was not to be, I was to go to The Royal Victoria Hospital in Netley, near Southampton. The better news was that I was to be promoted to Sergeant, only acting rank, but paid.

The RSM called me into his office as I passed by on my way back to work. He congratulated me on my imminent increase in rank and suggested that I speak to the unit tailor to see if he could make me a mess dress uniform. It would be cheaper here than in UK where it could cost over £200. RAMC mess dress consisted of navy-blue trousers with a cherry red stripe down the leg, short hip-length jacket with cherry red lapels and lining. It was worn over a white shirt, black bow tie and cummerbund.

The tailor had never made a mess dress before, but if I could borrow a sample, he would copy it. The RSM duly lent me his and the tailor made a fine, perfectly fitting copy for me. It cost me £50.

Packing our boxes started in earnest, our original three had increased to ten over the two and a half years in the Far East. I managed to strip down Jason's buggy and pack it into one of the boxes along with most of his light weight clothes. We would be returning home in late October and we had bought warm clothing for all of us. It never failed to amaze us how quickly it became to amass possessions. Our boxes were collected a couple of weeks before we were due to leave and we were left with just the essentials to see us through the fortnight, along with luggage waiting to be packed just before we left Singapore.

I had also ordered a new car for when we arrived home. It was a brand-new Ford Capri, the fashionable vehicle of the day. I financed it and obtained UK car insurance through the NAAFI and would collect the vehicle from a dealer in Birmingham as we were planning to spend a few days with our families.

The day came when we had to bid farewell to our friends at the hospital and our neighbours in Pasir Panjang. A minibus collected us from our house, and our neighbours came out to wish us a safe journey. Our amah Aminah turned up to see us off as well. I had given her a bonus and a reference, so I was certain that

79

she would find another family to take care of. We were sad to leave as we had really enjoyed our time in Singapore and hoped to return some day.

Our flight home from RAF Changi was uneventful, stopping over at Gan, Abu Dhabi and finally into RAF Lyneham. I had given Jason a mild antihistamine which would help him sleep during the long journey home. Apart from waking at the stops for a drink and a change he slept most of the way. We had to go through customs at Lyneham and I was a little worried as I had three cameras in my luggage. Fortunately, someone had advised me to keep the receipts for anything of value and to declare them to the customs officer. Telling the officer about the cameras I handed him the receipts, as the cameras were over 6 months old, he said there was nothing to pay. As I took the receipts back, he noticed the watch I had bought in Penang. "What about the watch?" he asked. I told him it was a gift from my wife, a belated birthday present. He was happy with the explanation, and waved us through. That Seiko chronograph would live a charmed life over the next few years.

We had written to our mothers to tell them when we were due to come home. We also told them not to meet us in Birmingham as there may be delays. As it turned out, they ignored our request. We left the station by one stairway as they made their way down another. We took a taxi to my mother's house in Alum Rock. My mother and I had been reconciled some time ago. Needless to say, there was no one in. Mo changed Jason on the floor of the back yard and we decided to make our way to Kingshurst and Mo's family. We had walked about a hundred yards down College Road when both mothers were coming up to meet us. After asking why they had ignored our request to stay at home, which went completely over their heads, as they were more interested in Jason than Mo and I.

We eventually made our way over to Mo's family in Kingshurst. All but one of Mo's siblings were at home to meet us. The exception was Mo's older brother, Alex, who had walked away from his job at the HP Sauce factory in Birmingham, and was now working in London. Jason was a hit with the family, if not a little bewildered by all the attention he was getting.

I picked up the car from a nearby dealer and decided to drive down to Netley, to run the car in and to see what was happening with regard to quarters. I was on disembarkation leave for a week and Mo was keen to see her family before leaving them for the south of England.

I had been to Netley three years previously when the old abandoned hospital was still standing. The hospital had since been partly demolished and only the chapel was left standing, but in need of renovation. The Royal Victoria Hospital was a large military hospital in Netley, the longest building in the world at the time, and it overlooked the Solent, near Southampton.

Construction started in 1856 at the suggestion of Queen Victoria but its design caused some controversy, chiefly from Florence Nightingale who was busily engaged in the Crimea and had no input into the plans of the hospital. Queen Victoria laid the foundation stone on 19 May 1856, concealing underneath a copy of the plans, the first Victoria Cross, a Crimea Medal and coins of the realm. In its day, it had its own railway station and jetty, both of which were much used during the evacuation of wounded to the hospital during the second Boer War and the First World War. The hospital treated 68,000 wounded troops evacuated there during the 2nd World War.

On arrival at Netley, I sought out the dispensary and the man with whom I would be working. This was Jim H, a staff sergeant, and between us we would run the dispensary along with the medical stores. Jim took me to meet the RSM and the quartermaster. The meetings were informal this time, just to welcome me to the unit, I would meet the commanding officer when I joined in a few days' time. The good news was that there was a quarter allocated to me, but it would not be available for a couple of weeks after I started work at Netley.

Chapter 10
The Bungalow, Swanmore, Hampshire

I drove back to Birmingham for Mo and Jason. We were staying with Mo's family as the house was larger than my mother's. We spent a couple of days visiting a few friends with whom we had kept in touch with letters and photographs from our time in the Far East. A conversation over dinner with Mo's family hi-lighted a deep lack of understanding of the life Mo and I had chosen. Mo's brother Douglas asked me what was next for me. I said that another foreign posting would be preferable, perhaps back to the Far East or Dharan in Nepal, but I would need to finish my time in Netley before that. Mo's mother leaned towards to her and said, "Isn't it about time Trevor settled down?"

I had to return to Netley in a few days and Mo would remain in Kingshurst for a week until the quarter was ready. In the meantime, I would stay in the Sergeants Mess until going back to fetch Mo and Jason. Meanwhile I had gone through the formalities of joining a new unit meeting with the RSM and the commanding officer. Also finding my way around the hospital which was now housed in low-rise buildings, originally built by American military as 'temporary' accommodation during the second World War.

I took over the bungalow in Swanmore in the middle of the week. It was much smaller than our house in Singapore but it had a large garden. Neither was it the best place we had ever had. The garden was overgrown and in need of some work to get it into shape. It was a hiring, the owners living abroad. The inventory was a mish-mash of odd and ends, mismatched cutlery and china, all appearing to have been bought from jumble sales. A number of items must have been bought by previous occupants as they did not appear on the inventory. Its saving grace was that the surroundings were pleasant, the garden was large for Jason to play in, and there was little traffic on the lane.

I bought and fitted a car seat for Jason and, with the help of Jim who was good with cars, then drove up to fetch Mo and our son to Swanmore. Mo was quite taken with the bungalow, which also had a dormer room with a single bed. Access to the dormer was via an open stair case from the living room. One of the first things I had to do in the garden was to build a fence to prevent Jason getting out and into the lane. The next item on the agenda would be to try and get the garden into some semblance of order, although this could wait until the spring.

Shortly after we moved in, there was a knock on the door and we met our next-door neighbour, Mrs Tanner. She was a widow and was immediately taken with Jason. She was to become an excellent neighbour, providing us with soft fruit from her garden, in return for apples and plums from ours. She was learning to drive and I offered to accompany her if she wanted to practice for an hour in her Morris Minor. I was still legal on my Singapore licence. She also had a telephone, which she agreed that the hospital could use to contact me when I was on call, provided it was not after ten o'clock at night, after that the hospital could send a vehicle for me. The main purpose of the hospital was psychiatric care and call-outs were rare.

My time on the Singapore driving licence was rapidly running out so I needed to get a driving test. I had taken a test in Birmingham while I was still on leave. I failed. The examiner was not a little perturbed when I removed the 'L' plates from my car and drove away from the test centre.

I had been out in my car with Jim a few times around Southampton. Fortunately, he had a friend who was a driving test examiner at the Royal Corps of Transport in Marchwood, across the Solent from Netley. He agreed to test me, although it would have to be in a Land Rover and not my own car. I made my way over to Marchwood and met the examiner and the Land Rover. We got in, and after a few false starts with an unfamiliar gear box, drove a couple of circuits around the camp site. We also performed an emergency stop, which I believe is no longer in the driving test today.

Exiting the barracks, we drove around the narrow roads of a local village for an hour and eventually came to a T Junction where the examiner instructed me to turn right. He was a bit late with his order and I asked him to watch me back while I reversed in order to make the turn. He told me not to worry and to drive over the kerb. I replied, "If I do that, you will fail me."

"No problem," he said, "you've already passed." So, I drove over the kerb, made the turn, and arrived back at the barracks, where I was given my pink slip, which I could use to apply for a full UK licence.

Our boxes arrived from Singapore at the beginning of November and we had our possessions to make the bungalow more comfortable. Mo had her food mixer and I had my dark room equipment which I set up in the dormer bedroom.

One of the things that I thought would brighten up the living room and Jason's bedroom was some new wallpaper. The paper in the living room looked as though it had been up for thirty years. It was dark and definitely needed something more modern and brighter. I bought some Tom and Jerry themed paper for Jason's room and brighter, floral-patterned paper for the main room. I then spent a couple of evenings stripping off the old paper and preparing the walls, then set to with wallpapering. The job took me a week of evenings, and by Saturday it was finished. Never having done decorating before I was pleasantly surprised by the result and standing back, admired my handiwork. Both rooms now looked bigger and brighter and certainly more welcoming.

Winter came before we knew it and the first snow fall of the season. Jason had never seen snow and the main priority was for me to build a snow man on the patio outside the kitchen. Jason loved the snow and ran about in the garden making footprints. Driving to work via Waltham Chase I had to be careful as the snow drifted over the road. The snow was short lived and soon disappeared which made the drive to work a lot easier.

The house became cold when the solid fuel boiler in the kitchen failed. I contacted the agent for the house who in turn called the manufacturers, only to be told that parts for the ancient boiler where no longer available. Fortunately, we had an open fire in the living room and I had boarded over the opening to the upstairs dormer to prevent the heat rising up and leaking out through the roof. I hadn't fixed down the boards in order to give us access to the upstairs room if we needed it.

The dispensary was not as busy as the one in Singapore. There were few outpatient prescriptions to dispense, but the bulk of the work was filling indents for our various outstations and medical centres. We also had to resupply our own medical requirements from DMED, which, because of their position in Ludgershall just 40 miles away, they would deliver to us. We had a fair amount of spare time which I spent exploring the vast area of the hospital grounds. There was a full-sized football pitch which, during the war was put to good use when a number of top flight teams played on it for the entertainment of the patients and staff. Aston Villa and Preston North End were a couple of the teams that played there.

Much of the area was heavily wooded and home to a couple of badger sets, foxes and rabbits. In a clearing in the woods was a Commonwealth War Cemetery which contained headstones from both world wars including those of some German Troops who died in the hospital.

Jim and his wife, Pat, lived in an Italianate lodge next to the entrance to the hospital. They had three children, all girls. Mo became friendly with Pat and they spent a good deal of time together. The house had great views over the Solent and several times we saw the QE II sail in and out of Southampton. The Solent was always busy with ships, both large and small. Later Jim and his family bought a house in Bitterne, a suburb of Southampton and moved out of the lodge.

The weekend before festive season was the Sgts Mess Christmas Draw. I had been told by someone in Singapore who had served at Netley that this draw was famous. Sale of tickets started in the previous June and went on throughout the year, including the infamous 'Swindle' which was effectively a draw for draw tickets. This meant that the draw fund amounted to over £1000 and thus quite a number of excellent prizes were to be had by the lucky winners. There were usually three top prizes and up to fifty or sixty others.

The attendance at the draw was open to all staff members and people from Netley village. Many were amazed at the buffet prepared by the hospital chefs of the Army Catering Corps, it covered four six-foot trestle tables and comprised a variety of dishes, from a realistic-looking army boot fashioned from an ox tongue, a whole decorated salmon, a sirloin of beef with a chef behind it to cut a slice or two. There were numerous side dishes of pickles and chutneys, salads and sweets. As usual the Catering Corps chefs had done a great job.

Mess protocol prevailed when the Mess president announced, "Ladies to the buffet." Once the ladies had taken their food, everyone else went up. After the men had served themselves and when all had finished their meals, the draw commenced.

Of the three main prizes, one was a brand-new moped. There were two drums, one contained all the draw tickets, the other the prize numbers. When each of the three major prizes and the winning tickets were picked out, they were placed in an envelope to be opened towards the end of the evening. This kept people waiting in suspense until the end of the evening for the winners to be revealed. I wasn't one of them, and didn't win anything that evening, although Mo and I thoroughly enjoyed the night.

Just after Christmas Mo told me she was pregnant with our second child. We were both delighted with the prospect of an addition to our family, boy or girl it did not matter. Mo had registered with a GP in Bishops Waltham, a couple of miles from Swanmore and it was there that tests showed she would be having our second child in August 1971.

I attended my first regimental dinner in the Sergeants Mess in February 1971 and wore my Singapore-tailored mess kit for the occasion. As I was the most junior member of the mess I was nominated as 'Mr Vice' which meant I had to stand at the end of the dinner and announce the loyal toasts to the Queen Mother, our Colonel-in-Chief, and the toast to the Queen.

Regimental dinners were a formal affair with everyone in mess kit or Number 2 dress. Tables were arranged in a 'U' formation, with the commanding officer, the RSM and the President of the Mess Committee, along with other special guests on the top table. The tables were covered with mess silver, candelabras and flowers. We were met at the door by the mess steward and waitresses with a pre-prandial sherry, or orange juice for the non-drinkers. Taking our seats, mine was at the far end, we were required to stand until the CO sat and the RSM announced we could take our seats.

Most of us had visited the Gents before finding our seats as mess protocol insisted that one did not leave the table during the meal, and the dinner would be seven courses, served with wine, followed by the port and the loyal toasts. After this, the RSM made the announcement, "Gentlemen, you may smoke," and at this, there was a dash for the loo.

Winter gave way to spring sunshine and it was time to take stock of the garden. Pretty soon the grass on the lawns started growing and the lawn mower in the garden shed was a rusted wreck, along with most of the other garden tools. Jim offered to help, he had a scythe and a Flymo, which he bought over one weekend. We set to, Jim doing the shorter grass with the Flymo while I tackled the long grass at the bottom of the garden with the scythe. We quickly had the lawn under control, Mo doing her bit to help, keeping us supplied with coffee or beer, and made lunch in the kitchen while watching Jim and I labouring away at the grass.

The fruit trees became covered in blossom. I had no idea what they were, not being a gardener. Mrs Tanner came to our rescue and told us they were apple and plum trees, and, judging by the abundance of blossom we were in for a good harvest.

The next job to be tackled was to prune the honeysuckle growing over the garden shed. I was about half way through cutting it back when the shed began to lean alarmingly. The honeysuckle was just about holding the shed upright! Mo busied herself in the front garden, weeding and planting a few flowers bought from a nearby garden centre. Within a couple of weekends of work in both the front and rear gardens, everything was looking reasonably neat and tidy.

Jason had the run of the back garden and it was safe to leave him to play as Mo could see him from the kitchen window. One day as she was ironing in the kitchen, she was distracted by someone at the front door. When she returned after a couple of minutes, Jason was nowhere to be seen. Mo thought he was down at the bottom of the garden and went to find him—he was not in our garden.

She could hear him chuckling at something and eventually, getting down on hands and knees spotted a small gap at ground level in the bushes which formed the border with our garden and those in an adjoining street. Looking through the gap she spotted Jason in one of the gardens accompanied by a large dog. Mo raced down the lane in panic to the house and rang the doorbell. The door opened and Mo was greeted by the lady of the house. Mo breathlessly explained to the lady that Jason was in her garden with her dog.

Mo was invited in, the neighbour explaining that she often saw Jason with his head through the bushes, but this was the first time he had managed to get into the garden. She assured Mo that the dog was a softy and would not harm Jason. The lady offered Mo a cup of tea and they sat in the living room and watched as Jason played in the garden. Mo said she would ask me to block to gap in the fence to stop Jason getting through into the neighbour's garden, and left to bring Jason home. With the aid of a few wooden stakes which I hammered in front of the gap, I solved the problem shortly after returning from work.

The Hawker-Siddeley company on the Hamble Peninsula was almost next door to the RVH. The company designed and built the Gnat Trainer, the jet aircraft used by the RAF Red Arrows aerobatic display team. The team had always promised to perform a display for the staff at Hawker-Siddeley who built their aircraft. True to their word they performed over the Solent. Staff from Hawker-Siddeley, together with patients and staff from the hospital gathered on the waterfront to see the spectacle.

A public address system had been set up and the announcer reported that the aircraft had left their base and would shortly be overhead. Within minutes, the nine Red Arrows in a diamond formation roared low over the hospital buildings and climbed high over the Solent trailing red, white and blue vapour trails to perform their display. The performance was a great spectacle, the roar of the aircraft deafening as they were so close to us, and we could see the pilots as the planes passed in front of us. We would not have had a better view of the display had we been standing on the runway at Farnborough.

Shortly after moving into their house in Bitterne, Jim received a posting order. He was to go to BMH Hong Kong in July 1971. Jim's wife was adamant— she would not accompany Jim on the posting. Mo and I tried our best to convince her that she and the girls would love the Far East, but she steadfastly refused to go. Pat was very much attached to her mother who lived on the Isle of White and could not bear the thought of being away from her for a couple of years. She would remain in the house in Bitterne with the girls.

Jim's replacement would be Dave Y, a staff Sgt whom I had briefly met in Singapore when he came down from BMH Kluang with medical equipment from the hospital which was closing down.

Mo and I kept in touch with Pat after Jim had left for the Far East, I said I would deliver any mail which arrived at Netley for Jim and herself. After a couple of months, I took some mail over to Pat who answered the door to me. "One from Jim for you, what's he got to say for himself?" I said.

She opened the letter and stood on the front door step, stunned, with her mouth open. "Oh my God," she exclaimed. "He wants a divorce!"

I murmured the usual platitudes and made my excuses to get back to work. My first stop when I got back to the hospital was to see the RSM. I told him what I had heard from Pat that her husband had asked her for a divorce and that there may be a welfare problem from Jim's wife. His first comment from to me was "And what was you doing there, Sgt Mansell?" I was a little taken aback and explained that I was just delivering her mail which had arrived at the hospital for her.

Working with Dave was a revelation. Once he had rearranged the office to his liking, he set about reviewing all the files, discarding everything older than three years and all irrelevant letters and circulars. By the time he had finished, our files occupied just one drawer in the filing cabinet instead of the three with which he had started. He then spent a fortnight visiting all our outstations and removing all what he considered to be an excess stock holding. He returned to our stores usually with his car boot full of medicines and medical equipment which we returned to our stock, or destroying any medicines which were found to be out of date.

He then, with the approval of the quartermaster, wrote to all the outstations advising them that their indents for resupply would have to be submitted to us by the first Monday of the month, we in turn would guarantee to fill their requests by the following Monday. Only demands for urgent items would be honoured outside of this time. The system worked well; we spent a week fulfilling orders and getting them ready for collection or despatch. The following week was spent on stocktaking and submitting orders on DMED to resupply our requirements.

Towards mid-July 1971 I received a call from the agent responsible for the bungalow at Swanmore that the owners of the property were returning back to the UK and would need to take possession of their house. The agent told me there was another bungalow available for us in Hedge End and we could move in at the end of the month so could we get the house in Swanmore ready for 'march out,' or handing over the property back to the agent.

We took a drive over to Hedge End to see our latest house. It was a relatively new, link-detached bungalow in a cul-de-sac. The owners were in and I knocked on the door and introduced ourselves as their potential new tenants. They were very pleasant and welcoming, inviting us in to show us around. The bungalow was a great improvement on our current place, with two bedrooms, large kitchen, living room, bathroom, and an attached garage. Mo would be happier here than in Swanmore, the shops were just down the road and, especially there was a gate on the garden which would prevent Jason from getting out into the road. I called the agent for the house in Hedge End and said we would be happy to take it.

We packed our possessions in the original MFO boxes in which we had bought from Singapore and was ready to leave once we had gone through the formalities of 'marching out.' The agent who did the march out was the same man who had taken over the bungalow in Swanmore about 15 years previously, and he admitted he had not visited the place since. I gathered from his remarks the house was in good condition all that time ago, but several occupants prior to us had let the place go, and consequently he wanted to know where the flower beds had gone from the front garden; who had redecorated the living room and bedroom? Why hadn't the grass been cut etc.

He was not happy that I had redecorated without permission. As for the garden, I pointed out the rusting lawnmower, the poor quality of gardening equipment and the broken boiler which had not been repaired or replaced since it broke down before Christmas, despite several letters to his office. He was beginning to annoy me; even more so when the inventory checks were completed, he presented me with a bill for about thirty pounds for damages. I signed the certificate and advised him I would be contesting the bill.

Chapter 11
'The Brambles', Hedge End,
Southampton, Hampshire

We moved into the Brambles on the first of August 1971 and made ourselves at home. This was house number ten but I can't remember the name of the road. We were getting quite adept at packing and unpacking boxes. Within a couple of days, everything was taken out of the boxes and put away either in the ample storage space in the house or in the garage. I received about £300 disturbance allowance and this was quickly put to good use, with some of it used to buy a twin tub washing machine from Rumbelows in Southampton. It was delivered next day and Mo soon got to grips with it. With another baby on the way within three weeks, it would soon earn its keep.

Mo's sister Anne was due to get married on August 6th so we took a drive up to Birmingham to help her and Derek celebrate the event.

Mo registered with a local GP and midwife as our second child was due towards the end of the month. Around this time Mo was feeling a little under the weather and went to see her GP. He decided that she was in danger of becoming toxaemic and said she should go immediately to the hospital in Winchester to have her labour induced.

She called me at work from the surgery and I left immediately to pick her and Jason up and take Mo to Winchester. We collected her ready bag from home and made the 15-mile drive to the hospital. She was admitted to the maternity ward where the sister told me to go home and ring the in the morning. She said she didn't expect Mo to give birth for at least a couple of days, but they would give her something to help things along later that evening. I gave Mo a hug, telling her I would call the hospital as soon as got into work the next morning, and drove back home. I fed Jason and put him to bed, I didn't sleep much that night.

I cannot recall who looked after Jason when I went off to work the next morning. He was probably with a neighbour. I walked into the dispensary to be greeted by Dave, who congratulated me on the birth of our second son and told me to get off to the hospital, and that I had a few days leave. I rushed back home collected Jason from whoever I had left him and drove to Winchester.

Jason and I went into the maternity ward where we found Mo sitting up in bed with our new-born son in her arms. Despite having given birth in the early hours of the morning, she was looking bright and cheerful.

Just after I had left the previous evening, Mo had been given a foul-tasting mixture of Castor Oil and orange juice to hasten on labour. Contractions started while she was in the ward toilets and was rushed to the labour ward where she gave birth after a short labour of 90 minutes just after midnight on 27th August 1971.

We had decided that the latest addition to our family would be called Justin Alexander. He weighed in at nine and a half pounds, another big baby. Mo would have to stay in hospital for another two days before being allowed home with Justin. Jason was at first confused with the new baby, but soon warmed to his new brother. We visited Mo and Justin in hospital until the day arrived when I could bring mother and baby home. In those days, there was no problem taking them home in my car and I drove very carefully back to Hedge End.

We had a number of visitors over the next few days, coming in to welcome our new arrival. We had flowers and cards in profusion. The midwife came to check both mother and baby and announced that they were doing well. After two or three days, I returned to work but nipped back home at lunch times to make sure all was well. It was only a 15-minute drive, giving me plenty of time to get Mo something to eat and to give her a short break from looking after Justin. He was a good baby and within a couple of weeks was sleeping through the night. We had none of the problems with his feeding as he took to his bottled milk with no problems. I used to watch the television with him sleeping on my chest.

Work in the dispensary was uneventful, especially with the regime implemented by Dave. We had plenty of spare time usually at the end of the month to pursue other activities. Dave bought an old Ford Cortina from the auction in Southampton and worked on it behind the dispensary building and out of the sight of prying eyes. Within a couple of weeks, it was running well after he had done a service, changed the brake pads and shoes. Jobs that needed a degree in mechanical engineering these days and cost a small fortune. Dave took it back to the auction and made a small profit which financed another car.

Dave and I were approached by the admin officer to ask if we were able to do something about the pigeons that were making a mess in some of the older buildings. Dave had a powerful air rifle, and there was a shotgun held by the quartermaster which would be able to make use of. The shotgun was an 'over-and-under' double barrelled Baretta 12 bore, a lovely gun and almost brand-new. We spent a few evenings in the following weeks shooting the pigeons and gradually cleared most of them out. We also ventured into the woodlands which were over run with rabbits. I shot a fair number of these which ended up in the Sergeants Mess kitchen for the chef to turn into rabbit stews for those living in.

Ladies' dinner nights in the mess were enjoyable events which took place a couple of times a year. It was a pleasure seeing Mo, stunning in a long evening dress, quite a few of which had been made by her seamstress in Singapore. We were able to obtain the services of one or two of the nurses in the hospital to babysit Jason and Justin for the evening. The dinners also gave Mo chance to meet with other wives and girlfriends of my colleagues.

Some of the wives were quite surprised to learn that Mo was not an ex-member of the QARANC (the Queen Alexander Royal Army Nursing Corps), as many medics were married to ex-nurses. The dinners were special occasions and slightly less formal than regimental events. There were the loyal toasts as usual, along with a toast to the ladies. I was no longer Mr Vice and it fell to another junior to propose the toasts. One raised a glass to the ladies with the comment, "A toast to our wives and girlfriends—may they never meet." This was met with a withering glare from the RSM.

I had a call from Mike asking if I could do him a small favour. He had agreed to photograph the wedding of one of the staff of the hospital. Unfortunately, Mike had been posted to Germany and would be unable to do the job. The wedding was to be in Brighton a month's time and I said I would be happy to do it. I contacted Sid, the prospective bridegroom, told him the problem and he was happy for me to be his wedding photographer.

I drove along to Brighton on the day of the wedding to meet Judy, the bride, along with her bridesmaids. It was a beautiful sunny day and I took quite a few pictures of the ladies in their garden. From there, I went to the church to photograph some interiors before the wedding party started to arrive. In the event, a good number of the friends of the groom were rugby players, many in the RAMC team. The church was packed and quite a few of the rugby players at the back were standing on beer crates in order to get a view of the proceedings. After the wedding ceremony was over, the vicar said that he had not heard a congregation in such good voice for a long time.

The X-ray department at the hospital was only part-time, so with the agreement of the radiographer I moved my photographic equipment into a locker in the darkroom. The arrangement was much better than working in our blacked-out bathroom, and Mo was pleased when the blackout in the bathroom was taken down, and the developer and fixing solutions were removed were removed from our refrigerator.

I processed the wedding photographs in my 'new' darkroom and prepared an album for Sid and Judy from the proofs they selected. I went with Mo to see Sid and Judy when I had completed the album. So pleased were they with the results that I went back to Brighton the following year to photograph Judy's sister's wedding. Mo and Judy became friends and visited one another frequently. Meanwhile, I had photographed a couple of other weddings of the staff of the hospital.

It was nearly Christmas 1971 and we had started to decorate the house ready for the festive season. The one part of the decorations I could not find was the Christmas tree. We had bought an artificial tree in Hong Kong and I thought we had packed it when we left the bungalow in Swanmore. I had a sudden flash of inspiration a few days before the holiday, I remembered I had put the tree into its box and put it up in the loft in the bungalow.

I drove over to Swanmore and knocked on the door. It was answered by the owner whom I had never met. I asked him if I could go up to the loft as I believed I had left our tree up there the previous year and I had forgotten it when we left. At the top of the stairs was a small doorway into the part of the loft that was not used as a bedroom, opening I found the tree and retrieved it. Going down stairs I stopped at the living room door to wish the family a Happy Christmas before I left and was amazed to see that the wallpaper, which I had put up had been stripped off and the room repapered with the same pattern of the paper on the wall when we moved in. I had to bite my lip to stop me bursting into laughter. Mo and I fell about with laughter when I told her what I seen.

My Seiko chronograph which was bought in Penang came with a 3-year warranty along with free 6-monthly services. I noticed that it was losing a few seconds each day and I took it along to a Seiko agent in Southampton. Showing the warranty and free service, I was disappointed to learn the service would be charged in the UK, and it would cost £30 and take two weeks. I left the shop and headed home. Along with the instruction manual with the watch were all the worldwide addresses of Seiko agents. I airmailed the watch to the Seiko building in Hong Kong with a note explaining the watch needed regulating and a service. The watch was returned, carefully packed, cleaned, regulated along with a bill for $5.00. The process took six days.

The hospital pathology laboratory had a couple of civilian scientists engaged in research into the causes of schizophrenia. One of these was a young female graduate called Merlin. She was a pretty, young lady, married to the son of a family who owned a vehicle service station in Warsash, about 6 miles from Hedge End. Over a cup of coffee one morning, she mentioned us that the garage owners were looking for a couple of part-time staff. Dave and I got the details and approached the owners of the garage who were happy to take us on for a couple of evenings a week. There was also the possibility of a few hours at the weekend.

We started at the garage in April 1972. We were shown how to work the petrol pumps and keep a note of sales. Takings in the evening, along with credit card slips were dropped into the night safe of the bank across the road. The pumps were still in pre-decimalisation and during our second week were replaced with new pumps. The owner showed us the new additions and exclaimed, "These new ones go up to a pound; whoever heard of petrol costing a pound a gallon?"

The job was easy, the pay was reasonable and we got a small discount for petrol for our own cars. Many of the customers were regulars with accounts and were pleasant to serve, most them giving us their Green Shield stamps. One of the customers was Tommy Sopwith, racing driver and power boat racer. One evening he bought his car to the garage for a service. The mechanics had gone home and I was alone at the garage. The car was a dark blue Jaguar E-Type, the latest version with the V-12 engine. He gave me the keys, bid me good evening, and walked away.

There was no way I could leave such an iconic and valuable car outside on the garage forecourt, so I got in and drove the car at about 2 miles an hour, the 50 feet into the workshop. Once inside I sat in the car for a few minutes savouring the luxury of being in one of the most famous vehicles in the world, one that I could never aspire to own. My reverie was interrupted by the arrival of a customer waiting to be served.

I was a keen fan of the Wimbledon Tennis championships. I couldn't play tennis but followed the fortunes of the players at the annual tournament. One of my favourite players was Ilie Nastase of Romania. He met Stan Smith, the American, in the final in 1972 and I was due to work at the garage on the Saturday, the day the final was to be played. I asked Dave to swap with me so I could watch the match on Saturday and work at the garage on Sunday afternoon. In the event, for the first time in many years, it rained heavily on the men's final day and the match was played on Sunday, the day I was at the garage. Stan Smith beat Nastase over 5 sets and I never saw a ball played.

Mo and I took the children on our first holiday for years. We booked a caravan in Ventnor on the Isle of Wight for a week in September 1972. We left for the car ferry across to the island on the Friday, a couple of days after the start of the Munich Olympics. The caravan was well-appointed with two single beds for the children and a double for Mo and I. It had a shower and a television so we could watch the Olympics in the evening. During our stay we visited the usual tourist spots, Godshill, Alum Bay with its coloured sand cliffs, the Needles, and Osborne House. The boys enjoyed the beach, building sandcastles and paddling in the sea.

We had a stormy night of the 4th of September which rocked our caravan. The next day the tragedy of the terrorist attack on the Israeli athletes gradually unfolded. The Black September group were holding the athletes hostage and demanding the release of Palestinian prisoners held in Israel. The attack ended with all the hostages and five German policemen killed in a failed rescue attempt. Mo and I were stunned by the attack which resulted in ending the lives of so many young people. The children were too young to understand.

We tried to get away for a day most weekends, visiting places along the south coast—Bournemouth, Brighton, Weymouth—surprisingly, Bognor Regis was one of our favourites with its pebble beach and pier. The New Forest was visited frequently along with its picturesque villages and wild ponies.

One Sunday we took a drive to Portsmouth and the naval dockyard. We were waved through the gates and parked alongside HMS Victory, Lord Nelson's flagship at the Battle of Trafalgar. Unfortunately, the ship was closed to visitors, so we wandered around the dockyard looking at the Royal Navy ships. After about an hour, the boys were getting tired and we decided to call it a day and returned to the car.

I had just started the engine when a navy police Land Rover pulled up in front and prevented me from driving off. Removing the keys from the ignition I stepped out and was confronted by two policemen demanding to know what I doing in the dockyard. I took out my army ID card and explained that we were hoping to visit the Victory, but as it was closed, we walked around to show the boys the ships. One of the policemen asked how we had managed to get in as we had no identity discs on the car. I told him we were simply waved through the main gate. They seemed satisfied with my explanation and told me we were free to go. I suspect the guard on the gate probably got a severe dressing down later on.

One weekday morning in September 1972, Mo and the boys went to visit Judy, whose wedding I had photographed and they had since become firm friends. Judy went into the kitchen to make coffee and returned and placed the drink on a low table. Mo turned to secure the gate across the stairs into the upstairs flat, and in the blink of an eye, Justin had reached up and grabbed the spoon in the saucer of the coffee cup. The coffee spilled over Justin's chest, soaking through his woollen top, and scalding the skin on his chest. Mo quickly ripped off his jumper and bathed the area with cold water, but soon the area blistered alarmingly. Both women were distraught and taking Justin, rushed to the accident and emergency department at Southampton hospital.

Justin was seen immediately by the staff of the department, was treated quickly, and given a mild sedative to calm him. Mo telephone me and I dashed to the hospital. By the time I arrived, Justin was calmed and sleepy as the effects of the sedative had started to work. His chest had been dressed and the doctor advised Mo to return to the hospital in a couple of days to monitor Justin's progress. Over the next weeks the scald had healed but the scar had become keloid and raised. We were advised to massage the area with lanolin in order to flatten the keloid scar. This only worked partially and Justin has the scar on his chest to this day.

Shortly after Justin's accident I had been painting the fence with wood preservative. When I had finished, I washed out the brush and left it to dry on the kitchen window ledge. The following day was bright and warm and Mo left Justin in his buggy in the garden while she busied herself in the house. Jason was in the garden with Justin, spying the paint brush he began playing with it and mixed up some earth and water.

Mo went out to make sure the boys were alright and was surprised to find a brown-faced baby sat in Justin's buggy. Jason had carefully painted Justin's face with the mud he had mixed. Mo told me in the evening she had trouble cleaning up Justin as she was hysterical with laughter. Meanwhile Justin sat there with a quizzical look on his face as if the whole incident was normal in the Mansell family.

I heard from a friend at DMED that there would shortly be a course to gain the medical storeman Grade 1, and wishing to extend my knowledge, applied to go on it. The course would last an intensive three weeks at the end of which would be a written and oral exam. I was due to started the course in September 1972, and headed up to Ludgershall. I drove to DMED via the scenic route through the Wallops-Over Wallop, Nether Wallop and Middle Wallop—the latter being the home of the Army Air Corps. The drive took a little under an hour as there was little traffic on the road.

Arriving at DMED I was shown to the Sgts Mess and allocated a room. I was just in time for lunch and some of the staff were coming into the mess, I knew several of them, a couple of dispensers and storemen I recognised from SMED in Singapore. After lunch, I walked over to the main building to meet a few more of the staff, including some of the section heads who would be the lecturers and examiners for the course. I was keen to meet the chief pharmacist, Mungo Malloch, with whom I had spoken several times on the phone from Netley. There were a number of people of whom I had heard, or spoken to on the telephone, but never met, I was a pleasure to put faces to names.

Over the following fortnight, I and my fellow students learnt more of the aspects of medical equipment and supply, accounting, surgical instrument recognition and maintenance.

I left Mo and the children in Hedge End with the intention of returning at the end of the first two weeks to take her with Jason and Justin to visit her family for the last week of the course.

After the first two weeks, I returned to Hedge End at the end of Friday lectures and on Saturday took Mo and the children to stay with her family. My mother had also moved to a new council flat in Kingshurst, just a short walk from Mo's family, so we spent some time over the weekend with her. I returned to DMED on Sunday afternoon to complete the last week of the course, at the end of which would be series of examinations. We all passed and were now Technical Storemen Grade 1 (the trade had recently been renamed). No extra pay for me, but those storemen who moved up from Grade 2 had an increase in pay. Now the course was over, I returned to the mess, packed my belongings, and made the trip to collect Mo and the boys and return to Hedge End.

By mid-1973, I was becoming bored with Netley and was hoping that a posting would come through soon. In October, I had been at the hospital for three years and was ready for a move. I asked Mo if I should get in touch with the records office and ask if there were any postings available. She was happy for me to do so. Meanwhile I was granted my substantive rank of sergeant and was no longer holding acting rank. In September, I made a call to the RAMC Records office, asking to speak to Mrs Robinson who looked after dispensers' postings.

I asked her if there was anything going and she told me the only posting available was to the ANZUK (Australia, New Zealand, and United Kingdom) Force at Changi military hospital in Singapore. I said I was seriously interested and she advised me to write and officially request the posting, she also said that it would solve a problem. I wrote the letter and the following week a posting order arrived for me to go to Singapore in January 1974. I telephoned Mrs Robinson to thank her for actioning the posting so quickly. She told me that by moving me to Singapore I was a piece of the jig-saw and she was able to move several more dispensers to various other postings.

Telling Mo in the evening, I was pleased to hear that she was happy to be returning to Singapore. We both loved this cosmopolitan, busy city and we were looking forward to our move in January 1974.

I was to take over from Tom in Singapore and I wrote to him to tell him we were coming. I received a letter from him by return saying that he was happy to be moving on as he had been in Singapore for three years, and would be getting a promotion to S/Sgt in his new unit.

Packing began in earnest in late October. We were now quite expert getting all our household packed into boxes, some of the bulky children's toys were stripped down to fit into the boxes, the most difficult being a go-kart we had bought for Justin and a bicycle of Jason's, both items bought as Christmas presents. Eventually everything we thought we could do without for a few weeks were packed up, boxes nailed down and labelled ready to be collected and shipped off to Singapore. Hopefully they would be waiting for us when we arrived. We were due to fly out to the Far East a few days after New Year 1974.

One major item I had to deal with was my car. It had to be sold. I had it serviced, I cleaned and waxed and advertised it for sale. I had few interested purchasers but none who were prepared to pay the price I was hoping to get. I took it to the auction in Southampton and waited anxiously for it to be presented to prospective buyers. Unfortunately, it did not reach its reserve and I had to withdraw it from the auction.

By a happy turn of events, I had a minor problem with the car and took it to the garage in Netley. The car was fixed and when I came to pay the bill, I asked the garage owner if he knew anyone looking to buy my car. I was surprised to hear that he was in the market for a car for his son and he asked the price, I told him I wanted £600 for it but I needed the car for the next two weeks. He was happy and, providing the car was still in one piece when I returned to him after a fortnight, he agreed to buy the car off me. We shook hands on the deal and I drove home to tell Mo the good news.

We had one last trip to make in the car, and that was to see our families. We went up to Birmingham on the Sunday before Christmas, taking the families' presents with us, and hoping that there were no bulky items they had got for the boys. Fortunately, they had done as we had asked and got light weight cotton clothing and teddies for Jason and Justin. There was also a lot of sweets and chocolate for them as well.

Our last Christmas dinner in UK, possibly for a couple of years, was enjoyable, turkey with all the trimmings and cooked to perfection by Bessie. The only member of the family not at the table was Mo's oldest brother, Alex, now living and working for Qantas in the States. My mother was invited to share with us, she was looking well, now in her 60s and retired from working. She was delighted to see her grandchildren and as usual, spoiled them. She would be a great help to us in later years.

We said our goodbyes on Boxing Day, the grandmothers with tears in their eyes as we loaded the car for the trip home to Hedge End.

The house was almost empty now that all our boxes were long gone on their way to Singapore. All non-essentials were either in the boxes or packed in suitcases. The washing machine had been sold and I had left my job at the garage. We had a couple of weeks before we left for the Far East at the end of the second week in January. My replacement arrived during the first week. This was Robbie, who was pleased to have got his third stripe along with the posting. He and I would be in touch a few years later when we were both serving in Germany.

I went back to work for a week after the Christmas break and then started my embarkation leave. I had said my goodbyes to friends at RVH, had my final meetings with the commanding officer, the RSM and my boss, the quartermaster, all of whom wished me and my family well on our travels to Singapore.

Jason was excited at the prospect of flying, but Justin wasn't sure. I was certain they would both enjoy their time in Singapore. Finally, the day arrived for the 'march out' of 'The Brambles,' our home for a little over two years. The much-loved Ford Capri had been handed over to the owner of the garage in exchange for £600 in cash. Everything was in order; the house was clean and tidy and nothing was missing from the inventory—except for one item—I could not find the keys to the garage door anywhere. We had searched high and low for them but they were gone. I ended up with a bill for £30.00, no doubt they would turn up eventually.

I can't remember how we travelled to RAF Lyneham for our flight. All I know is that we must have got there ready for the long trip. I had a few misgivings as to how the children would react. Jason had flown from Singapore 3 years ago, but would probably not remember it, and Justin had not been on a plane before. Mo was as excited as I was, and I think some of our anticipation rubbed off on the boys as we boarded the RAF VC10. We found our seats, Mo and the boys together with her in the middle seat. I was on the aisle seat in the row opposite. The flight wasn't full so we could mix and match during the flight.

Just before take-off one the cabin staff came round with boiled sweets and comics for the children. We had brought books and comics to keep the boys occupied, so we were well stocked. Justin howled as we roared down the runway and took to the air, but once the aircraft had settled into its cruising altitude and speed, he became calmer and soon fell asleep. Jason on the other hand was wide awake and curious, wandering up and down the aisles and stopping to talk to the other children on the flight.

We made the usual stops at Abu Dhabi and Gan where we could freshen up and get a drink and get a sandwich. At Gan, the boys were intrigued by the fruit bats in the palm trees. The flight was called and we boarded for the last leg of our journey—back to Singapore and our new home.

Chapter 12
2 Halton Road, RAF Changi, Singapore

Tom was waiting for us at the airport with a minibus to take us the short distance to our quarter. Within a few minutes, we were outside our new home. The house was a three-bedroom semi-detached, the living room well furnished with a rattan three-piece suite, three good-sized bedrooms so the boys could have one each. There was even an ahma waiting for us, curtesy of one of our neighbours. There was a small garden at the back and we had a veranda at the front. Best of all, our boxes had arrived—we would start unpacking tomorrow.

We were all suffering from jet lag after the long flight, and although the boys were excited, they were yawning. Upstairs the beds had been made by the ahma so we put the boys to bed, and went downstairs to sit and relax for a few minutes before going up ourselves.

We were all up early the next day and had breakfast on the veranda in the cool of our first morning in Singapore. Our ahma arrived shortly after and Mo asked her to clear away the breakfast things and to wash out the clothes we had travelled in. I had this first day to get settled in and to get our bearings around the base before going up to the hospital and going through the usual administration and formalities of joining a new unit.

I started on the boxes and asked Mo if there was anything she particularly wanted. She had a rough list the boxes containing essential items she would need to come out first. Amongst them was her food mixer and some of her clothes, along with the children's clothes and toys. I opened the first box she wanted and there on the top were the keys to the garage door at 'Brambles' in Hedge End! There was no point in returning them as it was over a month since the boxes had left for Singapore and the lock on the garage door had probably been replaced by now.

We met some of our neighbours. The quarters area was quite a cosmopolitan mix of Brits, Australian and New Zealand military families. The other half of our semi was empty, and another pair of semis were next door and with only one half occupied with an Australian corporal from the Royal Australian Artillery. He and his wife had three children, all girls, all born in the hospital here on the base. I later learnt that quite a few of the Aussies and Kiwis took advantage of a three-year tour of Singapore to have their children and dental procedures carried out here as it was a free service, as opposed having to be paid for in their home countries.

I had kept my olive-green tropical uniform from our previous time in Singapore and the ahma had run the iron over them. The only thing I had to get changed was the divisional flashes, I could get that done by the unit tailor once I had found him.

Tom called in and we went up to the hospital. First stop was the RSM who was surprised to see that I was wearing tropical green. I explained that I was at the BMH in Singapore three years ago and I had kept all my kit from that posting. I was introduced to the commanding officer who was British, as was the RSM. The admin staff was a mixture of New Zealand and Australian military, and after completing all the necessary forms and getting my beer ration card, Tom and I went to the pharmacy.

Here I met my boss, the pharmacist, an Australian Captain in RAAMC. There was also Mike, a New Zealand corporal, RNZAMC. Both were welcoming and friendly. The dispensary was quite busy, and, as the Mike was keen to learn, having recently qualified as a dispenser. I let him make up the prescriptions and I checked them thoroughly before handing them over to the patients. He rarely made a mistake which was very pleasing.

The pharmacist was often out of the dispensary, consulting with doctors and ward sisters about treatment regimes, thus myself and the corporal were mainly left to our own devices. The medical supply department was responsible for supplying the various medical centres around the island of Singapore and we completed requests by making up various lotions and potions required to complete their indents from the medical centres.

Mo found a swimming pool in Selerang, not far along the road from Changi. She went there a couple of times a week with the boys. There was a pool at the base, but it was very busy most days, particularly as it was open to the local civilian population. By contrast, the pool at Selerang was quiet.

Here she met a Chinese man who worked as pool life guard and swimming instructor. He was very good, and although Mo could swim, she was not very confident in deeper water. He quickly built up her confidence and soon had her diving off the side and off one of the low diving boards. I used to go with her and the boys, usually on Wednesday afternoons and weekends. Jason could swim quite well, but Justin had never been in a swimming pool.

The first day we took him, Mo had got him into his swimming trunks and his arm bands when he dashed out of the changing room and jumped into the deep end of the pool. The force of the water pushed his arm bands off and he immediately sank to the bottom in ten feet of water. Fortunately, I was already in the pool and I was able to dive down and fish him out. He was completely non-plussed, apart from coughing up half the pool he had swallowed, and once I had got his arm bands back on, he was quite happy to splash about.

Shortly after we arrived in Singapore it was our 8th wedding anniversary and we decided to go out for a meal to celebrate. We chose the Princess Hotel near Tanglin in Singapore city. The hotel had a revolving restaurant at the top called 'The Tiara Room.' I had booked a table for us and took the lift to the top where were met by a waiter who showed us to our table. The waiter was most attentive, bringing us a jug of ice water along with the menus and a wine list.

After all these years, I still have vivid memories of that evening. Mo ordered a crab salad in an artichoke heart; my starter was deep fried prawns with a chilli dip. I had ordered a steak for my main course; Mo ordered a red snapper. Once our starters were cleared away, our waiter bought my steak on a silver platter—it was raw! I thought I must have mistaken my order and as I took up my knife and fork, the waiter whispered, "Your steak, Sir. Chef would like to know how he should prepare it for you." Inwardly breathing a sigh of relief, I said that I would like my steak cooked medium rare.

As the waiter left to take my steak away to the chef, a sommelier arrived with a bottle of wine—Blue Nun Liebfraumilch. We were really pushing the boat out this evening! The sommelier was dressed in a leather apron with a tasting cup on the end of a chain. He opened the wine and poured me a splash in my glass for me to taste. I nodded that the wine was fine, and, after topping both our glasses, left us to await our main courses. The mains were excellent, and as we ate, and drank our wine, the sommelier appeared as if from nowhere, topped up our glasses and disappeared as mysteriously as he arrived.

Following our mains our sweet of crème brûlée we settled back to enjoy listening to a 4-piece band playing relaxing soft music. I took out a cigarette—it was allowed to smoke anywhere in Singapore back in the 70s—and before I could get my lighter from my jacket, another waiter appeared at my side with a Zippo and lit my cigarette. I have always been impressed by the service one receives in hotels and restaurants in Singapore and Malaysia, and the service in the Tiara Room was no exception. We had had a wonderful evening which has stayed in my memory after all the years since.

Changi was about 15 miles from Singapore city, and we decided we needed our own transport. One of our neighbours, an Australian, was due to finish his tour and had a battered Hillman Super Minx of about mid-60s vintage. He was anxious to be rid of it before he left to go back to Australia in a few days' time. I made a quick check of the car, kicked the tyres which were sound and had a good depth of tread on them. All the instruments worked, along with the windscreen wipers, indicators and the lights. I took the car for a spin around the base, the engine ran smoothly and quiet. The only problem I could detect was a slight rumble from the back end when I turned right.

I made him a paltry offer of a few dollars which he was happy to take so as to get the car off his hands. However, registering a change of the ownership of a vehicle in Singapore was an exceedingly bureaucratic exercise.

By the time I could get time off to go into Singapore to register the car in my name, the Australian had left for home. The local licencing authority insisted that both parties, seller and buyer, went to their office to complete the necessary paperwork. The fact that the Australian seller was no longer in Singapore added to the bureaucracy. There was also a fee to pay. This was based, not on what was actually paid for the car, but what the authorities told you what it was worth. This, and the price paid bore no resemblance whatsoever. There was also a sliding scale of fees based on the cubic capacity of the engine. This was in order to remove most of the gas guzzlers from Singapore streets, and it seemed to have worked. Most cars were of 1600cc of less.

The clerk and I completed the paperwork as far as possible in the absence of the seller. He then gave me an official looking letter telling me I had to go to across the road to a department at the town hall and find a Commissioner of Oaths.

Finding the receptionist at the town hall I asked directions for a Commissioner of Oaths. The town hall was a maze of corridors but I eventually found the office for which I was looking.

I gave the receptionist the letter and I was asked to take a seat. After about half an hour, the telephone on the receptionist's desk rang and I was shown into a sumptuous office with a large desk, behind which sat who I believed to be the Commissioner.

Rising from his desk he held a large Bible which he placed in my right hand. I was then told to raise my left hand and swear that I had bought the car from an Australian soldier who was now back home in Brisbane. Having sworn the oath, Commissioner signed and sealed a document which I then took back to the clerk at the licencing office. With more signatures and rubber stamps, I was now the proud owner of an old banger of a Hillman Minx and several hundred dollars lighter in the wallet.

I took the car to a local repair shop and explained that there was a rumble from the back end. Raising the car on the hoist the mechanic removed the sealing bolt from the differential gear housing and dipped his finger in the hole. Removing his finger from the differential, he held it up to me, "No oil, Sir," he said. I nodded and asked him to top up the oil. The rumble had disappeared when I drove away from the garage and went home. Here I managed to get the boot open which revealed half a set of golf clubs and a colony of cockroaches.

We discovered another minor problem with the car when we went into Singapore to see a movie. On the way home, it began to rain, which steadily became a tropical downpour. As we drove along, the driving rain forced itself up into the bottom corner of the windscreen resulting was a spray of water on the passenger side. By the time we got home, Mo was soaked. I took the car back to the garage next day to get the windscreen re-sealed.

Mo became friendly with our next-door neighbours and we used to share babysitting duties. They had some strange quirks. Tea was made in a billy can on the stove and was black and strong. Probably a hangover from their previous life in the outback of Australia. The husband was also extremely careful with water, insisting the children were not given too much as he was convinced it would make them fat.

One evening when Mo was babysitting, she went upstairs to check on the children, as she ascended the stairs, she was met by a 4-foot monitor lizard on its way down. Mo pressed herself against the wall and the lizard walked past without a backward glance. Mo wasn't particularly frightened, as she knew the monitor wasn't dangerous, but a little startled to see the lizard in the gloom of the stairs. Mo checked on the girls, the lizard had not been in the bedrooms as the doors were closed. How the animal got up the stairs in the first place was a puzzle.

Our neighbour's husband was also a fan of The Beatles and I gave him copies of the White album and Sgt Pepper on cassettes. He had recently bought a powerful hi-fi system which he played at high volume. One day Mo and I were returning from Changi village having done some shopping, and as we entered the main gate, we could hear the strains of 'Bungalow Bill,' a track on the White Album, coming from his quarter which was a couple of hundred yards from where we were. He was forever after known to us as Bungalow Bill.

A few weeks after we came to Singapore, my Kiwi corporal's wife delivered their first child, a daughter. Mo and I were asked if we would become proxy godparents at the Christening. We were honoured to be asked and participated in the ceremony at the garrison church. After the ceremony, we went home and to change into something less formal and went over to their house for a Sunday buffet and drinks to celebrate the Christening.

I had my introduction to Southern Comfort at Mike's house. As we walked into their house, he offered us drinks. I noticed an older gentleman lying on a settee with a drink in his hand and looking a little worse for wear.

"I'll have whatever he's having," I said, "who is he anyway?"

Getting me a glass of Southern Comfort, he nodded over to the gent on the settee and said, "Don't you recognise the vicar who christened our daughter this morning?"

Getting up and ready for work one morning, I was making a cup of coffee in the kitchen when I heard a plaintiff yowling coming from the ahma's room next door. The room had an Asian style squat toilet and a cat had somehow got in there and produced a litter of three kittens. One of the kittens had fallen into the toilet and was in danger of drowning. Mother cat was desperately trying fish to fish her kitten out of the pan but was unable to reach it. I pulled the kitten out, wrapped it in a cloth and gave it a good rub down and dried it. It must have just fallen in as it was still breathing and coughing up water. Putting her kitten back with its mother I found a cardboard box, lined it with an old towel and moved mother and kittens out of harm's way into the broom cupboard. As soon as the kittens were weaned, I took them and their mother to the local army vet, hoping he could find a good home for them.

The area around married quarters had a major problem with mosquitoes. Fortunately, Singapore was free of malaria, but dengue fever was endemic on the island and in Malaysia. Dengue can be fatal if not diagnosed early. Quite a few of the British contingent of ANZUK had tried in vain to get the area 'swing-fogged,' but requests had fallen of the deaf ears of the Australians who were responsible for maintenance and disease control in the garrison.

Swing-fogging was regularly carried out in the BMH and quarters area when we were there in 1970, and the Singapore authorities also swing-fogged the estate in Pasir Panjang where we lived. The operation left a lingering chemical smell of kerosene, but that was more acceptable that being plagued by biting insects. It was not until one of the Australian children became quite sick with infected mosquito bites that swing-fogging started on a regular basis. Within a few days, the mosquito problem had all but disappeared.

Mo and I had discussed the possibility of having more children in our family, but had eventually concluded that our two boys were ideal for us and we would try not to produce any more offspring. We made an appointment with the medical officer at the hospital with a view to me having a vasectomy. Mo was unable to take the contraceptive pill as it gave her unpleasant side-effects, one of which was a small lump in her breast. She had this checked in Chester but was dismissed as benign, although she continued to have it checked at regular intervals.

We were recommended counselling prior to me having the snip. Counselling was successful and I was referred to a female Australian surgeon who agreed to perform the operation and scheduled it for the following week. She explained that the operation would be performed under a local anaesthetic and I may experience a little discomfort afterwards.

The next week, I made my way over to the men's ward at the hospital and was prepared for the operation. After being given an injection of a cocktail of Diazepam and Pentazocine, I was wheeled into the minor operations theatre where my surgeon was waiting. By now, the drugs were taking effect and I had trouble focussing, it felt like the horizontal hold on a television was working overtime. I felt an injection of local anaesthetic into my nether regions and after a few minutes the surgeon began the operation. As she raised a scalpel, I remember saying to her, "For God's sake, don't drop a bollock now!" before lying back and thinking of England.

After what felt like only a very short time, the procedure was over and I was taken back to the ward for the various drugs to wear off. I was told to stay in bed for at least two hours before attempting to get up. I must have nodded off as when I awoke it was mid-afternoon and I felt fine. A little tender downstairs but I was ready to go home. One of the nurses came over and asked me if I was alright. I told her I was, but I needed a drink, and I asked if I could go home.

Over the next two or three weeks I returned to the hospital to see the surgeon. This was to check that the wound was healing properly and I had not developed any infection. I also had tests to determine if the 'snip' had had the desired effect. I was assured that it had—which pleased both Mo and I no end.

I dropped into the mess one lunchtime for a sandwich as Mo was out with Justin, Jason had recently started school and the amah had a day off. Here I met up with Bill Howard, a S/Sgt who worked in the laboratory. We were just chatting over our lunch when Bill bought up the subject of diving. I said that I was a diver and asked if there was a club nearby. He told me there was a club off the base, something I had not discovered, and that they met every Friday evening. He also mentioned the club was planning a diving expedition to one of the islands of the Malaysian coast.

I mentioned diving club and the trip to the islands to Mo over dinner that evening. She was pleased for me to go and I went to the club the following Friday.

I went with Bill to the club, remembering to take my diving log book with me and Bill introduced me to the club leader and the rest of the members. I told them it had been over four years since I had dived last and was told that if I successfully completed part of Test E of the 3rd class diver examination, I would be allowed to dive with them.

The test involved dropping all the diving kit into 10 feet of water—air tanks and demand valve, face, mask, fins, and snorkel—duck diving from the surface and putting all the kit on underwater. It was a hard test, but the trick was not to rush. Providing I could hold my breath long enough, the first thing to do was to get the air tanks switched on and get the mouthpiece into my mouth. Once this was done and I could breathe freely under the water, getting the rest of the kit on was easy.

I completed the test and was welcomed into the club. The leader told me the diving expedition was scheduled for the 11th April to 15th April and there was just one vacancy on the trip. I provisionally booked myself on the trip, because I had to ask for three days leave, and check with Mo that it was OK for me to go. In the end, my leave was approved and, more importantly, Mo was happy for me to go.

The dive site we were going to was off Tioman, an island in the South China Sea, sparsely populated and about 35 miles off the east coast of Malaysia. We boarded a coach at the diving club and headed off to the causeway into Malaysia. Our first stop was the army Jungle Warfare School in Kota Tinggi, where we loaded up with several cases of beer. Then on to Mersing to find our boat to take us Tioman.

Our transport to the island was small fishing boat, I could not believe this boat was big enough to take twenty of us with all our kit on the voyage to Tioman. We unloaded our equipment from the coach and began arranging it on the deck of the boat. Meanwhile, once the coach was unloaded a couple of our number took it away to buy ice from a freezer company.

The ice arrived in blocks, about 2-foot square and 9 inches thick. The blocks were wrapped in hessian and lowered into the hold. I was still a little bemused with the thought of all this ice melting in the tropical sun.

Our equipment was stacked on the deck and I was surprised to find that with a little moving around there was enough room for all of us to sit on the deck, and we made ourselves comfortable for the 4-hour trip to Tioman. We sailed away from Mersing on the late-night tide. It was a moonless and cloudy night, at least there was no wind and the sea was a flat calm.

After about an hour there was a knocking from the engine below the deck. The captain said something in Malay to the dive leader, who in turn told us there was a minor problem with the engine and we were heading to find the captain's engineer brother and get it fixed.

Bearing in mind it was the dead of night, cloudy, no moon and a serious shortage of sophisticated navigation equipment on our boat, other than a compass, we arrived at a small island and tied up at a jetty. From where I sat in the stern of the boat, I could barely see the bow. It still never fails to amaze me that our captain's navigational skills managed to find a small dot in the South China Sea with nothing more to guide him than a wheelhouse compass.

The engineer arrived and disappeared into the bowels of the boat. There was some hammering and banging for a few minutes, after which, the engine fired up, the knocking was gone and we were shortly on our way once more.

I dozed off where I sat and was awakened as the dawn broke and the boat was pitching in the swell. I could hear the crashing of waves and, looking to my left saw breakers hitting cliffs rising vertically from the sea. We were rounding the base of the twin peaks of the Gunung Kajang mountain, the highest point of Tioman at 3400 feet.

Soon we were out of the swell and into a sweeping crescent bay, about two miles long with golden sand. There is a story that this was the beach where the opening sequence of the movie 'South Pacific' was filmed. However, given the logistics of moving cast, crew and equipment 40 miles off the coast suggests this is unlikely and probably filmed on a beach on Hawaii.

The engines were stopped and the boat anchored in a couple of feet of water. The blocks of ice were thrown overboard and floated ashore. gradually all our equipment was carried up the beach. Most of us were tasked with erecting the tents, while a couple of the men were engaged in digging a hole in the at the top of the beach. Once the tents were up, I went to see how the hole was progressing. After all the hard work, the hole was now about 6 feet deep.

The sides were flattened and lined with the hessian, following this the blocks of ice were arranged around the bottom and sides. When this was complete, the beer and soft drinks were loaded into the hole, and surplus sand piled on top. I was told by the men who had dug the hole and prepared it for the drinks that the ice would stay frozen for at least a week, and this was the method used by the local fishermen to keep their fish in good condition before taking it to market on the mainland. All we had to do when we wanted a drink was to scoop away the shallow sand topping and retrieve a can or two, remembering to replace the sand afterwards.

Just before lunchtime, our encampment was complete and the compressor for filling the air cylinders was sited at the end of a small jetty about 500 yards along the beach. We had light lunch and after a short break got ready for our first dive. I dived with Bill, entering the water from the beach. My first dive in four years was wonderful. We went no deeper than forty feet but the variety of fish and coral was better than anything I remember from Hong Kong. We spent around thirty-five minutes, exploring the reef and collecting shells. Bill's underwater navigation was spot on, soon we were in shallow water and able to stand, our camp site was directly in front of us.

There were one or two nasties in the water we were advised to look out for. One was stone fish which were almost invisible when they burrowed into the sand. The only way to spot them was to look out for three spines sticking up from the sea bottom. Standing on them caused excruciating pain and in need of immediate hospitalisation.

The other dangerous creatures were moray eels which lurked in holes in the rocks and corals, waiting for prey to pass by when they would dart out and seize it with their razor-sharp teeth. A bite from one of these could inflict serious injury and we were warned no to put our hands into holes in the rocks. The only injury I suffered was from fire coral. I must have brushed against it during one of our dives and the skin on my arm came out in blisters, similar to nettle rash. The area on my forearm where I was stung still does not tan after 50 years.

On the duty roster, it was my turn to look after the compressor to refill the cylinders. For safety reasons, the compressor and empty cylinders were placed on the end of the small jetty, and well away from the campsite. There were six cylinders to fill which would take a couple of hours.

I started filling the cylinders, and while I waited leaned on the rail of the jetty. The water below was about eight feet deep and gin clear. There was a moving black shape in the water which I had not noticed when I came on the jetty. With the compressor humming along, the attached cylinder would take about twenty minutes to fill, I decided the black shape should be investigated, and dived over the rail into the sea below.

I was half way to the water when I realised I still had on my hat and glasses and as I hit the surface the force of the water tore both of them off.

The black shape turned out to be a shoal of millions of tiny fish. As I swam towards them the shoal opened like a curtain which closed behind me, leaving me surrounded by fish. I surfaced and climbed back up to the jetty, wondering if I would ever find my hat and glasses in the shoal. Peering over the rail, I was surprised to see both items clearly in the water, the fish forming a cylinder around them. The glasses were directly in line with one of the stanchions of the jetty.

The first air cylinder was full, so I changed it over for an empty one and started filling that. I found a face mask someone had left by the compressor and entered the water by the steps rather than dive in. I got my bearings on the stanchion, duck-dived into the water and I found my glasses straight away. I got my hat back 20 minutes later.

I got into some difficulty on my penultimate dive. Bill and I had been diving near a cliff face and had been down for about 40 minutes. We had started the dive off a small boat and we explored the undersea world with its coral and multitude of bright coloured fish. While we enjoying the dive and unbeknown to us quite a heavy swell had started. Bill signalled it was time for us to end the dive, and as I knew Bill's navigation was excellent, I expected our boat to be very close when we surfaced.

As we came up, we found that our boat had moved into the lee of the cliff where the swell had lessened, and about 200 yards from where we were. I had removed my mouthpiece and was just about use my snorkel when a wave broke over my head and I got a mouthful of sea water. I was choking and coughing and my diving equipment was pulling me under.

I twisted the cylinder on my life jacket and the 'O' ring seal blew out—my life jacked failed to inflate. Panic ensued and feeling I was about to drown I felt a hand reach down to grab the top of my cylinders and heave me up upwards. My head broke the surface and I emerged coughing and spluttering to get rid of the sea water I had swallowed. Bill turned me over onto my back and towed me the 200 yards to the boat. By the time we got there, I had recovered my composure and I was able to clamber into the boat with the aid of a gentle shove from Bill.

In hindsight, the answer to my dilemma was simply to replace my mouthpiece, breath air from my cylinders, and swim over to the boat. However, when blind panic sets in, reason goes out of the window.

The boat took us back to the beach in time for our evening meal, after which everyone started to get ready to leave Tioman the next morning. All our belongings and diving equipment, apart from our tents, were assembled on the beach. The ice pit was emptied of the last of the beer and soft drinks—there was not a lot left, although most of the ice was still there after five days of tropical heat.

Next morning, we struck camp and packed the tents and our remaining kit. Shortly after breakfast we saw our boat rounding the headland. It took about an hour to load up the boat for our trip back to Mersing and the coach home. This time the boat journey was uneventful and four hours after leaving the idyllic island of Tioman we were busy ferrying our equipment from the boat to our coach. I took time to thank our boat's captain for his service to us, tipped him a few Malaysian ringgit along with a pack of cigarettes before saying goodbye to him.

The island of Tioman was later to become a major tourist resort. There are a couple of 5-star resorts and many smaller hotels and camp sites. There are also regular ferry crossings to the island from Mersing.

All too soon we were across the causeway and on our way back to Changi. After helping to unload the coach at the club and saying goodbye to my fellow travellers, I threw my bag into Bill's car and we headed back to Changi and our families.

I had only been away for a few days, but in that short time we had become the owners of a dog. It was a mongrel and somewhere in his lineage was a dalmatian. Naturally the boys had named him Spotty dog. Justin was also covered in spots and calamine lotion. There was an outbreak of chicken pox among the children on the base and Justin had got infected. He seemed alright in himself, Mo said he had been a little miserable in the first two days, but now, despite the itchy spots, he was his usual cheerful self. Unfortunately, he would be unable to go swimming or to play out with his friends for a few days.

On Friday evening at the diving club, the president announced that there would be another expedition. This would be over a long weekend on Pulau Besar, another island off the coast of Mersing, but only an hour away by boat. Families would be welcome and I provisionally booked for Mo and the boys to go with me. Bill and his family would be coming as well.

Mo was thrilled at the prospect of a weekend away with the boys. I told them we would be sleeping in tents on the beach. That excited the boys as they had never been camping before.

The day before the expedition we packed our bags with light cotton clothing and swimming things, along with plenty of soft drinks. We were told fresh water would be available for cooking and drinking. Food would be provided in the form of army compo rations as on Tioman. There were just five divers on the trip, most of the single club members had agreed that this weekend should be for families. There were a little over thirty of us who boarded the boat for the hour-long voyage to the island.

We had a good break and I completed 4 dives off the island and saw many colourful fish and corals. The water was clear and was deeper than Tioman, and we got down to fifty feet. I was surprised to see how colour changed with the depth, the red of Bill's swimming trunks becoming darker as we descended. I later discovered that colours disappear in the same order as the spectrum.

Mo and the boys were enjoying the break, although Mo was plagued by sand fly bites. It was very hot with little shade so we spent a lot of time in the sea, cooling off and splashing around. Jason and Justin were intrigued with camping under canvas, but with all the running about on the island and in the sea, by the time it came to bed time, they both slept like logs.

All too soon the long weekend was over, and after loading up the boat with our equipment and belongings we sailed off to Mersing and our transport home. All agreed it had been a really enjoyable time, especially for the many children.

My last experience with the diving club was at the naval base in Sembawang. Six of us of went for a 'Pot' dive. We did not even get wet, the pot, as it was known, was a decompression chamber on the dockside. Its main use was as an emergency decompression unit into which divers who were suffering from the 'bends' (decompression sickness) were placed in order to remove nitrogen bubbles from their bloodstream. The bends were usually caused by ascending too quickly from depth. Bubbles of gas expanded in the bloodstream and joints and cause great pain and, in some cases, even death.

The pot was a steel tube with portholes and tubes and cables attached to it. All six of us squeezed into the cramped interior and the steel door sealed behind us. Once we were seated the compressors started, the noise was horrendous, which made it impossible to speak. A dial fixed to the wall of the pot gradually move to show our simulated depth (we never left dry land). Our ears popped and the temperature climbed into the eighties.

After about ten minutes, the compressors stopped and the dial indicated a simulated depth of a hundred feet. There was complete silence in the pot for a few seconds then someone spoke, "Thank heavens for that." At this, we all burst out laughing as his voice made him sound like Donald Duck. We were all the same, the air in the pot had become denser with the pressure. All our cackling voices were high and we sounded like a gaggle of hysterical chipmunks.

Soon the pressure in the post was gradually reduced. We extricated ourselves from it into the relatively cooler air of the dockside. The heat inside the pot had made us all dripping with sweat and we ducked underneath a standpipe to wash and cool off. We all agreed that it had been an excellent and amusing experience despite the noise and the heat.

In the middle of May, I was called to the office of the chief clerk. I was told that there had been a change of establishment in the pharmacy. My position was to be upgraded to S/Sgt, and as I was not sufficiently senior, I could not be given the rank and therefore I was to be posted—to Cyprus at the end of June. At least, that would give us a few weeks to get packed up and ready to move.

I went home at lunch time and told Mo the news. She was quite happy with the posting as she had heard good things about Cyprus from her many friends on the base. I was to go into the dispensary at the British Military Hospital in the eastern Sovereign Base Area of Dhekelia.

A couple of days after receiving the news of the posting, the RSM telephoned me asking me to join him outside the office of the commanding officer. Grabbing my beret, I made my way over to the office, the door of which was open. As I approached the CO called me and the RSM to come in. I entered and saluted. Bidding me to stand at ease the CO said, "I understand you have been posted to Cyprus."

"Yes sir," I replied, "there has been a change in establishment and I'm not senior enough to be promoted."

"Well," said the CO, "you've only been here for five months, and if you wish, I'll ask RAMC Records to reconsider the matter."

I was somewhat taken aback at this turn of events. "I'm very happy with the posting, Sir. This is my second tour of Singapore and I quite fancy a trip to Cyprus."

"Very well, Sgt," the CO replied, "if you change your mind, we'll keep it in abeyance for a week. Tell the chief clerk your final decision within a week. That is all." I saluted and thanked him and marched out of the office.

Later that evening when I returned home, I told Mo what the CO had said to me. I told her that there was the possibility of us remaining in Singapore or taking our chances and moving to Cyprus. She thought our posting might be good for Jason as the daily 40-minute trip to school in Serangoon was making him tired and she knew there was a primary school on the SBA in Dhekelia. She suggested we wait a couple of days and let the CO know we were happy with the posting. I agreed to this and two days later went to see the RSM and told him we were happy with the posting and to let the CO know my decision.

The following days were taken up with the administration needed to finalise the details of our move. Ordering another set of MFO boxes, applying for disturbance allowance, and requesting details of married quarters in Dhekelia. I also advised the pay office to make my final monthly salary in Singapore to be paid in sterling into the bank account I had kept open in Netley. I would need to open a new bank account in Cyprus as soon as possible after we had arrived. The

116

administration office sent a signal to the hospital in Dhekelia requesting a married quarter update—there was no email facility in those days and communications were made by telex.

There was complete silence from Dhekelia to three signals sent to them regarding accommodation in Cyprus, until 48 hours prior to our departure from Singapore. A signal consisting of one line which stated 'Suitable accommodation will be available on arrival' was all the information received from the hospital. When I mentioned this to Mo, she said, "Yes, a couple of chairs in the airport lounge!"

Our boxes were taken a couple of weeks before we were due to leave. The good news was that they were to be flown out to Cyprus on RAF transport. They would be on the island before us. I had sold the car to the local garage and made a small profit on the deal.

I went to my final Sgts Mess meeting before were due to leave. After all the formalities of the meeting, the mess treasurer giving a statement of accounts, and the entertainments committee report about upcoming events, the RSM reminded the members that I was leaving Singapore within a few days. He asked the president of the mess committee to award me a leaving present, thanking me for my support in the mess. I was given an engraved tankard made of Selangor Pewter, a gift I was delighted to receive. I thanked the RSM and the mess members saying I had enjoyed my short time with the ANZUK force, and hopefully I would meet some of them again in the future.

On the day before we left Singapore for Cyprus, I went down into Changi village and the local branch of the Chartered bank where I had my account. I believed that I had a couple of hundred dollars at the bank and I would draw out what remained and close my account. The clerk passed me a card with my account details and I was horrified to see that the pay office in its infinite wisdom had paid my final salary and allowances into the bank here, and not in the UK as requested.

Altogether my account amounted to almost the equivalent of over £700. I drew out all of it and closed the account, thanking the clerk for the service I had had from the bank. I took a taxi into the city and made my way into Change Alley. This place was in the banking district and there were many money changers standing around holding bundles of cash.

I found one of the most likely brokers and handed over most of my Singapore dollars, telling him to buy me as many Cyprus pounds as he could. Anything left he should be used to buy sterling pounds. I suppose that most people would be amazed at giving such a large amount of money to a total stranger, but the money changers in Change Alley had a good reputation for honesty and fair dealing. It was possible to get a better deal than going directly to a bank.

He returned fifteen minutes later, apologising that he was only able to get two hundred Cyprus pounds, the rest he had converted to British pounds, those I would have to convert those when I opened a bank account in Dhekelia.

Early the next morning we were all packed and ready for our flight to Cyprus. Spotty dog had been taken in by my Kiwi corporal and I gave our ahma, who had looked after us very well, a bonus and a letter of reference. The march out went without any problems and we were good to go.

My successor had arrived a couple of weeks previously and was at our house along with our friends and neighbours to wish us Bon Voyage. We had enjoyed our short time in Singapore and was sorry to leave, but full of anticipation about living and working in Cyprus.

We waved goodbye to Singapore, thinking we would probably never see the city again, not realising it would be 40 years until we saw the streets of the city once more.

The flight to Cyprus was routine for Mo and I, but the boys were excited. They had their books and small toys with them to keep them occupied, but soon their eyes drooped with tiredness and they slept for the first leg to Gan. We were on the ground for just a short time before we took off towards our final destination.

We arrived RAF Akrotiri in Cyprus shortly before 11 o'clock at night. After going through customs and immigration, we retrieved our luggage and went up to the arrivals lounge to find out how we were to get to Dhekelia. Gradually the lounge emptied of passengers until we were the only people left. I went up to an information desk and asked the RAF corporal what was happening. He checked a long list and then asked me who I was. I told him who I was and he consulted another list, telling me I was not expected.

I suggested he should contact the duty officer at BMH Dhekelia and ask him to resolve the situation. We could not stay overnight in the airport lounge, particularly as we had two young children with us. We waited about for another hour when the telephone rang on the desk. The corporal called me over and told me that a taxi would shortly arrive to take us to a hotel in Limassol for the night, and from there we would be taken to Larnaca the next day where there was a house ready for us.

We finally arrived at the hotel after about a half hour drive. The night porter showed us up to our room which had two double beds in it. We put the boys to bed and in minutes they were asleep. Mo and I fell into our bed, exhausted after the long flight, and stressed at the confusion at the airport.

It was about nine o'clock the next morning when we were awakened by the ringing of the telephone. The voice on the other end told me a taxi would take us to Larnaca and we should be ready to go at eleven o'clock. That would give us two hours to get organised, have showers and a leisurely breakfast before we needed to be ready for the taxi.

Our transport arrived promptly at eleven o'clock. The Greek Cypriot driver helped us load up our luggage and get the boys and Mo comfortable in the back seat. He told us it would probably take an hour to get to Larnaca. The day was hot but we were comfortable in the air-conditioned taxi.

The hour passed quickly and soon we were in the suburbs of Larnaca. The driver made a right turn and we headed down a road passing houses and shops. Just before the road ended, we stopped outside a detached house—this was to be our new home.

Chapter 13
Larnaca, Cyprus

I cannot remember the name of the road where our house in Larnaca was. It had three bedrooms, kitchen and bathroom. The living room looked out onto a large garden. Beyond the garden fence was rocky scrub land, which I came to know as 'The Bondu,' and was the name given to any similar area which was not farmland. The Bondu stretched for miles towards haze covered hills in the far distance.

Someone had provided us with a box of groceries, basic items such as bread, milk eggs etc, which would see us through for the next couple of days. Beds had been made and the house was clean. I would have to find out who had helped us settle into our place in Cyprus and thank them and pay for the groceries they had bought for us. Amenities such as gas and water were unusual to us. Water was provided by a bowser which came every four days and topped up the tank in the roof space. Gas was Liquid Petroleum Gas (LPG), kept in cylinders outside the kitchen door. We would have to get used to using water and gas sparingly and make sure we did not run short.

Our neighbours were all Greek Cypriots and very friendly towards us, especially when they found out we had two sons. The couple next door were in their late fifties and their garden was well stocked with vegetable plants—tomatoes, aubergines, and a grape vine. They were very helpful in advising us about the water and gas.

There was a folder in the house which, at first reading, was a little disconcerting. It gave advice as to what we should do in the event of an emergency. We should keep a suitcase or two packed and ready in case we needed to evacuate in a hurry. Make sure we had water and gas, and a plentiful supply of food was to be kept. Cyprus had been a trouble spot in earlier years but now seemed settled and peaceful. However, we decided to comply with the items in the folder.

The day before I was due to start work at the hospital, we received a visit from the RSM. He was friendly enough and welcomed us to Cyprus. He also told us that there was a community centre called Lion House about half a mile up the road where we could sort out problems with the house should the need arise. There were quite a few families living in Larnaca and Lion House was an important meeting place for wives and children to get to know one another.

I went to work the following day. The seven-storey hospital building in Dhekelia was high on a hill overlooking the expanse of Larnaca Bay. The foundation stone was laid in May 1955. The hospital opened to patients in September 1958 after much delay caused by unrest in Cyprus at the time. The ground floor contained the administration offices, reception, the accident and emergency department and the dispensary. There were ten wards above the ground floor, the hospital had its own laundry, and restaurant for staff and patients.

My colleague in the dispensary was Steve, whom I had known in Colchester while on the dispenser's course. He was most helpful in some respects in that he didn't mind running me about in his car if I needed him to. I would have to get some wheels eventually, but that could wait until we were settled in Cyprus and got to know our way around.

The hospital did not have its own Sergeants Mess, so the senior NCOs and warrant officers used the Garrison Mess. Given the number of members of this mess, the place was quite small and cramped, especially on meeting nights. Not the best Sgts mess I had ever been in.

Working hours at the BMH were from six o'clock until two in summer, and normal working hours in winter This was because the heat in Cyprus during summer months could get unbearable, and patients were seen early in the mornings. At least, the dispensary was air-conditioned.

We were not destined to be living in Larnaca for very long. On the second Monday in July someone from administration came to the dispensary to tell me there was a married quarter in Pergamos within the Sovereign Base Area if I was interested. I said I would like to get my family out of Larnaca and into the SBA and asked when I could take a look at the quarter. I was told I could go over to Pergamos at any time and Steve said he would take me there after work. He had telephoned the BIA (The person responsible for married quarters administration) at Pergamos to make sure we could have a look around the quarter before we set off.

Pergamos camp was a fifteen-minute drive from Dhekelia and we stopped at the barrier and asked directions to the BIA The guard on the gate pointed up the road, raised the barrier and we drove through. The BIA was waiting for us with the keys when we arrived, and we took a walk back the way we had come.

The house was a bungalow, the first quarter inside the camp, opposite the guard room and entrance barrier. My first impression was that this would be ideal for the boys. The only exit was via the barrier and the gate guard and the camp was surrounded by a high chain link fence.

Inside, the house was devoid of any furniture, the BIA explaining that it had just been completely redecorated and fire-proofed throughout, and furniture, fittings and household equipment would be supplied in the coming week. There were three bedrooms along with the usual bathroom, kitchen and large living room with an open fireplace. He said that if I wanted to take it, I could do the march in the following Monday 15th July. I provisionally said yes—I would have to get Mo to see it first.

Steve drove me back to Larnaca where I introduced Mo to Steve and told her a quarter had come available for us. I mentioned to her I thought it would be ideal for us and, especially for the boys and I had provisionally accepted it. She should come and have a look before I confirmed I would take it.

Two days later in the afternoon after work, Steve and I went to pick up Mo and the boys from Larnaca and drove us to Pergamos. We got the keys from the BIA and showed Mo around the house. She was quite taken with it, particularly as it was secure and freshly decorated. The only downside was the garden, which was rocky and scrubby, although she reckoned it wouldn't take much to tidy it up. We went back with the keys to the BIA and told him we would take it and agreed the march in would happen on Monday.

Over the following weekend we started packing our belongings ready to move to Pergamos. Fortunately, our boxes had not arrived from Singapore so we only had the things we came with. We were looking forward to the move.

I returned to Pergamos on Monday and started the march in. The house was now completely refurnished and all the necessary equipment was in place. The kitchen equipment, bedding, curtains and carpets were all brand-new. The BIA and I checked the inventory and when we were both satisfied that all was in order, we retired to his office to sign all the required paperwork.

We had almost finished the formalities when the radio which was playing music at low volume suddenly stopped and an announcement in Greek and Turkish came on. The BIA (who was a Turkish Cypriot) turned up the volume and listened intently for a few minutes and then went visibly pale. He then turned to me and said, "My God, they've killed Makarios, the President of Cyprus, and the army had taken over. You had better get back to Larnaca and get your family out. There is bound to be trouble."

My first reaction was which army had taken over. The British? The UN? Greek or Turkish? I got a lift back to the hospital, found the RSM and told him I had to get my family out of Larnaca, only to be told that no one was going anywhere as the Greek National Guard had closed the road in and out of the SBA.

We heard that Generals in the National Guard had attempted to assassinate President Makarios in his palace. Greek army troops in armoured cars swept up the drive to the presidential palace in an attempted coup. Loyal policemen and bodyguards opened fire, stalling the coup leaders at the top of the rise. The president, Archbishop Makarios, was entertaining a group of Greek schoolchildren from Egypt. He hurried them out of his office into the palace garden, fled down the back of the hill and escaped in a passing taxi. Arriving in Paphos, British forces based on the west coast helicoptered him to Akrotiri and then flew him off the island to Malta and safety.

It would be five days before I could get into Larnaca and be with my family. Meanwhile Steve and I stayed in the pharmacy. At least, Steve had a room in the Garrison Mess, but I slept on a camp bed in the pharmacy. I helped out in the hospital wherever I was wanted. I did a couple of spells in the laundry which was shorthanded as a lot of the civilian workers were unable to get into Dhekelia.

The large waiting room next to reception was set up as an emergency treatment area because casualties from the fighting were expected to make their way to the hospital. As a result of the attempted coup, many Greek Cypriots had used it as an excuse to get their shotguns and old Sten guns out from their hiding places and attempted to drive out Turkish Cypriots from their enclaves in towns and cities on the island.

One day Steve pointed out of the dispensary window towards Larnaca Bay and jokingly suggested that if the fighting continued, we could expect the Turkish Navy to be anchored in Larnaca any day now. His words were prophetic but the place was entirely wrong.

Saturday 20th July was hot even in the early morning. Shortly after breakfast I made my way up onto the flat roof of the hospital, at least there may be a cooling breeze up there. There were several hospital staff, both military and civilian, on the roof that day. A small group were gathered at one end, passing a pair of powerful binoculars around, and I went over to see what was going on. The binoculars were placed in my hands, and looking through them towards Larnaca I spotted a pair of National Guard gunboats just off Larnaca Point and shelling the Turkish Quarter.

The fires and smoke from the bombardment rose above the enclave. I have no idea how many Turkish Cypriots were killed or injured in the shelling, but it would have been many.

Of the civilians on the roof that day was one of the Greek Cypriots who helped out in the dispensary and I passed the binoculars to him and returned downstairs to the pharmacy, heartily sickened by what I had just witnessed.

The following Monday when I entered the dispensary, I heard one of the Greek Cypriot civilians who worked for us bewailing the Turkish invasion. He asked me why the Turks had come to his beautiful island. I told him they were there to protect the Turkish Cypriots.

"Why would they need to protect them?" he asked. "We Greeks are friends with the Turkish Cypriots." He was the one to whom I had passed the binoculars on the hospital roof the previous Saturday.

What we all unaware of was that in the early hours of Saturday morning, Turkish forces had launched an invasion in an area west of Kyrenia in the north. Following an amphibious assault on beaches near Pentemilli (Five Mile Beach), there followed air attacks and parachute forces. The force consisted of around 3,000 troops, 12 tanks and 20 armoured personnel carriers, as well as a dozen howitzers. The landing was not challenged until the first wave of Turkish forces were already ashore.

I cannot remember the exact dates when those with families outside the SBA were given safe conduct to go into Larnaca. The National Guard had lifted their road block into the SBA and I could get away into Larnaca and hopefully bring Mo and the boys into Pergamos.

Before leaving, our bus stopped outside the NAAFI where we could get much need provisions in case our families could not get out to the shops. I had no cash and many others were in the same situation as the banks had been closed a few days earlier.

I loaded up my trolley with basic foodstuffs such as baked beans, bread, eggs and bacon and some fresh vegetables, items that would keep us fed for a few days at least. At the till I my purchases were entered and I signed the till roll, half hoping and half expecting that I would get away with not getting a bill due to all the confusion. I had not considered the NAAFI's organisational capabilities—I got the bill a few months later.

I had a couple of days off with Mo and the boys and told her I was stuck in the hospital and could not get away to make sure they were alright. She told me they were scared at first when they realised what had happened in Cyprus, but hoped that matters would settle down now.

On the morning of the coup and unaware of the situation, she had taken the boys to walk up to Lion House. Shortly after leaving the house, she noticed there were no people about, many of the houses had doors and windows closed and she and the boys were being furtively watched through twitching curtains. She spotted a shop with the door half open and a sign outside advertising ice cream.

Entering the shop, she picked ice creams for the boys a bottle of squash and a pack of wax crayons. When she paid, the young girl in the shop hurriedly ushered her out with the words, "You are British, go home!" Mo thought the girl was being anti-British and, and as the boys were complaining of the heat, hurried back home instead of continuing on to Lion House.

When she got home, she turned on the radio to hear an announcement on British Forces Broadcasting Service (BFBS), advising families on the island to stay at home, move to the centre of the house and pack a bag in case they needed to be evacuated. Stunned by the news she realised that the girl in the shop was concerned for Mo's and that of the boys' safety. Had she continued to Lion House they would have been in danger as the building was caught in cross fire between Greek and Turkish Militias. Several people were trapped in there for a couple of days.

A few minutes after she arrived home our next-door neighbour came round with a basket of fruit and vegetables and to make sure everything was alright. Our Greek Cypriot neighbours turned out to be heaven sent. They were great comfort to Mo during the first days of the coup and assured her that all would be well. Their son took a risk and went shopping for his parents and picked up a few groceries for Mo. Apart from a few Cyprus pounds, Mo had very little money, and the neighbours waved away her assurances that she could pay them back as soon when she could.

A day or two later and to keep the boys amused, Mo suggested the boys could sit outside in the garden and draw some pictures with the crayons she had bought at the shop. This kept them amused for a while until they went inside the house to get a cold drink.

After about half an hour, they went outside to their crayons only to find they had melted into a multi-coloured heap in the middle of the table. Before they could get upset at the loss of the crayons, Mo spotted a group of armed men moving through the tall grass about half a mile away. There were shots fired as they moved along and Mo ushered the boys back into the house and comparative safety. They stayed inside for the rest of the day, not daring to venture out again.

During the coming days Mo spotted one or two groups of armed men on the Bondu at the back of our house. This time they were well away from habitation but Mo was wary of them. There was also the occasional shot to be heard, but nothing near the house.

Mo and the boys were pleased to see me when I got back to them. She was quite tearful at not knowing where I was or what was happening to me during the time when I had been unable to contact her. I assured her that we were all safe in the SBA and told her I would try and get her and the children out of Larnaca and to safety as soon as possible. The house in Pergamos was fine and ready for us to move into, all I had to do was to find a means of moving out.

I returned to Dhekelia after two days, promising to get them out as soon as I could. Meanwhile I would be able to get back to them in the afternoons after work. At least, the bank in the SBA was now open, but restrictions were introduced limiting the amount we could withdraw to fifty Cyprus pounds a day.

In the dispensary, Steve asked me if everything was alright with my family. I told him they were fine and the next-door neighbours were being good to them, my only problem was getting them out of Larnaca and into our house in Pergamos. He said he would help me at the weekend, only a couple of days away. He had a car, a small Datsun 120Y, and I thought it would take more than one trip get us and our belongings into it.

Early on Saturday morning we ventured into Larnaca, fighting was still going on in the north, and I was keen to get Mo and the boys out and into the relative safety of the SBA. We loaded up the car, packing the boot and roof rack with bags and boxes on laps of the passengers. Surprisingly we got everything in. I went next door to let our neighbours know we were leaving and to repay them for their kindness to my family, and to tell them we would visit as soon as matters settled down.

The heavily loaded Datsun drove well until we got to a hill leading up to the SBA. The car struggled up the road known as 'The Snake', but we finally arrived at the SBA and continued along the road to Pergamos and our new home.

Chapter 14
Number 1, Sycamore Road, Pergamos Camp, Dhekelia Sovereign Base Area

The first thing we noticed as we pulled up outside our new home was a pair of Scorpion Tanks parked outside. These belonged to the Blues and Royals, a Cavalry Regiment and part of the Household Cavalry.

We unloaded the tired Datsun and, thanking Steve for his help, moved into our new home. We were relieved to be out of Larnaca and into Pergamos which had a number of amenities, a NAAFI shop, swimming pool, and play areas for the children. Quite a few of my colleagues from the hospital lived in the camp, along with Dental Corps, Veterinary Corps, Engineers, Transport and Logistics Soldiers.

Mo and the boys welcomed the presence of the swimming pool and used it regularly. It was clean and cool with clear blue water and just what was needed during the heat of July and August. One morning, however, a sign outside the pool announced that the pool would be closed until further notice. The water was no longer clear blue but muddy brown. A strong wind during the night had blown dust and sand from the Sahara Desert across the Mediterranean, some of which had damaged the water filters. Without spare parts being available because of the hostilities, we would lose this popular facility.

Despite the loss of the pool the boys found plenty of mischief in Pergamos camp. Being a completely enclosed area with the only way out being the barrier next to the guard room, there was no way the children could 'escape.'

Our two lads, along with a few others managed to find a rubbish tip in a remote corner of the camp. There they came across a few half-empty tins of gloss paint, some of which had probably been used to decorate our quarter. They managed to get the lids off the tins and proceeded to throw the paint around completely oblivious to where it would land. Needless to say, most of it ended up on all of them.

A few days earlier Mo had gone to the NAAFI in Dhekelia and bought new shoes and trousers for our two and it was these Jason and Justin were wearing. As they wandered in through the front door, with paint splattered all over them, the air in the house turned scarlet. We could hear the other nearby parents also expressing their displeasure. They were grounded for a week, limited to the garden. I managed to get the paint off the shoes but both pairs of trousers were a write-off.

We still had a couple of Scorpion Tanks parks outside our front door. These were a magnet for the children who had never been close to a tank. One day Jason climbed up to get a closer look, was spotted by the corporal of the guard who ordered him to get down. Jason turned to him, spotting his one stripe on his uniform and told him his dad had three. Totally unperturbed by this remark the guard helped Jason off the tank and carried him into the guard room where he locked him in a cell for his cheek. Jason was only in 'chokey' for a few minutes, but I think he learnt his lesson.

Telling me of his experience later in the day, I walked across to the guard room to see the corporal. At first, he thought I was annoyed with him but we had a good laugh at the incident.

The British Military evacuated military personnel and dependants from Famagusta in early August, as it was certain that Turkish forces would attempt to take the city. We were just dropping off to sleep that night when I was awoken by hearing voices outside and by someone trying the door. I heard a voice say, "Break the door down, the house is empty." I got to the front door and opened it before someone kicked it in.

There were soldiers outside and a woman with two young children. I was told by one of the soldiers that this family had been evacuated from Famagusta and was to billeted on us. They thought the house was empty and apologised for disturbing us. We invited the family in and Mo made sandwiches and drinks for them while I made up beds in one of the rooms. I walked across to the guardroom and asked if they had any camp beds we could borrow for the night, telling the sergeant of the guard we had a family to look after. He gave me two telling me to hang on to them as long as I wanted them.

Justin had moved in with Jason, he had two single beds in his room. That left Justin's room with one single. I put the two camp beds together and made them up for the children. Once they had finished their drinks and sandwiches, they were all ready for bed and we left them to try and sleep.

We had all been settled for an hour when there was another knock on the door. I opened it to another pair of soldiers with another woman and her son. I got a further 2 camp beds from the guard room and moved our two boys in with us on two of them. Our new guest and her son got Jason's room with its two singles. Finally, after all the reorganising the sleeping arrangements I got a couple of hours before I had to go to work.

I managed to get a lift into work from one of my colleagues, but I would need to get my own transport sooner rather than later. Shopping in the NAAFI one day I spoke to the manager, a Turkish Cypriot if he knew of anyone selling a car. He said he would ask around for me.

The next time I was in the shop the manager told me he knew of a soldier in the Blues and Royals who was returning to the UK and had a car for sale. I contacted him and he told me there was still hire purchase on the car, and, if I took over the payments, I could have the vehicle. We went to the finance company, signed a few papers and I became the owner of his Subaru saloon.

One evening in mid-August I was on duty in reception at the hospital, and during a break went up to the roof. There were a number of people up there, most were looking towards the east and the road out of Famagusta. I could see a line of car headlights heading westwards into southern Cyprus. What I was seeing was the evacuation of this city, the citizens fleeing from the approaching Turkish forces. Many of these people entered the SBA and were accommodated in Athna Forest refugee camp.

The second phase of the Turkish Invasion began on 14th August. Fighting in the north continued, we could hear the noises of battles and air strikes. Gradually, the Turkish military ground down the Greek and Greek Cypriot forces and partly the Atilla Line, effectively cutting the island into two. Turkish Sabre jets regularly flew over Pergamos camp, lining up on Famagusta to fire off rockets and drop bombs into the city. Tension arose as Turkish forces fired tanks shells at the eastern edge of the SBA. Negotiations and navigational advice reminded the Turks where they were and the attack was not repeated.

In the early hours of one morning, we were disturbed by what sounded like someone or something digging in the garden. I thought it was probably one of a local farmer's goats and rolled over and went back to sleep. When we got up next morning to have a look at any potential damage to the boundary fence at the bottom of our garden, we found a couple of Gurkha soldiers in a slit trench armed with a General-Purpose Machine Gun (GPMG). Mo immediately went indoors and made them tea. The boys also went down to see them, taking sweets and chattering away. I told the boys not to bother them and so they only stayed a few minutes. The soldiers were only with us for two or three days and we were sorry to see them go.

One afternoon we were coming home from Dhekelia and saw that the wheat field on in the SBA had been harvested and the resulting haystacks were dotted around the field. Mo suggested that the Turks could hide an army in the hay bales as we drove past.

Later that evening her words became true. The security picket in the camp were doing their rounds late at night when they arrived at the camp fire station. One or two of the Turkish Cypriot firemen were chatting to a soldier on the other side of the fence. A double-take revealed that the soldier was Turkish.

The guard was alerted and we heard one of the Scorpion Tanks fire up and make its way out of the camp and into the adjoining field. The area erupted with Turkish infantry and armour.

What followed is probably apocryphal. The tank commander found the officer responsible who told him they were going to attack the Greek Cypriot village of Piroi at dawn. The Turkish officer was pointing at Pergamos village. The tank commander took the officers map and rotated it through 180 degrees, telling him he was about to attack a village of Turkish Cypriots. The village he was after was in the opposite direction. We heard tank and artillery fire the next morning as the sun rose. We assumed Piroi had been attacked.

As the Turkish forces advanced and neared the village of Pergamos which was also Turkish and lay just outside the SBA, a number of the village inhabitants came to the main gate of the camp and asked to be let in as they feared the approaching force was Greek.

Mo was outside at the time and stood at the barrier. One of the guards shouted at the villagers to go away. Many were crying in fear for their lives and one of the ladies held her baby up to Mo pleading for her to take it to safety. The guard then made the mistake of cocking his rifle. Mo stood there with her hands on her hips shouting and staring the soldier out until he lowered his weapon and went inside the guardroom to fetch the guard commander who managed to assure the villagers that they would be safe as the approaching force was Turkish.

Another apocryphal story follows a few days after the ceasefire and once the Turkish military had drawn the Atilla Line which effectively cut Cyprus in two. About a mile from Pergamos there was a taverna lying just off the SBA road. To the surprise of a soldier returning from Dhekelia he spotted a Turkish tank parked on the SBA road. Stopping at the guardroom, he told the guard commander, "There's Turkish tank parked in the SBA!" The duty officer (a second lieutenant) was then informed and he drove out in a Land Rover accompanied by one of the guards, both were completely unarmed apart from the officer and his swagger stick. Approaching the tank, he tapped it on the tread with his stick, whereupon the top opened and a Turkish soldier looked out.

"Look here," said the officer, "you can't park here, you know." At this, the Turk went for his pistol.

"And we'll have none of that either!" the officer replied, brandishing his stick.

At this, the Turk summoned his men from the taverna who clambered into the tank which then started off and rumbled away towards Pergamos village. If there is any truth in the story, only the British army could get away with it.

Just before the ceasefire, I was on night duty in reception when the telephone rang. An excited voice on the other end informed me that there was a wounded soldier being brought to the hospital helicopter pad. The casualty was a member of the Canadian United Nations contingent in Nicosia. He had been shot by a sniper and was seriously wounded.

I heard the helicopter approaching and I had despatched an ambulance out to meet it. The ambulance backed up to the entrance of the hospital and the rear doors crashed open to reveal what first appeared to be complete chaos inside. Apart from the casualty there were five others inside the ambulance, one of whom was kneeling astride the injured soldier and pumping his chest. Two others were holding blood transfusion packs aloft squeezing them in order to get blood into the soldier as fast as possible. The remaining two jumped down and pulled the stretcher with the soldier and the man off the back of the ambulance and all of them rushed down the corridor to the operating theatre suites, leaving a spattering of blood on the walls as they passed.

Half an hour later the five medics returned to reception. All were crestfallen as the injured soldier never regained consciousness and had died on the operating table. He had been shot with a 'Dum Dum' bullet, a projectile designed to expand on impact and cause maximum damage. They are prohibited for use in war under the Hague Convention of 1899, but are still used worldwide.

One morning in mid-August, we felt our house move on its foundations. My first thought was of an earthquake, but a few seconds after the shock we heard the sound of explosions coming from the north. The Turkish air force had dropped large several bombs on Nicosia Airport, some 30 miles away from us.

The ceasefire appeared to be holding, but the hospital was very busy. The accident and emergency area built after the attempted coup fortunately did not realise its potential for receiving mass casualties, although we had several through its doors after a major fire ripped through the refugee camp in Athna Forest. One of the doctors was heard to complain that he was geared up for gunshot and shrapnel wounds, but all he had seen was women bought into labour as a result of the bombing and shell fire.

Meanwhile, back at our quarter in Pergamos there were 5 extra mouths to feed. The NAAFIs both in Dhekelia and Pergamos were short of a lot of supplies. In order to alleviate this problem, the military arranged to issue compo rations at a rate of 2/3 ration. In this way, we received two ten-man ration packs every three days.

A ten-man ration pack was designed to feed a party of 10 soldiers on a high calorie diet for one day, and in addition to food, contained boiled sweets, chocolate, a can opener, tea, dried or condensed milk, and, most important of all, toilet paper. The food was canned and there was a variety in the various packs.

A four-tonne truck came round two days out of three and delivered the packs out the back, and we were asked how many were in the house. Because we were nine, we received two ten-man packs to last us for three days. One day the young boy of one of our lodgers was curious as to what was going on when the driver of the truck asked him how many were in the house and when he replied that there were nine, he was given another two packs—we got double rations that day.

We supplemented our supplies of compo by purchasing fresh fruit and vegetables from a trader from the local village. We also bough fresh milk from another trader. Pergamos was the first place we had been where we tasted fresh figs.

I made enquiries at work to find out if we could get our boxes delivered from Akrotiri. Unfortunately, very little information was forth coming and we were just about managing with the things we had bought with us. I bemoaned the problem with our MFO to Steve who said he would ring a friend in Akrotiri and see what he could fix. Steve had a wealth of contacts in Cyprus.

There was an airstrip in the SBA—Kingsland. It was mainly used as a glider club, but during the unrest it became quite busy as it was used to ferry in supplies to the SBA. It was not unusual to be stopped on the road by military police while we waited for yet another Hercules transport plane to come in to land. The airstrip was just a few yards from the edge of the road.

Arriving at work a couple of days after mentioning my MFO to Steve, he told me his contact at Akrotiri had fixed it for our boxes to be delivered. His friend had managed to get them on a supply flight arriving in Kingsland that day. I arrived home in the afternoon to find our boxes stacked on the veranda and I set about with a will to get them unpacked.

Gradually life slowly got back to some semblance of normality, although movement around the island was restricted. Our lodgers eventually were evacuated back to the UK and our house was back to being our own. The NAAFI shops in Pergamos became better stocked and we were able to resume a better diet after weeks of compo rations.

On Mo's birthday, we managed to get into Larnaca one evening and went to the Four Lanterns Hotel on the sea front. I remember that most of the menu was 'off' due to a shortage of supplies, but at least they managed to rustle up a dinner and a bottle of wine. It was not the most memorable meal we had ever had, but at least it was out of the SBA, if only for a few hours.

I went diving in Cyprus, but after the reefs and multitudes of fish of Malaysia I was sorely disappointed. The waters were clear to 50 or 60 feet but sea bed was sandy and barren of fish. There was really not a lot of interest in the areas where I went diving.

On one occasion, I was diving at about 50 feet with Steve and went to look at my watch to check the time we had been down. It was not there, and I assumed it had come adrift somewhere along where had been. I retraced the route I had taken in the forlorn hope of finding my Seiko chronograph. There was no sign of it and I surfaced and returned to the beach. Mo was sitting with the boys, and to my surprise was holding up my watch. She had been paddling in the sea close to where Steve and I started our dive. I was wearing a wet suit top and had clipped the watch over the sleeve. It was a tight fit and the watch strap had sprung open and dropped into the shallows before Steve and I set off. Mo found it while she was having a paddle. I was overjoyed at getting watch back and resolved to get a new bracelet for it as soon as I could.

I made only three dives in the Mediterranean, and the only one which was of any interest was my last one. We dived from a boat under the cliffs of Cape Greco. As before the water was gin clear and deep. We dropped down to 90 feet and could still see the surface, the waves breaking against the cliffs way above. The only problem with diving deep on compressed air is that one is limited to the time spent at depth. In this case, five minutes was the limit.

The other opportunity we had for recreation was the George Club in Dhekelia. This was mainly the sailing club which I joined and was allocated the last remaining sailing dinghy, an ancient Albacore. The boat must have been about 15 years old and in need of some TLC. It was heavy and certainly in no condition for competitions, although I did enter it into races occasionally, usually ending up at the back of the fleet. Despite this, it was fun to sail and could get up a reasonable turn of speed when conditions were right.

The club also had a bar which served drinks and snacks and was manned by Andreas, a local Greek Cypriot. There was a play area for the children and the small bay where the boats were moored was sheltered and safe for swimming. We used to go down to the club two or three times a week, I would sail while Mo and the boys enjoyed a swim or just a sit in the sunshine.

One afternoon after a race had finished, I was asked to sail out and bring in the course markers. These were essentially a plastic container tied to a breeze block and placed around the area to be raced. My crew and I had just pulled the last marker into the boat when there was a loud squishing noise and an octopus squirted itself out of a hole in the block. It lay in the bottom of the dinghy with its tentacles thrashing about. We got back to the club after about ten minutes and I called Andreas and told him we had an octopus and would he cook it for us.

After tenderising the animal by thrashing it on the concrete of the slipway, Andreas took the octopus up to the kitchen. Half an hour later he returned with several plates of grilled octopus tentacles along with lemon wedges and a salad. There were several members still enjoying the early evening sunshine, and most relished an early supper of octopus along with a glass of chilled white wine. There were one or two members who turned up their noses at the very thought of eating octopus. They obviously were not aware of what they were missing.

A squadron of the Royal Tank Regiment had taken over from the Blues and Royals in Pergamos, and evenings in their Sergeants Mess became the main source of entertainment in the camp. The men had come from a tour in Northern Ireland and were unaccompanied by their families so they were pleased to have female company in the mess.

There was a film night in the mess on one evening a week along with a buffet supper. A ladies dinner night was held every couple of months where we were greeted at the door with a sherry schooner containing a cocktail known as a 'Trankies' Belt,' a mixture of liqueurs carefully poured into the glass in layers which formed the colours of the RTR Stable Belt. The drinks were possibly Green Chartreuse, Grand Marnier and Drambuie. The drink was a great start to the evening.

I went to a regimental dinner in the RTR Sgts mess one evening. Once the formalities of the meal were over, there was a session of daft games. One was the Jacob's Cream Cracker challenge. This entailed two or three junior members being required to eat two cream crackers in two minutes, the first to finish given a small prize—no drink being allowed. The task was hopeless, as the crackers dried up the saliva in their mouths, making swallowing impossible. There were never any winners.

After this, and with great ceremony, the president of the mess announced another challenge had been received. The regimental 'Spoon Fencing Champion' had invited the most junior member of the mess to compete against him. I had never come across spoon fencing and I assumed it was possibly an RTR custom. This involved two men, one of whom was the most junior member of the mess, sitting closely opposite each other, each with a dessert spoon clenched between their teeth.

The senior of the two, a burly warrant officer, was introduced as 'The Royal Tank Regiment Spoon Fencing Champion,' as his 'second' stood behind him massaging his shoulders, as if this was a boxing match. The RSM appointed himself as 'second' to the junior, fanning him with a towel. The object of this game for each of the competitors to lean forward, one offering the top of his head to his opponent, who attempted to strike him on the head with the spoon held between his teeth. The first to submit being the loser.

The junior got the first try at bashing his opponent—he managed a gentle tap. Now it was the 'Champion's' turn. He raised his head back, spoon at the ready and made to strike. Unbeknown to the challenger, the RSM was holding a large catering serving spoon behind his back. As the champion went to strike, he pulled to one side and the RSM landed a hit on the junior's bowed head with the large spoon!

With a howl of pain, the challenger jumped to his feet, holding his head. He turned to the RSM, who with a wide grin on his face and holding his great spoon aloft, proffered the loser a pint of beer. With his shock and surprise eased by the beer, the loser shook hands with his opponent and joined in the laughter that rang around the mess.

The hospital did not have its own Sergeants Mess, but we made use of the Garrison Mess which was used by most of the senior NCOs of the smaller units. I used it infrequently as I did not particularly like the Garrison Sergeant Major (GSM) and it was too small and cramped to accommodate all the members. I spent more time in the mess in Pergamos than the mess in Dhekelia, although I paid my mess subs in the latter.

The only thing I did in the Garrison Mess was to organise the Whist Drive on a Tuesday evening. I bought the weekly prizes, took the subs, and played as well. There was a little déjà vu about this as my late father used to do the same when I was young. Like him I often won the prizes I had bought as I was a reasonably good card player having learnt to play bridge while on my course in Colchester, and managed to win the snowball one evening, pocketing £200.

Matters came to a head in late September at the monthly mess meeting in the Garrison Mess when the President of the Christmas Draw Committee outlined the arrangements for the Christmas Draw. The committee had decided because of the difficulties in Cyprus, they were unable to procure sufficient prizes. There were to be three large prizes only, and there would be two sittings a week apart in order to accommodate all the members. Duplicate draw prizes would be the same at both sittings. The GSM then stated that all mess members would be required to buy £20 of draw tickets.

The very thought of being ordered to part with my hard-earned cash riled. When my monthly mess bill arrived in November, I struck out the twenty-pound levy, paid the remainder, and waited for the fall out. It was not long in coming.

The GSM telephoned me a few days later and told me to come to his office in the mess immediately. I duly wandered over to the mess and into the see the GSM. I could tell by the expression on his face as I walked into his office, I was not currently his flavour of the month. I was subjected to a tirade of threats, telling me I was being disloyal to the mess and not supporting the mess committee. He then effectively ordered me to cough up the £20—or else!

"Very well, Sir," I replied, "I can see that you do not leave me much choice."

"No, I don't, do I?" he replied and told me to get out.

There is a system in the military to raise a complaint when one was believed to have been wronged. It is called a Redress of Grievance and I put in my request for a redress as soon as I got back to the hospital. I spoke to the hospital RSM and told him what I was doing, he was doubtful that I would be successful.

The next day I saw the GSM's car in the hospital car park, it was there for about half an hour and after it was driven off, I was summoned to the CO's office. I knocked on the door and was called in. I stood at the CO's desk and saluted. The CO told me to stand at ease and said, "I've spoken to the GSM and we have agreed that you should not have to pay the £20." I breathed a sigh of relief.

"However," he continued, "the GSM insists that you attend the Christmas Draw."

I thanked the CO for interceding on my behalf and assured him that I would comply with the ruling, I saluted and marched out of the office.

Arriving back to the dispensary, I immediately called a member of the draw committee and requested a pair of seats for the draw on Saturday evening. By this time, the first draw had already taken place on the previous weekend. The reply I received made my day.

"Sorry," said the voice on the telephone, "there's nothing available, the mess is full." That was a better result than I could have hoped for.

I had my second redress a week before Christmas when the duty roster for the Christmas break was published. I had been scheduled to be orderly sergeant on Christmas Day! I had been orderly sergeant only a week before, and the duty roster was supposed to be in strict rotation. I took up the matter with the RSM who told me the hospital administration officer had put my name forward. I duly asked to see the officer. I got to see him the next day and asked why I was nominated for duty on Christmas Day. His reply set me back on my heels.

"You are the only agnostic in the unit," he said, "therefore Christmas has no meaning for you."

"It has for my family." was my reply. "And it now appears that the tables have been turned and the Christians are persecuting what they view as the Barbarians."

I raised a request for a redress against the admin officer, and later appeared before the CO to explain my reason for not having to be on duty. The CO assured me he would look into the matter. The RSM called me later that day to tell me the roster had been rearranged and I would not be on duty. Another result against the establishment!

While all this was going on, Steve had received a posting order and his replacement had arrived. The new chap was Tony, whom I knew only by reputation. He was a couple of courses before me and therefore senior, although we were both sergeants.

Working with Tony was in complete contrast to working with Steve. Tony had a great sense of humour and found amusement in anything. He was unaccompanied in Cyprus and Mo and I had him over for a meal at least once a week.

On Christmas Eve, I also discovered he was accident prone. I took Tony out in the Albacore. It was a pleasant start but a squall blew up and we managed to capsize the boat. The dinghy was in danger of turning upside down and I called to Tony to grab the centre board before it fell inside, making the job of getting the boat upright more difficult.

Instead of grabbing the board he put his hand over the slot, the centre board dropped across his hand and he howled in pain. Despite this mishap, we got the boat upright, opened the self-balers and headed back to the club house.

As Tony was living in the mess and on his own, we had invited him to spend Christmas with us in Pergamos. He was nursing his fingers as we drove over to our quarter. I suggested he may need an X-ray but he said he could move his fingers and he would be OK.

Christmas in Cyprus was joyous affair. We had dinner with all the trimmings and Cypriot wine, a tree and presents. There was also a roaring log fire in the fireplace. Tony had managed to get a few toys for the boys and Mo. A bottle of Scotch for me. I ran Tony back to the mess on Boxing Day, suggesting he get his hand examined as soon as possible.

I went back to work on the Friday and, on entering the dispensary saw Tony with his arm in a sling. "Oh," I said, "you've had your hand looked at."

"No," he replied, holding up his originally hurt fingers, "these are OK now, I shut my other hand in a drawer this morning!"

In February, some travel restrictions were lifted in the southern half of the island. Although travel into the north was forbidden, so one Sunday we decided to take a day and travel along the south coast as far as Paphos in west. At the time, Paphos was a small fishing village where, legend has it, Aphrodite had risen from the sea.

We strolled along the sea front and around the back streets, finding it refreshing after being confined in the SBA for months. We had a lunch of fish and chips, sitting outside in the sun and watching ships passing by on the horizon.

There were a number of Greek Cypriots suffering from thalassaemia who attended a clinic in the hospital in order to get treatment for their illness. The disease is a genetic disorder and affects people of Greek, Italian, Middle Eastern, or South Asian origin. It causes a decrease in the production of haemoglobin and patients are treated with drugs and blood transfusions. The disease may also cause the bone marrow to expand and give rise to bone deformities especially in the face and skull.

Members of the military were often called to donate a pint of blood for transfusion into the person suffering from thalassaemia, the one proviso demanded for this donation was an equivalent pint of blood from an unaffected member of the patient's family. I donated on three or four occasions during my time in Cyprus, being only too pleased to offer my blood to help another.

Nine months had passed by since we arrived in Cyprus, we had survived the Turkish invasion and life had gradually developed into some semblance of normality, but I was getting itchy feet due to the still present restrictions, and I was hoping for a posting. Travel restrictions were still in place and there were shortages. For the most part, we spent most of our social life in the SBA, with just the sailing club and the Sgts Mess in Pergamos to relieve the boredom.

Our hopes were realised around the end of February when I received a posting order to the Royal Herbert Hospital, in Woolwich, south east London. Mo was pleased with the news that we were on the move again and wrote to her family telling them we would be back home in the middle of April.

I went through the usual administration form filling and requesting MFO boxes. We spent a couple of weeks packing our belongings, we were becoming a couple of experts at the job by now. Pretty soon we were done and dusted. The boys' bicycle and go-kart were the last things to be packed away, that would help keep them out of the house while we busied ourselves getting ready to move on.

The last thing I needed to do was to sell the car. I had made enquiries about shipping the car to the UK, only to find there were no agents for Subaru in the country, so I had to find someone to take the car off my hands. Again, the NAAFI manager came to my aid, saying that he would ask around. A couple of days later he came to our quarter to tell me he had a buyer, but it was in Pergamos village—outside the SBA.

A week before we were due to leave, I went down to the village with the manager to translate for me. There was a barrier across the road manned by a Turkish soldier. Stopping at the barrier I wound my window down and the manager spoke to the guard who waved us through. We drove a couple of 100 yards into the village and parked up outside the local police station.

We got out of the car and entered the station, making our way the office of the local Chief of Police. I must admit to being a little worried by now, apart from being completely out of bounds in Northern Cyprus, I was about to meet with the top policeman.

He was a large man with an impressive handlebar moustache and he greeted me with a beaming smile and shook my hand. He had a little English and asked if we could go outside a inspect the car. So, this was the person buying my vehicle. I had cleaned and vacuumed the car before bringing it into Pergamos After a brief inspection the policeman said he was happy with the car and we should return to his office to complete the necessary paperwork.

One of the documents stated in English, Greek and Turkish that once the political situation in Cyprus was resolved the buyer would go to the vehicle registration offices in Nicosia and formalise the sale. I doubted this would ever happen. We finalised the deal with a cup of strong Turkish coffee, the handing over of the sale price with no haggling, and a shake of hands.

The NAAFI manager drove me back home, dropped me off and returned to Pergamos with the car. I saw him later in the day and gave him twenty pounds for his help. All I had to do was to go to Larnaca and pay off the balance of the hire purchase. Once this was done, I found that I had made a small profit on the sale.

A couple of days before we flew out, a notice appeared on part one orders requesting anyone who had sold a vehicle into Northern Cyprus to contact the administration office to give details of the sale. I had heard from other units that those who had volunteered details of sales across the border had been fined. I decided to keep quiet and hope for the best. I breathed a sigh of relief when the plane left the runway!

Five years later I received a letter when I was working at the Cambridge Military Hospital in Aldershot. The letter asked for details of the car I had had in Cyprus. I replied that I had sold to it on a date I could not remember, to a person whose name I had forgotten and for a price I could not recall. I returned the letter to the sender and to this date have not heard anything further.

We flew back to England on a Britannia Airlines turboprop, landing at Luton. From there, we had railway warrants to Birmingham and our families.

I had a couple of weeks disembarkation leave and we stayed with Mo's family for that fortnight. I started looking for a vehicle and eventually found one which would suit us. It was a 2 litre Ford Corsair, old, but in reasonable condition, and the price was right. All I had to find was the money. Our account was still in Netley, but I approached a local branch to see if I could get a loan because I did not want to buy the car on hire purchase as the rates were exorbitant.

The bank was not too helpful, probably because I had not used my bank account for 15 months and had no credit history, being away in Singapore and Cyprus. I popped round to see my mother to make sure she was alright, and over a cup of tea told her about my problems in getting a loan for a car. She asked me how much I wanted, and when I said I was short by three hundred pounds, she disappeared into the kitchen, and following a rattling of pots and pans returned with a wad of twenty-pound notes from under the kitchen sink. I was extremely grateful, but annoyed that she was keeping a such large amount of money in the house.

I bought the car which ran well for a week, but then started to continue running on after the ignition was switched off. I mentioned this to a friend who knew about cars more than I did, and he suggested that the car needed a top overhaul. That meant taking off the cylinder head and removing all the carbon deposits from the engine, a seriously expensive business.

I took the car to a Ford service centre and asked about a top overhaul. The engineer to whom spoke told me they were very busy, but he would take a look at the engine for me. I turned on the ignition and the engineer listened intently for a few minutes. He told me there was no need for a major overhaul, but the carburettor needed replacement and he could supply me a refurbished one for £30. I bought the part and fitted it in the street outside my mother's house. With a little tweaking of the jets of the carburettor, the problem was solved and the engine ran sweetly.

My leave came to an end and I drove down to Woolwich and the Royal Herbert Hospital. The hospital was built on the authority of Sidney Herbert, responsible for sending Florence Nightingale to the Crimea, leader of War Office reforms after this campaign, and passionate about health care and reducing military mortality rates from diseases and ill-treated war wounds. It opened on 1 November 1865 as the Herbert Hospital and was renamed as the Royal Herbert in 1900. There was a huge portrait of Sidney Herbert in one of the stairwells of the hospital.

Entering the hospital through a portal in the façade of the hospital I made my way to the office of the RSM and introduced myself. I was due to start work the following day and he told me to report to his office the next morning, meanwhile I would have accommodation in the Sergeants Mess. I was shown to a room and went out to retrieve my kit from the car.

The next morning, I returned to the RSM's office and from there went through the usual administrative procedures before meeting the commanding officer. The good news I had from the admin office was that I would not have to wait long before a quarter became available. From there, I was shown to the quartermaster's office in the basement of the hospital. I had met the QM before and looked forward to working with him again. After a few minutes, we went further up the corridor and into the dispensary and medical stores.

Here I met my colleagues with whom I would be working for the coming two years. There were two Mikes, the senior being S/Sgt MW and the other Sgt MB, both dispensers. We also had a corporal medical storeman, a civilian storeman and a female clerk. Sgt Mike managed the dispensing while myself and the S/Sgt looked after the medical stores, although we all interchanged duties, when necessary, especially if the dispensing became busy which it often did. The dispensary waiting room held Mike B's pride and joy, a large aquarium full of fish which Mike looked after. It was a source of amusement to children who were waiting with their parents while their prescriptions were dispensed.

We did the routine work of servicing the outstations, stocktaking and placing orders for resupply on DMED. Our indents were usually processed quickly by DMED and delivered by truck into the back door of the stores. This often resulted in a pile of boxes and packing material lying on the floor of the cramped area at the rear. The stock was kept on mobile racking due to the area of the stores being limited in space and height. When two of us were engaged in the racking, it was not unusual for the shelving to move as another member of staff shoved the racking to one side to gain access. This was met with cries "Oi, I'm in here! to avoid being squashed."

I received a call from the housing department to tell me there was a hiring in Welling coming available if I was interested. I replied that I was I would go and have a look at it. Welling was a straight run from the hospital, and within 20 minutes I had found the house.

Chapter 15
77, Danson Lane, Welling, Kent

The house was semi-detached and from the outside looked as if there were three bedrooms. The location was ideal, just a short walk to the shops in Welling High Street, and only 20 minutes' drive from work. I went back to work and telephoned the housing rep, saying that provided there were three bedrooms I would take the house. He confirmed the number of bedrooms and suggested a march-in the following week on Friday morning. Perfect—I could take over the house and go straight up to Birmingham and collect Mo and the boys.

I met the BIA along with Mrs McDonald, the wife of the owner of the house, on Friday afternoon ready to take over the house. We checked the inventory as we moved through the house, the lady telling me her husband had retired from the Metropolitan Police and they were moving up the Isle of Skye. Mr McDonald was already in Skye getting their house on the island ready.

The house would be ideal for us. It had a good kitchen, dining room, a sitting room and three good bedrooms. It was also centrally heated. There was also a large garden complete with a greenhouse, a pond, and a tortoise. There was a fence at the back of the garden which had a gate giving entrance to Danson Park beyond. It had a garage which would have to serve as a shed as it was not possible to get my car into the garage as a step up to the back door blocked access. There was plenty of room on the drive so that would not be a problem.

Once the march-in was finished I jumped into my car and drove up to fetch my family to Welling. This was the time before the M25, and one or two of my colleagues at work said that the easiest way to the Midlands was to go through London via the Blackwall tunnel and Poplar. I was surprised that the traffic was light and made good time through London and headed north up the MI.

I spent Saturday with Mo's family and my mother and loaded up the car early Sunday morning for our journey back to London and Welling. I thought the boys would enjoy a boat trip so I drove back, passing Tottenham Hotspurs stadium at White Hart Lane. A few minutes later we were boarding the Woolwich Ferry for the short trip across the Thames. Half an hour later we were parked on the drive of our new home.

We unloaded the car and went into the house. The boys immediately dashed up the stairs to lay claim to their bedrooms, Jason generously letting Justin have the larger of the two singles overlooking the garden. Mo was quite taken with the house and garden, particularly the greenhouse. The garden was quite neat and wouldn't take much work. The boys had found the pond and declared that there were plenty of frogs in it. They also found the tortoise wandering around the small lawn.

We had a couple of days to find our way around Welling High Street. There was a good variety of shops, a cinema, and a branch of Lloyds Bank, to where I arranged for our account in Netley to be transferred. The local primary school was just a few minutes' walk from the house and Mo registered Jason there. There was also a play group for Justin in the park behind the house.

Our next-door neighbours called round shortly after we had arrived. They were Ron and Maureen, they came bearing a bunch of flowers and some young tomato plants, ready to be planted into the greenhouse. Being a complete novice gardener, they were most helpful in telling me how to plant and look after the tomatoes.

A few months after we had settled into Danson Lane and I was enjoying working at the Royal Herbert I got wind of a part-time job at a chemist's shop in Eltham. The shop was about ten minutes from home. I spoke to the owner over the telephone and was invited to go and see him.

We agreed a mutually convenient time and I drove round the following evening to meet Brendan Anglin, a tall, friendly Irishman. He told me the shop was extremely popular and busy as there were several group practices in the local area. The shop was open from 9 in the morning to 9 in the evening, Monday to Friday, and 9 AM to 6 PM Saturday. It also opened from 9AM until noon on Sunday.

Brendan said he was looking for a part-time dispenser for two evenings a week and the occasional Saturday. I told him I was well qualified as a RAMC dispenser and I was keen to keep my hand in as I was mainly involved in medical supply at the hospital where Mike B did most of the dispensing.

He showed me the dispensing area which was very narrow and a little cramped. He kept minimal stocks as he was well supplied by a number of wholesale stockists. There were usually three people engaged in dispensing, one of whom would be a pharmacist (a legal requirement), a senior dispenser, and the part-timer. Brendan offered me the job there and then and I was happy to accept.

I started the following Tuesday and Brendan was there to introduce me to the other members of staff. There was Jean who looked after the shop and took in the prescriptions, a locum regular pharmacist (Brendan did not work every day), and Bill the senior dispenser who had been with Brendan for years and knew where everything was. I got used to Bill after a while; not knowing where items were, I would ask, "Where's so-and-so?" Bill would grunt and point in the general direction of its location. After a couple of weeks, I got to know where everything was.

There were some differences in dispensing practices from that in the army. When the prescription was dispensed, it was marked with the pack size that was used to make up the order. For example, if we dispensed 50 tablets from a bulk pack of a thousand tablets, the figure 1000 was written the margin of the prescription. This allowed the NHS pricing authority to work out how much the pharmacy was owed for dispensing the prescription based on the price of the bulk pack. The prescription was also initialled by the person who made it up and checked by a second person. We also dispensed private prescriptions.

We regularly dispensed between 150 and 200 prescriptions in a three-hour session in the evenings, when the pharmacy was at its busiest. One of the most unusual items for which we were asked was a 'Brompton Cocktail'. This was a mixture of the patient's favourite tipple, maybe gin, vodka or whiskey. To this was added cocaine and morphine and was prescribed for patients terminally ill with cancer. Brendan took responsibility for preparing this, and if he was not in the shop that day, he was asked to come in to make up the mixture.

Shortly after I started at the shop, I was lucky at the Grand National when my horse L'escargot beat the field coming in at 14 to 1. I was pleased with my win and mentioned it to Brendan when I was in the shop on the following Tuesday.

"I had a winner on Saturday," I told Brendan.

"How much did you have on him?" Brendan asked.

I said I had had a pound each way. "Yes, good result for me as well," Brendan replied. "I had a grand on the nose!" My win just paled into insignificance.

One evening, just five minutes before we were due to lock up and go home, a man came into the shop. After looking around the shelves, he approached the counter where I stood with Jean and the pharmacist, all of us impatient to shut up shop and go home. I was about to ask if I could help him when, from underneath his donkey jacket he produced a sawn-off shot gun. I just stood there looking down the barrels of the gun and hearing the diminutive pharmacist whisper under her breath, "Oh shit!"

Two more men entered the shop and approached the counter, both carrying shotguns and wearing stocking masks over their heads and demanded the till to be opened. Jean immediately hit the 'No Sale' button and the man with the gun reached over and took all the notes from the register.

We were then herded into the stock room behind the counter, locked in and warned not to try and escape for at least half an hour. There was no need to try, the telephone was in this room and I immediately called the police, and then phoned Brendan. We also called our families to let them know that there was a problem in the shop and we would be a little late returning home.

Brendan and the police arrived and let us out of the stockroom, they took our details and told us that they would take statements from us the next morning and allowed us to go home. It was as well that Brendan was not working in the shop that night, as I was sure he would have had a go at the gunmen.

I got home about an hour and a half later than usual and sat with a drink telling Mo what had happened at the shop. I didn't sleep too well that night.

A detective from the local police force arrived early the next morning and while Mo took the boys over to the park. I gave a statement as to the events at the shop the previous evening. My description of the man with the gun was somewhat sketchy as my concentration was fixed on the shot gun. He asked me if the weapon was cocked and loaded, I told the detective that it was cocked, but I had no idea if it was loaded.

Once I had finished my statement, the policeman said, "Do you know what to do if someone points a shot gun at you again?" I said I did not.

"Well," he said, "all you have to do is stick two fingers into the barrels. If he pulls the trigger, you will lose your hand, but he will probably lose his head!" With that we shook hands and he left. I hoped he was joking about the shotgun.

147

The robbers were arrested a few days later after a failed bank robbery. The shotgun was fired at the time and fortunately no one was hurt. I never found out the result of their trial.

Shortly after all this drama, we took a holiday, spending a fortnight at Pontins in Southport. Our chalet was comfortable and clean, food in the cafeteria was very good, although by the end of the first week I was heartily fed up with the strains of a particular pop song sung by Pontin's Blue Coats before the start of every meal.

Southport was an ideal jumping off point for the various tourist and beauty spots within a reasonable driving distance from the camp. We visited Carnforth and the steam railway museum. Carnforth railway station was the setting for the film 'Brief Encounter', a memorable film directed by David lean and featured Celia Johnson and Trevor Howard. Jason and Justin had never seen a steam engine and both were impressed at the giant machines.

Windemere was another trip along with a side visit to Hill Top House, the home of Beatrix Potter. Most days were spent around the camp, making use of the many facilities. The swimming pool was the most popular with the boys, along with the playgrounds. Mo was asked to take part in a fashion show one evening in the camp theatre. She went along with it while I stayed to look after the boys. She returned late in the evening saying that she had enjoyed herself and was given one of the items she had modelled.

All too soon it was time for the long drive back to London. It would take at least six hours as this was before the motorway network. We left on the Sunday and traffic was light. At least, part of the way would be via the M1 to Watford. The car went well until we stopped at traffic lights on Shooters Hill when it died and wouldn't restart. Fortunately, we had stalled outside the entrance to the hospital Officers Mess and, with help from a passer-by managed to push the car onto the car park of the mess.

I found the mess steward and explained my problem with the car and said I would get the car moved as soon as possible. From there, I walked down the road to the married quarters were my colleague Mike W lived. I hoped he was in.

I was in luck; Mike and his wife had just finished their evening meal and he was only too pleased to help me out of my predicament. We drove round in his car and unloaded most of our luggage into his, non-essentials could wait until I could get my car started. Then, along with us crammed in we made our way the short distance home. Mike said he would come and get me the next morning and bring me to work. I was hoping to get my car working and moved out of the mess car park before too long.

Mike picked me up the next morning as promised and drove into the officer's mess car park. I jumped into my Corsair, inserted the key into the ignition, more in hope than expectation and turned the key. To my amazement the engine fired up first time. I got out leaving the engine running and found the mess steward to tell him I was leaving, returned to the car and drove it across the road to the hospital car park. At least if the car failed to start when it was time to go home, it would not be causing any obstruction where it was. Talking to Mike later, he suggested that the engine had possibly overheated with the long drive and cause a vapour lock, preventing fuel getting to the engine.

In early 1976, Anthony Nolan was seriously ill in hospital. He had been ill in hospital and had been suffering from a rare blood disorder, the only possible chance of saving his young life was a bone marrow transplant. Unfortunately, there was no compatible donor on the register set up by Anthony's mother. News of Anthony's plight gave rise to a large number of people coming forward to register and give a small sample of blood for tissue typing. Anthony died in 1979 without a suitable bone marrow donor being found.

The Royal Herbert Hospital helped with taking blood samples and a number of the hospital staff volunteered to have samples taken, myself included. I thought no more about it until I received a telephone call in May 1976.

The voice on the other end asked if I was the same person who had answered the call for possible transplant donors on the Anthony Nolan Appeal. I said I was, and how could I help. The caller went on to explain that they had a seriously ill South American girl in the hospital who was in desperate need of a donation of white blood cells and my blood was compatible with her. I was told the procedure was more or less the same as making a blood donation. I asked how much of my blood was needed and the reply came: "All of it!"

After a brief explanation of the process, I agreed to go over to the Hammersmith Hospital the next day, which just happened to be the same day as the FA Cup Final between Southampton and Manchester United.

I met with the consultant who took me to a treatment room equipped with an assortment of complicated-looking equipment. I was asked to get up onto a bed and a cannula was inserted into a vein in my left arm, a second cannula went into a vein on my right arm. I was told the process would take up to two hours as my blood would flow from my left arm into a machine which would filter out the

149

white cells and then return the blood to the vein on my right arm. I was assured that most of the body's white cells were in the bone marrow, and those that were removed from my blood stream would be replaced with 24 hours.

Shortly after the process started, a trolley with a TV set was wheeled in and I was asked if I wanted to watch the Cup Final. I was not a great fan of football but watching the final would certainly relieve the boredom of lying immobile on the bed for a couple of hours. I was given drinks and sandwiches while I watched the TV. I vaguely remember the match, which Southampton won 1-0.

After a couple of hours, the consultant came in and asked if I was alright, he said the process of extracting my white cells was complete and I could go home. I was detached from the machinery and got ready to leave when the doctor asked if I could come back again. I said I would be available at the weekends, but if it was urgent, he could telephone me and I would make myself available. In the event, I went back to the Hammersmith a further six times. I never found out if the girl had survived.

I was on duty one evening and was passing the time in the Sergeants Mess and chatting over a drink when to talk turned to sport, a common topic of conversation in messes around the world. I mentioned that I used to play rugby, but I hadn't played since leaving Keogh Barracks some years ago. One of the members asked me what position I used to play in. I told him I was a scrum half but I was long out of practice.

"That's a coincidence," said one of the group with whom I was talking, "we are short of a scrum half for Saturday, do you fancy a run out?" I said I wouldn't mind, and asked who I would be playing for. The RAMC had a rugby team made up of players from the Royal Herbert and the military hospital in Milbank. It was known as LAMS (London Army Medical Services). We had a reasonable season, won a few, lost a few, but rugby at the level we played was all about the banter and beer after the game.

My season came to an end in a game against Blackheath on a muddy pitch in September 1976. The opposition were much superior to us and ran us ragged throughout the game. I received an awkward ball from a line out in the second half and fell backwards as the Blackheath forwards came charging through our line. I managed to get the ball away and felt a sharp pain in my knee as one of their forwards caught me with the studs on his boot as he rampaged past me.

I sat up to examine the damage, and as I spread my fingers through the mud on my knee a squirt of blood erupted through the dirt. I was sure the studding had opened up my meniscectomy scar from an operation some years ago. Hobbling off the field, one of the RAMC spectators came over to me and bound up my knee with his handkerchief. He then helped me to his car and drove me to the casualty department at the nearby Sidcup hospital.

Unfortunately, this was the year that NHS junior doctors staged a strike and the hospital accident and emergency department was closed. My companion drove me to the only place in the area that had a casualty department we knew would be open—the Royal Herbert Hospital.

I was seen immediately by a doctor from Senegal who was on secondment with us. He was brilliant, cleaning up the mud and dirt from my knee and reassuring me that my scar had not been compromised. He worked steadily for an hour debriding the ragged cut and eventually inserting ten stiches into the wound. Finally, a nurse bandaged my knee and gave me a tetanus injection. I thanked my good Samaritan for his earlier ministrations and was driven home in an ambulance.

Mo was somewhat concerned as the ambulance drew up outside the house, but was relieved when I got out and made my way up the drive on crutches. I explained what had happened and said that my knee was a little painful but there would be no permanent damage, although I would not be playing rugby for the rest of the season.

I managed a reasonable night's sleep and my knee was a lot less painful on Sunday. I reckoned that if I rested it for the remainder of the day, I should be able to drive to work the next day. Sure enough, I had sufficient movement in my right knee to allow me to drive and brake, so I left for the hospital, driving carefully.

I made my way along the main corridor to the dispensary and was surprised to find Mike B with two black eyes and a cast over what I presumed to be a broken nose. He had taken a big hit in another rugby match somewhere else in London. At least, Mike W was in one piece.

Mike mentioned that the commanding officer was due to arrive on one of his regular inspection tours in half an hour. Sure enough, the CO, accompanied by the quartermaster and the RSM arrived at the medical stores to be met by the two Mikes and myself. Looking at Mike B and his panda eyes, and myself supported on crutches, he said that he had heard about our injuries and had not expected the pair of us to be at work on this day.

A few weeks later, Mike and I had fully recovered from our injuries, although Mike's nose was a little bent and I had a scar on my knee. Mike W was on leave when I had a call from the QM to come to see him. I duly walked down the corridor to his office where I met a couple of civilians who introduced themselves to be from the Greenwich Theatre, not far from Woolwich. They explained that they were part of the production team for a show by the comedian Max Wall, and were asking if they could borrow some medical equipment for a sketch.

The QM was happy for me to lend a few basic items and to make sure I got a signature for them. I lent them an equipment trolley, a stethoscope, a blood pressure monitor, and a head mirror, along with a selection of surgical instruments. They were happy with these items and gave me a pair of tickets for the upcoming show. Our next-door neighbour had kindly said in the past that they would be glad to look after the boys if we wanted to go out in the evening The Max Wall show was on the coming Saturday and Ron and Maureen were happy for us to take them up on their kind offer.

I found the show extremely funny as Max was on good form. The man sitting next to Mo thought so too, and rocked back and forth in his seat laughing his head off. Meanwhile Mo sat stony face and did not appear to be enjoying the evening's entertainment. Max did his stand-up comedy and paraded across the stage in his famous silly walk, he also performed a number of sketches including the one in the doctor's surgery where I recognised all of our borrowed equipment, and at the end of the show he made several curtain calls to great applause.

On our way home, I mentioned to Mo that I thought she didn't enjoy the show. She told me she was not a fan of Max Wall and had never found him in the least bit funny. However, she was happy to be out with me and pleased that I had had a good evening. I promised her that we would go to something she would enjoy next time.

Once my rugby injury had healed, and my rugby season was over I ventured onto the squash court again. I had learnt the game in Cyprus and enjoyed it, Mike B was also a keen played and we played together quite often. Once I thought my game was up to a reasonable standard, I joined the local league and eventually after a few months, more by default than skill, I found myself in the second division.

I returned to the office one afternoon after lunch in the mess and as I walked in Mike W was on the telephone.

"One moment," he said into the phone, "he's just walked in," and handed the receiver to me.

Taking the phone from Mike, I said who I was to the caller who replied that she was the Brigadier's PA and asked if I could I play the Brigadier at squash at 3 o'clock that afternoon. Cupping the receiver, I told Mike what the caller wanted and he said it was alright for me to go. I told the PA that I would be ready and waiting for the Brigadier at the appointed time.

Arriving at the squash court I met my opponent for the afternoon. He was short, about 5 feet 4 inches, with shorts down past his knees, thick pebble-lens glasses and plimsols. Thinking this was going to be a piece of cake, we shook hands and entered the court.

What followed was an object lesson in not judging a book by it cover. The Brigadier ran me ragged through five games. I managed to get three points off him over the match, and I think he was being kind to me. I don't believe he worked up a sweat whereas I was soaked through with chasing the little black ball around the court. He always managed to place the ball where I wasn't. After the game, I thanked him for the thrashing, shook hands again and left. I later learnt that he was his regimental champion.

The Sgts Mess was quite active in that there were games nights, mess dinners, lady's dinner nights and the traditional Christmas Draw. Police Officers from the local station on Shooters Hill were frequent guests at various entertainment evenings.

On one particular evening—a stag night—the entertainments committee had arranged for a couple of strippers for our delectation. They were terrible, but the many guests in attendance seemed to enjoy them. During the interval we were entertained by a local comedian whom I found very funny. It was a young Jim Davidson who would later go on to become quite famous (or infamous), and a good friend of the armed forces.

As I was a member of the Christmas Draw Committee, I was asked by the RSM to go round the tables and sell some draw tickets. Taking a large handful, I made my way around the tables and sold many books of tickets, some groups buying joint lots at £20 between them. I asked them to whom I should make out the ticket stubs and was surprised to be asked to note down various police departments such as 'The Murder Room' at one London police station, 'The Vice Squad' at another station, 'Traffic' at another, the mess was full of police officers enjoying the most awful strip show!

The next mess event after the Christmas Draw was a Burns Night in January 1977. The RSM was a Scot and the evening was in full Scottish tradition. Gentlemen were allowed to wear either mess kit or kilt with all the regalia, ladies wore evening dress. Mo, despite her Scottish ancestry, had never been to a Burns Night and was quite looking forward to it. As usual she looked wonderful in a full-length blue velvet dress with a broach complete with a sprig of heather.

It was fortunate the main room in the mess was quite large as the evening was well attended. The RSM was in full Scottish dress with kilt and Scottish Dirk (Sgian-Dubh) tucked into his sock. Once all the diners were seated and the starters were finished and cleared away, the RSM stood and asked for silence. At that point from the corridor leading to the dining room came to sound of bagpipes and the RSM asked us to stand and welcome the haggis. The piper entered followed by the mess steward bearing an enormous haggis on a silver tray.

The piper having finished, left the mess and the haggis was presented to the RSM who recited the address to the haggis, written by Robbie Burns. He managed all nine verses in the original vernacular before stabbing the haggis with his dirk. Once this was done the feast was served, haggis with all the trimmings, the wine and whisky flowing freely.

Port followed the main meal and dessert, and Mr Vice was called upon to propose the loyal toasts and a toast to the ladies. Mo and I took a taxi home after an evening which we both thoroughly enjoyed. Whenever I was in a unit with a Scottish RSM, Burns Night was always celebrated, but none matched our first at the Royal Herbert.

We frequently went into London on a Sunday with the boys. Their favourite places were the Natural History and the Science Museums and we usually spent most of the day in one or other of the two. At the time parking in South Kensington was easy as there was very little traffic on a Sunday morning in London and it was a good day to visit the sights of London and the outlying places like Kew Gardens, the Victoria and Albert Museum and the British Museum.

I was busy in the shed one afternoon when Mo called me into house. We went into the dining room and looked up the garden where we could see the greenhouse. Both the boys were in the greenhouse and appeared to be singing.

"What's going on?" I asked Mo. She told me there had been an item on the television recently about Prince Charles talking to the plants in his garden. The boys had seen this and were busily serenading the tomato and pepper plants. It must have had the right effect as we had an abundant supply of tomatoes and peppers that year.

We had a storm one night with strong winds and rain. When we got up the next morning part of the fence at the rear of the garden had been blown down in the night. The McDonalds who owned the house had left me the contact details of a solicitor in Welling who was managing their affairs regarding the house while they were in Scotland. I contacted the solicitor and told him that part of the fence had come down and that I was prepared to do the necessary repairs providing I would be reimbursed for the cost of materials. The solicitor told me to go ahead and to let him have the receipts; he was able to authorise this as he believed the repair would not cost too much.

After consulting my Readers Digest repair manual, I went out and bought the items I needed to fix the fence and had it upright and sturdy in one afternoon. The following week I took the receipts round to the solicitor who duly paid me from his petty cash, along with £20 for my work.

Apart from singing to the plants in the greenhouse the boys helped Mo and I in the garden. One of the jobs they enjoyed was cleaning out the pond. It had started to look a bit murky and we could hardly see the few goldfish swimming around. The boys got the job of fishing them out and carefully placing them into a bucket of clean water. They managed to catch 15 goldfish while I bailed out the pond with a bucket.

The pond was deeper than I first thought, although the bottom six inches was a sticky sludge. As I was clearing this out the sludge came alive with frogs and newts, wildlife I wasn't fully aware of. The three of us were up to our wellington tops trying to catch the writhing and jumping amphibians. Among the many newts were several of the Great Crested variety; today they are protected and one is not allowed even to handle them without a special licence—we had at least ten in our garden pond, along with about 30 frogs. I was amazed that such a small pond—it was only about 5 feet square—would harbour such a quantity of wildlife.

We soon had the sludge and silt out of the bottom of the pond and we refilled it with clean water, Ron from next door leaned over the fence and advised us to leave the water to stand for a few hours to allow the chlorine to evaporate off and for the water to become a little warmer before we put our frogs, newts and goldfish back.

Mo discovered a yoga group in Welling and went along one evening try it out. She was quite taken with it and joined the group, finding the yoga exercises to be quite relaxing, in fact she quite often fell asleep during the warm down after the class. She also went away for a weekend a couple of times for periods of yoga and relaxation.

My mother came down for a long weekend visit, bringing with her presents for her two grandchildren, a kite for Justin and an Action Man doll with a lot of extras for Jason, and, of course sweets for both of them.

There was a good breeze that day, ideal for kite flying, so we went through the back gate into the park. We were saddened to see many of the elms had been cut down because of Dutch Elm Disease that was spreading through the country. At least, the Charter Oak, a 200-year-old tree, was still standing.

We managed to get the kite up and flying high. Justin was able to get it going himself after a few attempts and was happy and laughing as his kite flew higher and higher. Jason was running about with his Action Man making machine gun noises.

Leaving the boys in sight, Mo, myself and my mom took a gentle stroll around the park with its boating lake and splendid old Danson House. It was a really pleasant area of park land and we were privileged to have easy access to it via our back garden gate.

Jason and his friends frequently went through our gate and spent a lot of time running around the park. One Sunday he had gone through the gate with his Action Man and water bottle for adventures. He had told us where he was going and we reminded him that Grandma was leaving later and not to spend too much time away.

He turned up a couple of hours later looking flushed, distinctly bleary-eyed and unsteady on his feet. Mo asked him if he was alright and he said that he was a bit tired and was going for a nap. "Do you want a drink?" Mo asked him.

"No thanks. I've had some from my water bottle," he replied and tottered off upstairs for his nap.

Mo took his water bottle and started to empty the contents down the kitchen sink when she noticed a particular smell. She bought it to me and asked me to take a sniff. There was a distinct smell of gin. Jason later told us that he thought that mixing gin and orange juice which Grandma liked would be OK to take to the park for refreshment. When he got up a couple of hours later, he was suffering from his first hangover!

Mo visited the local GP for a regular check-up on the breast lump she found when we were living in Chester and which was dismissed as nothing to worry about by a few male physicians over the intervening 7 years. On this occasion, she was seen by a female GP and she told Mo that she was not happy about any abnormalities in the breast. The GP referred Mo to a surgeon at Guys Hospital in London who in turn decided that the lump should be removed.

Mo was admitted to Guys a fortnight later and after surgery, spent the weekend on the ward to recover. She got the results of the pathology on the lump, which turned out to be benign, and I collected her from the hospital on the Tuesday. When the stitches had been removed the skill of the surgeon was apparent. A faint, barely visible scar was the only evidence that Mo had had an operation.

Mo had routine mammogram screening when we were in the UK, and later, after I had retired from the army, another lump was detected and this was also successfully removed and shown to be benign.

Justin was seen by our local GP as the scar on his chest had developed into raised keloid scarring. He was seen by a burn specialist at a hospital who recommended regular massaging with lanolin. Mo religiously applied lanolin twice day for several weeks, and although the keloid tissue flattened somewhat, she took Justin back to the GP who suggested Triamcinolone injections which may reduce the scarring. The GP made a referral to a specialist at Guys Hospital with a view to Justin having this treatment.

A few weeks later we received an appointment, but on the day, Justin had a heavy cold and we cancelled. Shortly after this, other matters came up, and we decided not to subject Justin to what we were told could be quite painful.

The Royal Herbert was due for a visit from the London area commander the coming fortnight. This meant an intense period of cleaning and tidying the whole building ready for the commander and his entourage to make his visit to the hospital a success. The medical stores and dispensary were in good shape anyway, and little in the way of cleaning and tidying was necessary. However, this did not stop Mike W insisting that we kept the place in pristine condition. I took to carrying out my work with a yellow duster in my pocket just in case I spotted on offending particle. By the end of the week, we could have performed brain surgery in the place as it was practically sterile.

After the first week of constant tidying, all of us apart from Mike W were heartily fed up. The visit was scheduled for Tuesday the coming week and I had hatched a cunning plan.

I knew that DMED would have, by now, processed the orders we had sent off to them in recent weeks and I telephoned a contact in Ludgershall and asked him if our consignment was available for despatch to us. My contact said that it was apart from one or two items and would be completely ready by early next week. I asked him to arrange the delivery in the morning of the commander's visit, not telling my friend the reasons for the request, he said he would do his best to arrange the shipment to us.

The morning of the commander's visit arrived, and while our S/Sgt was in conference with the quartermaster, a four-tonne truck arrive at our back door with our order from DMED. Mike B, myself, and our corporal set to unloading the truck into the medical stores and started unpacking the boxes.

DMED used a lot of wood shavings and sawdust as packing materials at this time, and our load was no exception. Pretty soon we had a lot of the boxes unpacked along with the packing material which littered the floor and caused a cloud of dust.

About 15 minutes before we were due the visit Mike W came back to the office and saw the mayhem at the back of the stores. He just stood there glaring at the three of us, ankle deep in wood wool and sawdust along with a pile of empty boxes.

"You buggers," he cried. "You've done this." We expressed ignorance feigning surprise and carried on unpacking.

10 minutes later, the commander and his entourage along with the QM and the CO arrived. We stopped unpacking and walked down and stood to attention in front of the visitors. Looking over my shoulder and surveying the jumble of boxes and packing material up the far end, the commander turned to Mike W and said, "Oh, I see that you're very busy so I won't detain you, I'll leave you to your work."

With that, the group turned and made their way out of the stores, but not before the CO had looked over at Mike W and said, "Well done, Staff W, good show." The compliment went some way to placating Mike and he eventually saw the funny side of things.

We opened up one Monday morning to a disaster in the dispensary waiting room. The front panel of Mike's aquarium had exploded and there were dead fish, gravel, and dead plants all over the floor. The burst panel must have been quite powerful as gravel and fishes had been fired through the dispensary hatch into the office.

I gave Mike a hand to clear up the mess, mopping up the water and sweeping up the gravel which had got into all the nooks and crannies of the waiting room. Fortunately, clinics were not opening for an hour or two so we soon had the area clean and ready for patients coming in for their prescriptions.

Just as we had finished cleaning up the QM called in for a quick visit and was just as saddened as we were at the loss of the aquarium. He suggested that he might be able to get some money from a contingency fund to replace the tank and to restock it with a few fish. He said he would speak to the CO.

Mike B got the go-ahead from the QM to cost a replacement aquarium and new stock, and eventually we had a new fish tank in the waiting room. Mike had spent a few hours one Sunday morning setting it all up, ready for Monday morning. He did a fine job, the replacement aquarium looking far superior than its predecessor.

When we first arrived at RHH building work on the new military hospital, The Queen Elizabeth, had been underway on the site of the old Shrapnel Barracks since 1972. It was to be a 456-bed hospital and designed to replace the Royal Herbert, which, being over 100 years old was beginning to show its age, and also a successor to the Queen Alexandra Military Hospital at Milbank, London. The new hospital was being built off Stadium Road not far from RHH.

In the spring of 1977, we had gradually begun moving medical equipment and some drugs across to the medical stores and dispensary at the new hospital. While there, we had a wander around the hospital which was nearing completion. The stores and pharmacy were finished, as was the pathology laboratory. The hospital was to be fitted with easy clean carpeting throughout, but I found this to be tiring to walk on.

In the autumn of 1976, we received a telephone call from the McDonalds' solicitor in Welling asking us to visit as he had some news for us. Wondering what the news was all about we made an appointment and visited the solicitor in his local office. The news was that the McDonalds' bank manager had advised him that keeping the house in Welling was not economically sound, and he should consider selling it to raise capital to support their business venture on the Isle of Skye.

The McDonalds had agreed to sell the house, giving us as sitting tenants first refusal on purchasing the property. We left the office with mixed feelings, namely the prospect of becoming house owners or that of having to leave a home that had been a happy place for over a year.

We checked our finances and later visited a building society with evidence of my earnings to enquire as to how much we could raise as a mortgage. Along with any savings we had, the most we would be able to manage would be a maximum offer for the house of around £12,000. On top of this, we had allowed for solicitor's and survey report fees.

We made our offer to the solicitor who promised to call us back within a few days. As it turned out, our offer was refused, the McDonalds were asking £13,500, and were not prepared to go any lower. Mo was dead set against approaching our families for help. My mother had very little money anyway being retired and receiving only a state pension. Thus, it would appear, we were on the move again.

Within a few days, I received a call from the housing officer telling me the solicitor had advised him of the situation and that we should vacate the house in Danson Lane within a month. He also said he had a suitable house for us in Eltham which we should take a look at as soon as possible.

The house was an end-terrace semi-detached property on a corner. It appeared to have quite a large garden at the rear, but we were unable to see as there was a high wall running along the adjoining road. The house was not far from Eltham railway station, a doctor's surgery almost opposite, and a nearby shopping centre.

I took over the house in mid-September 1976 and our belongings were moved by a local firm. As usual I had kept our boxes and the only large pieces we had were a freezer and a washing machine.

The 'march out' from Danson Lane was the easiest we had ever experienced. The housing officer and Mr McDonald started checking the inventory in the kitchen. After 10 minutes, Mr McDonald said he was satisfied that all was in order and he was quite content to sign that we had left the property in good condition. I believe he was intending to clear all of the furniture and other items from the house shortly after we had left anyway so checking everything off would be a waste of time.

Chapter 16
19, Well Hall Road, Eltham, London

The house was quite large with three good bedrooms and a spacious kitchen. It was carpeted throughout with light cream coloured shag pile carpet, not the best colour with two young children running in and out. As we thought the garden was very big but over grown, it could probably wait for our administrations until spring.

We discovered one major drawback after we had moved in. The whole house had just 6 electrical plugs! 3 were upstairs in the bedrooms, one in the living room and thankfully, two in the kitchen. Most of our electrical appliances were plugged into extension leads and adapter plugs. Not the ideal from a safety point of view.

There was no central heating in the house, the only place which was warm was the kitchen where the heat came from the gas range which also heated the water. Luckily, I found a fairly new paraffin heater in the loft which we used to heat the living room.

The move was not a good one. We went from Kent, just 3 miles from Welling, into London and as a consequence Jason had to change his school and Mo had to give up a part-time job at a green grocer in Welling High Street, and her yoga group and there was no bus service between Eltham and Welling.

Jason started at a local primary school a short walk from the house. The headmaster was related to Robin Cousins, the British Figure Skating champion who later went on to winning a gold medal in the Olympics in 1980.

We continued our forays into London at the weekends visiting the many sights of the capital. The boys still enjoyed the Natural History and Science museums.

December soon came along and with it the usual Christmas festivities. The boys were up early as usual tearing open their presents from under the tree in the living room. We sat down to breakfast together only to find that we had almost run out of squash for the boys.

There was one place I knew would be open on this day—the chemist shop. I waited until 10 o'clock and jumped into the car and drove the short distance to the shop to find Brendan on his own and the shop crowded. I took off my jacket and went behind the counter to help him out. Most customers were after things they had forgotten, as had I, but there were one or two folks with prescriptions.

I suggested Brendan should look after the dispensing while I saw to the customers wanting over-the-counter medicines such as aspirin or indigestion remedies.

I managed to get a quick telephone call to Mo to tell her that it was mayhem at the shop and I would probably be a couple of hours before getting back home. Mo was happy with this and said she would see me when I returned home.

After about an hour and a half, the rush subsided and the crowd in the shop became more manageable. There were still a few prescriptions to fill by Brendan while I served the diminishing number of customers. Finally at mid-day I served the final packet of aspirin, turned the door sign to 'Closed' and latched the door.

Brendan emerged from the dispensary breathing a sigh of relief, but with a smile on his face. He walked over to me and thanked me for helping out. He then disappeared into the stockroom and returned with a large box of chocolates.

"That's for your wife when you get home," he said as he punched the "No Sale" key on the till, and handed me £30. "And you have a very Merry Christmas." I returned the compliment and went home to Mo and the boys.

In the New Year, 1977, work continued with the gradual movement to the Queen Elizabeth Hospital. The new hospital would not open fully until all the patients from the Royal Herbert and the Queen Alexandra Hospital in Milbank had been transferred. Meanwhile one or two outpatient departments in the QE were functioning and I worked in the dispensary at the QE on an ad hoc basis when I went across to deliver items they needed from us. I usually stayed on to help out in either the pharmacy of medical stores as we at RHH were not too busy.

Although the hospital was fully up and running by late 1977, it was officially opened by The Queen on 1st November 1978. The QEMH was named in honour of Queen Elizabeth the Queen Mother, who was also the RAMC Colonel-in-Chief at the time.

We received a posting order in early February sending us BMH Hannover at the end of April. We were quite pleased to be on the move again and started the business of applying for quarters in Hannover and MFO packing boxes. We decided to take a minimum of stuff with us to Germany. A fair number of things we reckoned we could do without we would put in storage, so we ended up with two piles of belongings, one pile for Germany and another for storage. The two major items we had to have with us in Germany were the freezer and the washing machine. We had these crated by the local storage company we had selected to take our second pile.

Our pile for storage included a lot of our vinyl LP records, our wedding photographs, along with cooking pots and pans and crockery, items which would be available in the quarter in Hannover.

Gradually we were all packed up and the MFO disappeared on its way to Germany. A few days before we were due to leave the storage items were taken by the removal company to their depot in Sidcup. I sold the car for not a lot of cash, after all I hadn't paid a great deal for it in the first place and it had been reasonably reliable—apart from one or two hiccups—in the two years we had had it.

We had called round to our neighbours Ron and Maureen in Danson Lane to thank them for their friendship and to say goodbye. They kindly gave us their telephone number so we could keep in touch with them. That telephone number proved to be most useful in a few months' time.

I called into the chemists shop to say goodbye and wish them well. I had enjoyed the part-time job and the company of the staff. My replacement at the RHH had taken over from me in the shop as well.

It was also time to say goodbye to Well Hall Road. We would not hear about it for 15 years when 19-year-old Stephen Lawrence was murdered in a racially motivated attack, just a 10-minute walk from our old home.

Our flight to Hannover was from Luton Airport. Armed with railway warrants we boarded a train from Eltham station. Two hours later, via New Cross and London Bridge Station we were at Luton Airport.

The flight to Hannover was on a chartered Britannia turboprop which took just a little over 2 hours. The landing was a bit bumpy as the turbulence moved the aircraft around, but we soon were down safely in Germany.

The four of us went through the usual formalities of arriving in a foreign country, passport control and immigration (we had arrived at a civilian airport), and finally on to collect our luggage. My boss, Chris H, was there to meet us. I was surprised to see him as he had a full beard. Something I had never seen in the RAMC before.

Chris helped us to load our cases into his car and drove us from the airport through the suburbs of Hannover to our new home in Weidetor Strasse. Chris told us that we were just a few minutes' walk from the hospital and that he had done the march in on our behalf. Everything was in order; the flat was clean and most of the furniture was new. Having unloaded his car, Chris left us to settle into our new place, telling me he would come and collect me early on the day after tomorrow.

Chapter 17
Flat 2,20, Weidetor Strasse, Hannover, West Germany

The ground floor flat was spacious and spotlessly clean. From the front door, a corridor with three bedrooms and the kitchen off, it led down to the large, bright living/dining room. There was a glass door out to a balcony which looked out over a grassed play area.

Of the six flats in the block, four were occupied by medics and their families. Directly opposite was the hospital chief clerk; and in the two top floor flats above lived Barry D, the sergeant medical storeman who would be one of my colleagues. Opposite Barry was Dave L, one of the administration clerks.

The block had a cellar with six storage rooms—one for each flat. Some were larger than others and it was traditional for the larger ones to be passed over to the other residents when the 'owners' of the room moved on. We got one of the smaller rooms but this would be adequate for storing boxes and Jason's bicycle and Justin's Go-cart.

The only part of the flat that needed attention was the kitchen. Chris had mentioned that the units were due to be replaced in the next week or two. That would be an advantage as the worktops in the kitchen when we moved in were quite low, and we could get the fitters to raise the new units to a height that would suit Mo and I as we were both quite tall. In the event when the fitters arrived, Mo asked them to build the units high enough to suit her. They did just that and the new kitchen, with a brand-new sink and taps was completed in just one day.

Chris came for me as promised and we drove the short distance to the hospital. Here I went through the usual administration, met the RSM and the commanding officer. After this, I went with Chris to the medical stores down in the cellar. The stores occupied a good L-shaped space and unlike the Royal

Herbert had plenty of headroom. All the pharmaceutical supplies were in one leg of the L, and medical instruments and equipment were in the other.

Here I met my neighbour Barry and two British civilians, Dave was a general labourer as was Tommy. There was also a secretary, Debbie, and a couple of Portuguese labourers. Chris then took me up to the dispensary where I would be working. This was a large and spacious room with floor-to-ceiling windows and an adjoining waiting room with a glass-partitioned stable-type door.

The hospital had no Sergeants Mess, but across the car park there was a building which contained a senior ranks club. It functioned as a mess but had no official standing as such. It was essentially a place to relax at lunch times and was not big enough to hold large functions, thus the senior NCOs and warrant officers of the hospital were members of the Garrison Sergeants Mess.

The public transport system in Hannover was excellent and cheap. There was a bus stop not far from our flat and the service connected with the trams into the city. Our first foray into town was amusing. With my limited German, I asked for two tickets into the town, handed over the fare and sat back to enjoy the ride. After about twenty minutes, we found ourselves at a terminus out in the countryside. I approached the driver who was enjoying a break with a cup of coffee and asked him where we were.

The driver turned to an older lady at the back of the bus and beckoned her forward. She spoke to us in good English and asked us where we were going. When I told her we were trying to get into town, she told us to follow her when she got off.

Not long after the bus started off, we stopped in an area with tram tracks. She motioned to us to get off and follow. She took us to a tram stop telling us that the tickets we had were good for the tram and it stopped outside the main railway station in the centre of town. We thanked her profusely and waited for the tram.

Hannover is a beautiful city, mostly completely rebuilt after the war. There were many excellent department stores, small shops and street vendors selling various food—bratwurst, currywurst, chips, and my favourite, a ham and cheese filled pastie, the name of which I have forgotten. The city had a wealth of places to eat, Italian, French, Greek, and many Oriental restaurants, along with others from around the world.

After a bite to eat, we made our way to the Commerzbank to open an account. I had remembered to take my last few pay slips to prove I was earning and the process of getting an account was quite easy. I changed my remaining sterling into Deutsch Marks and made our way home on the tram and the bus.

The first priority after a couple of weeks of settling in, was getting the boys into school, and finding our way around, was to look into buying a car. The local overseas allowance, my salary and there being no taxes and duty to pay on the purchase of a new car looked like a good investment and a considerable saving on the prices back home. Not only would we save on the price of a car, but we were allowed to purchase a ration of 200 litres tax free fuel a month.

My first choice was a top of the range Ford Cortina, but any Ford car meant nine months waiting list. I investigated Mercedes (too expensive), most Japanese vehicles, Peugeot, and many others over the next few weeks. Eventually, Dave drove Mo and I out to a Chrysler dealer in Langenhagen having suggested a Chrysler Alpine. I wasn't too keen at first but taking one for a test drive I was convinced that this was the car for us. Mo and I discussed the car at length and decided that we should go ahead and order one. The main advantage was that it could be made available within a fortnight.

Two weeks later the dealer delivered our new car and invited Mo and I out for a drive to familiarise me with the controls. The first thing I had to master was driving on the 'wrong' side of the road. With the car being right hand drive, it was easy to keep close to the kerb, but I was confused when we turned at a T Junction and ended up on the left with a lorry heading towards us. The dealer sitting beside me leaned over and eased the steering wheel over to the right, saying that head-on collisions tended to give him a headache!

I had a day off and with the boys at school I used it for our first trip out in the car to the barracks at Bergen-Hohne, about 45 miles from home and home of a Dutch tank regiment. I had heard that the Dutch version of their NAAFI were doing a special sale of hi-fi equipment and my cassette recorder needed to be upgraded.

Once we were out of the suburbs of Hannover the road to our destination was quiet with birch forest on either side. As we neared our destination, Mo turned to me and said, "I find this area a bit creepy. It's making the hair stand up on the back of my neck." Just then, we made a turn in the road and there, on the left-hand side of the road, was the Bergen-Belsen Memorial.

We were both shocked to come across this infamous place, not realising it was close to a large city like Hannover. We agreed to stop off and see the memorial on our way home.

We continued on our way to Bergen-Hohne and found what I was looking for. I had bought an Akai cassette recorder and was pleased with the price I had paid.

We made our way back to the car and returned to the Belsen Memorial. We parked up and went into the information room with its many haunting photographs of the camp before and after it was liberated by the allies in 1945. From there, we went into the grounds following the paths around the many mass graves with the plaques indicating how many dead were interred in them. There were few other people about and the site was so silent and haunting, and, despite the nearby forest, we could hear no birdsong. We stopped at the main memorial and stood in silent contemplation before returning to the car and making our way back home, we had no words between us for what we had just experienced.

I was in the medical stores chatting to Dave and telling him we had been to Belsen when Tommy walked in. Tommy was in his 50s and ex-military himself having fought in the war. He overheard the conversation with Dave and coming up to us said, "Yes, I remember Belsen, I haven't been there since I was there on the day it was liberated on 15 April 1945." With that, he disappeared into the stores, leaving Dave and I standing with our mouths open.

Dave was keen to move on from general labouring in the stores and asked me if he could help in the dispensary. I was happy to have him with me as I was alone in the pharmacy, and it would be nice to have someone to talk to. I told him he should speak to Chris first, but to say that I would be pleased to have him upstairs with me.

Chris was OK to let Dave go on the condition that he could have him back downstairs to cover for leave, or when they needed an extra pair of hands to deal with deliveries from DMED.

Dave was a quick learner and after a few weeks showing him how to use the equipment, make up the ward baskets, and prepare bulk stocks. I made up prescriptions which Dave handed out to the patients. Controlled drugs were my responsibility and were subjected to checks by the orderly officer and the commanding officer when he came on his regular inspections.

Dave lived in the attics of the hospital and had made a comfortable room for himself. Most of the furniture, including his bed had been scavenged from unwanted items left outside houses for bulk rubbish collection. Dave usually accompanied the driver on his regular run in a four-tonne truck to replenish the hospital medical gases supply, which is how he managed to transport the larger items of furniture back to the hospital and his flat.

Dave was from London and had decided to hitch-hike around the world. When he arrived in Hannover, he found his brother working as an army cook at the hospital and he stayed. When I first met him, he had been in Germany for a couple of years and his intention to travel the world had long since been placed on hold.

One of the first trips we made from Hannover with the boys was to the city of Hamelin, which was about an hour's drive away. We went on a Sunday as the re-enactment of the Pied Piper legend happens in the town square as we wanted to get a good view of the proceedings.

We found a parking space close to where the play was to take place and had a good view of the setting. The story commemorates the events of 1284 when the town was infested by rats and a musician guaranteed to get rid of them by playing his pipes. He led the rats to the river Weser where they were all drowned. When he presented his bill to the local council, they refused to pay, so the piper led all the children of the town to a nearby mountain where they disappeared, never to be seen again.

The re-enactment starts with a narrator telling the story, this is followed by the townspeople dressed in period costumes lamenting about being overrun by rats, portrayed by children in rat costumes running about the stage. The story is well performed, the children playing their part exceptionally well. Although mostly in German, it is easily understood as the story is well known.

When the play ended, we made our way through the town looking in the shops, a lot of them selling souvenirs of the pied piper. We bought the boys a toy rat apiece and we found a café for elevenses before heading to the river side. Here we boarded a small boat for a trip along the Weser. As we got aboard Justin dropped his rat into the water, fortunately it floated and one of the crew fished it out. Justin had a genuine rat, one that did not perish in the river Weser.

Following the boat ride and a bite of lunch we made our way back to our car and drove the hour to Hannover and home. We all agreed we had had a good day out and seen a little of Germany, and we would certainly see more in the coming months.

A few days after our visit to Hamelin, Mo told me she was worried about Jason, as he didn't appear to be happy at school. He came home grumpy, dropping his bag in the hallway and disappearing into his room. I popped in to see him and to ask him what was wrong. Jason just shrugged and said nothing. I could understand why he was unhappy; he was eight years old and in his fifth school. Our moving around had done him no favours.

I suggested to Mo that we should consider a boarding school for Jason, possibly in or near our parents in Birmingham. Mo wasn't keen on the idea, but agreed that we should look into the idea.

There was a community centre near the NAAFI which had a reference library, and there were one or two books giving details of boarding schools in UK. After pouring over the books in the evenings after the boys were in bed, we had a short list of three schools which we considered suitable. There were two in Birmingham and one in Wolverhampton.

I had advised Chris that I would be needing a few days off to go back to UK to sort out a school for Jason, but I didn't have any dates until making appointments to see the heads of the schools we wanted to visit. He was fine with this and said he would cover the dispensary as I was only going to be away for 5 days and two of them would most likely be over a weekend.

I wrote to the heads of the schools requesting an appointment and giving details of Jason's education to date, and the dates when I expected to be available for interviews. While I was doing this one evening, Jason woke up asking for a drink. Coming into the living room and seeing the books and correspondence on the table he naturally asked what I was doing. I told him I was looking at a change of school for him as didn't appear to be happy where he was now.

"You're not thinking of sending me to boarding school, are you?" he asked.

I replied that we were just thinking about it at the moment and deciding what would be best for him.

"Wow, great!" Jason exclaimed. "When can I go?" This was completely unexpected. I was sure we would have tears and not happy anticipation of going away to school. I told him we were going to England as soon as I had appointments to see the schools we were interested in, and he would have part of the decision whether or not he would be happy to go to one of them.

We had replies from the three schools quite quickly. We had an appointment for the school in Wolverhampton for a Friday in two weeks, and the other two in Birmingham on the following Saturday morning. The timings could not have been better for us. We could leave Hannover on the Wednesday evening, take the midnight ferry from Zeebrugge and be home by lunch time of the Thursday afternoon.

At the time, P&O ferries were offering a five-day return fare for about £50 for 4 people and a car. The midnight ferry took 6 hours to do the crossing to Dover as the port did not open until 7 o'clock. We had booked a cabin to get some sleep after the long drive to the ferry terminal.

We left at 6 in the evening from Hannover having filled the car and two jerrycans with petrol earlier in the day. The trip would be about 350 miles and would be the first long distance journey we had made with the car, so I allowed us 6 hours to do it.

We stopped after a couple of hours at a service area for a bite to eat and drink. We were making good time on the fast autobahn, clocking around a steady 90 miles an hour, and we were half way into our journey. After our break, we continued on, stopping only to top off the petrol tank just before the Dutch border, near Venlo.

Crossing into the Netherlands we were waved though by the border guards, not even having to show our passports. From there, we passed through into Belgium and onto the port of Zeebrugge via Antwerp. We finally arrived a little after 11.00 PM. The trip including a stop had taken just over 5 hours. I was looking forward to having a sleep on the ferry before we arrived in Dover.

After going through the formalities of tickets and passports, I drove onto the ferry, parked up and we climbed the stairs to find our cabins. Having got the boys settled Mo and I turned in for the night crossing, I was asleep within minutes, and the next thing I knew was a knock on the door as we approached Dover. We got the boys ready and made our way down to the car deck, ready to disembark.

Once through customs and immigration at Dover we were on our way to our families in Birmingham. The drive up to the Midlands seemed to take an age after the fast journey from Hannover, but we were with Mo's family at last. Tomorrow we would visit the school in Wolverhampton, but now it was time to relax and catch up. A further reminder that Mo's mum had no idea of our lifestyle. When she asked us about our plans and we told her we were home to look at boarding schools for Jason, she said, "Oh, that's not for the likes of us!"

We went to Wolverhampton the next day and was shown around the school by the head mistress. We were reasonably impressed by the facilities, but were a little disconcerted when the head dressed down a pupil while we were with her. We left the school with mixed feelings, but looking forward to seeing the two places the next day.

I can't remember the first place we went to except that it was out in the countryside and its curriculum seemed to be mainly agriculturally based. Our final appointment was at the Blue Coat School in Harborne, not too distant from Birmingham city centre.

Our first impressions were favourable. The grounds were well tended and the school's 1930s buildings were solidly constructed of red brick. I knew the area from my youth, as my school had its playing fields a few hundred yards from the Blue Coat School's main gates.

We found the reception and the headmaster, Mr Bissel, instead of showing us into his study, welcomed us and proceeded to take us on a tour of the grounds with Jason at his side. We came across several of the boys on our walk, and the head greeted them by name. He seemed to know all of them as we passed them.

Eventually we re-entered the school building at St Martin's House, which we were told, would be the house in which Jason would enter should he join the school. Here we met the housemaster, Mr Gray, in the common room, where he told us the boys could play table tennis, snooker, or just relax and read. From there, we went upstairs to the dormitory where the boys would be sleeping. It was spacious and bright with long windows letting in the light.

We asked Mr Bissel what the boys would be doing at weekends, he told us that it was still school on Saturday mornings and a chapel service on Sunday mornings. If the boys had a weekend pass (an exeat) to stay with parents or relatives, they could leave after lessons on Saturday, but must be returned by 8.00 PM on Sunday.

Having spoken for quite a while to Jason, the head said that he would be writing to us in the next few days to advise us of his decision regarding Jason coming to Blue Coat School for the start of the winter term in September. We thanked him for seeing us and returned home to Kingshurst and Mo's family. On the way, Jason was enthusiastic about going to boarding school, and of the three we had visited, Blue Coat was the favourite.

We spent Sunday with Mo's family and my mother was invited to lunch with us. With all the running about visiting schools, we hadn't had time to visit her as she was still living in Alum Rock. I would run her back home in the car when she was ready to leave.

We left for Hannover in the small hours of the next morning, intending to get to Dover for the early ferry back to Zeebrugge. I didn't bother to fill up the car with petrol as I believed we would have enough in the tank and in the two jerry cans in the boot to get us from Birmingham and across into Germany before we needed to get fuel for the final leg of our journey.

We arrived back in Hannover late that day, feeling completely jaded from the journey and the busy weekend. At least, the boys had slept for most of the drive and woke bright and breezy the next morning, and ready for school.

The following Monday, the post corporal came into the dispensary and handed me three thick A4 envelopes. Opening them, all were offering Jason a place at their schools for the coming September term.

When I got back home that evening, I told Mo we had had offers for Jason from the three schools we had visited and should we let Jason decide if he really wanted to go to boarding school and if so, which did he prefer?

Jason was outside playing and we called him in. We all sat round the dining table with the three information packs and told him he had been given a place at all three, and asked which one he would like to go. His reply was immediate— the Blue Coat School. Mo and I were happy with his choice as we were impressed with that school.

I wrote to all three schools, accepting the Blue Coat, and rejecting the other two, but thanking them both for their offers. One of the advantages of the Blue Coat was the issue of Jason's first school uniform. This was to be supplied by an out-fitters in Birmingham. We ordered Cashes name tapes and Mo started sewing some of these into Jason's clothes he would be taking with him. I would be doing the rest once I had Jason's uniform when I went with him to Birmingham, just a few short weeks away.

I bought a trunk for Jason at our local NAAFI shop. I tried it in the boot of the car before buying it to make sure it would fit. It would be large enough to take Justin's belongings should he go to Blue Coast, as well in the future. The hospital sign writer kindly made me a plaque with our surname on it.

Jason was so enthusiastic about going to the Blue Coat that I had visions of the bubble bursting as we got nearer to the point when I would have to leave him at his new school. Soon that time came around, it was time to leave Mo and Justin and head off down the autobahn and take the ferry over to Dover and north up to Birmingham.

The following day after spending some time with families, we went into Birmingham to get Jason fitted out with his new school uniform. He got a blazer, shirts, jumper and corduroy shorts. Most of his clothes were bigger than needed, a size the outfitter suggested Jason would soon grow into. When we returned home, I spent a few hours sewing in the name tags and packing them into his trunk.

On Tuesday, it was the first day of the new school year and we drove to the Blue Coat School, where we unloaded the trunk from the car and, escorted by Mr Gray made our way up to the dormitory. There were a number of other boys in the room, some, like Jason, here for the first time. We found his bed in a corner by a window and started unpacking.

When I felt I had got Jason settled into his new surroundings, I said I must go back to Mum and Justin in Hannover, and he should come down to the car and say goodbye. He followed me downstairs where I asked him if he was going to be alright. He gave me a hug, said, "I'll be fine, Dad, see you at Christmas!" and with that dashed off to meet his new friends. I just stood there for a few minutes, mouth open and with a tear in my eye at leaving him, before starting the car and heading back to Germany.

Jason wrote to us once a week, I believe the house master had the boys sit down after school on Saturday and write to their parents. His letters gave us the satisfaction that he was happy and enjoying boarding school life. The two grandmothers had been to visit the school a few times, usually on Sundays where they attended the service in the chapel. We were looking forward to seeing him at Christmas.

At the start of October, I received a telephone call from Mrs Robinson at RAMC Records. She called to ask me if I would be interested in a posting to Dharan in Nepal. I asked when that would be and she said that it would be in January 1979. I told her I would call her back later in the afternoon as I had to speak to Mo.

I went home at lunchtime, telling Chris about the call I had had, and that I might be late back. He was OK with that and said he would cover the dispensary until I returned.

I told Mo that Mrs Robinson had called and that my immediate thought had been to take the posting. However, I had to talk to Mo, as the posting for the dispenser at BMH Dharan had to be accompanied, and anyway it was only for a year. My second thoughts were that I should turn it down. This particular posting had that option.

Mo and I agreed the posting was out of the question given our circumstances at the moment, and I went back to work and called Mrs Robinson. I told her Mo and I were in a difficult position having just put Jason into boarding school, we had not long bought a car, and we had only been in Hannover a few months. I also told her I would ring around some of my contemporaries suggesting one of them would be interested.

In the event, I rang Robbie in BMH Munster. Robbie was a year behind me as a dispenser and he had taken over from me when we were posted from RVH Netley. He was a sergeant and married with no children. He sounded definitely keen having been in Munster for a couple of years. I gave him Mrs Robinson's extension number at RAMC Records and to let her know he would like the posting. This he did and he went to Dharan in 1979. Everyone told me I was mad to turn down the posting, especially as it was one place I had always fancied. As things turned out, it was a fortuitous refusal.

My upstairs neighbour, Dave was an ice hockey fan, and followed the fortunes of the Hannover team. He asked Mo and myself if we would like to go to a match, adding that it would be OK to take Justin along as well.

The stadium was open to the sky, and there were a few inches of snow in the stands. There was no segregation of the fans and alcohol flowed freely. I was surprised at the fans were not segregated as they were in football, given the violent nature of the game, I was expecting the aggression to spill out into the crowd. There was a group of opposition supporters behind us, and when we had soundly beaten their team they leaned forward and congratulated us on the result.

I had no thermal underwear but I was wearing snow boots so my feet stayed warm, although my body felt the cold. I had been issued with two pairs of 'long johns' as part of my kit when I enlisted. I took one look at them and decided I would not be seen dead in them. One night in a freezing, open-air ice hockey stadium changed my mind.

I had never seen ice hockey, except briefly on television, it looked quite violent, as indeed it was. Mo, myself, and Justin loved it. It was fast-moving, with frequent changes of teams on the ice, either defence or attack. As we watched I forgot the cold in the excitement of the game. After the game, Dave introduced us to a German business man friend of his, who was a sponsor of a number of Canadian players in the team.

We followed Hannover ice hockey team throughout the season, with Jason with us when he came home for the Christmas holiday. He even got a puck which came over the barriers into the crowd, it was handed to him by one of the opposition supporters. At the end of the season, Hannover gained promotion to the next division, and the stadium was rebuilt with a roof and more comfortable seating, not that the seats were often occupied, as nearly all the spectators were on their feet for most of the game.

Jason came out to us for the Christmas holiday. He was escorted onto buses and trains and eventually to Luton Airport by a company called Universal Aunts. I am ashamed to say that I did not recognise him as he came into the arrivals area at Hannover Airport. His hair was longer and he had grown a couple of inches in the short time he had been away.

He told us he was enjoying school and the grandmothers came to see him, or he went to them on some weekends. He had made friends and the teachers were kind and understanding, especially his house master, Mr Gray. It was a couple of days into the holiday before he got out of the habit of calling me 'Sir' when he spoke to me.

Snow had started to fall in November, so I bought sledges for the boys as one of their many Christmas presents.

Over the holiday we made a couple of trips to the Hartz Mountains, one of which was organised by the unit as a ski training exercise. It took about ten minutes to realise that skiing was probably not for me, but I persevered and after half an hour of falling over, the decision was made—I abandoned skiing for those who were more able. Meanwhile, I went and found the boys and fought them for a sledge, they had to give in, mainly because I was bigger than them.

The sledges were fun, sturdily built from beech wood and with metal runners. They remain in use today by our grandchildren, some 40 years on, and I still enjoy speeding down a snow-covered slope in a local park.

Our neighbour, Dave, introduced us to his second love—Opera. He had four tickets for Tosca at the Hannover Opera House and invited Mo and I to accompany him and his wife. We had seats high up in the gods, it felt like we were sitting on the edge of a cliff, but we had a great view of the stage. Mo and I loved the opera, the stage sets and performances were wonderful. Dave had a recording of the opera which contained copy of the libretto in English so we could follow the story.

The back of the programme listed the forthcoming productions for the season. On that caught my eye was 'Hansel and Gretel' by Humperdinck, with a performance on Boxing Day. I thought it would be interesting for the boys as part of the Christmas celebration. When I got into work the next day, I asked Debbie, who spoke good German, to book me four tickets for the opera.

She got the tickets which cost about £20.00. I assumed that they were for seats up in the gods because they were very cheap by UK standards. There was even free parking underneath the opera house. When we arrived, we made our way upstairs and presented our tickets to the door man. He shook his head and directed us down to the ground floor, explaining that our tickets were for the stalls. Our seats were four rows from the stage.

The production along with our view of the stage was excellent, the children playing the hero and heroine had good voices and the action was easily understood as we knew the fairy tale. At one point, the auditorium filled with smoke from the oven, and when the witch smashed a pot with her broomstick, most of the broken pottery ended up in the orchestra pit.

Winter, along with Christmas, was our favourite time in Germany. The local council kept the roads clear of snow, although residents were required to clear snow and ice from the pavements outside their house and flats. We had a rota in our block and we took it in turns to clear snow and keep the stairwells clean.

Shops in the city closed at lunch time on Saturday and didn't open again until Monday, four weeks before Christmas this changed, and they stayed open until late evening. There was also a Christmas market (Christkindlesmarkt) during the period of Advent, selling seasonal items—Christmas decorations, Christmas trees, street food such as bratwurst, and glühwein, usually with a tot of brandy added. Of all the cakes on sale my favourite was Stollen with its marzipan filling. There were also street entertainers and puppet show. The boys loved the markets with the bright lights, decorations, and entertainers.

Mo had been on a trip to West Berlin with wives' club earlier in the year, travelling on the military train through East Germany to the British sector of the isolated and divided city. She remembered the blinds were drawn shut, carriage doors were locked and the East German police on the train walked through and checking passports and running dogs under the train checking for any persons hiding there.

Mo and her friends stayed in Edinburgh house for the three days they were there, and visited many of the sites of the city, including a visit into the Russian sector of East Berlin. She told me the place was grey and foreboding with few people about, and most of the shops had little to offer, including one in which the only display in its windows was one solitary boot. She noted that many of the buildings were still disfigured with bullet holes, a legacy of the second world war and the fighting of the Russian military when they entered the city in April 1945.

In December of 1978, all of us had travelled by car along the corridor from the border checkpoint Helmstedt-Marienborn or Checkpoint Alpha, one of three crossing points from the West into occupied East Germany. A few weeks before we went, our passports were sent away to be checked and travel documents were issued. The documents had to be identical to our passports, even down to the spelling of our names in English, essentially as both were checked by the Russian border guards who, it was assumed, would compare both visually as they could only read Cyrillic script.

At Helmstedt, our documents were checked again by British military police who found a mistake on Mo's papers. Her name on the passport was in capital letters whereas the documents showed her name in lower case. New documents were issued in a hurry as we had to attend a briefing before we passed through the border.

The briefing consisted of slides showing the various junctions on the autobahn where we could accidentally exit the road and find ourselves, illegally, in East Germany. I was told the minimum time to make the journey to Berlin was a little over two hours, any less than that may result in a speeding fine, any longer than six hours and the military police would come and find us. We were not allowed to stop anywhere along the autobahn. If we broke down, we were to stay in the car, lock the doors and windows and wait for rescue by the military police.

At the end of the briefing, I was handed a hard backed, A4 dossier containing all of the briefing notes and photographs. At the middle of the book was a centre-fold notice to be displayed in the windscreen should we be stopped by the East German police which were not recognised by the West. It consisted of a Union Flag and a message in German and English which stated, "I am a British Soldier, in possession of valid travel documents. Please fetch an English-speaking Russian officer." We were advised to lock the car doors and pull across and block the two lanes of the autobahn. It was suggested that once there was a couple of miles of tail-back the police would relent and send us on our way.

We were waved through Checkpoint Alpha and drove a short distance to the border post of East Germany. We were stopped and our documents examined by the border police—all the time being scrutinised by armed police on a gantry above us. The low barrier was raised and were waved through towards the

Russian checkpoint a few yards further along the road. I stopped at another low barrier which was about 3 or four feet off the ground and appeared to be made of steel and the thickness of a telegraph pole. I later found out the barriers were so designed as to prevent low sports cars from driving under them.

The Russian soldier, impeccably dressed in winter grey and fur hat, beckoned me to get out of the car. I approached him carrying our travel documents with me. As I neared him, he came to attention and saluted me. I returned his salute although I was dressed smartly in civilian clothes, and handed him our documents. He accompanied me back to my car and checked my family, nodded, saluted again, returned my documents, and directed me to a hut on the side of the road. I again returned his salute and made my way to the hut.

The inside of the hut were bare walls apart from a picture of Joseph Stalin. In front of me was a window reminding me of a railway ticket office, except that the window itself was completely blocked and I could not see inside. I placed my documents on the shelf below the window and a hand appeared and took them inside. It felt completely surreal, like the hand of a toy money box, when, at the touch of a button a hand comes and takes your money away. After a few minutes, the hand reappeared with my papers and I left the hut and got back in the car, the barrier was raised and we were on our way to Berlin.

The drive was uneventful as there was not much to see. We saw Leipzig in the distance, but not much else. Most of both sides of the autobahn were tree lined, giving little in the way of a view from the road.

We made good time and went through the document checks in reverse order before finally entering the city. We stayed at Edinburgh house for our long weekend intending to see as much of the city as we could in those few short days. We visited Mike B and his family who we had known in Woolwich, and they were happy with their life in Berlin.

We walked around the city, visiting the wall and the Brandenburg Gate, the checkpoints into the East, and looked over the wall from a viewpoint at Checkpoint Charlie in the American Sector. On the other side of the wall was a hundred yard No-Mans land with minefields, tank traps, barbed wire and a double fence patrolled by armed guards with dogs. We felt sorry for the East Germans trapped in their own country.

Shopping was also on the list, The American PX for King Edward cigars for Dave at work, 50 for 5 dollars. Shopping in the PX was all in US Dollars so we had to exchange our Marks on the way in. We also went to the French Economat for wine and cheese.

West Berlin was a vibrant city, both by day and night. Brightly lit at night in comparison with the darkness of the Eastern Sector. We didn't venture into the East, essentially because we had the boys with us and, as a soldier, I was required to wear uniform if I went across.

We left Berlin for Hannover just as it was starting to snow. We went through the check points with no problems and soon we were on our way. The road was clear but the snow fell heavier as we went along so the journey was slow. After about an hour, my windscreen washers froze up and I had to make frequent stops to clear my windows of ice as the temperature had dropped sharply.

Despite the slower speed and stops, we made the border after about three hours and stopped at Checkpoint Alpha where I got some hot water to thaw out the windscreen washer container. Once that was done, we made our way home, relieved to be off the autobahn corridor and with a clear windscreen.

Heavy snow continued over the next three or four days and, although the roads were kept clear by snow ploughs, I hadn't driven my car during that time as I had a few days off work. Gradually my car was buried in a huge pile of snow and before long it would possibly be hit by a plough and I decided it was time to dig it out and move it out of harm's way.

After an hour or so, the car was clear of the snow and I got in expecting not to be able to start it as it was also very cold. To my surprise it started first time and I drove it around the block and parked it out of the way of the snow ploughs. Barry, the medical storeman offered me a lift into a work as his car was free of snow as he had been working, so my car stayed where it was at the back of our flat while I went off with Barry. Come the weekend, we decided we must go and get some Christmas shopping, and went round the back to get the car warmed up. It wouldn't start!

I popped round to one of the Royal Engineer vehicle mechanics who lived nearby and told him the problem, mentioning that it had started easily when I had dug it out, although I had had to use the choke. Asked how far I had driven I told him it was just around the corner to the back of our flats.

That was the cause of the problem he told me. The short drive in the cold weather had caused petrol to condense on the spark plugs and stop them from working. The remedy was to remove the plugs, dry them thoroughly, replace them and try and start the car using no choke.

It didn't take long to get the plugs cleaned up and have a go at starting the car. Sure enough, after three or four goes the engine fired and I left it running to warm up before heading off to the NAAFI. That taught me not to drive a car for short distances in cold weather.

Between Berlin and not long after digging out our buried car, we celebrated our first Christmas and New Year in Germany. Christmas morning was the same as most people with children. We were up early watching the boys ripping off the wrapping from their presents which were piled up under the tree. Apart from the usual gifts of sweets and chocolates, we had got them typical German warm winter clothing and snow boots. One particular item we had bought Justin was a set of junior skis, which had to be tried on as soon as breakfast was over.

Directly opposite our block of flats was the Messe Schnellweg built on a high embankment about 30 to 40 feet high. This was Justin's nursery slope, and he became quite good at skiing down it and not falling over too often. He was able to develop his skills better over the following few days later.

On New Year's Eve, we were invited across to one of our neighbours to let in the New Year. There were quite a few people celebrating the arrival of 1978 and just before midnight it started to snow quite heavily. Having let in the New Year we finally left the party at around two in the morning and trudging through a couple of feet of fresh snow across to our flat.

New Year's Day was bright sunshine but very cold. At least, the snow had stopped although three feet had fallen during the night. We had breakfast and decided to drive to the Hartz Mountains, knowing the snow ploughs would have been out in the early hours clearing snow and ice from the roads and I had no worries about driving 70 or so miles to a village called Silberhütte.

The autobahn was clear and the drive was trouble free, even the road up to Silberhütte had been ploughed. Had there been any problems further up the road the police would have a check point and ascertain that there were snow chains in one's car, if not, one would not be allowed to go further.

We parked up at a nearby café and made our way up to the ski slopes, Justin with his new skis and Mo, myself and Jason with the sledges. There was quite a crowd of people at Silberhütte that day, skiers, sledgers and folks just enjoying the snow. After a couple of hours, we packed up the car and went to the café for a late lunch before making our way back home. We had had a lovely day in the sunshine and snow.

The time came for Jason to return to school. We were pleased that he was happy to be going back to meet up with his friends and his grandparents. We drove to Hannover Airport and left him in charge of a stewardess on the aircraft, along with other children going back to school, and waited for his flight to take off. Mo shed a few tears on the way home, which was understandable, but she was reassured with knowing he was happy with his school and his new found friends.

It was also time for me to reclaim the cost of storing our household items held in storage in Sidcup. The problem I found was that I had no receipt for the previous bill I had paid in September. I checked through my most recent bank statements and was unable to see when the cheque I had sent off back then had not cleared.

The mystery deepened a few days later when my September cheque was returned to me. I decided I would telephone our neighbours in Danson Lane and ask Ron if he would make some enquires for me.

I received a letter from Ron the following week telling me he had gone round to the removal company and discovered that they had gone into receivership and a lien had been placed on the business. This meant that all our items in storage were lost.

Fortunately, we had taken out household insurance with a company in Salisbury and I contacted them and explained the problem. They asked me to prepare a list of items that we had lost. Most of the things we had left behind were inconsequential and of no great worth, but a few were of sentimental value. Our wedding album, family photographs, a lot of vinyl records, and my shooting trophies. We were particularly sad at the loss of our album, as they were gifted to us by one of Mo's colleagues at work. All was not completely lost as Mo's mother had a small album from our wedding.

The insurance company paid up with a couple of weeks, but for several months after either Mo or I would ask one another if either of us had seen a particular item, only to get the answer that it was probably lost in storage.

A short time after Jason left for school, I was in the Sergeants' Club at the hospital to say goodbye to one of our colleagues who was posted. The RSM presented him with his 'Hannover Horse,' a memento of his time at the BMH. We were having a few celebratory drinks when the duty medical officer came in to say farewell to the sergeants with whom he had been working. He also told us that the temperature had dropped suddenly and the phenomenon of freezing rain had started and we should get ready to leave before it got any worse.

I left about ten minutes later and slipped and slid over to the where I had parked my car. When I finally got there, the car was covered in clear ice and looking as if a layer of Perspex had been sprayed over it. I managed to get into the car and sat in it while the heater came on full. I then drove off very carefully, the roads on the way home were like skating rinks. For the only time we were in Germany, the local authority had closed the Schnellweg. I later found out that the medical officer who had warned us about the weather had slipped on the step on his way out of the club and broken his arm.

When winter had passed and spring returned, Mo's mother came over for a visit. I took a few days off and did the tourist stuff. We visited Celle, a beautiful town north of Hannover. Down to Hamelin for the Pied Piper, a scenic drive through the Hartz Mountains, and a day out in Brunswick. Bessie enjoyed her time with us, being quite impressed with the places we visited and the friendliness of the people we met.

Eileen also came out to us and I drove the 80miles to an RAF airbase at Gutersloh where she was due to arrive. In the event, there was a problem with her aircraft and she was 12 hours late getting to Germany. I slept in the basement of the base while I waited for her plane to come in. When she finally arrived, I was reasonably refreshed and ready for the drive back to Hannover. We stopped on the way to have some breakfast as Eileen had had little to eat during the long delay of her flight.

We went to the same places we had taken Mo's mum, but with one addition. We were coming back to Hannover from a trip to Goslar, a mediaeval town of half-timbered buildings, and a church with beautiful stained-glass windows. Eileen was a regular church goer and she was quite taken with the old church. On the way back, we spotted a castle high in the hills. Consulting the map, I found it to be Schloss Marienburg, a 19th century castle.

Making our way along the road up the hill we eventually came to the castle, and were just in time to join a guided tour of the building. The tour of the castle was quite cheap but very informative. I well remember the vaulted ceilings, typical German furniture, and the portraits of the previous occupants.

The most memorable and beautiful were the inlaid wooded floors which must have taken craftsmen an age to complete. We were all required to cover our shoes with large felt slippers and encouraged to slide the over the floor which went a long way to keeping the marquetry of the floors in pristine condition. Eileen said that we all looked like Mickey and Minney Mouse with our over-large slippers, and giggled her way around the Schloss.

One of the other places we visited was the Herrenhausen Palace and gardens in Hannover. The place was originally the summer residence of the House of Hannover. It was the home of the elector George Louis, who in 1714 succeeded to the British throne as King George I. He was also responsible for adding the water features of the garden including a fountain which shot a jet of water some 50 feet into the air.

During World War II Herrenhausen Palace suffered immense damage in a British bombing raid on 18 October 1943 and the ruins of the palace were almost completely torn down after the war. Prince Ernest Augustus of Hannover sold his remaining property at Herrenhausen Gardens in 1961, but kept the nearby Princely House, a small palace built in 1720 by George I for his daughter Anna Louise. It is now his grandson Ernest Augustus's private home, along with Marienburg Castle.

The gardens occupied over 50 hectares and had an open-air theatre. There were also frequent spectacular firework displays accompanied by classical music. On one memorable evening, there was a firework display held during an eclipse of the moon, the accompanying music was Beethoven's Ninth Symphony.

Both the boys had Lego bricks and, when Jason came home for the Easter holiday, I took weeks leave and we went to Lego Land in Billund in Denmark. I decided to take a couple of days to do the trip as it was almost 300 miles. Too far to do in one day, especially with the boys.

We left in the morning and took the E2 towards Hamburg and onto Flensburg where we crossed the border into Denmark. With one or two stops on the way, it was just past noon when we crossed into Denmark and found a small town with a nice-looking guest house overlooking the town square. We booked two rooms with breakfast, and leaving our luggage went and found lunch at a nearby restaurant, followed by a wander around the town. We returned to the hotel in the evening, and after a light supper, had an early night.

We rose the next morning to a bright sunny day. We had a leisurely breakfast on a hearty Danish repast of cold meats, cheeses, cereal, soft bread rolls, coffee and orange juice. It was excellent and would set us up until lunchtime. We made a few sandwiches of the leftover cheese and meat, paid the hotel bill, and left for Billund, the home of Legoland.

It was a mid-morning by the time we had packed up the car and headed north. After a couple of brief stops, we arrived in Billund around lunchtime and the first priority was to find somewhere to spend the night and freshen up after the drive, then find a bite to eat. We found a welcoming guest house that would provide both beds and lunch. Once we had settled in and eaten, we made our way to Legoland.

Legoland was brilliant. We were all amazed at what could be built with thousands of plastic Lego bricks. We took a boat ride around the various items built of Lego bricks—Abu Simbel, the Taj Mahal, the Danish Parliament Building and Buckingham Palace. There was also an amusement park which the boys made full use of. Jason managed to get a Legoland driving licence. All to soon it was closing time and we left and retired to our guest house for an evening meal and bedtime.

We returned to Legoland the next day after checking out and spent the morning and half the afternoon enjoying the park before heading back south. We had decided to stay at the same hotel in Denmark as before, having booked in before we left a couple of days previously.

We had just dropped off to sleep when we were rudely awakened by the loud noise of motor cycles revving their engines, accompanied by the beat of rock music. There was a group of around thirty or so motor cyclist gathered in the town square below us for a party. The noise was deafening and the Danish triple glazing did little to mitigate the cacophony. It was well after midnight before Mo and I managed a few hours' sleep. The boys, who were in a room opposite us, heard nothing and had slept through the night.

Although feeling a little jaded after only having a less than restful night, Mo and I were reasonably refreshed after another large Danish breakfast along with several cups of strong coffee. We left Denmark around mid-morning and were soon on our way for the five-hour drive back to Hannover.

We had one last Sunday before it was time for Jason to return to school and we went to a town in the Hartz Mountains called Braunlager. We walked to the top of the hill overlooking the town where the was an abandoned ski jump. We soon saw the reason why the structure had been allowed to fall into disrepair. Any ski jumper using it would have landed across the border into East Germany.

The high fence and watch towers in the valley below were clearly visible from where we stood.

We descended the hill and found a quiet area on the outskirts of the town where could have our picnic. There was a small clear stream where we placed a bottle of wine and soft drinks to cool. A narrow-gauge railway line ended abruptly on the edge of the stream where there was evidence of a bridge across, the line continued on the other side. It was then we noticed that the East German border fence and watch tower was about half a mile away from where we were getting our picnic ready. Meanwhile the boys had crossed over the stream and were chasing one another around the field beyond.

A middle-aged couple approached us and spoke to us in a mixture of German and broken English, urgently telling us to call the boys back to us. They were concerned that the eastern border guards would let their dogs loose on them, or worse, come across and kidnap the boys. Mo and I thought that very unlikely but in order to calm the couple down we called the boys back to us. Once Jason and Justin returned across the stream the couple calmed down and went on their way. I retrieved our drinks from the stream and helped Mo get the picnic ready, after which, we packed everything up and made our way back to Hannover.

After the Easter break, Jason returned to school and, after his flight to Luton, escorted by a member of Universal Aunts, was eventually met by my mother at the station in Birmingham. We received a letter a few days later telling us that all went well and there were no hitches on his journey back to school. He was becoming a seasoned traveller, which would serve him well in the coming years.

In late September, shortly after Jason had returned once more to the Blue Coat School, we received a posting order, sending us to the Cambridge Military Hospital in Aldershot. This was good news as we would be able to have Jason with us more often, both during the regular holidays and in the half-term breaks. The other good news was that I would get a promotion to staff sergeant. We were pleased with news, the routine of completing the paperwork for the move could wait until after Christmas. That would give us plenty of time to get organised.

Just after the end of the festive season, I was dispenser on call when I received a telephone call in the early hours of the morning. I dashed into the hospital and directed up to men's surgical ward where I was met by the on-call surgeon. He asked me for a supply of dexamethasone injection as he had a soldier injured in a car accident who had developed a serious complication which would require massive doses of the drug to alleviate.

I went down to the medical stores and grabbed all the dexamethasone we had in stock and took it up to the ward. The surgeon said that he would need a greater amount than I had in stock so I said I would call round the various military hospitals and get more. My first call was to BMH Rinteln where they got Mike B out of bed. He had a small supply and I asked him for all of it. He agreed and arranged for the military police to pick it up in one of their patrol cars and deliver it to us. BMH Munster couldn't help but I finally located a large supply in Monchengladbach, the only problem being the nearly 200 miles down the road between me and the drugs.

My colleague on the other end of the phone said he would call someone else and call me back in a few minutes. He was back in 10 minutes. "Problem solved," he said, "I've called in a favour and a helicopter is on its way with the drugs and it will be with you in just over an hour." The military police arrived within the hour, blue lights flashing and carrying enough dexamethasone to tide us over until the chopper came with the rest. The MPs had covered the 60 miles from Rinteln in 40 minutes. The helicopter delivered 30 or 40 vials of the drug and left with profuse thanks from myself and the surgeon.

The patient was showing signs of improvement by the time I left for home. The doctor thanked me for my efforts and said he thought we had managed to stabilise his patient and said, "I think we've saved him, but if he dies by the morning, I shall be seriously annoyed!"

I went back to work the next morning and made a number of calls to those who had helped us out and letting them know that the patient was stable and expected to recover.

We were due to move at the end of March, and, checking the calendar, that would be shortly before the Easter holidays. Justin had also said that he would like to join Jason at the Blue Coat School as soon as we could arrange it.

I duly wrote to the headmaster advising him that we would be posted to Aldershot in March 1979 and asking if Justin could join the school after the Easter break. In reply, he suggested we should visit with Justin a couple of days before the Easter holiday as he would like to speak with Mo and I and Justin before a decision could be made to let him join the school after the break. I would have about 10 days leave after arriving in Aldershot and we could add a few days, provided the unit agreed, to go to Birmingham, see the headmaster and collect Jason for the Easter holiday.

All too soon Christmas came and Jason was with us. He was taller and more confident, although he still called me 'Sir' for the first couple of days. We spent the holiday in Hannover and the Christmas market, ice hockey at the new covered stadium, and sledging in the Hartz Mountains.

Shortly after Jason returned to school, we started packing up some of our non-essential items, mostly the boys summer clothes and their bikes which we had bought them the previous Christmas, the sledges as we didn't think we would be going back to the Hartz before we left for Aldershot. I went along to the Sgts Club for to say farewell to friends and colleagues. I had asked for and been given a departing gift of a boxed collection of Beethoven Symphonies, and along with a model of the Hannover White Horse mounted on a wooden base. This was about a foot high and had a inscribed plaque from the club members giving my name, rank and the dates I had served in BMH Hannover.

We made a final trip to Bergen-Belsen on morning in February. It was a bright but cold sunny day when we left, but it became overcast as we approached the memorial. Walking amongst the burial mounds with their plaques numbering the dead interred within, it started to snow. From the distance, we heard the sound of tank fire from the ranges at Fallingbostel. It bought home to Mo and I the despair of those unfortunate souls confined in this awful place.

I received a message from the Cambridge Hospital that we had been allocated a quarter in Salamanca Park, just off Gun Hill and a short walk from the hospital. The other good news which came our way was that our good friends, Mike and Midge, were also in Aldershot, Mike had been recently commissioned and was the training officer at the hospital, and Midge was working at an engineering company in Fleet. Mo and I were looking forward to meeting up again.

The MFO boxes were finally packed up and shipped off the UK. All that remained was to clean and tidy up our quarter and get it ready for the 'march out'.

We had removed some pictures from the wall which left an outline of their places. Mo decided that she had to wash the wall down and remove the evidence of the pictures. Unfortunately, the original emulsion paint had not been of the best quality and the wall was left streaky. The BIA on the march out told us we should have left it as it was, but still charged us £30 to have the wall repainted. At least, that was the only cost levied, and we believed we had left the quarter in a better state than when we took it over.

I had arranged for Mo and Justin to fly out of Hannover and onto Aldershot, while I drove our car home. I had packed the car with most of our electrical items and a couple of jerry cans of fuel, topped off the petrol tank, said goodbye to Mo and Justin as they left for the airport and headed for Zeebrugge and the overnight ferry to Dover. The drive to Zeebrugge and the ferry was uneventful and with a couple of stops for a rest and refreshments made the ferry in good time. I had booked a cabin for the overnight sailing; the trip would take around six hours as the ferry sailed slowly towards Dover.

I took the items to declare at the customs post at Dover, presented the customs officer with a folder of all the receipts for the items in the car along with my vehicle. He was happy that all the goods I was carrying were bought within the time limit allowed and waved me through without having to pay any duty.

The drive to Aldershot took about two and a half hours and I arrived at our quarter in Salamanca Park around 10 o'clock.

Chapter 18
7, Salamanca Park, Aldershot, Hampshire

The house was a three-bedroom, semi-detached, with a large lounge-dining room. It had a reasonable sized kitchen and bathroom upstairs. A door from the lounge led out to a postage-stamp sized garden with a couple of small flower beds and a rotary clothes line. The house was newly decorated throughout with standard issue magnolia emulsion.

Outside via a door in the kitchen and built on to the kitchen wall was a good-sized store room which would accommodate the freezer when it arrived with the MFO. There was a hard standing outside with three parking spaces.

I was happy to be with Mo and Justin again. They had arrived in Aldershot in early evening, found our new home and the keys with the next-door neighbour. The quarter had been taken over by a colleague and his wife from the hospital who had made up the beds and left a supply of groceries. I would settle up with him when I went up to the hospital the following day.

I walked up to the Cambridge the next day and called into the dispensary. Here I met the pharmacist, Jan Sobzuk, he would be my first experience of working with the new breed of commissioned pharmacist the RAMC was now in the process of recruiting. There was also a corporal and a female civilian with whom I would be working. From there, I went to check in with the RSM. He greeted me with the news that I was to be the mess treasurer for the next three months. Fortunately, I had recently completed a course in Monchengladbach so I would be coming fresh to the job. The bad news was that my predecessor had been posted a couple of weeks prior to my arrival. There would be a lot of catching up waiting for me in the mess office when I came back from leave.

I went back to Jan and told him I needed to add a couple of days on to my disembarkation leave to go to Birmingham and meet with the Headmaster of the Blue Coast School regarding Justin's admission after the Easter break, and also to collect Jason a couple days later. Jan was alright with this and I went to the company office to arrange the extra days.

Next on the list was the medical stores down a hill from the hospital to meet with the staff. Tony BR was the warrant officer in charge and had both military and civilian staff under him. I had met Tony in Ludgershall some time ago and knew him to be a friendly sort of guy. I would be working indirectly with the medical store staff so I considered it prudent to introduce myself to them.

Finally, I found the office of the training officer and knocked on the door. A familiar voice called for me to come in. I entered and found Mike who I had known since our course in Colchester. "Ha ha!" he exclaimed. "It's the blonde one, welcome to Aldershot." I asked him about Midge and their two children and he told me they were all well and we passed a few minutes talking about old times in Singapore and Hong Kong. I mentioned our plans for the next 10 days and he said we would have to meet up when I was back at work. With that, I said my goodbyes and headed off home to Mo and Justin.

Our boxes arrived during the week and we set about unpacking once again. I reassembled the bikes while Mo put away clothes and linen in the ample storage cupboards and wardrobes around the house. Justin had already decided on his bedroom and was helping to put his things away. His room looked neat and tidy and I wondered how long this would last.

Once we were completely unpacked and everything tidied away, we left to visit our families in Birmingham and to eventually to see the headmaster at Blue Coat School to get Justin into the school after the Easter break.

My mother had moved from her terrace house in Alum Rock to a ground floor flat in Kingshurst, a few minutes' walk from Mo's family. This move would be very good if and when both boys were at the Blue Coat as they would be able to see both sets of grandparents on their weekends out. The two grandmothers could travel together to the school when they went to the Sunday morning service in the school chapel.

The meeting with the headmaster went well, Mo and I with Justin at first, then the head spoke with Justin on his own for about 15 minutes. Mo and I were called back into the head's study where he told us that he would be pleased for Justin to start at the school after the Easter holiday. We were granted a free issue of school uniform which we would sort out over the weekend.

We had ordered Cash's name tags in the anticipation of Justin getting into Blue Coat and, having got his uniform over the weekend, Mo and I bent to the task of sewing in the labels. On Monday, we said goodbye to our respective families and went to pick up Jason and the trunk from school and headed back to Aldershot. I was great to have both the boys at home in our latest house.

I went to the hospital on Tuesday morning and said my good mornings to Jan and the other two in the dispensary before going off to see the RSM. He pointed me in the direction of the administration office where I went through the usual documentation procedures before being wheeled into meet the commanding officer. Here I was welcomed to my new posting and I replied that I was glad to be in Aldershot as I would be able to see more of my children and our families. I also mentioned that I was looking forward to working with the pharmacist in the dispensary.

The dispensary was quite small but well laid out with a central bench and racking around the walls containing all of the pharmaceuticals we would need. Bulk preparations were made in the workroom at the back, which also contained the controlled drugs cabinet to which I had a key. Stock from the medical stores were delivered by truck to the parking space outside which gave access to the rear workroom.

We were kept busy dispensing prescriptions as the hospital treated civilians from the surrounding area as well as military personnel. The hospital was very popular with the civilian population. Shortly after starting work in the pharmacy, a familiar face appeared at the window with a prescription. I immediately recognised him as Arthur English who I remembered from television and radio. He was at the time appearing in the television comedy show, "Are you being served?" He was a regular visitor to the pharmacy as he was being treated in the hospital for a chest complaint. I also met him a couple of time on Aldershot station on his way to London.

Shortly after we arrived in Aldershot, the Conservative Party won the General Election in May 1979 and Margaret Thatcher became Prime Minister. We were living in an era of high inflation, in 1979 it was almost 14%. As a result, the value of the salaries of the military were being rapidly eroded. We had not kept up with wage inflation in industry caused mainly due to the power of the unions. The Conservative government remedied military pay by awarding a large pay rise. It was a win-win situation for me, a pay rise and my promotion to S/Sgt increased my take home pay considerably.

After the Easter break, we went back up to Birmingham to take the boys to school and to see our families again. On Sunday morning, we arrived at the Blue

Coat School and met the housemaster, Mr Grey, who took us all up to the boys' dormitory. Justin was next to Jason and near the widow where we placed the trunk. Mo and I unpacked some of the items from the trunk while Jason took Justin down to the house common room to meet some of the other boys.

After about 20 minutes, Mo and I decided it was time for us to leave for Aldershot and we went down to the common room to find the boys. Justin was at the snooker table, lining up a shot on the black. We called out to him that we were leaving, he looked up from the table and replied, "OK, see you at half-term!" and went back to lining up his shot. Jason came out to say goodbye assuring us he would look after Justin and we left the school, pleased in the knowledge that Justin would be alright.

One evening, Mo and I went to the cinema in Aldershot, I can't remember the film we sat through, but when the lights went up, we immediately recognised a couple in the row in below us. It was Brian and Anita whom we knew from Chester. We caught up with them before they left the cinema and went for a drink at a local pub. I had heard that Brian had become the RSM at BMH Rinteln a few years previously but had now retired from the army and was working as a representative for a drug company.

We chatted for a while, talking about our experiences, Mo and I in the military, Brian and Anita their life in civvy street. They were now living in Ash Vale and invited us over for a meal the next weekend. Brian had also worked in the Middle East during the time when many hospital projects that were being built in that part of the world during the late seventies and early eighties. There were quite a few RAMC ex-dispensers and medical storemen working in the Arab countries in the Gulf States (usually retired senior NCOs or warrant officers).

I was interested in furthering my qualifications which would stand me in good stead in finding employment when I left the army. I found an evening course at a reasonably local college which would, if I was successful, give me full membership of the Institute of Purchasing and Supply. Having qualified as a medical storeman I already held associate membership of the Institute. I attended the course for the two years we were in Aldershot, getting good grades in the examinations, before we left for pastures new.

I was due to be on night duty as Orderly Sergeant Major at the hospital when I received a phone call in the afternoon from John P, a retired dispenser working for a group which was heavily involved in hospital builds and supply of equipment in the Middle East. John told me he had a problem with costing a hospital equipment supply as many of his staff were off work with flu and he was struggling to meet a deadline.

He explained that he needed an inventory of drugs to be costed which the company for which he worked was tendering to supply to a hospital in United Arab Emirates. If I was amenable, he would furnish me with the list along with a copy of a publication called 'The Chemist and Druggist' which listed all drugs and medicines available in the UK along with pack sizes, and trade prices.

All I was required to do was to go through the tender document, price the pack sizes, quantities needed, and add his company's mark up. This sounded easy enough and as my night duty usually was trouble free, I thought I could work on the paperwork through the evening. I agreed to give it a go and John told me the documents would arrive by courier within the hour.

As promised the courier arrived just before the dispensary closed for the day. He came to the hatchway, asked for me and presented me with a bulging foolscap envelope. Opening the package, I found a hundred-plus pages of the tender document and a current copy of The Chemist and Druggist, along with brief instructions on what I was to do.

The document was and alphabetical list of all the drugs and medicines John's company was tendering to supply to their potential customer. The process of costing it would be easy enough, if a little tedious. Before working on the tender, I did my rounds of the hospital to make sure there were no potential problems on the horizon, and letting reception know where they could find me if needed, and I retired to the dispensary office and started with the job of working through the list and quantities with a calculator.

Fortunately, I had no interruptions and finished the work around three in the morning. I did another wander around the hospital and fell into bed. I was awake at seven, went to the mess for breakfast, after which I returned to work in the dispensary. Jan commented that I looked tired, I told him I had had a busy night, but not what I had been doing for most of it. I called John just after nine to tell him I had completed the work while Jan was out doing his rounds of the hospital wards.

Another courier turned up an hour later. I handed him the documents and in return he handed me another, smaller envelope containing a several £20 notes. John phoned me later in the week to say thank you and that he was pleased with the result. I replied that he knew where he could contact me if he needed my help again. I met him in person a few years later by which time I had retired from the service.

There was a shooting group within the hospital. I made enquiries and met up with an officer from the X-ray department who was the organiser and coach. I didn't mention that I could shoot, particularly as he told me they were using .22 rifles with which I had no experience. The group used the range at Keogh Barracks on Tuesday evenings, and due to security reasons, we had to use three cars to get there. One car for the rifles, another for the ammunition and the third for the rifle bolts.

The rifles we used were Lee Enfield Mk 8, fitted with Parker Hale rear sights and an aperture front sight. The rifle was completely different to the .303 Lee Enfield Mk 4 rifle I had used previously, mine was standard army issue with its original standard sight. It was going to take practice to get used to the smaller .22 Lee Enfield, and my first attempts were not very good.

We were shooting over 25 yards at paper NSRA 2510BM targets which had 10 smaller targets printed on them, 4 top and bottom and two across the centre. The centre 4 concentric circles were black and white, and appeared to just fit into the front sight aperture. The maximum score one could achieve on this type of target was 100.

Gradually over the next few weeks I became more adept with the rifle and was regularly scoring in the high nineties. My best was 98 and I made the team for a competition which we went on to win.

I drove up to Birmingham to collect Jason and Justin for the half-term break between the Easter and Summer holidays. I popped into to see my mother and Mo's family before going on to the Blue Coat School and the boys. Mo didn't come with me as she was now working as a receptionist in Fleet at the same company as Midge.

I picked up the boys in the afternoon and headed straight back to Aldershot. I got back just as Mo was returning from work and helped her get our evening meal ready. Mo told me we were invited to dinner with Mike and Midge the following day at their new home, one they had recently bought in Coronation Road in Aldershot. Midge had hinted that I was expected to sing for my supper, and I would find out when we got to their house.

When we arrived, we found Mike's two boys playing on an early computer, I think it was an Amstrad. The game simulated table tennis and our two boys were fascinated with it.

Mike was outside in the garden and it was here I found out what he and I were going to do before dinner. Mike had started to build a breeze block wall along the boundary between his house and next door. I had no idea about brick laying and worked as Mike's labourer, mixing mortar and handing him bricks. We worked steadily until Midge called us in for dinner, by which time Mike had managed to lay half the length of the garden with a wall about 5 feet tall. We both stood back to admire our labours before getting washed and ready for dinner.

Dinner was excellent as Midge was a very good cook. We said our goodbyes and headed back home, Mike saying he had a few of days off and would continue building the wall over the coming days. He returned to work on the Wednesday and I popped down to his office to ask about progress with the wall.

He told me he had just laid the last brick when his neighbour looked over and told him the wall had encroached over the boundary at the top of the garden by a few inches Mike would have to move the wall back to the boundary line. Fortunately, it was only the last few feet that needed to be moved and Mike had fixed the problem.

Another time we went to their house, Mike called us into his shed, telling us there was quite a large spider living behind a sheet of plywood. This one was particularly large, and Mike had christened it 'Incy Wincy.' We were over there a week later, and as we went in Mike said to Mo, "Come and see, Incy Wincy's had babies." Mo went with Mike to the shed while I chatted with Midge. I heard Mo scream and dashed outside to find Mike and Mo laughing their heads off. Incy Wincy was long gone, and Mike had substituted a huge black rubber replacement, behind the plywood sheet where the original spider had been. Hence Mo's scream when he revealed the black rubber monster.

Some years later we visited Mike and Midge when they were living in Farnborough and the house in Aldershot was distant memory. It was just after October 1987 when the UK had been hit by a hurricane and winds had reached over a hundred miles an hour in some places. There was much devastation and 15 million trees were blown down, along with the garden wall in Coronation Road. Mike said he was pleased to inform me that the wall ended up in next door's garden.

It was time to take the boys back to school after the half-term break. Again, we went through the routine of driving up to Birmingham and staying with Mo's family before heading off to the Blue Coat School on Sunday. We stopped off at

Gino's pizza restaurant in the city centre before taking the boys back to school. This became a tradition over the next few years, pizza with wine for Mo and I along with soft drinks for Jason and Justin before returning to school.

The next few weeks passed quickly and we soon were back up to Birmingham to bring the boys home for the summer break. We returned to Aldershot with the trunk in the boot, and lifting it out, I heard Mo groan in pain. She had hurt her back as she lifted the trunk. I helped her into the house and sat her down, getting her as comfortable as possible, got her a coffee and a couple of paracetamols to ease her pain.

After an hour or so, Mo complained that her pain was no better, so I rang the hospital and asked if the duty doctor could call and examine her. The doorbell rang within 15 minutes, and by chance the on-call doctor was an orthopaedic surgeon, who after a quick examination suggested Mo had possibly slipped a disc in her lower spine. He told me to get her into bed to lie flat for at least a week, and if possible, put some bed boards under the mattress. I would have to see if I could borrow some from the hospital. Meanwhile I took the door off the kitchen as a stop-gap until I could get some boards.

I couldn't get any leave over the next week as Jan was away. I would have to look after the pharmacy as I was the senior dispenser. There was no alternative, I would have to get my mother to come down and look after the boys and Mo while I was at work.

We had been back a little over a couple of hours and I got the boys together and told them I was going to get Ethel to come and look after Mum, I would be away for at least five hours but I would see if I could get help. Meanwhile they should keep an eye on their mother.

I drove round to Coronation Road to enlist the assistance of Midge who had been a nurse in the QARANC before marrying Mike. Midge said she would come over immediately and stay with Mo until I got back with Ethel.

As it was a Sunday, traffic on the way to Birmingham was relatively light and I was knocking on my mother's door in a little over 2 hours. I had phoned Mo's mum and asked her to call round to Ethel's flat to tell her I was coming. She was ready with her bag packed and happy to come down and help out. We were back on the road within 20 minutes.

The round trip took just under five hours and I was pleased to see Midge, who had made the boys and Mo some supper telling me Mo was sleeping. I thanked her for troubling her and she left to go back home.

Over the coming week Mo gradually improved, her pain eased and she was able to get out of bed for a wash and to use the toilet. Mother cooked and cleaned for us and looked after Mo's every need. On Friday the doctor came to examine Mo and told her she was much improved and could get out of bed. The pain in her back was almost gone, but she was not to lift anything heavy. She was to take things easy for at least another week, by which time she should be fully recovered.

At the end of the two weeks, Mo was much better and able to move about without pain. She said she was able to manage if she was careful, remembering not to lift anything heavy. My mother was taking a short holiday in the coming week so I took her back home on the Sunday and we thanked her for all the help she had given us.

One Saturday during the summer break we took a trip to Bognor, a resort we had enjoyed visiting when we were in Netley a few years previously. The boys had been with us but didn't have any memories of going there.

We spent a couple of hours wandering around the town and along the beach, it was a warm day and the boys went for a swim in the sea. Mo and I paddled in the shallows, keeping a careful eye on the boys. After an hour, we continued along the sea front and we spotted a poster for the Selsey Summer Fete and decided to drive the short distance to see what it had to offer.

We arrived just in time for the fete to be officially opened by none other than Patrick Moore, the presenter of the long running TV programme 'The Sky at Night.' After a short speech to open the fete, Mr Moore wandered through the crowd chatting to people. We had recently bought a telescope and as Mr Moore came towards us, I held out my hand and introduced myself and my family.

He had a larger-than-life appearance and was very friendly. I mentioned that we had recently acquired a small telescope and he surprised me by offering me his card saying that should we be in Selsey again we should visit his house and he would be happy to show Jason and Justin his collection of telescopes. His house on Selsey was called Farthings (Far Things). We never did get to visit but I wrote to him a year later.

1978 came and went, Mo had a couple of jobs one in Farnham as a receptionist for a building company, and when she left that after a few months, she got a job at United Dairies in Aldershot, again as a receptionist. That was more convenient and better paid. She could walk to the job, which was just 10 minutes from our quarter in Salamanca Park.

Mo's mum, Eileen, and my mother visited us a couple of times while we were in Aldershot. I coupled their visits with collecting the boys from school for the half-term breaks. We took them round to various places in the surrounding area, Guildford was a pleasant town to visit, along with trips to the coast.

We had a scare one Saturday morning. The heating in the house was by warm air through vents around the house. I was up early getting breakfast before we went shopping. I heard the heating fire up and within minutes the house was filled with smoke. I opened the door which concealed the heater for the warm air to find it was on fire. I pulled the fuse for the heater and turned off the gas. Mo had come running downstairs to find out what was going on.

I called the housing office to tell them we had a major problem with the heater in the house and detailed what had happened. I was amazed at the reply from the person with whom I had spoken who told me that sort of incident was impossible because of the fail-safe systems within the heater. I suggested he get round to our house and see for himself. If we had left the house and the fire had started while we were away matters would have been pretty serious. The house would probably have been burnt to the ground as the fire would have travelled through the warm air ducting into all the rooms of the house.

A gas engineer turned up a few hours later and immediately condemned the heater. We were issued with a couple of portable heaters until the heating system had been repaired.

Eventually the heating system was replaced by a boiler and radiators a few months later. The installers were very good, they turned up just before we went out to work and were gone by the time we returned. They tidied up after themselves and apart from new radiators fixed to the walls one would never know anyone had been in the house. The central heating was far more efficient than the old warm air system.

Mike and Midge had booked a couple of weeks at a caravan park in St Ives in Cornwall and were going to make the drive overnight so as to be early at the park and secure a good site for the caravan. We invited them over to dinner on the evening to spare them having to cook before setting out on holiday. Mo and I were also on leave for two weeks and I jokingly said we might drop down to Cornwall and sleep in the caravan awning.

They left around 9 o'clock to make the final preparations for their trip. Shortly after Mike phoned us and said he had had a flash on inspiration. They had a couple of tents, their boys, Shane and Darrel, along with our two boys, could sleep in the tents and Mo and I would be in the caravan with Mike and Midge. We would share the expenses and cooking and we did not need to be asked twice to join them.

We packed quickly and left Aldershot shortly after midnight for the drive to St Ives in Cornwall. With the roads at the time, despite low traffic in the early hours, I calculated it would take at least 6 hours of steady driving to do the trip. I was not far off, we arrived at the caravan site around 7 o'clock and found Mike having just set up the caravan and the awning. Mike's two sons had erected the tents and Midge had breakfast on the go. The smell of bacon and eggs was most welcoming.

Midge showed us round the caravan which was quite spacious. Mo and I had bunk beds, the boys would be outside in tents with camp beds and sleeping bags. In fine weather we could all gather around a table in the awning for meals. We had a wander around the camp site to scout out the facilities. There was a small shop, showers and toilets, and a laundromat. The beach was just a short walk down the hill.

The weather during the first week was fine and warm. The four boys spent time on the beach and swimming in the sea. I had long since declined venturing into the sea as I found the waters around the British Isles too cold even in summer; I had become too used to the warm seas in the Far East and the Mediterranean. Mike had bought a stunt kite which we all spent hours flying until the guide strings got tangled.

We explored the north coast as far as Newquay and Padstow, south to Lands' End and the Lizard Peninsula. We went fishing for mackerel and caught enough to provide dinner for all of us. Getting around was easy enough as Cornwall, although popular was nowhere near as crowded in summer as it is today.

At the start of the first week, we had rain throughout the night of Sunday. One of the tents had sprung a leak and some of boys' bedding had got damp. We decided to move the all the boys into the caravan and Mike and I would use the dry tent for the Monday night. We would be able to use the sun loungers and sleeping bags. There was a little rearrangement of sleeping in the caravan and after dinner we all retired for an early night. There was a wind blowing up which rattled the tent but I was soon asleep.

It was around 5 o'clock when I was startled awake by two loud explosions and the noise of high winds. I leaned over towards Mike to see if he had heard the noise as well, but he was not in the tent. It was then I noticed the main tent pole was bent and the tent was in danger of collapsing. I got up and dressed quickly and went out to find Mike. He was sound asleep under the awning and was completely oblivious to the noise of the explosions which I later learnt were maroons alerting the lifeboat crews.

It was the night of the Fastnet disaster. A worse-than-expected storm on the third day of the race wreaked havoc on over 303 yachts that started the biennial race, 19 people lost their lives. Emergency services, naval forces, and civilian vessels from around the west side of the English Channel were deployed to aid what became the largest ever sea rescue operation in peace-time. This involved some 4,000 people, including the entire Irish Naval Service's fleet, RNLI lifeboats, commercial boats, and helicopters.

I later asked Mike why he had done a 'Captain Oates' on me (a member of Scott's ill-fated Antarctic expedition who walked out of the tent during a storm saying he may be away some time—and never returned). Mike said he had woken up and saw the tent pole bending, and seeing I was sound asleep, left me snoring away and went and to sleep under the caravan awning. We managed to get a new tent pole and fixed the tent, and along with finding the leak on the other tent and repaired that one. Once the bedding had been put through the tumble dryers in the laundromat the boys could move back in.

Following the storm, the weather cleared and the summer sun made a reappearance. We continued exploring Cornwall, visiting Newlyn on the south coast and Peranporth on the north. Mo and I would go back to this picturesque town many years later to visit Bill H (who had rescued me on Tioman), and his wife Isabel.

Soon it was time to pack up our things and head back to Aldershot, as it would be soon to take the boys back to school for the autumn/winter term. We said goodbye to Mike and Midge, saying we would meet up again back in Aldershot.

Not long after Easter in 1981 and the boys had returned to school, I received a call from Malcolm in Catterick, again I knew of him but we had never met. It almost was a repeat of the call I had made to Robbie from Hannover when I was offered the posting to Nepal. Malcolm had been asked by Mrs Robinson at RAMC Records if he would take the posting to BMH Dharan in September. He was in an almost identical situation to me in Hannover when I was asked—he was moving house, his two daughters were at important points in their school education and he had recently bought a new car.

The establishment in respect of the rank for the posting had been uprated to S/Sgt, and I was certainly interested. I asked him to give me half an hour to make a phone call to Mo, and assured him I would get back to him.

I called United Dairies and Mo answered the phone. I told her the situation and she was enthusiastic at the prospect. I warned her that there was no school for children over the age of 11 in Dharan, and that would be the most difficult part of the posting. She was sure that would not be a problem and I should call Malcom and tell him we would take the posting.

I phoned Malcolm as soon as I got off the call to Mo, telling him I would call records and ask them if I could have the posting. I did this, and speaking to Mrs Robinson told her I was keen to get the Dharan post and would she let me know as soon as possible. She called me back with the hour telling me the posting order would be in the post that day and hoping we would enjoy Nepal.

The next day and I got a call to go to the company office where I was informed that a posting order had arrived. I said I knew about it and the chief clerk's eyebrows raised at my comment. I told him about the telephone calls between Malcolm, myself, and Mrs Robinson. He replied that us dispensers were not ones to let the grass grow under our feet.

The posting order came complete with an information pack, telling us all about Nepal and along with a long list of what we should take with us. This included things like a year's supply of toothpaste and cosmetics, sun screen, camera film, warm clothing for winter, mosquito repellent etc. The information pack would be interesting reading over the next few days. We decided we would tell the boys when they came home for the half-term break.

The posting was originally scheduled for mid-August and I had asked for this to pushed out to mid-September to assist with getting the boys back to school after the end of the summer break. I was also told we were allocated a two-bedroom quarter, and I asked if a three bed could be allocated. Within a few days, both requests were agreed.

The current NCO in the medical stores in Dharan was Tony B who we knew from our time in Cyprus. I wrote to him telling him we were looking forward to coming to Dharan in September and meeting up again. He wrote back telling me he had asked for his posting to be pushed out to early December and we would therefore have a lengthy handover period of about two months with which he was happy. He would explain the reasons for the change in his plans when we met in Nepal in October. We now had five months to get ourselves organised.

I fetched the boys home for the half-term break and when we sat down for our evening meal on Saturday, I suggested that we might only be able to have corned beef sandwiches for Christmas dinner this year. This was met with a pair of quizzical looks from both the boys. I told them about our posting to Nepal in September and that I was only joking, at worst we might get a chicken. They were keen on the idea, but I had to stress that they would have to stay at school in England but they would be able come out for the main holidays.

I had also written to Patrick Moore telling him we were going to Nepal for 12 months and asked him what we should look out for in the skies in that country. I received a reply just a few days later, obviously written by himself on his trusty Remington typewriter. In his letter, he told me what to look for, and ended by wishing us a good time. His finishing words were "I envy you the skies of Nepal."

Mo and I went up to Birmingham with Jason and Justin and back to the Blue Coat via Gino's Italian restaurant with my mother. We had pizza, but mother whose tastes were more conservative than mine and the boys settled for an omelette. We dropped the boys off at school and I returned my mother back home. On the way, she told me she was worried about taking the boys down to London for their flights out to us in December. She said she did not think she could cope with the escalators in the Underground. I assured her that I would sort something out to make things easier for her.

I had already booked the flights for the boys in December and I had a thought that it may be possible to fly the boys out from Birmingham to Heathrow for their flight to India. When I got to work on Monday, I called the movements people to suggest this and told them the problem with my mother and the London Underground, and could the boys fly to London from Birmingham and I would pay the difference in costs. To my surprise the person to whom I had spoken told me a flight from Birmingham to Heathrow would be a better option for all concerned, it would be safer, more convenient and there would not be any extra charges involved. Their tickets would be held at the check-in desk at the airport.

I called my mother with the news that the boys could fly from Birmingham. She told me she was relieved and she would be able to take them on the bus, or possibly ask one of Mo's brothers to drive them over, it should not be a problem either way, the airport was just 5 miles from Kingshurst Estate and easy to get to.

With the boys back at school, it was time to start packing in earnest. We had just eight weeks to get organised. We had bought walking boots for us all in a shop in North Camp, a suburb of Aldershot. As we expected to be flying during our stay in Nepal, we thought it prudent to contact a solicitor and make our wills.

I had ordered 10 MFO boxes which I reckoned would be sufficient for us, anything left over could go into storage. There was a long list of what to take with us. Clothing was a priority, mainly cotton along, with warm items for the winter. Mo took this as the authority to buy a completely new wardrobe. We also had to make several copies of the contents of the boxes for Nepalese customs.

By now, we had the packing off to a fine art; bikes were stripped down to fit, electrical items were carefully wrapped as were all other breakable items. We also made a comprehensive list of the items going into storage, hoping that lightning was not going to strike for a second time. The boxes were packed, screwed down, labelled, and shipped off within three weeks. Items for storage would go a week before we were due to fly out. We hoped it would not be too long before we saw them again. A contact at DMED suggested our boxes might be flown out with the medical supplies due for Dharan in the next few weeks. With any luck, they might be waiting for us when we arrived in Nepal.

Half-term came three weeks before we were due to fly out to Nepal. We spent the time with the boys assuring them that all would be well and they would be looked after while we were away. I took them to Heathrow Airport as they had developed an interest in plane spotting.

Security around the airport was nowhere near as tight as it is today. We went up to the roof of Queens Building where there were many other spotters with their binoculars and cameras. We saw Concord and quite a few Boeing 747s. It never failed to amaze me that the latter ever left the ground, it was so big. Mo and I would be on board one of them on our way to Nepal before long.

We drove up to Birmingham and stayed with Mo's family. Once the boys had gone to bed we chatted with our families about Nepal and what we were expecting when we got there. I had to admit I didn't know a great deal, only what I had read in the information pack sent to us from RAMC Records. Our only worry was leaving the boys, when they went back to school on Sunday that was the last time we would see them until they came out to us for the Christmas holiday.

Just then the living room door opened and Jason popped his head round. I asked him if he was alright and he told me he was fine but that Justin was upset and crying. I went upstairs to find out what was going on. I found him in bed with tears rolling down his face.

"What's up? Is there a problem?" I asked him.

"I don't want you to go away, I want to come to Nepal with you and Mum," he said between sobs.

"I thought we had sorted all this out," I said. "You know there's no school for you and Jason in Dharan."

He then reminded me of our visit to Heathrow Airport to watch the planes from Queens Building. "It's such a big place and me and Jason will be on our own, and we might not hear our names called, and I'm worried we'll get lost and miss the plane. And we will never get to Nepal."

I had a vision of two schoolboys at the end of the runway at Heathrow trying to thumb a lift from a passing jumbo jet bound for India.

I hugged him to me and told him everything would be alright.

"It's been fixed for you and Jason to be flying from Birmingham to Heathrow," I assured him. "Grandma or Andrew will take you to the airport, hand you over to a lady, probably one of the airline's cabin staff who will check in you and your luggage and make sure you get on the right plane."

"When you arrive in London, there will be another lady with a big sign with yours and Jason's name on it. She will stay with you until you get on the aircraft to India. That will stop in Delhi and again someone, probably me or Mum, will be there to meet you and take you on to Dharan. You and Jason will never, ever be left on your own to look after yourselves."

By now, Justin had stopped crying and I asked him if he was reassured by what I had told him. I said it would be a great adventure for both of them, something that few others would ever experience. He told me he felt a lot better and he would be alright now that he knew what was going to happen. Jason came over and we had a group hug. I tucked Justin back into bed and went downstairs to let Mo and the family know what Justin was upset about.

The boys went back to the Blue Coat School on Sunday, as usual via the Italian restaurant for pizza and salad. Mo and I had said farewell to our families before heading off to Harborne to drop off the boys. We gave Jason and Justin long hugs as the next time we would see them would be in India. Justin was fine and Jason was eagerly looking forward to the adventure. We left them in the capable hands of their housemaster and drove out of the school and off to Aldershot.

The only problem remaining before we left was selling the car. Usually when words get round that there was a dead line with the sale of a family car, the bottom falls out of the market. I had had one or two enquiries, but nothing definite, However, a friend's misfortune became our saviour. He had been on holiday in Cornwall when he was in volved in a bump in his car. The damage was minor and, with the aid of a few lengths of string and some heavy-duty adhesive tape he was able to continue with his holiday, intending to have the repairs done on his return home.

He was driving the car round to the garage for the repairs when he was hit again. This time the damage was terminal and his insurance gave his pride and joy the last rites and wrote it off. His next stop after seeing his car taken off to the scrap yard was to my front door and make me an offer for mine. After a minimum of haggling and a few drinks we shook hands on the deal and our Chrysler Alpine had a new owner.

I was visiting one of the wards later that afternoon when I met Brian L who was attending a clinical meeting at the hospital. We stood chatting for a while and he asked me if everything was arranged for our trip to Nepal. I said that all was fixed except for getting to Heathrow, whereupon he suggested he would take us. He had to go into London anyway as that was where he worked. We had an early afternoon flight to Delhi and, from there, an onward flight to Kathmandu. We could stay overnight with him and Anita and travel to the airport the next day. He had a big car which would take us and all our luggage and get us to Heathrow in plenty of time. I readily accepted the offer and thanked him profusely.

Our tickets to Nepal arrived the following week, the time had come to say goodbye to friends and relatives. We did our final packing of suitcases and checked around the house to make sure we hadn't left anything behind. We completed the march-out of our quarter in the afternoon just as Brian arrived to take us to his house in Ash Vale.

We spent a pleasant evening with Brian and Anita, promising to write as soon as we arrived in Dharan. We retired to bed early, I certainly had trouble sleeping, thoughts of our adventure to come in Nepal swirling around in my head.

We were awake early the next morning, and, after a hearty breakfast, set off for Heathrow and our flight into unknown territory.

Brian got us to Heathrow in plenty of time. We thanked him for bringing us to the airport and his hospitality the previous evening, said our goodbyes and made our way to the check-in desks. This was long before the airport security we have today. There were no armed guards on the doors, no three-hour check-in, and no hand luggage screening.

We were flying with British Airways and quickly found the desk. A young woman in front of us was flying to New York and had her baggage on the scales. The attendant calmly informed her that her excess baggage charge would be £95. She was obviously bemused at this saying she had only paid £99 for her ticket on Laker Airlines. While she was in conversation at the desk next to us, we had loaded our baggage onto the conveyor for weighing. Mo had a larger baggage allowance than usual due to the circumstances of our posting. The attendant told us the excess baggage charge would be £740. The lady who was still remonstrating with her check-in attendant stopped mid-flow with her mouth hanging open. Meanwhile, I was a little perturbed at being told the cost of our luggage when the attendant, who had been leafing through our tickets whispered to me that there was a voucher in the booklet which would cover the charges and all was in order, and our luggage would be booked in all the way to Kathmandu.

Our luggage was checked in it disappeared along the conveyor. We were almost on our way. We made went up to the departure lounge and wandered around the duty-free stores. I got some perfume for Mo which was all we bought. I had bought a dozen rolls of film in Aldershot and was pleased to see that the same item was more expensive in the duty-free shops. I checked the departures board and saw that we had about an hour to wait before our flight was called. That last hour seemed to last forever.

Finally, we were called for the flight to Delhi and after final passport checks we boarded the Boeing 747 for our 8 hours flight to India. I hadn't really looked at our boarding cards, and I was therefore surprised when we were shepherded into BA Club class. With our previous experience of long-haul flights, we were in for a period of luxury. The seats were comfortable and wider and we had a lot of leg room as our seats were in the area next to one of the emergency exits. I opened the in-flight magazine and was pleased to see that the drinks in Club class were complimentary.

We taxied out to our take-off position. The engines roared, the breaks came off and we were on our way down the runway and into the air—we were off into the unknown.

Our only stop was in Dubai, far from the enormous hub it is today, Dubai Airport in 1981 was a collection of low-rise buildings housing minimal facilities for travellers. At least, it had a duty-free shop where I managed to get through the crush and buy a litre bottle of Scotch for £1–50. A couple of cups of barely drinkable coffee a few minutes later cost twice that. Soon were back on the plane and on the last leg of the flight.

Apart from a little turbulence as we flew over the Gulf, the flight was uneventful. The cabin staff came around with drinks and food which helped to pass the time. I dozed off for half an hour during the in-flight movie, read the newspaper and attempted the crossword. The flight was a few minutes over four hours and seemed interminable. We were pleased when the captain announced that we were making our approach to Delhi. It was one thirty in the morning local time and the temperature was 28 degrees.

We disembarked from the aircraft and made our way to a waiting bus which ferried us to the airport terminal. Here we went through customs and immigration, getting the first of many stamps in our passports. I saw that our flight to Kathmandu was not due to leave until 8 o'clock so we would have a 6 hour wait in the transit lounge. We decided 6 hours was not enough time to leave the airport, find a hotel and have a couple of hours sleep, so we made our way to the transit lounge.

The facilities were hopeless. Hard plastic chairs, an empty vending machine and no catering—it was going to be a long wait. Thankfully, facilities at Delhi Airport have long since seen major improvements since the early eighties.

Our onward flight to Kathmandu was called at 6.30 in the morning. We eased our tired bodies out of the plastic chairs and made our way to the Nepalese Airlines desk. From there, we were directed to an airport bus which ferried us out to the far side of the airfield. I was not quite sure what to expect by way of aircraft, I had imagined something old and dilapidated and was pleasantly surprised to see a modern Boeing 737.

Once we had boarded the flight, the aircraft taxied out to the runway and soon, we were on our way to Nepal. The aircraft captain informed us that the flight would take a little under 2 hours. The seats were reasonably comfortable and I managed to snatch half an hour's dozing. Looking out of my window I could see the flat plain known as the Terai which is the area of northern India and southern Nepal leading up to the foothills of the Himalaya.

We were flying eastwards and gradually the Terai gave way to the foothills which seemed to be reaching up towards us as we flew on. Soon the pilot announced we were on our approach to Kathmandu; I could see nothing from my window apart from snow-capped mountains in the far distance. We felt the aircraft beginning a tight, slow turn which continued as we lost altitude. Below I could see houses and farm land, and then Kathmandu came into view.

The city lies in a valley and flying into its airport is not without its difficulties. A multitude of temples stood up above the low houses, high on a far hill top stood a solitary temple, which I was later told was Swayambunath. The sight was a city scape unique in the world and one which I would never forget.

Finally, we were on the ground after a smooth landing and gathering up our belongings made our way on foot to the ramshackle buildings which were the airport terminal.

We were met by Major Ganesh, a retired Gurkha officer who supervised all the movements of British and Gurkha troops, their families, and equipment into and out of Kathmandu. Bidding us welcome to his homeland, he arranged for our luggage and passports to be quickly cleared by customs and immigration, and made us comfortable in his small office.

Our flight to Biratnagar was scheduled to leave in a couple of hours at 2 o'clock so we had another period of hanging around. At least, this time the seating was comfortable and refreshments were freely available.

Major Ganesh appeared half an hour later. "I'm afraid there has been a minor difficulty," he said. "The nosewheel of your aircraft has had a puncture and has to be repaired. That will probably take less than an hour."

True to his word we were called to the flight at 3 o'clock and we went forward through minimal security and baggage checks. We climbed the steps onto a twin-engine Avro and settled down for our short flight to Biratnagar.

The engines were roaring away and I glanced out of my window to see the pilot looking doubtfully at the repaired nosewheel and shaking his head. A few minutes later came an announcement that due to technical difficulties our flight would be delayed until the following day. We had just been introduced to the vagaries of flying in Nepal. The 'technical difficulty' amounted to the pilot believing the nose wheel was possibly only good for one landing.

There was one other person and his wife also due to travel to Dharan. He introduced himself as Lt Colonel Scotson, and he would be the Chief of Staff in Dharan. Mo and I were due to stay in a hotel called the Nook in the city, but the Colonel suggested to Major Ganesh that the Everest Sheraton where he and his wife were to stay would be better for us. The major agreed and we all got into a battered taxi and drove off through the dusty streets of the city, our heads turning this way and that as we surveyed the buildings and street hawkers of this mediaeval city.

When we arrived at the hotel, the driver leapt out with a brick in his hand and quickly placed it behind the back wheel of his taxi. We got out quickly and retrieved our luggage. I glanced at the brick behind the wheel. "Handbrake not working, Sahib," he told me as I paid the fare.

The hotel was new, opened only a few months ago, and was apparently owned by the Queen of Nepal. I checked in and was shown to our room by a bell boy dressed in what I believed to be Tibetan dress. I tipped him a few rupees which I reckoned to be about a pound sterling, he thanked me profusely, and with his hands together in the Nepali fashion, backed out of the room.

The first thing to find was the bathroom as we both needed a shower after travelling and waiting around for the best part of 36 hours. The bathroom was splendid, expertly tiled and with gold fittings all round. I tested the shower and after a while a flow of steaming hot water flowed. I left it running and called to Mo that she had first dibs. She came in dressed in one of the luxurious complementary bath robes and shooed me out. I could hear the groans of pleasure as she luxuriated in the shower.

She emerged after about 20 minutes, drying her hair and said she would lie down on the bed for a while. I had my shower and when I emerged, Mo was fast asleep on the bed, still in her bath robe. Once I was dry, I lay down beside her and was asleep in seconds.

After what seemed to be only a few minutes, but was in fact quite some hours, we were awakened by giggling. I opened my eyes to find two chambermaids standing at the end of the bed and wanting to turn the bed down for the night. I told them not to bother and asked if the restaurant was still open. They assured me that it was and backed out of the door, still giggling. Mo said she thought she was hallucinating when she woke to find the girls standing at the foot of the bed.

We found the restaurant and sat down to a light supper. I had just lifted my knife and fork when the lights went out. A waiter appeared bearing a couple of candles. "Not to worry, Sahib, Memsahib," he said, "power cut. Hotel generator will start shortly." We ate our candlelit supper, and had finished by the time the generator fired up and the lights came back on. Power cuts in Kathmandu were common and the power was disrupted over varying sectors of the city most evenings.

Returning to our room, I found a note slipped under the door. It was from Colonel Scotson advising us that we should be ready to leave by 8 o'clock the next morning, as our onward flight was scheduled to leave at ten.

We were ready and waiting after a quick breakfast. The hotel and service were excellent and it would be many years before we would be able to experience first-class luxury again.

We returned to the airport to find our plane waiting for us to board. I had a quick glance at the nose wheel, it was sporting a brand-new tyre, which boded well for our flight and landing. As advised, we got seats on the left, Mo next to the window. The flight was about two thirds full with only about 25 passengers.

After a bumpy ride down the runway, we were on our way. A stewardess came round with a selection of boiled sweets and cups of orange juice. The captain announced that our flight would be about 45 minutes, the weather was good and we would be flying at 12,000 feet.

Once we had settled into the flight, I asked one of the cabin staff if I could go up to the cockpit. She said she would go and ask and returned after a few minutes. She beckoned me to follow her to the front of the plane. There was no door to the cockpit, unlike the armoured steel door on aircraft today, on this flight all that separated the passengers from the pilot was a thin curtain.

The stewardess pulled the curtain aside and told me to step inside. Both the pilot and co-pilot turned to greet me with the customary 'Namaste.' I was surprised to see both the pilots with their feet on the instrument panel and reading newspapers. Glancing over to the altimeter I could see that we were flying at 12,000 feet. I assumed the aircraft was on auto-pilot.

The co-pilot rose from his seat and pointed out of the left window. "You should just be able to make out the Everest massif," he said. "Everest is the black triangle in the distance, Lhotse, Nuptse and Makalu are nearby. The mountains you can see are over 80 miles away. Further to the east, you can just make out Kanchenjunga."

I was completely enthralled at what I was seeing; The mightiest mountain range in the world, hundreds of miles of the Himalayas were laid out running west from Pakistan to Bhutan in the east, as far as the eye could see. I had never seen snow-capped mountains before this day, and I took several photographs of the view.

"You are lucky today," said the co-pilot. "The monsoon rains have washed the dust and haze out of the air making the view of the mountains very clear. But you must return to your seat now as we will be landing in Biratnagar shortly."

I thanked them both for showing me the most spectacular view I had ever seen, and returned to my seat. I was later to fly along this route several times during our stay in Nepal and the sight of these majestic heights never failed to stir my imagination.

I sat and pointed out the mountains to Mo through her window. She was just as amazed as I was despite the view from her vantage point not being as good as I had just had.

Our pilot came over the PA to announce our imminent arrival at Biratnagar. The flight had been smooth and the views unforgettable, however, the landing was somewhat bumpy.

The Avro taxied back towards the airport terminal (in reality Biratnagar Airport was in 1981 just a grass strip with a group of untidy buildings which served as its terminal). We disembarked from the plane and made our way to the terminal. The change in the atmosphere was considerable. The fresh spring-like air of Kathmandu was replaced with the warm humidity of the Terai.

Waiting for us at the terminal, Mo and I immediately recognised Tony B from Cyprus in 1974/75. He was unmistakeable with his thick glasses and blonde hair.

We loaded our baggage on to the roof of the waiting Land Rover and joined Tony and his wife for the drive to the cantonment. The journey would take about 40 minutes, Tony pointing out places of interest as we passed. The first major landmark was the Dubi Bridge, being built by British engineers and local labour. Two previous bridges had collapsed during heavy monsoon rains, and it was hoped that the new bridge would withstand the power of the river in full flood during the monsoon.

The major town was Itahari, which sat at a cross road on the East/West Highway, the main arterial road to Kathmandu and was intended to eventually span the entire length of the Kingdom. It was the first stopping point for travellers arriving from the eastern crossing point from India at about 120 miles to the east. The noise of the town was punctuated by the roar of the exhaust of buses and trucks.

We soon left Itahari behind, the area through which we travelled was mainly farm land, much rice paddy with farmers driving buffaloes harnessed to wooden ploughshares. Eventually we were flanked on either side by forest, white-faced monkeys watching us from the tops of the trees, and occasionally we slowed as a troop of them crossed the road in front of us. After passing under a stone archway, indicating the road continued onwards to the village of Dharan about a mile along the road. Here the Land Rover made a sharp left turn and we drove along a narrow winding road. Rounding a bend we saw the main gate of the Cantonment, emblazoned with the crossed Kukris of the Brigade of Gurkhas. As we drove through a smart Gurkha soldier in slouch hat and burnished kukri on his belt, smartly saluted and waved us through. We had entered Dharan Cantonment, home of the Ghurkha recruiting base and our new home for at least the next twelve months.

Chapter 19
October 1981–October 1982

Dharan Cantonment, Nepal

The minibus and Land Rover came to a halt next to a short pathway up to the front door of a large sprawling bungalow. Then house was spotlessly clean with a large garden laid out with flower beds and manicured lawns. Those responsible for this were waiting outside, three Nepalese people, two women and a young man, they were all holding garlands of flowers. Tony said we were at our house and he would introduce us to the staff.

First was Martha Tamang, our housekeeper and cook. She was tubby with an engaging smile and had been the dispensers' house keeper for the last 15 or so years when we inherited them from Tony and Sally. She greeted us with "Namaste, Sahib and Memsahib," and placed garlands over my and Mo's heads. Next was Tika Rai, our 'ayer,' nannie, laundress cleaning lady. Tika was the opposite of Martha, slim and tiny and would rush around the house like a frightened mouse. As an ayer she was second to none, no stain was Tika-proof even if it meant a hole where the stain used to be.

Lastly was a good-looking young man who Tony introduced as Raj Kumar; he was what was known as my 'Bearer.' He kept the garden in good order, cleaned our shoes and ran the errands. At just 21, he was the most willing helper one could wish for, forever smiling and singing while performing his many and varied duties in and around the house.

Mo was a little wary at first, not being used to having full-time help around the house but she soon came to not having to stand over a hot stove in the heat, or having to wash and iron when she had better things to do.

We were shown into and around the house. The main room was large and airy and led out onto a veranda and the garden. There were two medium sized single rooms and our bed room which was a large double, with a door leading out to the garden. The kitchen was at the end of the house and had an electric cooker and a large chest freezer which was well stocked. There was also beer and soft drinks in the refrigerator. Tony had placed an order with the local store for an assortment of groceries, and meat in the freezer came from the Ordnance Corps butcher. Tony also mentioned we would see the bill at the end of the month.

The house was spotlessly clean and well furnished with a rattan three-piece sweet, similar to the one we had in Singapore. I looked at Mo, she had a broad smile on her face and was obviously pleased with her immediate surroundings.

Tony had done the 'march in' on our behalf and assured us that all was in order. He also told us that there was a slight change in their arrangements. Martha had been the dispenser's house keeper and cook for over 15 years and she was now ours. Tony and his wife were without any staff and could they take their main evening meal with us? Mo and I were happy with this arrangement, Tony saying anything they had in way of groceries he and his wife were willing to share with us.

Martha came into the living room to ask us what we would like for our evening meal. I suggested something quick and easy, as Mo and I were very tired and slightly overwhelmed with the travelling and our new surroundings. Tony said Martha had cooked a beef curry earlier that day, and would we like that? That would suit us fine and we agreed on a time later for dinner.

Martha asked us if we wanted to be awakened in the morning with tea in bed. We both declined, saying that I would probably be up early but Mo would sleep in. With that, Marth disappeared into the kitchen. Mo said she would go and unpack some of the cases and went off down the corridor to our bedroom. She reappeared a few minutes later. "That was quick," I said.

"It's done," replied Mo. "Most of our cases have been unpacked and our clothes have been put away in the wardrobes, though I can't find your uniforms."

I said I would ask Martha if she had moved them and I went into the kitchen.

"Martha," I asked, "do you know where my uniforms are? I shall need one for tomorrow."

"Tika has them, Sahib. She will starch and iron a set for you to wear tomorrow." With that, Martha pointed out of the kitchen window where a set of my light khaki shirts and olive-green trousers were hanging up to dry in the garden. Tika later appeared outside the living room window on the veranda and spent some time ironing my uniform ready for the next day.

We had a thousand questions for Tony and his wife, but they would wait for the next few days. The couple left for their house and Mo and I sat in the cool of the bungalow until it was time for dinner.

Martha popped her head around the kitchen door and asked if we would care for a drink. I had a locally produced Cola while Mo opted for a 'Nimbu Pani' made by Martha. It was a refreshing ice-cold lemon drink.

Over the next few weeks, we found Martha to be amazingly resourceful. She could read and write English, although some of her spelling was amusing and, unusually in the Hindu Kingdom of Nepal, she was a Catholic Christian.

Martha and Tika lived next door to us in the servants' quarters, and Raj lived 'down the lines.' We later found out that Raj was acting as an unpaid servant with the person with whom he shared a room and who was not very kind to him. It was Martha who bought this unhappy state of affairs to our attention and it was decided to see if we could move Raj up to the bungalow.

Martha kept the kitchen well stocked with seasonal fruit and vegetables from the local market, and cooked dishes for the freezer. She went out once or twice a week to the local market in Dharan village, never asking for more than 100 rupees (about £2.50), always bringing change and showing Mo the shopping list she had taken with her.

Later in the evening Tony and his wife arrived for dinner, Martha served up the beef curry, along with rice and Naan bread. It was delicious. Martha hovered around us while we ate.

"Don't mind Martha waiting," said Tony, "she is just checking on how much you two eat, so she doesn't prepare too much and ends up wasting food."

With dinner over, Tony and his wife left for their own house. Tony said he would come and get me at 8 o'clock the next morning and take me up to the hospital. I asked Martha to call me at seven in the morning, and Mo and I had an early night, falling asleep to the sound of tropical insects chirping and buzzing in the night.

The next thing I heard was a knock on the bedroom door and Martha calling out, "Seven o'clock, Sahib." Mo was still sleeping soundly and I got up, washed and shaved, and quietly retrieved my freshly washed and starched uniform from the wardrobe. I could not find my shoes.

Martha was waiting by the dining table, wished me good morning, and asked what I wanted for breakfast. I requested a soft-boiled egg, with toast and coffee. she disappeared into the kitchen to be replaced by Raj who was carrying my shoes. These he placed carefully beside my stocking feet ready for me to slip on and tie the laces.

I had just finished breakfast when Mo appeared looking refreshed from a sound sleep. She had a cup of coffee and said she would have breakfast later, and asked Martha about where she would get groceries. Martha replied that there was a store in the cantonment and if Mo gave her a list, she would send Raj with it and have the groceries delivered later that day.

Tony arrived promptly at 8'oclock and he and I walked the short distance to the hospital, about three hundred yards from our front door. Our first port of call was to meet the hospital administration officer. This was Ranjit Singh Rai OBE, a portly gentleman who had been in office for a long time. He stood up as we entered and proffered his hand, welcoming me to Nepal.

During my time in Dharan I got to know Ranjit well. He was an amiable fellow with a broad grin. He was also a Christian, a rarity for a Christian to be holding high office in this country.

Tony told me later that Ranjit disappeared on occasions and was found to have been arrested and in the local jail. It was allowed in Nepal to be any religion, but attempts at conversion and proselytising was strictly forbidden. People jealous of his position would spread rumours about him which resulted in him being detained by the local police. The commanding officer of the hospital would then go and demand his release.

From Ranjit's office, we moved on to visit the CO. This was Lt/Colonel Stevens, a general surgeon. He greeted me and welcomed me to BMH Dharan. He gave me a brief run-down of the hospital staffing. There were two other RAMC medical officers—an anaesthetist and a physician. There were five QARANC nursing sisters and a matron. The hospital had 70 beds, 69 of which were usually occupied, the remaining bed was kept for any one of the British contingent who may become ill enough to be hospitalised. The hospital was always busy, the operating theatre was in use usually three times a week.

Of the non-commissioned RAMC personnel, along with myself there were three others, a radiographer, laboratory technician, and an operating theatre technician, all were staff sergeants.

Our next stop was to the pharmacy and medical stores. Here I met the Nepalese dispensers, Arun Chettri was the senior of the three who worked in there. Of the other two, there was one recently qualified and another, younger Nepali who helped with cleaning.

Next door was my air-conditioned office. There were two Nepalese members of staff, both clerks, both were called by their initials as most Nepali names were a bit of a mouthful. Senior clerk was 'BB,' the junior was 'MB.' Both were welcoming towards me and I greeted them with a 'Namaste' and a handshake.

As we made our introductions, there was a knock on the door and an ancient Nepalese man entered carrying a large jug of tea which he poured into mugs on the three desks. I noticed he had a large dent in his skull and was missing three fingers on his right hand.

"Who was that?" I asked Tony as the old fellow left.

"That was Haki, the chai wallah," Tony replied. "He comes around about this time every day. He also does some odd jobs around the hospital."

Tony also told me that when he first encountered Haki, he was convinced the fellow had leprosy due to his missing fingers and until he learnt the truth about the old boy, he had poured away his tea and carefully washed his mug.

It was BB who had enlightened him. Haki was a poacher before he came to the cantonment. He had been loading his old gun when it misfired and he lost some of his fingers. He ended up in the local hospital and when he was discharged, went on a bender, got hopelessly drunk and fell into a monsoon drain, fracturing his skull, hence the dent in his head.

A year later, Ranjit called Haki into his office, suggesting that Haki was over retirement age. Haki disagreed suggesting he had another four years left before it was time for him to retire. Ranjit demanded to see a birth certificate which Haki produce the next day. Ranjit carefully perused the document, asking Haki to confirm his birth date, to which Haki replied it was 1931, which made him 52 years old.

"Oh," said Ranjit, "so ball-point pens were around in 1931 then?" The birth certificate was an obvious forgery, the ball-point pen not being in common use until the 40s, and certainly not available in Nepal. In the end, Ranjit took pity on Haki, but told him he would have to retire at the end of 1983.

We went into the medical stores which was comfortably air-conditioned. It was well stocked with pharmaceuticals and medical equipment, and well laid out. It was also clean and dust free. I spotted a couple of boxes on a high shelf and asked what they might be. Tony told me they belonged to an officer in the RCT, Maj Tim K, and the boxes contained his artists' materials, water colour paintings and photographs. He kept these in the air-conditioning during the monsoon when the high humidity would have damaged them at home.

We returned to the medical stores office and Tony gave me a quick run-down of the accounts and the methods used for resupply. I knew that I would be able to cope with the accounts, the major problem was that we were on the end of a 7000-mile supply line, and matters could go wrong. I would need my problem-solving skills if matters took a turn for the worst.

Having met the people with whom I would be sharing my life over the months to come, we visited the operating theatre. It was a non-operating day when we went there, and found Ron D, the theatre technician, having a smoke and a cup of tea in the rest room.

There was a number of photographs that caught my eye in a corridor. They were a series of before and after surgery of a young girl who was attacked by a bear. In the first, her main injuries to her face and were appalling; but after many operations her face had been repaired, it was not perfect and she would bear the scars for life. I believe a max/facial surgeon from Hong Kong was bought in to help reconstruct her face. I mentioned the pictures to Tony who said we may meet her if we go up to Hille, a Tibetan settlement, a day's walk from Dharan. Her name was Nepte.

Mo and I spent some time finding our way around the cantonment. It was beautifully laid out with neat white washed bungalows and Swiss style chalet houses. There was an oil-fired power station which generated electricity across the entire area, a water treatment plant which produced water that could be drunk straight from the tap, possibly one of the very few places on the entire Indian sub-continent. Everywhere were trees and flowers of many varieties, and a profusion of birds flew and sang over our heads. Eagles and vultures were as common as sparrows, and peacocks strutted their stuff on the golf course.

For recreation, there were squash and tennis courts, a golf course, and a swimming pool which was next to our house. There were horses in the stables which were available to ride in and around the cantonment. All the houses had a loudspeaker which was wired into the radio studio.

The cantonment was in essence a square mile of Surrey, completely self-contained and transplanted into the mountain Kingdom of Nepal in the late 1950s It was opened in 1960 as the eastern recruiting centre for the Brigade of Gurkhas.

There was another base at Pokhara in the West. Outside in the villages were little of the conveniences and comfort we take for granted back in the UK. Few houses had electricity or safe running water. Telephones were few and far between and medical facilities were scarce or non-existent. Inside the fence surrounding the cantonment we had all the things we considered to be essential for our western lifestyle. The hospital, though small by western standards was probably the best equipped in the country. It was originally intended to look after the welfare of the British and Nepalese staff of the cantonment, but soon it was thrown open to the local population. The only thing missing was television and I did not think we would miss it.

On Friday evening during dinner with Tony and Sally, Mo and I were asked if we would like to visit the Tamur base camp. Tony explained that British engineers were constructing a road north to connect Dharan with Dhankuta, which used to be, until 1963, the administrative centre for the whole of eastern Nepal. It was still an important town in the area. We said we love to go with them, and looked forward to the trip out and see the surrounding area.

Tony had booked a Land Rover and driver for the journey. (None of the British contingent were allowed to drive in Nepal due to the roads being so dangerous). We would go to the top of the Sanguri, the ridge that rose to 6000 feet, high above the cantonment, and he would pick us up at 8 o'clock the next morning, all we would need to take with us was a plentiful supply of water.

We left promptly the next day in a Land Rover drive by a Gurkha driver. The drive took us through the village of Dharan and up the first stage of the Dhankuta Road which twisted and turns through many hairpin bends. The views back over the Terai were spectacular. The cantonment was easily identified as it was surrounded by forest which gave way to the flat treeless plain in the direction of the border with India.

The drive took about an hour and we stopped just before the crest of the ridge. Tony pointed out a stepped pathway, at the top of which was a low construction with a crenelated border. We made our way up the steep path and finally reached what appeared to be a patio about 10 feet square with battlements. This, Tony explained, was 'Charlies Point.'

A year previously, Prince Charles had visited the cantonment and taken to where we were. Previously, engineers had taken top off a small knoll and built a viewing platform for the prince to see the mountains. Mo and I stood where the prince had stood a year before and gazed open-mouthed at the incredible sight before us. Stretching for miles and clear in the sparklingly clear air, east to west were the snow-capped peaks of the mighty Himalaya. Directly in front was a black peak with a cloud of snow blowing off the top. That was Mount Everest, 80 miles to the north. We were seeing the south face, which does not get much snow, and so appears black. Tony pointed out Makalu to the right of Everest, and Lhotse to the left, three of the fourteen over 8000-metre-high mountains.

Coming down from Charlie's Point we got back into the Land Rover and headed down towards a river we could see in the distance. We could also see a cluster of buildings set back from the river. This was the Tamur base camp, temporary home of the road builders. On the way down, we spotted Nepalese women on the side of the road breaking rocks into smaller and smaller pieces and piling them into pyramids on the side of the road to be collected and eventually form part of the road base being built.

Where the road ended was a Bailey bridge, lying parallel to the river and not connected to the road across to the other side. We left the Land Rover and made our way towards a collection of prefabricated buildings up on a slope away from the river. Here we met a group on engineers having lunch. We were invited in for tea and sandwiches. Tony asked how the project to build the road was progressing and was assured that it was going well, all they had to do in the next day or two was to put the bridge back and connect the two sections of road.

The engineers could then move their heavy machinery across and continue building towards Dhankuta, work that would take at least another year. I asked why the bridge had been taken down in the first place.

"You've not been here during the monsoon, have you?" one of the men replied. "We bridged the Tamur River when we first arrived here. Then the monsoon came, and one morning we got up to find the river had risen several feet during the night and demolished the bridge. We found most of it a couple of miles downstream. So now we take the bridge down at the first hint of the monsoon starting."

He also told me that when the river was in full spate, it carried huge boulders along its bed. The crashing and banging was enough to keep everyone awake at night.

Lunch was soon over and we returned to our vehicle. On the way, Tony pointed out a suspension bridge high above the river. "That's the Mulghat Bridge. If we go up to Hille, we will cross that to meet the path up to Dhankuta."

Tony left for Kathmandu on Monday morning. He had had an accident shortly before we arrived, having fallen off his bike after a couple too many cordials in the mess. He had hit his head and had since been suffering with severe headaches and blurred vision. Tests at the hospital had discovered nothing to cause the problems from which Tony was afflicted, so it was decided for him to see a consultant ophthalmologist in Kathmandu.

As we saw him off, he joked that it was just his luck that he would probably return with a guide dog, one that was almost certainly rabid.

He returned a few days later and looked quite fit and happy. He regaled us with the story of meeting the ophthalmologist who, after examining Tony's eyes, ushered him into a windowless room lit with a single light bulb. At one end of the room was an eye test chart and Tony was asked to read from the card. At that precise moment, the room was plunged into darkness—a power cut in Kathmandu. There was complete silence for a minute or two as they waited for the power to be resumed. Tony then heard a clicking from the far end of the room as the ophthalmologist illuminated the chart with his cigarette lighter. This was just too much—Tony collapsed in hysterical laughter, tears running from his eyes. He recovered later after the power was resumed and the eye test was completed.

Following the examinations and tests, a diagnosis was eventually reached. It transpired that when he had fallen from his bike, the frame of his thick, pebble-lens glasses had become distorted and this was what was causing the headaches and blurred vision. Simply straightening the frame was an instant cure. So, Tony returned to Dharan without the possibly rabid guide dog. His accident proneness had not diminished with age.

There were a number of newcomers to the cantonment, some having arrived a few weeks before Mo and I. We were invited to an evening buffet at the house of the Chief of Staff, Colonel Scotson. It was here that we met and mingled with people we had seen about around the cantonment, but not to whom we had spoken. Some were British officers and senior NCOs; others were officers in the Brigade of Gurkhas.

One priceless piece of information we were given was not to fly the boys into Delhi, the way Mo and I had travelled. The reason being was that the airport was often closed during the monsoon period. Most families flew their children in via Calcutta. I was advised to contact the movements office and get the boys' flights changed as they were due to come out to us for the Christmas holidays.

I went to the office the next day and spoke to the chief clerk who told me he would organise all the necessary documentation required to change the boys' flights and he would let me know the arrangements as soon as he had them.

Tony and Sally asked us if we would like to go up to Hille for the weekend. It would be a day's walking to get there and we could start at the Tamur base camp which meant we would not have to climb the Sanguri ridge to start. Hopefully there would be room at one of the inns in the village.

We set off early on Saturday morning and were driven to the base camp. We had taken a small amount of things with us, a pack of sandwiches, water, some warm clothing as we would be at an altitude of 6500 feet in Hille in the evening, and it would almost certainly be cold in early November. We also took our sleeping bags with us.

From the base camp, we made our way along the river bank to the suspension bridge at Mulghat, and crossed over the Tamur River. The bridge swung in the light breeze as we walked over it. From the end of the bridge, there was a well-trodden steep pathway which was the main 'road' to Dhankuta.

The pathway was rocky and uneven and the going was quite slow. After about half an hour, Mo said she didn't think she could go on. I made her rest for a few minutes and Tony mentioned that there was a 'Tea Basha' about a quarter of an hour away. Mo recovered and we carried on upwards.

There was a sharp turn in the path and there before us on the bend was the tea basha, a shack built out over the drop below, cantilevered away from the path. Looking somewhat rickety as it was built from bamboo and old planking. Tony and Sally walked onto the bamboo floor and order tea for the four of us from the young woman who was busy fanning a fire in the middle of the floor. Mo and I trod gingerly to a table set close to the edge of the shack. We could see the vertiginous drop into the valley below through the gaps in the floor.

Sally assured the place was perfectly safe as they had come this way on a number of occasions. She also jokingly told us Tony was madly in love with the lady making the tea.

The Nepalese way of preparing tea was totally different to anything I had seen before. A kettle of water was set on the fire and all the ingredients added, tea, sugar, and milk. The whole was bought to the boil for a few minutes before being strained into glasses. Despite the method of preparation, the drink was delicious and welcoming after the hard climb up the pathway. Just before we left

Tony dug into his pack and produced a pair of part-worn trainers, these he gave to young lady who received them gratefully, waving away payment for the tea.

We continued on our way, the path now less steep and easier as we continued towards Dhankuta. Mo, suitably refreshed after our short break and tea, was happily striding along having got her second wind. We eventually arrived at the town of Dhankuta after four hours of steady walking. The Danroaders, as the British road builders were called, regularly made this journey in a little under two hours and set a record of an hour and a quarter for the trip down. Apart from the necessity of keeping fit, the prime reason for making these exertions turned out to be a couple of hotels in the town which sold cold beer.

Tony retrieved various odds and ends from his and Sally's pack. There were tennis balls, T shirts, and old, but serviceable trainers. These he handed out to the children in the village who were following us as we walked on by.

"Saves us having to throw this stuff away, when someone could make use of it," said Sally, giving another child a nice clean T-shirt. Both of them were walking jumble sales, every item given away was with grateful thanks.

Carrying on our walk, we passed by the local jail. Looking over a low wall, topped with broken glass we spotted a few prisoners in the courtyard below. Several of them had a ball and chain fixed around their ankles. It gave the impression that escape was not an option. I threw half a pack of cigarettes for them and hurried on past the jail.

The path taking us onto Hille had been hacked into the cliff face above a river a couple of hundred feet below, and was quite busy with porters carrying heavy loads of farm produce for the markets in Dhankuta and Dharan. We had to step to one side to let them through, pressing ourselves against the rock wall as they passed. We also met a farmer driving his goats down the path. Everything that came and went to and from the hills had to be carried on the backs of porters, there being few roads at the time running from the south into the north. Any item found in these parts had at some time been on the back of a porter. From a nail to a brick, parts of suspension bridges, food stuffs, even the beer favoured by the Danroaders, all had to be carried on the backs of porters.

Evening was fast approaching as we neared Hille, it was also becoming significantly colder as the sun dropped below the horizon. Tibetan prayer flags fluttered at the entrance to the village sending up their messages on the breeze to the heavens. Hille was just one street with shops and a couple of hotels. The population was largely Tibetan wearing traditional dress with felt hats and warm sturdy boots. They had different facial features to the Nepalese. It was obvious we were in a culture that was markedly different to those of Nepal.

First stop for us to rest our weary legs was one of the hotels, Tony saying he hoped Tunkulamas had a couple of rooms for the night. We were in luck, the manager, Mrs Tunkulama, welcomed us in with a smile and seated us by an open fire.

"She obviously likes the look of us," said Tony. "I'll get us drinks and some food, and see if there is any room at the inn." With that, he called Mrs Tunkulama over and was given a menu, surprisingly written in almost English. He pointed out a dish and ordered four, along with four pots of 'Tongba.' This, he explained to us was a Nepalese beer brewed from fermented millet.

The Tongba arrived first, in turned, cylindrical wooded pots, about eight inches tall, topped with a lid through which was a wooden straw. The waitress removed the lid and poured boiling water over the millet. We waited a few minutes for the beer to cool and then sucked on the straw. The taste was quite pleasant and faintly alcoholic. As we drank the waitress added more water until the beer was no more than warm water.

I mention to Tony that I thought I had seen our waitress before. He told me I had seen her pictures in the operating theatre—this was Nepte, the young girl savaged by a bear. In the poor lighting, I could see the faded scars of the operations she had undergone. She was still a pretty young woman despite the scars.

Nepte bought our food, I have no idea what it was that we ate, except that there were pieces of chicken in with the noodles, however it was tasty and filling.

After we had finished our supper, we were all very tired from the walk up to Hille and decided it was time to get some sleep. We were shown to our rooms at the rear of the hotel. The room was very basic, just the four walls and a barred window, more like a prison cell than a hotel room. There were two beds, essentially tables piled with several Tibetan carpets which served as mattresses. The room was lit with an oil lamp which gave us enough light to unpack our sleeping bags and climb into them.

Despite the hard surface on which we were lying we both slept reasonably well. I awoke just as it was getting light and I was desperately in need of a toilet. I tried the door, only to find it firmly locked. I was going to have to cross my legs until I could get out and find the loo. I must have been hopping about for half an hour when I heard a noise in the courtyard outside the room.

It was Nepte, making, what I later found out to be yak butter in a cylindrical churn. I managed to attract her attention and asked her to unlock the room. This she did and I made the necessary gestures to her, which she understood and pointed to the toilet. This turned out to be a lean-to shack with an Asian style pan and no flush. At least, I was able to take a pee, the relief was overwhelming. I used a bucket of water and ladle to flush the pan, which no doubt emptied into a hole in the ground below.

Going back to our room, I told Mo where the loo was to be found, mentioning that it was not the most salubrious she had ever used. She duly went and returned to say that my remarks were a considerable understatement.

Tony and Sally were in the main room of the hotel when we went in. He had ordered breakfast which consisted of hard-boiled eggs with flat bread and tea. There was also yak butter and a jar of jam which went well with the bread. Replete with the food, we packed up, paid the bill, and started to make our way back down the hill and home.

Going down from Hille was a lot easier and faster than the climb up although the path was rocky and we had to be careful not to trip. We passed by the jail in Dhankuta and entered the main square which was covered with red chillies drying in the sun. It gave the appearance of a red carpet spread out to welcome us to the town.

Soon we were back at the Tamur base camp where our Land Rover and driver was waiting to take us back to the cantonment. We got back by lunchtime and asked Martha to make us some sandwiches and coffee. She told us she had made a steak and kidney pie for dinner and asked what time we would be eating. It was rapidly becoming obvious that Martha would be heaven sent during our time in Dharan.

The walk to Hille had taken us most of the day. When the Dhankuta Road was completed and later, a road connecting on to Hille, the journey to the town would take a little over 2 hours by Land Rover. Dharan to Dhankuta was only about 20 miles as the vulture flies, the road surface in contrast was over 50 miles, with numerous hairpin bends as it made its way up the hillside.

Tony and Sally were going on trek the following week and reckoned they would be away for about ten days, so I would now be left to my own devices in the medical stores. The butcher had returned from Calcutta, and apart from meat and fish supplies he had also bought anti-rabies vaccine and snake bite anti-serum from the centre in Calcutta.

I spent most of the morning stock taking the pharmaceuticals in the stores and flagging items which needed to be replenished. Haki came round with the tea and I checked into the dispensary to see if there were any problems, of which there were none.

At home, Mo had prepared a shopping list for the butcher and made a start helping Raj to clear out the store room behind the kitchen. Martha had told Mo about the problems Raj was having with his room-mate and had suggested that he move in with them. Seeing that Martha, her husband and 3 children were living in their small quarters Mo, had decided that that would be most unsatisfactory, and to see if she could convert the store room into a place for Raj, but without mentioning her plans to him.

I had spoken to the BIA and arranged for a single bed, mattress, blankets and a locker. These were delivered the next day while Raj was out on his errands. We also managed to obtain a fan from the market in Dharan.

Moving Raj into the room was Mo's project and she and Martha had schemed to keep Raj busy and away from the house while his new 'digs' were made ready. Without Raj knowing what was going on, the store room was swept and cleaned, windows polished, and the bed erected with its new mattress. All was ready for Raj to move in.

I was home in the afternoon when I heard Martha calling Raj, telling him that the Memsahib wanted him. He duly appeared from the garden and Mo told him to follow her to the newly converted store room.

Mo opened the door and turning to Raj, told him this was to be his new home and he could move in as soon as he could get his possessions together. She stressed that it would be his responsibility to keep it clean and tidy, he would have his own key and could come and go as he pleased. The look on his face was one of complete surprise and he clasped his hands together thanking Mo for her kindness. He moved in within a couple of hours.

I took a call in at work from the movements office to let me know that the boys' flights had been rearranged and thy would be flying in to Calcutta in early December. They also added that if I was intending to go and meet them, I would require a Darjeeling permit and I should go and see Ranjit Singh soonest, and get this organised as the wheels of bureaucracy in Nepal and India ground ever so slowly. The movements people had arranged for the boys to have permits well before they were due to make the flight out to us.

We heard of an Indian circus coming to Itahari just after Tony and Sally returned from their trek. We organised a mini-convoy of Land Rovers to take us and several other folks from the cantonments along with some of their household staff to visit the circus. None of us knew what to expect from the circus and in the event, we were not to be disappointed. The big top was illuminated with bright coloured lights and surrounded by a fairground with a shooting gallery, hoopla stalls and, wonder of wonders, a Wall of Death.

Graham, our Royal Engineers postman, made a beeline for the shooting gallery and soon had a crowd of locals gathered around him as he knocked down target after target. The stall owner, delighted at the prospect of having more customers, encouraged Graham to keep on shooting in the hope of winning a prize. Finally, he laid down his rifle and was presented with his winnings—a large packet of Rinso washing powder!

We were all keen to sample the delights of the Wall of Death and made our way through the crowds of people to the entrance. Just outside was the man who was preparing to perform the feat of riding around the walls. He was surrounded by a collection of parts of an ancient Villiers motor cycle. We left him to his ministrations and wandered off to visit some of the other stalls, returning to the Wall of Death after about half an hour.

The motor cyclist had now finished re-assembling his machine and was now trying to coax it into life. A few kicks on the starter and the Villiers spluttered and back fired into action in a cloud of smoke from the exhaust. We exchanged glances with one another, it would be a minor miracle if the bike managed to stay on the wall.

We paid our entrance fee and climbed the spiral staircase to a balcony overlooking the walls around which the intrepid motor cyclist was to perform his dare devil ride. He entered the arena, revving his machine which sounded as if it had a death rattle.

Then he was away, building up speed at the bottom of the walled cylinder. He drove up the sides, round and round he sped, the whole structure rocking and groaning under the strain. I began to wonder who was in more danger, the spectators, or the driver as he roared around the walls. He was definitely not dressed for the part. Anywhere else in the world he would be dressed brightly coloured leathers, crash helmet, leather gloves and boots. Not our performer, he chose to demonstrate his skill still clad only in khaki shorts and a singlet, both of which were stained with the oil from the servicing of his machine.

He bravely went through his performance, driving up and down, first with one hand and then none, standing on the saddle waving to the crowd. All the while the crowd roared and applauded their appreciation, and the Wall of Death rocked back and forth. Finally, he slowed down and drove to the floor, stepped off the bike and bowed to the wildly cheering audience.

We made our way down the rickety stairs of the Wall of Death and joined the crowds waiting to be admitted to the big top and the start of the circus. For the princely sum of 35 pence each, we secured ring-side seats and we entered the tent and found our places. We were almost in the ring itself, only a circle of six-inch wooden blocks stood between us and the arena.

Looking up into the top of the tent I could see that air-conditioning had been thrown in as part of the entrance fee. The roof of the tent was a series of holes held together by strips of canvas. We hoped it would not rain. Suddenly, the resident four-piece band struck up with a fanfare of Indian music to announce the start of the entertainment for the evening.

There was none of the glitter and fanfare associated with circuses in the west, no ring master, no light show; just pure entertainment. There were high wire walkers, trapeze artists, a knife thrower, tumblers and acrobats, a performer who drank a full two gallons of water from a fire bucket, clowns who spoke in Hindi, but were still hilariously funny even though we could not understand a word they said. There were animal acts in profusion—elephants, horses, camels and even a goat which walked the tightrope.

The high light of the evening was introduced with yet another fanfare from the band. Two clowns came on carrying a couple of large, painted wooden stakes, a giant wooden mallet, and a length of heavy rope. A huge cage covered in plastic sheeting was trundled in on what appeared to be square wheels and stopped in the centre of the ring behind the clowns. The clowns proceeded to hammer the stakes into the floor of the ring with the great mallet, and ran the rope between the stakes.

The sheet over the cage prevented the audience from seeing what was in it, and another piece of rope was passed underneath the cover which was then whipped off to reveal—a lion!

It was the oldest and most threadbare lion I had ever seen, but it certainly looked very, very angry. The lion was probably not annoyed because of toothache as it didn't appear to have any teeth. Even so it would probably have given one a very nasty suck.

One end of the rope had been clipped to the collar around the lion's neck, the other end had a metal clip which was attached the rope strung between the two stakes in the ring floor. Another two long ropes were attached to the collar and the cage door thrown open.

The lion leapt out of the cage and performed its tricks tethered to the rope and restrained by the extra leads which were held by the two clowns. There was no protection for the audience which clapped and cheered as the animal went through its paces. Tony and I discussed the most effective means of escape should the lion break free of its restraints. We decided that the safest thing to do was to make a mad dash for the lion's cage, slam the door and hide.

Apart from a few short interruptions when the power failed, once in the middle of a high wire act, the performances lasted for four hours. It was the best circus I have seen before or since. All through this time the four-piece band played continually, mainly Nepali or Indian tunes. Every now and then they would break into a few bars of something which just recognisably western. Whether this was part of their repertoire or for our benefit, I don't know. I do know that whenever they gave us a rendering of 'The shadow of your smile' or 'Tea for two,' we all fell about laughing as they managed to play the tunes half a tone flat or in Indian musical style.

Tony had organised a dinner in the mess the following Friday and he was mulling over the possibility of hiring this four-piece band to play background music during the evening. The thought of these musicians done up in evening dress, sitting amongst an arrangement of potted palms, and belting out western tunes, all flat, had me rolling about in hysterics.

The dinner in the mess was a great success, the senior NCOs wore mess kit and the ladies were all in their fine evening dresses. The circus band did not play the background music which was provided by a tape recording of various cocktail lounge tunes. If Tony had managed to get the band, I do not think I would have got through the first course.

Tony and Sally left for home the next day. They had converted their baggage allowance to cash and, taking the minimum of luggage, were intending to fly east to west back to England, via Malaysia, Australia and the USA. They were seen off by a crowd of people, and garlanded with flowers, and boarded the Land Rover for the airport. I would see Tony again three years later.

Mo and I were having our lunch one day when there was a knock on the door. Mo went and was met by Maxine, the wife of one of the British Gurkha Welfare officers on the cantonment. Mo invited her in and offered her a cup of coffee. There followed a somewhat unreal conversation.

"I've just popped round to see you," said Maxine, "to ask you if you would like to come with us tomorrow to help pick out an elephant."

Mo looked a little bewildered. "Why do you need an elephant?" she asked Maxine.

"Oh," Maxine replied, "it's not for me, it's for the children's Christmas party when the kids come here from the UK for the holiday. We have elephant rides on the golf course. It would be most of the day out and we'll take a picnic with us. If you want to come, there will be half a dozen of us."

"You have just got to go," I said to Mo, "it would be a wonderful experience for you to get out of the cantonment for the day and meet some more people." Mo told Maxine she would love to go and Maxine told her to meet her at the Officers Mess the next morning.

Mo told me she had had a great day with the other five ladies when she came home in the evening.

Our house had a large garden in which Raj worked hard keeping the lawns cut and the flower beds well stocked. We were able to buy potted plants from the nursery, as well as cuttings and bedding out plants. We had an aspidistra which we reckoned gave a good case under the Trade Descriptions Act against Gracie Fields. There was a Jasmine under the bedroom window which filled the room in the evening with its delightful aromatic perfume. There was also a Frangipani which seemed to be in flower all the year round. The one thing that would set the garden off and lend a focal point was a water feature with fishes and frogs.

One of the previous occupants of our house had had a sand pit built for his young children. Our two boys were well over the age for this sort of amusement and Mo and I decided to convert it into a pond. Raj did the work of digging out most of the sand, and losing it somewhere. He left about an inch of sand in the bottom, so we now had a rectangular pit, about eight feet by four feet, and around 18 inches deep.

I approached Brian, the warrant officer in charge of the ordnance depot to ask him if he had any heavy-duty polythene. He came up trumps with a couple of large sheets which, when joined together with waterproof tape, fitted the repurposed sand pit perfectly. Raj then turned on the water and we hoped the liner was waterproof.

We left the pond to stand for a few days to allow the sterilising chlorine to evaporate and to make sure there were no leaks in the polythene lining. The water level remained static, which pleased Raj and I no end. From the nursery, we obtained some ferns and other tropical looking plants which we planted around the edges of the pond. We then stood back and admired our efforts in creating a garden pond out of the sand pit.

Martha, however, was not impressed and was showing her displeasure by rattling her pots and pans in the kitchen, as she was wont to do when she was not happy. Her main concern, she told Mo, was that frogs would be attracted to our pond. "Frogs come, Memsahib, frogs talking all night and keep Sahib and Memsahib awake. Also, snakes like to eat frogs."

True, the pond was quite close to our bedroom window, and in the warmer weather we kept the door to garden open at night, the screen door allowing better ventilation. As the nights in Nepal rang with the continual noise of crickets and other insects we were not overly concerned with a few frogs and their mating calls, and anyway they might do something about the cricket population. Snakes were another matter, but we only ever had one in the garden and this one was quickly despatched by Mo with a spade.

Shortly before Christmas I was enjoying a welcome cup of coffee in the office with Ron from the operating theatre when the telephone rang. It was Ranjit asking for a volunteer to escort the provisions for the festive season to the embassy in Kathmandu. As we were not very busy at this time of year, I suggested to Ron that we might both take advantage of a trip to the big city. Ron had been to Kathmandu a couple of times and knew his way around so we could see the sights together and maybe pick up a few Christmas presents at the same time.

I called round the see Colonel Stephens to ask if it would be alright for both Ron and I to be away at the same time. After getting his nod of approval, Ron and I presented ourselves to Ranjit and said we would be only too pleased to escort the diplomatic turkeys and Christmas puddings to Kathmandu, and what time did the flight leave?

"Oh, no flight," said Ranjit. "You will be going in the four-tonne Bedford. There is too much weight to fly and it would cost a fortune to get it there."

There was an audible groan from Ron as he knew too well what we had let ourselves in for. Dharan to Kathmandu is a little over 350 miles along some of the worst roads imaginable. We were in for a bumpy ride.

At 5 o'clock the next morning, we found ourselves outside the butcher's shop in the chill of the late November air. Bill was inside unloading his freezers of the packing cases and cold boxes containing the makings of the Christmas feast at the British Embassy. The luxuries had arrived from Hong Kong a few days previously and we were to see them safely to their destination.

With the lorry loaded with the help of a couple of Gurkha soldiers, our Gurkha driver drove us out of the cantonment and down the road towards Itahari. Here we turned right on to the East-West Highway; only 15 hours and we would be in Kathmandu.

The main road had been built with aid from various countries including India, the Soviet Union, China and Great Britain. At the start of each section of road was a large sign telling which nation had been responsible for the building of that stretch of highway. We could see by the changing design of the many bridges that we were entering another country's building section. Most of the bridges were in a good state of repair, although some looked decidedly rickety. In one or two places, the bridges had collapsed in the monsoon floods and a detour through the river bed had to be negotiated. There was just enough room on the road for two vehicles to pass, although it was not advisable to travel with an arm out of the window while overtaking.

The main method of transporting goods along the road was by the ubiquitous Ta-Ta trucks which were built in India. All these sported intricate designs, many of them looking like mobile Christmas trees with tinsel festooning the windows. Pictures of Hindu gods, elephants and peacocks adorned the sides as they thundered along the road throwing up clouds of dust in their wake.

The state of disrepair of some of these vehicles was alarming. The bright and gaudy paintwork covered a multitude of patched body work, tyres were repaired by bolting a strip of old rubber over the damage; and exhausts belched black smoke. It was not unusual to see lorries being stripped down and practically rebuilt on the side of the road. It was a tribute to the engineering skills of these drivers that these trucks continued to ply their way along the highway.

We pounded along the road at a steady 30 miles an hour, the highway passing through the many villages and hamlets that had sprung up along the way. The first 150 miles ran along the Terai with its rich farm land tended by farmers with their ploughs drawn by a couple of buffaloes. Gradually the gradient increased as we were heading into the low foothills of the Himalayas, it was time for a stop for refreshments.

We pulled off the road and parked up next to a tea stall in the small town of Muglin. Evening was approaching and the mist rolling down from the hills bought a sharp chill to the air. We made our way into the tea house, glad to be able to stretch our legs after 8 hours in the cramped cab of the four-tonne Bedford truck.

We were relaxing after our meal when a British Army Land Rover drew up. It was driven by Fred, the garrison engineer from the cantonment. He was on his way from Pokhara, the western recruiting base, and on his way to Kathmandu. He had pulled in for a cuppa before making his final run to the capital.

Fred stayed and chatted for a while asking what we were doing in Muglin. When we told him, we were on our way in the four tonner to the embassy with the Christmas goodies, he laughed and told us we had hours before we reached our destination. He promised to let our hotel know we would be arriving late and the night porter should expect us well after midnight. With that, he left in his vehicle and disappeared into the falling shadows of the evening.

By the time we were ready to continue our journey it was dark and we clambered back into the cab with our driver. There were no street lights or cat's eyes to guide us as we droned on into the night. In the distance, we could see a weak light bobbing away in the distance and as we got nearer, we managed to discern the large shape of an elephant lumbering along with a torch held firmly in his trunk. As we passed, we saw his mahout had also tied a red light to his elephant's tail! Ron suggested that sight would cause a stir on the M1 and we fell about in fits of laughter.

We finally ran out of metalled road about seventy miles from Kathmandu. We had come to the start of a section known as the Chinese Road being hacked out of the side of the hills and spurs by bulldozers, the spoil being dumped into the valley far below. The surface was just about drivable with deep ruts and potholes, and there were no lights nor safety barriers on the side of the road to prevent vehicles going over the edge. The road graders had not yet started on levelling the road bed and we bounced along at a steady 20 miles an hour, hanging on to anything fixed in the cab.

After a couple of hours, we saw a light waving in the gloom on our side of the road. We slowed to a stop beside a Land Rover pouring smoke while Fred walked alongside kicking at the wheels. He was not happy. Apparently, he had been making good progress along the road when, without any warning, the clutch had given up the ghost and the Land Rover was going nowhere.

Fred was extremely lucky that we were travelling the same road as the local drivers were reluctant to venture this way in the dark. Fred would have faced the prospect of having to spend the night in his vehicle on the side of the road. He suggested we tow the Land Rover to Kathmandu behind the Bedford. Our driver was none too keen at the thought of towing a ton of Land Rover behind our vehicle for the sixty or so miles to Kathmandu. Fred assured our driver that the Bedford was a good workhorse and could do the job easily, our driver finally relented and got a chain and tow hook out of the Bedford's tool box.

With the dead vehicle securely attached behind us, the driver gingerly pulled away to make the upward journey to Kathmandu. The road climbed steadily, weaving its way around the spurs that jutted down from the hills above. The surface never got any better and we continue to bounce around in the cab. We never got out of second gear or going any faster than 15 miles an hour.

After about an hour of steady progress, we vaguely made out a dark shape lying across the road and blocking our way forward.

Inching forward, we saw in the lights of our truck, an empty petrol tanker lying on its side across the road. We all got out and went forward to see if there was anyone in the cab or under the tanker. There was no one, the driver had either gone over the edge of the road or he had left to find shelter somewhere.

The driver of our vehicle edged forward to see if he could manoeuvre past the tanker. Finding he could not, he backed off a few yards, revved the engine and drove at the back of the tanker. Ron and I seeking protection behind a large boulder. The impact was enough to nudge the stricken tanker a few inches back, allowing enough space between it and the edge of the road for the Bedford to get past, the nearside wheels scattering stones down into the valley below. We were safely past and on our way to Kathmandu.

Fred said we had about forty miles to go and before too long the road we were on had a metalled surface. The Chinese Road surface had finally met the main road to Kathmandu. I turned to look at our driver who had a broad grin of relief on his face now that he had a reasonable surface on which to drive. I clapped him on the soldier and told him, "Well done." He had driven with great skill on a barely driveable road in the dead of night. We picked up speed and we were in the outskirts of Kathmandu, dropped off the Land Rover and headed to our hotel.

We finally pulled up outside the Nook Hotel at 2.30 in the morning. We had been on the road over 18 hours and were both totally knackered. The night porter let us in and showed us up to our rooms where I was asleep within seconds of falling into bed. The next thing I knew was Ron knocking on my door to tell me the Bedford would be back in 20 minutes to take the goods to the embassy. A quick wash and shave were all I had time for before the lorry turned up, without the Land Rover in tow, and we were off to the embassy.

The embassy compound was only a few minutes away and the Christmas provisions were quickly unloaded by the staff. Then it was back to the hotel to see if they could rustle up some breakfast. We were in luck, a couple of boiled eggs and a pile of toast with local marmalade. That would keep us going until we could stop for lunch. We spent a couple of hours in New Road, had a light lunch and went to find the truck and make our way back to Dharan.

We returned the way we had come and joined the Chinese Road once again. At least, this time it was in daylight and we could see where we were going. The petrol tanker was still there along with its hapless driver. We stopped and our driver spoke to him in Nepalese. The tanker driver said he had lost control on a bend; he was not injured and had found shelter for the night. What was more disconcerting was where we had negotiated our way past the night before. There was a shear drop off the side of the road of at least a thousand feet into the valley. One minor miscalculation by our driver, and truck and Land Rover would have gone over into the abyss.

We made good time and came into Muglin in time for a bite to eat. After a lunch of chicken curry and Naan bread accompanied with a bottle of local beer set Ron, myself and our driver were ready for the drive back to Dharan.

We arrived back home just after 9.30 in the evening after 12 hours on the road. All I needed was a light supper and my bed. Fortunately, it was Saturday the next day so I could have a lie in.

It was mid-morning when I woke, the past 48 hours had been exhausting and I promised myself that I would never travel to Kathmandu by road again. (A promise I would not keep.) I had breakfast, and Mo and I sat in the garden where she told me that Pat, the wife of the paymaster had called round yesterday. Two of her children, Mark and Samantha were on the same flight to Calcutta as Jason and Justin. There was also a fifth child, that of Pushpa and Raj Kumar, the Gurkha Major.

Pat had said as there were five on the flight, they would be allowed 3 escorts for the children and would she like to come with her and Pushpa to meet the children in Calcutta. Mo told Pat that she would ask me if I was happy for her to go. I said she should get round to the movements office and apply for a Darjeeling permit as soon as possible, as the children would be travelling in a couple of weeks' time.

Pushpa had done the trip before and knew what to expect at the border between Nepal and India. And forearmed, the passage through customs and immigration on both sides were without any undue hold-ups. They got to Bagdogra Airport, which was a combined military and civil facility, in good time for their flight to Calcutta. The flight to Calcutta was uneventful and they arrived in good time to meet the BA plane with the children.

They were at the airport half an hour before the children's plane landed. The arrivals board showed the flight to be on time. Making their way up to the observation deck, they spotted the aircraft coming in to land and taxi to the terminal. Pat was first to spot her two children, Mark and Samantha, coming down the steps, followed by Pushpa's daughter and then our two boys. We all waved but the children had not seen us in the crowd.

They dashed down the stairs to wait for the kids to come through immigration and customs, and finally, accompanied by one of the airline cabin staff, they came through the doors and into the arrivals area, where they were met with hugs and kisses from their respective mothers.

The flight back to Bagdogra was early the next day and they were taken short taxi ride to the Fairlawns Hotel. After they had had a bite to eat, Pushpa took them all to see the delights of the markets in Calcutta. Mo told me having Pushpa with them was really helpful. She shooed away beggars with a loud burst of Hindi, and haggled in the markets getting good prices from the traders for Pat and Mo.

After they had finished their shopping, they returned to the Fairlawns for a light supper and bed—they would be up early next morning.

They were soon on their way to the domestic departures to catch the flight to Bagdogra. They had an hour to wait, but that passed quickly with all the talk about school, how much they were looking forward to Christmas and their stay in Dharan. The children were told they still had a long time to go before they were home in the cantonment, but they were just excited about the coming three weeks with their parents and meeting new friends.

They boarded the flight and had a smooth ride to Bagdogra and were soon on their way in a Land Rover to the Indian border with Nepal. With cursory checks at customs and immigration at both the Indian and Nepalese sides, they were driven from Kakarbhitta the 2-and-a-half-hour trip to Dharan and home for the 3 weeks of the Christmas holiday.

It was great to have the boys with us, although only for the short Christmas break. Once they had met Martha Tika and Raj, they were off to pick out their bedrooms. Justin bagged the bigger one with the air conditioner unit (although we did not mention that we did not use the A/C as they were far too expensive to run). Mo and I sat and chatted with them for a while and it soon became obvious that they were jet-lagged and ready for a sleep. After something to eat, they went to bed and were soon fast asleep.

Everyone was up early the next morning and we had breakfast together. A couple of days before the boys had come out, I had reassembled their bikes as soon as our boxes arrived and were unpacked. Jason and Justin said they were off exploring on them, there was almost no traffic in the cantonment but I told them to be careful. I also told them they were not to leave the cantonment under any circumstances, the guard on the gate would have stopped them anyway.

They were away most of the morning and returned just as I came home for lunch. They had been all over, the Royal Engineers compound, butcher's shop, the Dharan club for cold drinks and crisps, inspected the swimming pool which was currently empty prior to being cleaned, and the stables to see the horses. They had been 'down the lines' and made friends with a few of the Ghurkhas' children. Evidence that they had visited the farm was Jason bringing home the runt of a litter pigs of. It went back to the farm after lunch.

Christmas was only a few days away and preparations were well in hand. We had had a tree delivered and Martha and Tika were busily decorating it. We had also bought some of our Christmas decorations along with tree lights, and bought balloons from the grocery store.

The prospect of corned beef sandwiches for dinner was thankfully not to become a reality as the festive fare had been sourced and delivered from Hong Kong. Bill the butcher had been busy making Angels on Horseback, the sausages made with his own fair hand, he had also made stuffing for the bird. Turkey with all the trimmings was on the menu for Christmas Day, along with plum pudding for afters.

On Christmas Day, Mo helped Martha prepare the dinner. Mo was effectively relegated to sous chef as Martha had had 15 or more years' experience in preparing a Christmas Day feast.

I had written to the boys before the holiday to ask them to bring out a few items we could not get in Dharan, a selection of cheeses were top of the list along with chocolate digestive biscuits. These they had bought with the help of my mother. Jason had also purloined a few miniatures of whisky from the drinks trolley on the plane.

Christmas Day came and the boys were up early looking for their presents. A couple of weeks before the big day, one of the hospital staff had gone to Hong Kong to get items for the Christmas Draw in the Sgts mess. I had asked him to get a Sony Walkman for Justin and a pair of binoculars for Jason.

Once breakfast was over and presents unwrapped, the boys disappeared to see their friends and to compare Christmas gifts. They reappeared just before lunchtime. This tended to be the norm over the holiday, they were out most days except when we all went out together.

Boxing Day saw the elephant, which Mo and the other ladies had selected a few weeks previously, arrive on the cantonment with his mahout. It was beautifully decorated with garlands of marigolds and words in Sanskrit, as was the Hindu custom. There was a large gathering of adults and children on the golf course and the elephant took most of the children on rides on it around the course. Jumbo was fed an enormous amount of fruit and bananas as a reward.

Towards the end of December, the day was bright and sunny and we suggested to the boys that they would like to see the mountains from the top of the Sanguri ridge. We decided we would walk and took some sandwiches and water with us. We said the walk to the top would take about an hour and a half.

Leaving the cantonment, we walked through Dharan village and past the water catchment area which served both the cantonment and parts of Dharan itself. Soon we were on the path and we had a steady walk to the top of the ridge. Jason went on ahead and was soon high above, leaving Mo, Justin and myself well behind. The path itself wasn't difficult and there were many people travelling up and down. After 45 minutes of steady walking, we reached the top—Jason was nowhere to be seen! I went down the other side of the ridge and spotted another European couple coming up. I stopped to ask if they had seen him, but they hadn't. Jason would not have been difficult to notice, a boy of 13 years old with light coloured hair being a rarity in these parts.

I went back up to Mo and Justin who were, by now, getting worried. There was a branch in the path which went along under the top of the ridge to a chalet belonging to the cantonment. We decided to make our way to it and find the

Nepalese caretaker and ask him if he had seen Jason. He said he hadn't but had heard someone on the path below the chalet but he offered to come with us to help us look for Jason.

We made our way along the path which was narrow with drops into the forest below. Finally, we came on the Dhankuta Road and there he was, completely oblivious of the worry he had caused us. I was really annoyed with him and berated him for going off alone. He had no water or food with him and he could have tripped and fallen off the path. Suitably contrite he apologised saying he was sorry he had worried us. I turned to thank the caretakers for his help, but he had disappeared back to his duties at the chalet.

After telling him never to go off on his own again, I told him we were at the place where we would be able, hopefully, to see the mountains. Just above us was Charlie's Point and we climbed up the few steps to the viewing point. It was a beautifully clear day and the mountains in the far distance were visible in all their magnificence. We had the Christmas binoculars with us and I pointed out the well-known peaks, including Everest, 80 miles away on the horizon, a plume of snow blowing off its summit.

New Year's Eve parties marked the end of the festive season and it would be soon before the children started to return to school. Wesley, the paymaster, and I said we would escort the children back to Calcutta for their flight to England. We had applied for and had our Darjeeling permits ready for the journey to Bagdogra.

We took a Land Rover with a Gurkha driver for the journey along the East-West Highway to the border with India at Kakarbhitta. That part of the trip was about 70 miles and took a couple of hours. Pushpa mentioned that it would be a good idea to take the precaution of filling out Indian immigration forms before we left as this would save time when we got to the border. In the event, we were the only people there when we arrived.

Having passed through immigration and customs on the Nepalese side without any delay, Wesley and I went to see the Indian immigration officer whose post was a large tent on the side of the road. Inside the 'office' was a desk with a couple of chairs and, behind, were several book cases filled with large leather-bound ledgers. We wished the officer 'Namaste' and took the seats. The gentleman was a Sikh, very pleasant with a broad smile. He carefully examined our passports with their permits and turned to take one of the ledgers from one of the bookcases. I noticed that all of the ledgers were all marked with the name of a country.

The officer turned pages of the ledger marked 'Great Britain' and eventually came to the page with mine and Wesley's names written in beautiful copper-plate handwriting. Against our names were the corresponding numbers of our Darjeeling permits. How the information got to him was a mystery, there was no telephone or fax machine in his tent. Satisfied that all was in order he stamped our cards and passports and handed them back to us. We thanked him, wished him a good day, and made our way over to the customs post where the Land Rover was given a cursory glance and we were waved through into India proper.

Our final leg in the Land Rover was to Bagdogra Airport. This served as a civilian and military airport and security was much in evidence. Handing over our tickets at the departures desk we received another stamp in our passports to go with those from Nepalese customs and immigration, Indian customs and immigration. Two pages of our passports covered with stamps; I would need a new one the following year.

The flight to Calcutta was on time and took a little over an hour. The landing was smooth and our descent to the airport was accompanied by a flock of vultures! We were quickly off the plane, through customs and immigration (again, more stamps) and out into the concourse of the airport.

We made our way to the international departures area and found the BA desk, the children's flight home would be in a couple of hours. We checked in the kids' tickets and baggage, found the lounge and waited around for the flight to be called. While waiting for flights, trains or buses, time passes slowly. The children wandered around the lounge, Wes and I keeping an eye on them to make sure they didn't go missing. A few minutes before the flight was called, a BA steward came towards us and told us it was time for the children to board the plane, they would get on first and avoid the crush. I will be ever grateful for the way our offspring were so well looked after by BA staff whenever they travelled alone.

With last hugs and kisses, we waved goodbye to our children. We would see them again in 13 weeks' time when they came out for Easter, as far as I was concerned that could not come soon enough. Wes and I went up to the observation deck to see the plane leave, and left the airport to find our hotel for the night as we would be leaving for Dharan the next morning.

Our hotel was directly across the road from the airport but we would have to get a taxi as crossing over the dual carriageway to the hotel was impossible because the central reservation was blocked. A little haggling over the taxi fare and we eventually got a ride for a pound for the 400-yard trip to our hotel.

We had a minor problem at check-in as we told the receptionist that our bill would be paid in Indian rupees, and not in US Dollars as was the usual method of payment in hotels in India at the time. Payment by credit card was then not common in India. The manager was sent for and we explained the situation again.

Fortunately, we had a letter from the British embassy in Kathmandu pointing out that neither myself nor Wesley had access to foreign currency in Nepal other than Indian rupees. The manager was duly placated and we were shown up to our room.

The room overlooked the swimming pool which looked inviting and I asked Wes if he would like to have a dip in the pool. Wes said he was going to have 40 winks but I should go if I wanted. I had bought my swimming trunks with me so I popped down to the pool and spent a pleasant hour in and around the pool and relaxed with a cold drink.

When I got back to the room, Wesley was up and dressed ready to go down for dinner. I got ready and went with him to the hotel restaurant. After dinner, we went to the bar for a couple of drinks before retiring for the night.

We had booked an early call and after a hurried breakfast we returned to the airport for our flight back to Bagdogra. There was no interminable waiting as there is today and we were boarding the plane within an hour of getting checked in.

Shortly after we were airborne, our pilot announced that there was a storm brewing in our path and we should expect some turbulence, and we should keep our seat belts fastened. True enough within 20 minutes the aircraft met the edge of the bad weather and we had a bit of a roller coaster ride for a short while. I looked behind me to see a Buddhist monk in his saffron robes, eyes tightly shut and sitting cross-legged on his seat furiously working his prayer beads as the plane bucked in the turbulence.

Eventually we had passed through the storm and were making our final approach to the airport. Once we were off the plane, and retrieved all the luggage we exited the airport to see the Land Rover waiting to take us homewards to Dharan. We passed through Indian and Nepalese customs and immigration in the reverse of 24 hours previously. Another page of passports stamped and we were on our way home.

Soon we were at the gates of the cantonment, the Gurkha soldier on guard recognising Wesley, snapped up a smart salute. I was exhausted after all the travelling, fortunately it was the weekend tomorrow and I could have an easy day.

There was plenty to do in the cantonment when I wasn't at work. I took to playing golf on the nine-hole course, which had nine holes and 18 tees. I played with another member of the Dharan club, and we took a caddy each with us, and they were good at recommending which club we should take. It was quite a demanding course with narrow fairways, some quite close to the boundary fence. I played most days, mainly to keep fit as I never got any good at the game, but I enjoyed the hour and a half it took me to go round the nine holes.

There was a competition every Saturday which attracted most of the cantonment golfers. If you won, your name went onto the board in the Dharan club. I played in all the competitions and eventually won a match and got my name on the board.

The course was effectively two courses in one. When the monsoon arrived, the grass grew quicker than it could be cut and handicaps tumbled like a stone in the months between July and September. Once, in a break in the selection of recruits for the Gurkhas, the intake of applicants were given sickles and set to work cutting the rough on the first fairway. In the space of a morning's work, they found 600 lost balls.

There was competition during this period, it was match play called 'Monsoon Madness' and there was only one local rule that differed from the norm. That was once you had entered through the gate onto the course, you and your opponent had to complete at least nine holes. The only time play could be abandoned was if lightning occurred.

More than once, having teed off on a glorious sunny afternoon, the clouds rolled in, and half way up the third fairway the heavens opened and the deluge went on and on. Within minutes, the sixth fairway became a river and the monsoon drain (known as the Nullah), which ran across the first and ninth fairways was three or four feet deep with water.

Having completed our nine holes, my opponent and I would shake hands and leave the course looking like a pair of drowned rats, much to the amusement of the non-golfers who used the club as their local bar.

There was also a BFBS (British Forces Broadcasting Service) studio on the site. What originally started some years previously with one of the medics drilling a hole in the party wall between his quarter and next door, passing a cable through and connecting a speaker so he and his neighbours could listen to music, the idea eventually morphed into purpose-built studio.

The studio had a mixing desk, a pair of Garrard turntables. a Ferrograph reel-to-reel tape deck, a cassette recorder, and a short-wave radio receiver on which we received the news from the BBC World Service at 10 minutes past six every evening (Nepal was 10 minutes behind India time). There was a library of hundreds of BBC Transcription Service discs and tapes of drama, comedy, and short stories.

I and a number of others had a 'DJ' spot in the evenings. The Nepalese members had the studio in the mornings. I had a spot on Friday night from shortly before 6 o'clock until 11 o'clock. I opened up the studio, woke up the desk and introduced the evening.

BFBS engineers had made me a jingle which I used as the start to my session. It was a clip from the lyrics of 'Stereophonic Sound' from the movie 'Silk Stockings.' I began my session by announcing myself and saying, "Good evening from BFBS Dharan, coming to you in—glorious technicolour, breath taking cinemascope and stereophonic sound!" The irony being that all the houses had only one single mono loudspeaker connected to the studio.

Following the news from the BBC, I had a 45-minute slot when I could play music of my choice, usually a varied selection of easy listening, classical and pop. I had a large collection of my own long-playing records and these frequently formed part of my programme. BFBS shipped a tape (probably in a diplomatic bag to the embassy in Kathmandu) of the previous week's Archers omnibus which was usually the fare for Sunday nights. There was serious discontent among the Archers fans if the tape turned up too late for the Sunday broadcast. I don't believe it ever failed to arrive at all.

Apart from the late arrival of the Archers for the Sunday broadcast in April 1982, the other cause of concern was the matter of the Falklands war which was to have major knock-on effects for me in February 1983, more of which later.

Agra or Bust

We used to get a film in the mess once or twice a week, and after one such evening, Mo and I were having a drink when we were joined by Mike and his wife, Ursula. Mike was a REME vehicle mechanic, and he and his wife along with his 5-year-old son, Michael, were planning a trip to Agra to visit the fabled

Taj Mahal. Mike asked us if we would like to join him and share the cost. The provisional date for the trip was over the Easter break when the boys would be coming out to us for the holiday and it would be a great opportunity for them to see a little of India.

Mike had already done some groundwork for the journey which would involve hiring one of the welfare Land Rovers for the 12 days it would take. One of the two vehicles available would be ideal for the seven of us. It had a roof rack with space for our luggage, and a few jerry cans for petrol. We also had to have a driver as most of us were not allowed to drive in India or Nepal. The reason for this being that the roads and local driving habits were so bad that we were considered to be at risk on our own.

Mike was the exception because the nature of his job required him to road test vehicles that had come to his workshop for servicing. It was handy having him around in the unlikely event of our vehicle breaking down. Our vehicle for the journey would be a Series II, long wheel-base Land Rover built in the 1960s It was quite old but it had been lovingly maintained by the various REME vehicle mechanics during its life. It was in good condition despite its very high mileage, just a bit short of a quarter of a million miles, and we would be adding another 1500.

Travelling by road to Agra had been done a few times before us and those before us had made a vague itinerary of directions which was not very accurate. It was suggested to us that we should rewrite it for future reference.

There were no maps available and we were to rely heavily on our driver's memory. He said he knew the road as far as Lucknow and he was sure he could find his way to Agra. At least, he spoke the language and could ask for directions.

Raj had asked for a few days off to visit his family in the hills while we were away. We were happy for him to go, and gave him a kilo of salt and few bars of Lux toilet soap to take with him. His family were some three days walk away from the cantonment and he hadn't seen them for some time.

We decided we would keep the trip a secret from the boys, we would be leaving two days after their arrival from England, and swore everyone on the cantonment to secrecy. When they arrived, we told them we were going for a picnic around the area near the Khosi Barrage, about 40 miles along the East/West highway. They had been there before and knew it would be a good spot for bird watching and fishing.

On the day we left, the boys must have had an inkling we were not being entirely truthful about the final destination of our 'day out.' They thought it a bit strange that we were loading several suitcases, five jerrycans full of petrol and three cooler boxes, and they finally asked us what was going on. We let them in on the secret, telling them we were off on a 1500-mile round trip to Agra. We would be seeing the Taj Mahal, and returning via Pokhara and Kathmandu, and we would be away for about twelve days. To say they were delighted and excited at the coming adventure was an understatement.

We left the cantonment in the fully loaded Land Rover and soon, after joining the East/West highway, our vehicle ate up the miles. Lunchtime saw us in the town of Hetouda, home of the Star Beer brewery. We sampled a bottle or two of the local brews in a wayside restaurant and bought a bag of oranges before turning south towards the town of Narayangarh on the wide Kali Gandaki River.

Our driver had told us we would have to cross the river on the ferry, and naturally we were expecting something akin to a cross-channel boat. We were to be a little disappointed.

On our arrival at the ferry 'terminal,' the boat was making its way back from the opposite bank loaded with a bus and a couple of lorries. The ferry consisted of two large wooden boats joined together with lengths of heavy planking forming the 'deck' on which the vehicles were loaded. The power to propel the ferry was provided by the muscles of half a dozen oarsmen.

By time our driver had negotiated the fare for us and our Land Rover, the ferry had docked and discharged its passengers and vehicles. He drove down the stony bank and took his position on the deck. With our transport safely loaded, we boarded the boat.

The river was about 300 yards wide and flowed rapidly, its surface broken by a number of ragged boulders around which water surged, forming small whirlpools.

With the ferry finally loaded with several cars and a bus, we were cast off into the current. The oarsmen strained to pull us upstream against the rapidly flowing water and I was surprised at the steady progress we were making. We finally reached the centre of the river, about 150 yards above our landing point, when the rowers stopped and shipped their oars. The helmsman steered the ferry towards our destination.

The current took us in a wide loop and we hit the landing site with remarkable accuracy and only the gentlest of bumps. I was amazed at the simplicity of the operation, the strength of the oarsmen along and the skill of the helmsman. A minor error in his navigation would have had us drifting off downstream. I had visions of a boat load of passengers and vehicles floating out of control down the river to be eventually washed out to sea. Once off the ferry we continued on our way to Lumbini. Buddha was born in town of Lumbini in Nepal in 632AD and the town was our last stop on this leg of our journey.

We arrived at the border town of Bairawha (also known as Siddharthanagar) just after nightfall and drove on to the Everest View Hotel. Somewhat mis-named, as there was certainly no view of any mountains, let alone Everest. We hadn't made any advanced bookings for hotels along the way and we hoped there would be rooms for us. Fortunately, there were two doubles available and dropping off our overnight bags went and found the restaurant. The food and drink were excellent even if the service was a bit slow. None of us lingered too long over supper as we were all shattered after our long drive of more than 300 miles.

Leaving the restaurant, we could hear the sound of children laughing and shouting outside. Venturing over to see what was causing the excitement. We came across a group of youngsters playing in and around a clump of bushes growing along the hotel driveway. They all were carrying jars from which emanated a bright yellow glow. In the bushes, we could see a myriad of bright pinpoints of light flashing on and off in the darkness.

It was the signals of fire-flies and the children were collecting hundreds of them in their jars and were using them as primitive torches. The light given off was bright enough to light up the happy expressions on the faces of the firefly hunters, one of whom placed one of the glowing insects on the palm of my hand. I had never seen one before and expected there to be some heat from the light in its tail, but there was none. It was a strange experience to see this odd creature running around my hand like a demented torch bulb. Suddenly it flew off into the night, its flashing light becoming fainter as it rose into the warm evening air.

We left the happy children to their game and made our way up to our rooms. The furnishings were spartan but at least the beds were clean and had fresh linen. There were half a dozen small lizards on the ceiling and corners of the room, always a good sign as we had a collection of mobile mosquito killers to keep the room free of these annoying insects, particularly as the fly screens were full of holes. Also thrown in free of charge as an added bonus was a dead mouse under Justin's bed.

We rose early in the morning and after a light breakfast went to find our driver and Land Rover. We never did find out where he spent the nights throughout the trip, but he was always waiting for us the next morning, uniform neatly pressed and the interior of our vehicle cleaned and tidy and ready for the next leg of our journey. He had also filled up with fuel as the gauge showed the tank to be full.

We all had had a good night's rest, especially Mike who had been suffering from a stomach upset for some days before the trip started. At one time, it was doubtful if he would be coming with us as he had been quite ill and had lost weight.

We were soon on the road, hoping to arrive early at the border crossing point into India, 30 minutes' drive away. We were third in the queue when we got there and waited for the check point to open.

Indian immigration officials were notoriously slow at processing documents and passports, especially if one complained about the service. We always found that a little courtesy and patience with the machinations of Indian bureaucracy tended to oil the wheels and speed one's passage through customs and immigration.

It was a few minutes before 9 o'clock when the immigration officer set up his table on the veranda of his office and carefully arranged his piles of documents, rubber stamps and ink pad ready for his day's work. I walked over to his desk and, wishing him 'Namaste,' asked for a handful of immigration forms. We could be filling these in while we waited for us to be called forward.

We had had the luck to arrive at the border a few minutes before a bus load of German tourists so we were hopeful that we would not have too long to wait. Finally, with the pink forms all completed, it was our turn. I walked over to the official at his desk and presented the forms and our passports. True to form, he turned every page in every passport before finally placing his rubber stamp on a virgin page in each one. He handed the passports back to me and I thanked him, wished him 'Namaste,' and made my way back to the Land Rover.

At least, the border crossing was quick and painless, which is more than can be said for the time we spent on the next leg of our journey. The distance to Lucknow was about 270 miles and it took a long time covering it. By the time, we reached our destination I was convinced we had been driving over corrugated iron all day. Some of the potholes were so deep we all bounced around inside the Land Rover, even banging our heads on the roof. Needless to say, we were all suffering from either a sore bum or a headache, or both, by the time we reached our destination.

We almost paid the price of not booking hotel accommodation ahead of our trip. We tried several hotels and guest houses; these were all fully booked, expensive, or totally unsuitable for our needs. Our driver was unable to help as he was a stranger to the city himself. We asked at the local Sheraton for their room charges and decided they were well outside our budget. After a couple of fruitless hours, Mo and Ursula were beginning to rebel and threatened to take themselves and the children to the Sheraton anyway, and leave Mike and I to fend for ourselves. Just then a local rickshaw driver must have overheard our heated conversation and offered to guide us to what he assured us was a good hotel.

He gamely pedalled his trishaw in front of our vehicle and led us along the unlit backstreets of Lucknow. The chain came of the rickshaw and he made running repairs by the headlights of the Land Rover. After about half an hour, we entered the driveway of the Grosvenor Hotel, a magnificent old sand stone building in the style of the Raj. They had a couple of large family rooms at a fair price which we gladly took. We gave the rickshaw driver a generous tip, which was probably more than he had earned that day and waved him on his way back to the city.

The lobby of the hotel was spectacular with a curving marble staircase on either side of the desk. There were two large glass cases, one each by the side of the stairs, one housing a huge stuffed black bear, the other a stuffed tiger showing its terrifying teeth.

Our rooms were enormous with high ceiling fitted with a polished brass fan which cooled the air. The bathroom was a leftover from the Raj. The bath stood on a marble plinth and so big all four of us could possibly have fitted in comfortably. While Mo was having a soak, I called room service to get some refreshments for us. I had barely replaced the receiver when there was a knock on the door. I opened the door thinking it was Mike, only to find a chai wallah (tea boy) bearing a silver tray with my order for tea and cokes.

After we had washed off the grime and dust of the journey, we ventured down to find the restaurant where we enjoyed a good supper, before wandering out into the hotel grounds. The front lawn was covered in carpets leading up to a large marquee. The noise and flash of camera flashes suggested that there was a party in full swing. Our curiosity got the better of us and we took a peek inside the tent. The party turned out to be the reception for a Moslem wedding and we were cordially invited to meet the groom and the guests.

There were tables full of food and sweetmeats which were offered to us and which we sampled with thanks. There was much celebration as the groom had taken a fourth wife. Our question as to which of the many beautifully dressed young ladies present was met with amusement. The bride, we were told, was not usually present at the wedding feast and was in her room in the hotel with the Moslem equivalent of her bridesmaids. There was a possibility that she may put in an appearance, but this was unlikely.

We were the only white, westerners in the marquee and the groom came over to introduce himself. Mo asked him if he came from Lucknow, only to be told in a broad Midlands accent, "Oh no, I'm from Wolverhampton!" The world, it would seem, was growing ever smaller.

We all slept well and woke refreshed early the next morning ready for the final leg of our journey. After a substantial early breakfast, we went down to find our driver and transport for the drive to Agra. He was waiting for us, smartly dressed as usual with the Land Rover washed and cleaned. He had directions for the drive to Agra, which was a little over 200 miles. He reckoned would take about four and a half hours as the road was much better than that of yesterday.

We drove through central Uttar Pradesh. In many places, the highway had extensive wheatfields on either side, the state being known as the bread basket of India. One of the towns we passed through was Cawnpore (Kanpur today) which became one of the most important commercial and military stations of British India. The city is now famous for its leather and textile industries.

We passed through many small towns and hamlets, and as we entered one there was a sharp crack from the roof rack. Our driver stopped and got out to find that part of the roof rack had collapsed and needed a welding job. After speaking to a passer-by, he said there was a garage just around the corner.

We drove round and found a mechanic who said he could fix the problem straight away. We unloaded the rack and the mechanic set to work with his welding equipment, his eye protection only consisting of a pair of aviator sunglasses, despite this, he made a first-class job of the repair, and once cooled we reloaded the roof rack and we were on our way within half an hour.

Just after mid-day, as we neared Agra, we had our first sight of the Taj Mahal in the distance. Pretty soon we were in Agra city and found the hotel which had been recommended to us by past visitors from the cantonment. Again, there were two double rooms available and we unpacked our belongings and settled into our accommodation for the next three nights. We had decided that we would explore around the hotel and the city and go to the Taj the next day.

On a hill not too far from the hotel was the ruins of a house that looked as if it dated from the days of the Raj. The next morning, well before the others were up and about, and the early morning light was just right for photography, I took a walk up to the ruined house.

Just outside what would have been the entrance, was a memorial to a Major John Jacob Petrus of the Indian Army. He had been killed in Agra by the rebels during the Indian Mutiny in July 1857. He had left behind a wife and daughter. Despite the house being a complete ruin and dangerous, the memorial was in good condition and no attempt had been made to desecrate it.

By the time I got back to the hotel, everyone was at breakfast. I had mine and we made ready to go and see what we had been driving towards for the past three days. We arrived there to find that the Taj Mahal was closed for the morning! The Sultan of Brunei was visiting, and he was been granted a personal tour of the monument for only himself and his entourage until mid-day.

We drove to a Holiday Inn Hotel a short distance away to while away a couple of hours before the general public would be allowed into the Taj for the rest of the day. The restaurant was almost empty and we got a table by a window which gave us a perfect view of the mausoleum which was at the time shrouded in with a haze of pollution from a nearby power station.

We ordered coffee and sandwiches and lingered over these while we waited for mid-day. Gradually the haze cleared as the wind changed direction and the upper part of the Taj became visible in all its glory. Just the dome and the tops of the four minarets, gleaming in the sunlight.

Shah Jahan was the Mogul emperor when his beloved wife, Mumtaz Mahal, died giving birth to their 14th child. Shah Jahan was heartbroken and vowed to give his wife a monument that would be the envy of the world. And so began the planning and construction of one of the seven wonders of the world.

We made our way back to the entrance of the Taj just after it opened to the public. Paying the admission price of a few pennies each, we entered through the red sandstone gate and stood in awe at the sight that greeted us. There is no photograph that does justice to one of the world's most iconic buildings. The afternoon sun lit the brilliant white marble of the mausoleum and its four minarets. Already there were crowds of people making their way to the Taj proper and we followed them through the garden to get a closer look.

We climbed the steps up to the marble square on which the main building stood in front of the arched entrance. The main gateway of the Taj Mahal is one of the five main elements of this magnificent monument. Adorned with Moslem motifs, the Taj gateway is a tall niched doorway in the shape of an arch that rises up the mid-height of the structure. It is bordered with inlaid black marble Arabic calligraphy of verses from the Quran. An optical illusion makes the size of the letters appear in such a way as for them to seem consistent all over the arch from top to bottom.

With our feet clad in old sacking so as not to damage the marble floor, and with an English-speaking guide, we entered through the doorway into a huge chamber with a decorated arched roof. Inside, surrounded by an octagon of perforated marble screens, were the false tombs of Mumtaz Mahal and her husband Shah Jahan, both of whom are buried below. The tomb of Mumtaz was sited directly below the centre of the dome, the inclusion of the tomb of Shah Jahan destroyed the perfect symmetry of the chamber.

The marble screens around the tombs took two years to make and are inlaid with semi-precious stones in the shape of intertwining flowers and more-precious stones. The whole building took 22 years to complete and employed over 20,000 workers, including many artisans such as stone masons, workers in precious stones, and sculptors from around the Mogul Empire.

There are many myths and legends surrounding the Taj, one being that all the people involved in the planning and construction were put to death in order that they could not produce an equally exquisite structure. Another is the planned building of a black copy across the river which would be the shadow of the Taj and the eventual tomb of Shah Jahan. Neither has any evidence in fact, although they serve to heighten the romantic drama.

One documented story surrounds the wooden and bamboo scaffolding after the building was completed. The Shah was told it would the several months to dismantled, which displeased him. He decreed that the scaffolding would be given away free to anyone who could carry it away. All of it disappeared within two days.

Our guide took us around the building and indicated the best places to take photographs. We sat on the bench that was later to be known as 'Diana's seat' a few years later. But it was ours first.

On either side of the Taj are two other buildings, to the west were apartments in which visitors stayed when coming to view the Taj. On the eastern side is a mosque with a sandstone courtyard, about 50 yards square. We decided to have a look at the mosque, but first we had to remove our shoes. There was a gate into the courtyard, a good 50 yards away from the main entrance, so we ran across the scorching stones. It bought a whole new meaning to running hot foot!

Having finished our tour of the Taj, our driver took us to the Agra's Red Fort. It was the main residence of the emperors of the Mughal Dynasty until 1638 when the capital was moved from Agra to Delhi.

In September 1657, Shah Jahan fell seriously ill. This set off a war of succession among his four sons in which his third son, Aurangzeb, emerged victorious and usurped his father's throne. Shah Jahan recovered from his illness, but Emperor Aurangzeb put his father under house arrest in Agra Fort from July 1658 until his death in January 1666.

Our guide showed us around the fort, describing the various rooms and gardens and his main stock in phrase was 'and the fountains played.' Unfortunately, they no longer did; however, a lot of the beautiful Mogul architecture survives. We saw the imprisoned Shah's apartments where he was able to see the Taj Mahal on the banks of the Jumna River. For a small tip, the guide took me up onto the roof where I was able to take more photographs of the Taj and the surrounding countryside.

We left the fort and returned to our hotel to change out of our sweat stained clothes and freshen up for the evening. When we left the Holiday Inn earlier, I had spotted and advertisement for an evening of Indian music and dance. The admission price included a buffet supper. I suggested we should have dinner at the hotel and the entertainment would make a fitting end to our visit to Agra.

The entrainment of the evening was excellent with a young and gifted Sitar player, accompanied by tablas, harmonium, flute, and a singer. The dancers appeared on stage dressed in brightly coloured costumes and performed traditional Indian dances. During a short break in the performance, I managed to approach the performers and asked if I could take photographs. They were happy for me to do so and I have many happy memories of that day.

Finally, when the music and dance had ended to much applause, and we had sampled the buffet, we left the hotel where our driver was waiting for us. It was a bright moonlit night and the Taj had to be seen in the moonlight. As we neared the main sandstone gate, we could feel the heat of the day radiating from the brickwork. Evidence as to how hot the day had been.

The Taj Mahal by moonlight is an unforgettable sight, one I shall never forget, the marble dome and minarets sparkling in the cool evening air. There was a light breeze and the reflection of the Taj shimmered in the lake, causing the whole scene to have a magical atmosphere.

All too soon we had to tear ourselves away and return to our hotel for the last night before heading on to the next part of our adventure. I had told the hotel manager we would be leaving early the next morning and he should have our bill ready. As it turned out there was a problem—our bill was presented in US Dollars.

Explaining to the manager that we had no access in foreign currency and we were only able settle our bill in Indian rupees. He was quite adamant this was not acceptable. We offered an alternative—Nepalese rupees, as this was the only other currency we had. Neither Mike nor I had credit, cards and the hotel did not accept them anyway. In the end, he relented and agreed to accept Indian currency at a higher figure that I knew was over the official exchange rate.

Our driver was waiting for us, immaculately dressed as usual, and once the Land Rover was loaded, we headed back on the road and to Lucknow. This time we had taken the precaution of booking ahead before we left the Grosvenor Hotel.

We were just 5 hours on the road, but it was a hot and dusty drive and we were relieved to arrive at our hotel. After freshening up in the shower to wash off the dust from the journey, we stretched our legs around the hotel gardens. Of the wedding celebrations a few days before, there was no sign.

We had our evening meal; I was the only one who had the fish. It was delicious but I was to pay for it the following day. I went out early the following morning to take photographs before the light became too intense. When I returned to our room, Mo had packed up and we were ready to leave, but I suddenly had an attack of 'Delhi Belly,' I had been free of upset stomachs since arriving in Nepal. Mo came to the rescue after I emerged from the bathroom and gave me a couple of tablets of Lomotil, an anti-diarrhoeal drug, a combination of diphenoxylate and atropine.

The tablets took effect within 20 minutes and the griping pains in my stomach eased. The last thing I wanted was be suffering from the dreaded lurgy during our 7-hour drive to Lumbini. One of the side-effects of the drugs was to make me incredibly thirsty, and it was well we had plenty of filtered water with us. Fortunately, I had no further attacks of the runs during the long journey, although the Lomotil gave me a really dry mouth and I was grateful for the water.

We reached Lumbini back in Nepal in the late afternoon and immediately went to get some food in the hotel restaurant. I had no appetite, and all I wanted was some soup and a beer, a pint of which went down in one go. The soup with bread was welcome and I went up to our room, showered and fell into bed exhausted. I remembered nothing until the next morning when I awoke. My stomach no longer felt as if it was being held in a vice and I was starving. The Lomotil, soup or the beer, or a combination of the three, had cured my gippy tummy.

We had another long drive ahead of us, our driver reckoned on it being around 7 hours. We were making for Butwal which was the last town on the Terai before we made our way into the Mahabharat Lekh, the low foothills running across Nepal from Pakistan in the west to Bhutan in the east. Until 1960 it was only possible to reach Pokhara on foot from Butwal, but in 1968 the Siddhartha Highway was completed to allow motor vehicles access to the town.

The drive uphill from Butwal was a switchback with hairpin bends and precipitous drops in deep valleys. At least on this road there were regularly spaced concrete blocks which would prevent a vehicle from going over the side. We had just crossed over one of the many bridges when the Land Rover spluttered to a stop. It was not a fuel problem as the gauge was indicating we had plenty of petrol.

We all got out to stretch our legs while Mike and the driver lifted the bonnet and peered into the engine to see if they could find the problem. I had visions of being stranded on the road, miles from anywhere. After about ten minutes, Mike called out that he had found the cause of our Land Rover breaking down. A thin wire which was supposed to be connected to the distributor had worked loose. Mike reconnected it and our driver tried the ignition. The motor fired up first time and we were on our way. That was the one and only time our vehicle had let us down over the whole journey. I was thankful Mike knew what to look for in order to get us back on the road.

After what seemed to be a permanently uphill drive, we reached the outskirts of Pokhara and made our way for our hotel where we would be staying for 2 nights. It was late in the afternoon and there was heavy cloud which obscured a view of the mountains to the north, they had been this way for a couple of months.

After a shower and dinner, we all went up to our rooms to sleep off the hard day we had all had. Before going up, I had sought out the night porter and asked him to wake me if the mountains were visible in the early morning.

I was awakened by a heavy banging on the door—it was just after half past four in the morning. I went and opened the door to find the night porter.

"The mountains are out, Sahib!" he said excitedly. I went over towards the balcony, opened the French windows, and stepped out onto the balcony. It was a cloudless sky, the sun just above the horizon to the east. There in front of me was the Annapurna massif, snow-capped and glinting in the sunshine.

Machapukhare, the fish-tail mountain was just 16 miles away, but I had to tilt my head back to see the peak. It was massive, rising high above the surrounding mountains, all of its 23,000 feet towering over Pokhara. I called Mo and the boys to come and see for themselves. They came out onto the balcony and stood open-mouthed at the sight before them.

Machapukhare is at the end of a long spur ridge, coming south out of the main backbone of the Annapurna massif and has never been officially climbed as the Nepalese government will not issue a permit due the mountain being considered sacred.

I believe Chris Bonington had climbed the mountain to within a few feet of the peak, respecting the Nepalese request that it should not be summited. Annapurna itself was first climbed by two French mountaineers in 1950, it was the first peak over 8000 metres to be successfully conquered.

After breakfast, we explored around Pokhara and took canoes out on the Phewa lake. The surface of the lake was placid, and the mountains were reflected in the clear waters. After dinner, we ventured out to visit a cultural centre for an evening's entertainment. We had to find our way by torchlight as there was no street lighting. The evening diversion was a Celebration of Nepalese music and dance, with Limbu drummers and dancers.

It was still pitch black when we left to return to our hotel, and, looking up into the night sky, I remembered the last line of Patrick Moore's letter to me— "I envy you the skies of Nepal." The stars appeared brighter and more numerous than I had ever seen before. The band of stars that comprised the Milky Way, stretched across the heavens like a silver, sparkling river.

The next morning, we packed up again, ready for the next leg of our journey, which would take us on to Kathmandu. It would be about 7 hours driving, but we could stop for lunch at Muglin, where Ron and I stopped on our way to deliver the Christmas fare to the embassy. From there, it would be 4 hours to Kathmandu.

We arrived in Muglin in time for lunch and a beer. Chicken curry and flat bread for us all, including our driver. Mike was looking a bit under the weather and Mo and I suggested we extended our stay in Kathmandu by an extra day for him to rest up. We could stay at the Nook, which was reasonably priced and comfortable; our budget could stand the extra, and we could contact the cantonment via the embassy to let them know we would be returning a day late.

We made it to Kathmandu at around 6 o'clock and checked into the Nook. A shower and change of clothes were the first order of business before heading out into the city to find dinner. There were plenty of good restaurants in and around the area of the Nook and we settled for Chinese, which would make a change from curry.

There was plenty to do and see in Kathmandu, our first stop being New Road, the main road in the city, to have a look at what the shops had to offer. From there, we went to Boudhanath Stupa, one of the largest Buddhist temples in the world. It was decked with prayer flags, we walked around clockwise spinning the prayer wheels.

The next day we visited Swayambunath stupa, set high on a hill and visible for miles around. It is said that every religion in the world is represented in this temple.

From there, it was just a short walk to Durbar Square, a UNESCO world heritage site. Surrounded by over 50 temples, palaces, pagodas, narrow streets, and courtyards, dating from the 12th to 18th centuries the square has examples of the fine architecture of Royal Nepal and its cultural heritage. Along with many other buildings in Kathmandu, Durbar Square suffered serious damage in the earthquake in 2015.

The next day was the last day of our holiday and we made an early start as our drive home would take eight or nine hours to cover the almost 250 miles back to Dharan. The first part of the trip and the hardest would be to Mithila. From there, we would join the east/west highway and we would make better time.

We got back home in late afternoon having covered nearly 1600 miles in our trusty Land Rover along with its faithful driver. We unloaded our belongings and gave the driver a tip equivalent to a couple of a couple of weeks pay, he had certainly deserved it and had served us well, always cheerful, flawlessly dressed every morning, and our vehicle cleaned and ready for another day of hard driving.

Martha, Tika and Raj were waiting for us when we got in, the first thing we were asked was what we would like for dinner. Martha said she had a steak and kidney pie waiting to go in the oven which we said would be most welcome, but first we had to change out of our sweaty clothes and shower the dust of the road off us. Tika was going to be busy with the washing and ironing over the next few days. I asked after Raj's family and he said they were well and they thanked us for the salt and soap.

The next day was Sunday and I walked across the road to see how Mike was faring as he was not looking too bright when we got home. Ursula said he had gone up to the hospital as he was suffering from stomach cramps. I said I hoped he would get better soon.

Unfortunately, matters did not turn out well for Mike. After a series of examinations and tests in the hospital, he was diagnosed with cancer. He and Ursula and little Mike returned to UK for specialised treatment of his cancer. Despite the heroic efforts, he died not long after. Everyone in the cantonment were devastated with the news.

The boys returned to the UK a week after we got back from our trip to Agra. Wes and I went with them as Mark and Samantha, Wes's children, were also travelling home. We had our permits and went along the long road to Kakarbhitta and to the airport at Bagdogra. Our passage through the check points were quick as we were becoming friendly with the immigration officer.

The flight from Bagdogra to Calcutta was on time and we had a couple of hours to wait before seeing the children on to the BA flight to Heathrow. When their flight had left Wes and I checked in to the airport hotel, as due to a change in scheduling, our return to Bagdogra was the next morning. We had a bite to eat and went to explore around the local area.

Not far from the hotel was a large steel works and we wandered along the road adjoining it. I was a little disconcerted to see the communist emblem of the hammer and sickle all around the area and began to wonder if we were safe being there.

My concerns turned out to be unfounded as we turned a corner to find a village surrounding a large lake on which there were several small boats fishing. Wes and I walked through the village lanes and most of the people sitting outside their houses smiled back at us as we passed.

Everywhere there was a patch of grass between the houses, children were playing cricket. Groups with a makeshift wickets and home-made bats. Some of the groups were just three of four, others were twenty or more, and all were playing happily together. Most of the bowlers bowled slow spinners as there was not enough room for a fast bowler to run up.

I took photographs as we went around the village, always asking the residents if it was alright. Most were happy for me to photograph them, particularly the fishermen landing their catch of small fishes.

We returned to our hotel in time for dinner, and after a leisurely meal retired to our room and to bed. We were up early the next morning to get our flight to Bagdogra and back to Dharan.

Colonel Stevens and his wife were posted back to the UK, and he was replaced by my new boss, Major Peter G. I found him to be a most pleasant officer, and on my tea breaks with Ron in the theatre rest room, learnt that he was considered to be a fine surgeon by those who assisted him at the operating table. I was to find out how good he was shortly after he came to the cantonment.

The telephone rang in my office one morning, MB answered and passed the phone over to me saying it was Major G for me.

"Hello, Staff," he said, "do we have and hip replacements in stock?"

From memory, I said that we had several of different sizes on the shelf and asked what he needed.

"Would you bring a few of them around to my consulting room?" he asked. I told him I would be there in a couple of minutes.

I took three Charnley artificial hips round to his consulting room and knocked on the door. He called for me to come in, and entering found Major G, Ron D, and the radiographer, along with a little old lady who was wrapped in a blanket and seated in a corner on the floor. Above her was the X-ray viewing box with pictures of a pelvis and a what looked to me like a dislocated hip.

I placed the metal hips on the Major's desk and he pointed to the X-rays.

"That's a seriously arthritic hip, and I'd like to replace it with this one," he said, holding up the Charnley replacement hip. Turning to Ron, he asked, "Have you seen a hip replacement performed before staff?"

259

Ron replied he had worked with a senior orthopaedic surgeon at the Royal Herbert before he came to Nepal and he had assisted in several dozen. I knew the surgeon Ron spoke about, having had orthopaedic chisels returned to the medical stores for shipping off to DMED for the cutlers to re-sharpen.

"Very good," said Major G, "at least one of us in theatre will know what to do!" He had never performed a hip operation. To Ron, he said, "I have some reading to do, we will do the hip on Friday. Thank you, gentlemen." The three of us left the consulting room and I turned to Ron asking if the hip replacement was a difficult procedure. Ron replied that it was but he reckoned Maj G was very good and he had every confidence that the Major would do a successful job.

The operation took place three days later; after a week, the old lady walked out of the hospital, albeit with a slight limp.

The hospital was always busy. The ward master, a Nepalese who had been there for many years, had the task of making his way up to and outside the north gate to the crowds of people waiting to see a doctor. It was his job to vet those waiting and issue a ticket for them to enter.

Quite a few of those waiting had travelled for miles to the cantonment in the hope of getting treatment for their troubles and injuries. His years of experience allowed him to spot those who should be seen immediately by a physician or surgeon, and those who could wait a little longer. Others were patients returning for appointments to see a physician or surgeon. Some of those whose condition was not as serious as others he would direct to the local hospital in Dharan, or tell them they may get seen the next day.

I was amazed at the patience of the people waiting, many of them squatting on the floor outside the pharmacy or consulting rooms for hours. In my first full year in Dharan, the hospital had over 80,000 patients through its doors. Tuberculosis was endemic and prescriptions for anti-tuberculosis drugs were numerous. Burns, often in children who had fallen onto open fires, were common, as were fractures from falls and other accidents. The operating theatre was kept busy.

I was called out one evening by the anaesthetist who was also on call. When I arrived at the pharmacy, he told me he needed anti-snake venom in a hurry. As I unlocked the refrigerator, he explained that a young woman from the village had been bitten in the ankle by a cobra, the most feared of all snakes in the sub-continent. I got a bottle of anti-venom and accompanied the doctor to the treatment room where the young woman, who had stopped breathing within 20 minutes of being bitten, was being resuscitated by one of the nursing sisters.

The doctor got a line into a vein and started administering the anti-venom via a saline drip. Within a few minutes, the woman started breathing on her own and was started on oxygen. The doctor was satisfied his patient would make a recovery from the snake bite, but would need further treatment in the hospital over the next few days, particularly as a cobra bite causes the tissue around the bite to die. She would probably need skin grafts to repair the damaged tissue of her ankle.

Not long after this I was again called out one Sunday morning for anti-venom. As I rounded the corner of the pharmacy block, I could smell the unmistakeable odour of gangrene. The patient was a woman in her thirties who had been bitten in the hand by a snake. All snakes in Nepal were considered poisonous by the locals.

The woman's husband had applied a tourniquet to her upper arm as soon as she had been bitten, however he had failed to loosen the tourniquet briefly since applying it five days previously. As a result, all the tissue below the tourniquet had died and become gangrenous. She would lose her arm in theatre the following day.

There was plenty of entertainment to keep us occupied. We had a film in the mess once a fortnight, the films being sent to us from Hong Kong. About every two months we had a regimental dinner and, given the relatively small numbers of senior NCOs and warrant officers, these were usually turned into a ladies night. The kitchen staff in the mess were very good, and could turn their hands to most dishes, dependant of the availability of ingredients.

The entertainments committee had to be inventive; we had a disco in an empty 50,000-gallon water tank which had just been cleaned. The tank was underground and very spacious with access via a ladder. The bar being positioned on the top next to the manhole. Drinks orders were lowered down by a tray on a rope. When we first entered, the acoustics made the place echo, but the sound was deadened with the addition of a number of mattresses, which also caused a rethink by the committee who turned the evening into a Roman night, with guests lounging around on the mattresses.

Barbeques were always popular, usually shortly after the butcher had returned from his trip to Calcutta. They were held in the Mess, the Dharan club and we even had one in the swimming pool—one around the pool area and another actually in the pool itself when it had been emptied for cleaning and maintenance.

There was a wealth of talent amongst the British contingent, amongst them was 'Val the Voice.' She had been a professional opera singer and was married to Frank, a Royal Engineer warrant office. Often she treated us to a rendition of a classical piece in the mess after a dinner or film night. Her singing of 'Summer Time' from Porgy and Bess will stay with me forever, and whenever I hear it, I am immediately transported back to Dharan.

We had a few soirees in various houses when guests were required to 'Sing for Their Supper.' On one occasion, I was dressed as a vicar about to preach a sermon when I was interrupted by Ian, the lab technician dressed in rags as Quasimodo, complete with hunch back, and ringing a hand bell borrowed from the school. The punch line was "Evenin' vicar, lend me a quid 'til I get straight!" I flourished a pound note from my pocket and Quasimodo dashed out, ringing his bell as he went. There was also a piano and cello recital that evening, along with Val and others singing.

On another weekend evening, Mo and I and the boys were invited to Major Peter G's house for drinks and nibbles. Quite a few of the hospital staff were there and Mo and I mingled with everyone. Mo was in conversation with Judy, Peter's wife, when I noticed Jason was missing.

I heard the rustling of pages from a downstairs room and gently pushed the door open. Jason was inside with Major G, pouring over an open copy of Grey's Anatomy. Jason was telling Peter that he was going to be a doctor when he was older. I asked Jason what he was doing in Peter's study. Peter assured me that it was alright, and if it was OK with me Jason could join him in the operating theatre on Monday. I said it was perfectly fine and Peter told me that I could stand behind Jason, ready to catch him if and when he fainted. So, both of us would be in theatre on Monday.

At precisely 9 o'clock on Monday morning, Jason and I were scrubbed and gowned, and shown into the theatre. There was a full complement of staff, Major G, Major Chris P the anaesthetist, the theatre sister and Ron the theatre technician along with a pair of Nepalese theatre nurses.

The first patient was lying on the table, and Maj G motioned for Jason to stand slightly behind him and to one side so he would be able to observe the operations. The first three procedures were routine, a couple of patients undergoing a 'Z Plasty,' a plastic surgery technique that is used to improve the functional and cosmetic appearance of burn scars. A third having a skin graft to repair a burn on his upper arm. A patch of skin taken from his thigh to cover the burn area.

After each procedure, swabs and instruments were carefully counted to make sure nothing had been left behind. The fourth operation was to be more complicated. The patient had been attacked by bandits and left with a depressed skull fracture. This had left him paralysed along one side of his body and the diagnosis was that there was a blood clot beneath the fracture creating pressure on the brain.

A flap of skin was made over the area of the fracture and the bone of the skull exposed. The theatre sister stood on the opposite side of the table ready to hand the surgeon the instruments he would be needing. Major G was handed a drill and made four holes in the bone surrounding the depression. All this time Jason stood at Major G's shoulder and listened intently as the details of the operation were pointed out.

Major G took a Gigli saw, a length of toothed stainless-steel wire with loops on either end, and passed it through one of the holes in the patient's skull and out of another. Two handles with hooks were produced and attached to the exposed ends of the wire. With a sawing motion, the two holes were joined with a saw cut. This was repeated three more times until a square of bone could be removed exposing the membrane (the Dura Mater) surrounding the patient's brain.

The membrane was carefully snipped to make a flap which, when lifted, exposed the brain and the large blood clot that was giving rise to the pressure on the patient's brain causing his one-sided paralysis. Major G carefully washed the clot away, and with very small stitches, carefully sewed the dura mater back in place. All that remained was to replace the square of bone back into the patient's skull with bone cement, and to sew the flap of skin back in place over the repaired bone.

Once complete, the operation was finished and the patient wheeled away to recover from his injury. Jason and I were suitably impressed with the surgeon's meticulous work, and of the way the theatre staff all worked together in assisting him. The whole operation took place in almost complete silence, only broken when the surgeon asked for an instrument to be passed, or the work area to be swabbed clean of blood, of which there was very little.

At this point, I whispered to Jason that we should leave and let the staff get on with the rest of the day's work. I thanked Major G and the theatre staff for allowing in to watch their work and left quietly for a welcome cup on tea in the rest room.

Maj Tim K came along to medical stores to collect his artist's materials and pictures once the monsoon had finished. I asked him at the time if he ever considered selling some of them. I had had a look through them while they were in the stores and was impressed with them. He replied that he didn't think they were good enough.

He must have had second thoughts, for a few weeks later a notice appeared in the mess to the effect that there would be a viewing of his work at his house. Mo and I went along and browsed along with others from the cantonment. I was taken with quite a few and so were the others. Soon a number of red dots appeared on the paintings and, being keen to acquire at least one, I spotted three watercolour paintings of work on the Dhankuta Road. I immediately placed a red dot on them. I still have them, in their original frames, and they have pride of place on my living room wall.

Life in the cantonment was certainly not a round of entertainment. Work proceeded in the in the various offices and workshops. The farm provided instruction on agricultural methods for Gurkhas retiring from the army. The REME workshop maintained the various vehicles and gave training to young Nepalese keen to learn how to service and repair motor vehicles.

My work in the medical supplies department kept me busy maintaining the stocks of pharmaceuticals, instruments, dressings, and various items needed to help keep the hospital functioning efficiently as possible.

Contact with the outside world was by signal, essentially telex. Eric who was single and lived in the mess, was a Royal Signals sergeant who dealt with these and had been in Dharan for quite a few years. These were the days before the internet and fax machines, mainly because the telephone system in Nepal was practically non-existent. Anything urgently needed from UK was requested in the form of a telex, although I used the system on a couple of occasions for urgent drugs from the medical supply department at BMH Hong Kong. I could usually get a supply from them within 72 hours, via civil airlines into Kathmandu and internal Nepalese flights to Biratnagar.

The most unusual application I received from the physician was for the drug Thalidomide. Despite its reputation for causing birth defects, it had been shown to be effective in the treatment of leprosy which had failed to respond to other drugs. I believe the request raised a few eyebrows at DMED, but we got a supply within a week, and the physician started his patient on the drug immediately and with satisfying results.

We had a short break for the Whitsun holiday in May, Mo and I took a long weekend in Kathmandu. We travelled down to Biratnagar and took a flight on a Swiss made Pilatus single engine aircraft. There were ten other passengers and the pilots flew with the curtain to the cockpit open. I was interested to watch them fly the small aircraft in such a relaxed manner.

We were to stay at Dwarika's Hotel, just outside the city. Built by Mr Dwarika Das Shrestha and in an attempt to preserve the Kathmandu Valley's heritage, he had salvaged much of the architectural heritage of the Newari civilisation. The intricately carved wooden treasures, with each artifact being an original, are built into the hotel structure. The hotel was surrounded by expertly landscaped gardens and secluded courtyards.

We were shown into our comfortable room and the porter pointed out the stained-glass Newari window set into one wall. The window dated back two or three centuries. The roof of the veranda outside our room was supported by beautifully carved Newari temple struts, no doubt rescued from a building site.

The hotel was not far from Pashupatinath temple which was classified as a world heritage site by UNESCO in 1979. It is a Hindu temple precinct and is a collection of temples, ashrams, images and inscriptions raised over the centuries along the banks of the sacred Bagmati river, alongside which is a funeral ghat, a place where the bodies of the dead are burnt on funeral pyres. It is one of seven monument groups in UNESCO's designation of Kathmandu Valley and is the oldest Hindu temple in Kathmandu, construction starting around 1692.

I walked up to the temple shortly after breakfast the next morning. The temple doors were guarded by armed police and non-Hindus were not allowed to enter. I crossed over the river where I could see the funeral ghat. I was just in time to witness a funeral where many mourners were bidding a final goodbye to their friend and relative whose body shrouded in white was lying on top of the funeral pyre. The fire was lit and soon became an inferno, the perfumed sandal wood smoke drifting over the river as the body was consumed in the flames.

When I returned to the hotel, Mo was ready to go into the city for a little retail therapy. Kathmandu bustled with Nepalese and many tourists and it made a pleasant change from the ease of life in the cantonment.

We wandered through the alleyways and eventually found ourselves in Bhaktapur. Down one of the side streets off Durbar Square we came across the famous peacock window set into the ground floor wall of a house. The window is 15th-century and is often referred to as the 'Mona Lisa' of Nepal. It is one of the most precious and highly regarded artworks of Nepal and to find it unguarded in an unprepossessing street filled me with amazement. It is still in on view today in the more secure Pujari Math building which serves as a wood carving museum.

One of the main reasons for our visit to Kathmandu was to buy a carpet. We visited several places and eventually found a large shop occupying a corner position out of the main city. The shop appeared deserted, there was no assistant ready to help us choose one of the many rolled up carpets lined along the walls. Mo and I set to in the absence of the shop owner and began unrolling carpets onto the floor.

After a dozen or so, we found a seven foot by four-foot carpet we both liked. A finely woven example with the images of three Tibetan coins woven into the pale cream background. We rolled it back up and placed it back against the wall where we would be able to find it amongst the hundreds of others when we returned to the shop later in the day.

We stopped for lunch at a nearby restaurant and Mo asked me if I thought the carpet would be expensive. I said it was a good quality item and it probably would be. I could see she was really keen on having the carpet.

After a couple of hours, we ventured back to the shop and found a young Nepalese woman inside. We wandered around for a few minutes picking out a few carpets and looking interested. Finally, we retrieved our favourite, unrolled it onto the floor and expressed our delight at it. The young woman came over to us and told us the dyes used were natural in origin and would not fade. If it did, I could bring it back for a refund. I asked how much for the carpet.

"That one is 3000 rupees, Sahib." (About £40 at the current exchange rate.)

"That's very expensive," I replied, "I'm not a tourist, I live here in Nepal in Dharan."

She was totally unimpressed. "I know you're not tourist, Sahib," she said. "If you were, my asking price would be 4,500 rupees!"

Forty pounds for this fine carpet was a steal. I could not refuse it and, taking out my wallet, gave her the 3000-rupee asking price for which she thanked me. She re-rolled our purchase and wrapped it carefully in plastic sheeting. We thanked her and left the shop, pleased with our carpet and my negotiating skills. I didn't feel like walking through the streets of Kathmandu with a heavy carpet over my shoulder so we hailed a passing Ambassador taxi and headed back to our hotel.

We bought another, smaller carpet the next day. Walking along a main street in the town, I spotted a carpet featuring a Chinese dragon, hanging out of the third-floor window of a building down an alley. There was a sign with an arrow pointing upwards over the entrance to the building indicating carpet sales. Making our way up a rickety staircase we found the carpet shop and asked about the dragon carpet. The owner retrieved it from the window, told us the price, and, after a little haggling, I handed over a small amount of rupees and went on our way with our latest purchase.

Both the carpets are still in pristine condition, the Tibetan coin carpet, which still looks as if it had been bought the day before, adorns the living room in our house in Stourbridge to this day. The dragon lies at the foot of our bed.

We had several visitors to the cantonment, one husband and wife who stayed with us worked at the Britain/Nepal Medical Trust, which had an office in Biratnagar. The husband, Alan, had a nasty looking growth on his upper arm and had come for a consultation with Major Peter G. The growth was diagnosed as a melanoma (skin cancer), and the recommendation that it should be removed as soon as possible. Surgery was scheduled for the next operating day.

The melanoma, which was about two inches long was excised a couple days later, along with a fair amount of surrounding skin and muscle, to make sure as much, if not all of the cancer was removed. The area was repaired with a skin graft and Alan and his wife stayed with us for a few days to recover from the surgery before returning to Biratnagar.

We also entertained an Indian man and wife from Darjeeling. They were a couple of tea planters who were in the cantonment for a golf competition. They stayed with us for three days and were generous to Martha and Tika who had looked after the cooking and their laundry. They also gave us a gift of a pair of 2.5 Kg tea chests of Black Gunpowder tea from their estate. This is made by rolling the tea leaves to form tiny pellets, it is also known as Pearl Tea and originated in China. It made for a delicious tea. We gave one chest to be shared with Martha and Tika, no doubt Raj would get a few cups of tea as well.

One of our overnight guests was a geologist from the Dhankuta Road builders. He had come to the hospital for a minor procedure and stayed with us for a couple of nights until one of his colleagues would come to collect him. Tika washed his laundry and as usual, Martha cooked us excellent evening meals. At the end of his short stay, he offered to pay us for our hospitality, but we refused, telling him to give Martha and Tika some money for the cooking and laundry. He gave us a carving of talc stone which he had fashioned from an outcrop of the mineral he had found while working on the road, and he had made it for us as a gift. It was of two hands held in the Nepalese greeting of 'Namaste.' We still have it.

Overheard conversation of a western tourist in a restaurant in Kathmandu by one of our number in Dharan.

"The Nepalese must have very good eyesight as you don't see many of them wearing glasses." The tourist had no concept of the poverty existing in the country as a whole.

The truth is that many Nepalese with poor eyesight could not afford spectacles to correct their vision. The average per capita income of the Nepalis in the eighties was a little above $1 a day. With a pair of glasses costing the equivalent of several weeks income, it was hardly surprising that few of them could afford to buy glasses.

With this in mind, Mo mentioned to me that she thought Martha's eyesight was not very good. She had started dropping things, and although she could read English, Mo noticed Martha was holding a book close to her face.

I approached Ranjit at the hospital and asked him if I could get Martha's eyes tested. He in turn asked the Nepalese doctor who got Martha to read an eye test chart. It turned out her eyesight was not too bad but she needed glasses.

Mo did no more than to arrange transport for herself and Martha to visit an optician in Biratnagar. Mo went shopping in the town while the optician performed an eye test and wrote a prescription to correct Martha's eyesight.

Marth waited for Mo to return from the shops and they went to the shop next door to the opticians to get her new glasses. Martha tried on several pair and chose one she liked. To Martha the price was equivalent to two month's wages and she was despondent at the cost, but Mo waved her worries away and paid for the spectacles and the opticians fee which altogether, to us, was a just few pounds.

The effect on Martha was instant, no more dropped cutlery in the kitchen and she read our recipe books without having them up to her nose. She also looked good in her new spectacles.

I returned to the optician a few weeks later as my own glasses were becoming a little worse for wear. I read the letters on the chart which were on the back of a Sanskrit version, after which the optician opened his wooden box of various lenses for me to try. After a few minutes, I could read the bottom line of the chart and a prescription for new lenses was written for me to take next door to the optician's cousin.

I picked out a set of frames and asked the technician if he could obtain photochromic lenses for me. He said he could but they would have to come from Kathmandu and would take a fortnight. I replied that that was no problem, left a small deposit and returned two weeks later.

The technician in the shop greeted me with a cheery 'Namaste' and said my lenses had arrived. He retrieved a box lined with tissue paper and unpacked my new lenses. My mouth dropped open as he showed me what had been delivered. The lenses were the size of saucers and I wondered what exactly I had ordered.

Without another word, the technician turned to a foot-pedal operated grinding wheel, overhead of which was a single 40-watt light bulb. He pedalled energetically, holding each lens in turn against the stone wheel. After about 20 minutes, he pronounced he had finished and taking my new frames popped the newly shaped lenses in. They fitted perfectly first time. I tried them on and after a couple of minutes, my eyes adjusting to the new prescription, I looked outside. My new glasses were great and the photochromic lenses immediately became active.

I spotted another pair of frames that would be useful as a spare pair and asked if the lenses in my old glasses would fit. Comparing old and new frames the technician relied that he would make them fit and returned to the grinding wheel. A few minutes later and after a quick polish I had a new spare pair of glasses. The whole cost of new glasses and the spare pair blew a hole in £30!

The Blue Coat School was 'feeder' school for Old Swinford Hospital School in Stourbridge in the West Midlands. The head of Blue Coat had suggested some time ago that it would be a good place for Jason as he was doing well at school.

Mo and I had visited in Old Swinford 1980 with Jason and we were impressed both with the school, its surroundings, and its academic record. The headmaster, Mr Potter seemed a kindly man, and dependant on Jason's record at Blue Coat suggested there may be a place for him in 1982 when Jason would be 13.

Shortly before the boys had left for England at the end of the Easter holiday, I received a letter from Mr Potter offering Jason a place at his school in

Stourbridge. Jason was keen to go to Old Swinford and I replied to the effect that we would be pleased to accept Mr Potter's offer of a place.

The move to Old Swinford would take a little organising. I would be granted leave to accompany the boys home to England and help Jason move to his new school when they left Nepal after the summer holiday.

One evening in the mess we got chatting to a couple who were going to Darjeeling for a long weekend. Mo and I thought a trip to this town in the hills for a few days would be of interest to the boys in the summer. From there, we could go onto the Tollygunge Club in Calcutta before the boys and I flew back to England.

After checking dates and times, I asked the couple going to Darjeeling if they would make a reservation for us at the Windamere Hotel. Another contact in the cantonment was able to get in touch with the Tollygunge Club and make us a booking.

We told Martha of our plans for the holiday, and, as she had family in Darjeeling, suggested to her that she and her husband might wish to visit them. They could travel with us to the town in a cantonment Land Rover. Tika had family in the hills as did Raj, so they could all take a holiday while we were away.

Just before we had left for Agra, we received a consignment of stocks for the medical stores. Everything came packed in heavy-duty cardboard boxes which were carefully opened. These would be packed flat, some used to send supplies up into the hills for the many welfare centres, but the majority would be sold for a few rupees. Because of their robust nature the boxes were prized by porters. I had seen my boxes on the backs of porters on the pathway when walking up to Hille.

The other item that made a small amount of cash was old X-ray films. This was sold by weight and was burnt, the ashes processed and the silver recovered. The cash we made from selling boxes and film went into the patients' comforts fund to buy small items such as toiletries and special food items. Drugs which were getting close to their expiry date were given to the local hospital or to the Britain Nepal Medical Trust in Biratnagar.

The spring weather gave way to the heat of summer and the busy work in the hospital carried on. BB had retired and MB became my chief clerk. My afternoons were spent on the golf course, particularly when work in the medical stores became routine and there were just a few odds and ends to tie up. MB would look over to me, his glasses perched on the end of his nose and say, "Go play golf, Sahib." He knew where I would be if I was needed before closing time, as did most of the staff of the hospital.

Our reservations at the Windamere and Tollygunge were confirmed, all we needed was to obtain the necessary visas and permits and we could travel when the boys came out for the summer holiday. I had also applied for a flight back to UK to accompany the boys back home and to see Jason into his new school. We would fly out from Calcutta while Mo would return to Dharan.

Meanwhile, the boys came back to us for the summer holiday. I went down to Calcutta to collect them, going through the usual rigmarole at the customs and immigration at the borders. Another two pages of my passport used up. By now, I was just about on first name terms with the Indian immigration officer.

Back at home the boys were keen to get some fish for the garden pond. It was at the time populated with frogs which Raj frequently cleared out, although most of them found their way back. Justin was looking a bit peaky when they arrived, and my mother had written to say he had been under the weather recently and he had had a few tests but there were no definite results.

Mo decided to take Justin up to see the doctor up at the hospital. The anaesthetist, Major Chris P, was on duty that day and he gave Justin a thorough examination. When this was done, he suggested to Mo she should keep Justin indoors, give him painkillers and plenty of fluids and to return if there was no improvement.

Mo was just about to leave when Major P asked her to wait a moment, as he had a flash of inspiration and said he would take a small blood sample from Justin. This done, he told Mo a test would take a short time and he would call her at home when he had a result.

He called a couple hours later to tell Mo that Justin had glandular fever. There was no treatment apart from taking care of him, such as getting enough rest, eating a healthy diet, and drinking plenty of fluids. He thought the disease may be in its final stages and Justin should be better in a few days.

The next morning Raj came to say that he knew a place where he could get some fish and could he take the boys with him and a couple of friends to get some stock for the pond. Justin was still under the weather, so Jason, Raj and a couple of Nepalese boys went off in a rickshaw into Dharan and from there took a bus towards Itahari. I gave Raj a few rupees to get some food and to pay for the transport and off they went.

I was having a cuppa in the operating theatre rest room when Ron came in after returning from a few days in Kathmandu. "Hello," said Ron, "do you know where your kids are?"

I said Justin was at home and Jason was off somewhere with my gardener and his mates looking for fish.

"I thought as much," replied Ron. "I've just come up from Biratnagar, and on the way, I saw a bunch of kids in a paddy field up to their waists in mud. I did a double take and realised one of the kids was yours!"

Jason and Raj returned from the fishing expedition in the afternoon, both of them wet and covered in mud. Mo banished him to the shower for a good scrub, hoping he hadn't picked up some horrible disease, Martha doing the same with Raj in the garden with a hose pipe.

When I got home, I was shown a bucket of water containing quite a few fish, amongst them was a catfish about 6 inches long. They were all about to be consigned to the pool when I suggested the catfish would eat the smaller fishes and we kept it separate for a couple of days before gently adding the rest to the pool. There was around a couple of dozen assorted fish and they appeared to be happy in their new surroundings.

The pool was a great success, especially after a few clumps of water hyacinth had been added. This would give some shade during the hot weather, but would have to be controlled as it grew very rapidly, and would cover the pond surface quite quickly. Another fishing expedition added a few more fish to the stock.

Meanwhile, Justin's glandular fever appeared to be subsiding, and within a few days he seemed to be his normal self. Mo spoke to Major Chris P, telling him Justin was on his way to recovery and thanked him for his timely diagnosis.

****

Tragedy Strikes

It was a Saturday morning in late August. Most of us golfers were getting ready to play in the board competition when the accident occurred. Major G's boys were riding their bicycles around the cantonment, normally a safe place for children as there was very little traffic.

The dustbin lorry was doing its rounds travelling at a leisurely 5 MPH on the road from the golf club as both boys came through the ordinance depot yard into the path of the lorry. One of the boys managed to stop, but the elder boy, Peter was going too fast. He dropped down, laying his bike down and slid beneath the lorry. Apart from a bad case of gravel rash he would have been safe, but the lorry struck an electrical junction box and bounced back, its front wheel crushed the boy's head, killing him instantly.

Someone must have seen the accident as an ambulance was on the scene with a few minutes. The boy's inert body was removed from beneath the lorry and moved gently into the ambulance which returned to the hospital. The lorry driver was distraught but was comforted by some of the wives who had come to the scene. He was later absolved from any blame.

The death of Peter was only the second fatality among the British contingent of the cantonment, and the first within the confines of the base. The first was the wife of a UK soldier who drowned in the Dudh Koshi at Tribeni a few years previously.

The following few days saw a pall of sadness hang over the cantonment when all of us were shocked over the tragedy. Ranjit took charge of preparing Peter's remains for return to the UK. The body was sealed in a metal coffin and stored in a freezer until flights back to the UK for the family could be arranged.

The Major, his wife Judy, and son, along with the body of Peter, left the cantonment for England soon after. Everyone came to wish them a fond farewell, although sadness was in the air as they drove out of the cantonment.

Mo and I and the boys left for our trip to Darjeeling a week later.

****

We travelled in a cantonment Land Rover with a driver. Martha and her husband Michael accompanied us on the 5-hour journey, along with another Gurkha soldier and his wife. We passed through Nepalese and Indian customs and immigration quickly and started the long climb up to Darjeeling.

We drove quite close to the track of the 'Blue Train,' narrow-gauge railway and frequently saw it puffing its way through the trees. The road and railway track went through several small villages, the track passing close to the front door of some of the residents.

Soon we reached Darjeeling, which at almost 7000 feet above sea level, was established as a hill station where employees of the British Raj in Calcutta could spend the hot summer months of the city in the relative cool of the hills. Evidence of this can be seen in some of the colonial style houses in the town. The British also planted many tea estates in the region, Darjeeling Tea rapidly became famous throughout the world.

Arriving at the Windamere Hotel, we said goodbye to our travelling companions, and told our driver to collect us three days later. Martha and Michael would make their own way back to Dharan later in the week.

The Windamere Hotel, one of the oldest in Darjeeling was owned and run by a Tibetan lady by the name of Mrs Tenduf La, affectionately known as 'Mrs Tender Flower' by the guests. She had managed the hotel since the 1930s after her husband left for America, never to return. The hotel was built in the colonial style and had roaring fires in the rooms as, despite it being mid-August, the evenings were quite cool after the heat of the Terai. Our rooms were comfortable and the food was excellent. British staples such as steak and kidney pudding, jam roly-poly and custard, along with traditional Indian cuisine were on the menu.

We spent our time wandering the hilly streets of the town, visited a tea plantation, and a Tibetan refugee centre. On our final morning, one of the hotel staff knocked on our door very early to tell us the skies were clear and views of the mountains could be seen from Tiger Hill.

We dressed hurriedly and made our way to Tiger Hill which has the best views of the mountains. From there and over 40 miles to the north, we could see the massive bulk of Kanchenjunga, the third highest mountain in the world at a little over 8,500 metres and known as the 'German Mountain', due to quite a few failed German attempts to reach its summit, The mountain was eventually conquered in May 1955 by Joe Brown and George Band. This was after several failed attempts by various climbers over the previous 100 years.

One morning, while Mo and the boys went to a local market, I ventured off to visit the Himalayan Mountain Institute Museum. On my way there, I saw a Nepalese gentleman coming towards me. I immediately recognised him as Tensing Norgay who, with Edmund Hilary, had successfully conquered Mount Everest in 1953.

As he came close to me, I greeted him with 'Namaste' and held out my hand. He took my hand in his and with a broad smile welcomed me to Darjeeling asking me what I was doing in the town. I told him I was on holiday with my wife and children, and I was on my way to the museum.

"Make sure you see Mallory's ice axe." He replied, and wishing me goodbye he continued off down the hill.

Mallory and his climbing companion Irvine, were lost on Everest in 1924, and were last seen approaching 28,000 feet when they disappeared into cloud. The ice axe, reputed to be Mallory's was found in 1933; Malloy's body was discovered in 1999. He was identified by the name tags sewn into his clothing. Irvine's body has not been found. It is not known whether they reached the summit.

After seeing the mountains, we returned to the Windamere for breakfast and got ready to check out. I settled our bill with Mrs Tenduf La with Indian rupees and a bottle of Johnny Walker whisky (the latter paying for the boy's room). Our driver was waiting for us as we left the hotel to make our way to the airport at Bagdogra and on to Calcutta.

We arrived in Calcutta in the early evening rain and, fighting our way through the porters who wanted to carry or bags, eventually found a taxi to take us to the Tollygunge Club. I sat in the front seat with the driver and asked him to set the meter. He told me the meter, which was already showing several hundred rupees, was broken, although it continued to click over as we drove on through the rain and the crowded streets of Calcutta.

We eventually reached the Tollygunge after what seemed to be an interminable drive. Looking at the meter I saw that it registered just short of a thousand rupees, the driver asked me for 850. Telling him to wait, I got out of the taxi and went to reception. There I asked the clerk to tell me the fare from the airport to the club. He told me it would usually be about 250 rupees. Returning to the taxi, I unloaded our cases from the boot, stuck my head in the driver's window and gave the driver 300 rupees, and suggested he be on his way, mentioning that had his taxi number.

The first thing I had to do in Calcutta was to confirm mine and the boys' flights back to UK. After breakfast, while Mo and the boys were in the pool, I took a taxi to the British Airways office in the city. To my astonishment I was told that our three seats had been double booked but we could fly out from Delhi the same day we were booked from Calcutta. I said that would be in order and was told to return the next day to confirm.

It suddenly dawned on me that there were three vacant seats on the flight out of Calcutta. The boys and I were originally on the same plane as Major G and his family who were going to UK to visit family; but they had flown out a few days after the death of their son a couple of weeks before. Movements in Dharan had not cancelled the first booking.

All of us went to the BA office the next day, only to be told that all the flights out of Delhi were fully booked. I mentioned seats booked for Major G and his family, but the clerk in the office insisted they were still valid. However, we could get on a flight from Madras if that was acceptable. I told him I would be happy with any airport if it meant me and the boys could get home in time. He said he would contact the Tollygunge Club as soon as he knew anything.

The following day we were up early and spent a couple of hours on the golf course, playing 9 holes before returning to the club house for a spot of breakfast. The waiter had just taken our order when well-dressed Asian gentleman approached and asked if he could join us. He mentioned that he had noticed my Dharan Golf club sweat shirt I was wearing and asked if I knew Jimmy Lys.

Jimmy was a retired colonel in the Gurkhas who ran a farm in Pakhribas, near Hille. Here he and his wife taught farming methods to retired Gurkhas on how to farm their land. He was also an active member of the golf club in Dharan and often played at weekends.

"Next time you see Jimmy, tell him Lenny sends his regards," said the gentleman. I replied that I would be almost certainly see him soon after I got back to Dharan when I returned from the UK.

We sat and chatted over our breakfasts, and after coffee was served, he signalled to a waiter. I noticed the gold cufflinks and the expensive Rolex on his wrist as he raised his arm. He gave the waiter a set of keys and asked him to go to his car and fetch his briefcase, mentioning that the car was the black Mercedes on the car park. I had assumed that Lenny appeared to be a successful Indian business man—I could not have been more wrong.

The waiter duly returned a few minutes later with Lenny's briefcase—an understated Gucci number. "I Think you may like to see these," said Lenny as he opened his case and produced a packet of photographs. We passed the pictures around; they were mainly of Lenny on a hunting trip in the Himalayan foothills, snow-capped mountains were in the background. There were pictures of him with his foot on a dead bear; a dead deer, and many birds having been shot from the skies.

I handed him back his sheaf of photographs, saying it looked like a very interesting trip. He looked at his watch and said he must be going; he was flying to Australia that afternoon. He thanked us for our company but just before he left, I asked him what he did for a living.

"Oh, not much," he said, "I'm just the King of Bhutan's uncle!" and with that he was gone.

Shortly after I returned from England, I met up with Jimmy at the Dharan club. Over a drink in the bar after the game I mentioned that we had met Lenny in Calcutta.

"Lenny," said Jimmy, "the King of Bhutan's uncle." I asked him if that was true.

"Certainly," he replied. "I knew him from Kathmandu. He was at one time listed in Playboy Magazine as one of the top ten most eligible bachelors in the world. We became friends when I was the military liaison officer at the embassy there. He and his cronies had been involved in a coup against his uncle and Lenny had been exiled to Nepal. My good lady used make tea and scones for him and his cronies in the kitchen of our house while he continued to plot against the king."

"Recently, he and the king had become reconciled, and the last I heard he was engaged to be married to the king's daughter."

In the afternoon, Mo and I were with the boys in the swimming pool at Tollygunge when one of the staff came to tell me there was a telephone call for me. It was from the BA office advising me that unfortunately the Madras flight to England was full, but they had provisionally got the boys and I seats on a flight from Bombay, and which they would confirm as soon as possible.

The flight was confirmed within the hour and I was asked to come to the office to collect the tickets. I did this and found tickets for a domestic flight to Bombay leaving the next morning and a flight to UK the following day at 6.30 the in morning, a day later than I had originally intended. There was also a voucher for a hotel for an overnight stay.

While I had been in town collecting the tickets, Mo had been busy packing most of our belongings as we were both flying out of Calcutta early the next morning; Mo to Bagdogra and home to Dharan, and myself and the boys to Bombay and England.

When I got back, we spent the afternoon on the golf course. The course was beautifully laid out and maintained, the fairways lined with many mature trees such as oak, beach and yew planted by the course architect almost a hundred years before we played on it. It was difficult to believe we were quite close to the centre of one of India's largest cities.

The club house itself is over 200 years old and built in the colonial style, and here we retired for dinner after the game. We all agreed the holiday had been a success, apart from the problems with flights, but that had been resolved—and we had enjoyed the time we spent in Darjeeling and the Tollygunge Club.

We were up early the next day and made our way to Dum Dum Airport and checked in. Our flight to Bombay was before Mo's and we waited for a little over an hour before boarding. We saw the BA plane, which was the one we should have flown in to UK, arrive from Dacca, just as our Bombay flight was called. I kissed Mo goodbye, and the boys gave Mo a hug, and we made our way to the departure lounge.

When I returned to Dharan a few days later, Mo told me that as our flight took off an announcement on the PA system called the boys and I to the BA desk. There she told them we had just left for Bombay, and the clerk at the desk said we had been allocated three seats on the flight from Calcutta!

The flight to Bombay took a little over two and a half hours. Our luggage had been booked all the way to England so we didn't have to go through the baggage collection, we just had overnight bags each. We left the domestic side of the airport and took a taxi to the international departures.

When we arrived, the place seemed deserted and it took me a while to find someone to direct me to the BA desk. The departure hall was also completely empty of people, no one manning the any of the desks. I found BA office and knocked on a door which opened to reveal four BA staff playing cards. I told them who I was and introduced the boys. One of the men took out a folder and told me they were expecting us, asking which hotel we were booked into. I told him, and he said the Holiday Inn would be better for the boys as it had two swimming pools. Picking up a telephone he called the hotel and confirmed they had a couple of rooms which we could have. I told him that would be great and he gave me a voucher to cover the hotel and meals for the time we were staying.

Looking through the folder he mentioned the flight was due to leave at 7 o'clock the next morning, and we should be at the airport no later than 4.30. When I asked why, he said I would find out when we got there. He then arranged a taxi to take us to the hotel. I thanked him profusely for his help in fixing everything for me and the boys, he wished me a pleasant flight home and returned to his card game.

The taxi took us the 20-minute drive to the hotel where we checked into our rooms, only unpacking our swimming trunks, after which we explored around the building and grounds. We found the important places—restaurants and the swimming pools.

The hotel was next to the beach, which was crowded with hawkers and beggars, the beach and sea did not look particularly inviting, and we decided to give it a miss. We had a couple of hours to kill before it was time for dinner so we went to the pool for a little relaxation for me and a splash about for the boys.

We spent a leisurely time over dinner and went to our rooms afterwards for an early night. I booked an early call in the morning and ordered a light breakfast from room service. I had checked out before we went to bed and paid the small difference between the bill and the BA vouchers. We were all tired out after the travelling and the early start in Calcutta. I saw the boys to their room, made sure they were comfortable and left for my own room next door.

I must have fallen asleep as soon as my head hit the pillow, for the next thing I knew was the telephone ringing for my wake-up call at 3 o'clock. When I was washed and dressed, I went next door to wake the boys, telling them to come to my room for breakfast as soon as they were ready.

Breakfast over, we went down to reception to wait for our taxi back to the airport. When we arrived at the international departures desk, I found out what the man at the BA office meant when he had told us to get there early. The area was packed with people checking in. Immigration was the same, processing was incredibly slow, with every passport meticulously checked, this was the days before computerisation and self-check-in.

By the time we got through, we had an only an hour before our flight was due to leave and we were able to go through to the departure lounge before boarding our flight to the UK.

Fortunately, we had been allocated seats in BA Club class and boarded after the first-class passengers. The flight was full, and the crowds at the airport suggested that most flights westward were much the same. The captain announced, as we taxied out to the runway and take-off, that our flight would take approximately 10 hours and was non-stop to Heathrow.

We had second breakfast an hour into the flight after which we settled back into our seats and tried to relax for the long journey homewards. At least, we had plenty of leg room as our seats were in front of the bulkhead. The boys had their Asterix comic books and I had a novel to keep us occupied.

Soon the boys were asleep, but I rarely slept for more than a few minutes at a time during flights. The journey, apart from the toilets being awash after a few hours, was uneventful if interminable. At least, the cabin staff kept us fed and supplied with drinks, a couple of gin and tonics eased the boredom, and at last we were at London, Heathrow.

We passed through baggage claim, and passport control a lot quicker than at Bombay. A British Midlands flight to Birmingham, a bus to Kingshurst and Mo's family home. As I had hoped, Mo had managed to inform her family we would be arriving a day later than expected. My mother was there and was pleased to see the boys. She would be coming with us the next day to see Justin back to the Blue Coat School and then on to Jason's new school at Old Swinford Hospital.

My mother, along with her pensioner's bus pass, travelled everywhere by public transport around Birmingham, and knew the best way to get to our destinations. First to Harborne to see Justin settled in for the winter term. We met Mr Gray who wished Jason well at Old Swinford. Then back to Birmingham for a bus to Stourbridge and Jason's new school.

The bus ride from Birmingham to Stourbridge took an age, and we walked up the hill to Old Swinford, me carrying Jason's luggage in my old army suitcase. I had a good sweat on by the time we got to the school. We found reception and the first person we met was Jason's house master, who took us to Jason's new surroundings. Here Jason met some old friends from the Blue Coat School, which would ease him into his new school. Once he was settled in, we hugged him and said goodbye telling him, as usual to write soon, and we were looking forward to seeing him and his brother back in Dharan for the Christmas break. He said that with his old friends he was sure he would be OK, and he was gone.

I had a couple of days before leaving for Nepal, and I was looking for a set of golf clubs for Mo and I. Looking through the Birmingham Mail I spotted an item for the Robin Hood golf pro shop, which was having a sale. I set off for the course the next day and, browsing around, spotted a set that looked as though they would suit me. They were heavily discounted in the sale, so I approached the professional telling him I was interested and did they have a half set for my wife.

He said he had a half set in the same and found them out from the many sets in the shop. I ended up with a set and a half of John Letters Master Mex. The woods were blue on my set, and pink on Mo's. I paid with my credit card, the first time I had used it in over a year, telling the pro I was taking them out of the country the next day and would he provide a VAT invoice for them, which he duly did.

I went with my mother to Birmingham airport and took a British Midlands flight to Heathrow. My only luggage was my small suitcase and the golf clubs. I eventually found the VAT refunds desk, where I was told the clubs had to be out of the country for a certain time, otherwise I may have to pay back any refund.

I had recently applied for, and been granted, an extension to my posting to Nepal so I was certain I would be out of the UK for the required time. I filled in a form and posted it off to the tax man.

I checked in at the BA desk for my flight to Calcutta, and incurred a small charge as my clubs put me slightly over my baggage allowance.

The flight was, as usual, boring, but at least it was non-stop to Calcutta, and on time. I would have just a short wait for my connecting flight to Bagdogra. My golf clubs arrived unscathed, but my suitcase did not appear. I found out later that it gone on to Daca in Bangladesh and it turned up in Dharan about three weeks later, along with an apology from BA.

The Land Rover from Dharan was waiting for me at Bagdogra and, after passing through Indian and Nepalese customs and immigration, I was on my way back to Dharan after a hectic 4 days in the UK. I was happy to be back in the cantonment with Mo.

My first stop the next day was down to the movements office where I asked about the flight from Calcutta the previous week. They assured me they had contacted BA with regard to the cancellation of the seats for the Major G's family but had received no confirmation until after my flight had left without me. In the end, everything all had turned out alright, if a little hectic—apart from my missing suitcase.

On Monday morning, I returned to my work in the medical supply office. I went for a cuppa at 11 o'clock in the operating theatre and there I met the lady surgeon who was to look after the surgical needs of the hospital while Maj G was away. This was Major L D and she would be with us for around six weeks.

I was sat at home enjoying my lunchtime sandwich when the telephone rang.

"Hello Trevor," said the voice at the other end. "It's Mike Templar, I've just got in from Hong Kong. I will see you on the first tee at 3 o'clock."

"I'm a bit busy at the moment," I replied. "I've been away for a couple of weeks. Perhaps in a day or two."

"No, no," came the voice at the other end. "First tee, 3o'clock."

"I don't know, Colonel," I said.

"I presume you know why I'm here."

281

"Yes," I said, "with Major G away, you've come over to watch the shop."

"That makes me your boss then."

"Yes, it does," I replied.

"Well then, first tee, 3 o'clock."

I knew when I was on the wrong end of an argument. We played together several times over the next three weeks, neither of us were very good at the game, but the banter between us made for an enjoyable round of golf.

Mike Templar was a full colonel and physician. We had served in several hospitals together. He often popped into the dispensaries where I worked for a chat over a cup of coffee. He always reckoned he was the dispenser's friend, as he only knew the name of six drugs, and three of those were insulin. Not true, of course. He had a reputation of being a fine doctor and was well liked by his patients. I once asked him if he was busy. To which he replied that he had a great filing system—"In, out and too hard. The latter holds most of my files." Knowing his reputation, I did not believe that for a minute.

Shortly after the Colonel had arrived, two young girls were brought to the hospital. They were sisters who had been abandoned by their family and had been taken in by a couple in another village. While they were out playing together, they were both savaged by a rabid dog. The younger of the two was bitten in the ankle, but the older girl was attacked about the face. It was she who was showing signs of rabies, a totally fatal disease once the symptoms had manifested themselves. The virus attacks the nervous system and eventually, the spinal cord and the brain.

The older sister was barrier nursed in isolation, while Mike attempted to save the life of the younger girl. She was given a series of anti-rabies injections and started to recover; antibiotics prevented further infection of the dog bites. Soon she was sufficiently well, and showing no symptoms of rabies, was allowed to go home to her adopted family. Meanwhile, her sister gradually deteriorated and was heavily sedated, within a week she died, albeit peacefully.

On a lighter note, Pat and Wes held a supper party to which they invited Mike as he was leaving shortly to go back to Hong Kong. Pat had made a kipper pâté and offered Mike a sample. Mike told Pat he very rarely ate fish, but as she had gone to the trouble of making the pâté, he would try a little.

After all the guests had gone, Mike and Wes sat chatting, and over the next couple of hours had demolished a bottle of whiskey, before Mike retired to the Officers Mess. The next morning when Pat was riding her bike on her way to open the radio studio, she met Mike, looking a little worse for wear and on his way to work. Mike flagged her down and said to her, "Pat, I will never eat pâté in your house ever again, I feel bloody awful this morning!"

Mike left a few days later, we were to meet again in Hannover a little over a year later.

Chapter 20
October 1982–October 1983

Dharan Cantonment, Nepal

October 1982 saw the celebration of Dusshera which was spread over several days, culminating in the ritual sacrificial offerings of many animals. The dates of this festival are determined by the phases of the moon and stars. The previous year Dusshera had occurred in early October and we had missed it.

All male members of the British contingent were ordered to attend, none of the British females were allowed because several years previously, one of the British wives had disrupted the proceedings with a one-woman protest. We were also required to wear a suit and tie, despite the heat of the day, even in the early morning. An area the size of a tennis court was roped off and a number of Hindu officials wandered around inside.

The proceedings started with a Hindu priest blessing the arena with lots of water being cast around. The first animal, a goat, was brought in on a length of rope which was passed through a hole in a tall, decorated pole in the middle of the arena. While two men held on to its tail, the rope was pulled taught through the hole in the post. Another man stepped forward, armed with a large Kukri, and brought the blade down quickly, severing the goat's head with a single stroke. This was thought to be auspicious; the head being lopped off with one strike of the blade.

There then followed a succession of animals, goats, sheep, chickens and ducks. All these were offerings from local people, all hoping for a successful single strike to appeases the gods and bring good fortune for the coming year. The more expensive the animal, the brighter the prospects for good fortune. Within a few minutes, the arena floor was awash with blood, those officiating the sacrifices paddling around in it.

The ritual went on for about an hour and a half, culminating with the main event—a bull led in to be sacrificed on behalf of Gurkhas around the world. The beast was huge, its neck was easily 18 inches thick. After being blessed by the priest along with much splashing of water, and with three burly Gurkhas hanging on to its tail, the bull was tethered by a rope through its nose ring being passed through the pole. Three more Gurkhas held on to the rope, the bull's neck being pulled rigid.

Gurkhas are usually thought of as being small and wiry, but the one that stepped into the ring was the size and build of a present-day England rugby forward. He carried with him an enormous ceremonial Kukri, the bright steel blade of which was easily four feet long.

The swordsman stood to one side of the bull, facing us in the front row of spectators. When he had composed himself, he raised the Kukri high above his head, the blade glinting in the mid-day sun. Then, with one swish of the blade, he severed the head in one slashing strike, blood spurting everywhere, and a great cheer went up from the crowd. Following the successful sacrifice of the bull, a signal was sent to all the Gurkha units in the world telling them of the result, and of great auspices for the coming year.

Very little of the meat of the slaughtered animals and poultry went to waste. Once the ceremony was over, we retired to the Ghurkha Sergeants Mess for drinks while we waited for beef, goat and chicken curry to be served.

The pay office in Dharan served as a bank for obtaining rupees, paying our various bills from the grocery shop, the Dharan club and the Sgts Mess. All our purchases in the bar the Sgts mess and grocery shops were signed for, very little cash was used apart from paying our household staff.

The pay office also paid Gurkha pensions. There was a set day for pensions paid to retired Gurkhas and widows. Pension paying day was a day to avoid the pay office as the queue outside was infinitely worse than those at a UK post office on pension day.

The pension queues around the time of Dusshera were enormous, as many of those that could afford to, allowed their pension to build up over the months, so they would have a larger sum around the time of the celebration. The queues would have been even longer a few years previously. Since then, the Gurkha Welfare Trust of Canada had funded the construction of over twenty welfare centres in and around the foothills of the Himalayas. Many of these were able to pay pensions to local pensioners who lived within a few days walk of the centre to collect their pensions.

The amount of money paid out during this time was eye-watering. Pensions were paid in cash and the pay office funds were kept in safes in cells in the guard room. It was an indication as to how much money was involved in that the local bank had the same arrangement with the guard room, although they had two safes for their funds, the pay office had three!

The notes paid to pensioners were expected by the recipients to be new and unmarked in any way. Bank notes were issued in stapled in blocks of a hundred, and, while checking the blocks of 1000 rupee notes, Dave, the warrant officer, noticed that one of the notes had been cut short by half an inch at the printers. Knowing this note would be unacceptable, he popped next door to the bank to exchange it. The manager took one look at the note and offered Dave 800 rupees for it! Dave declined the offer.

Shortly after Dusshera I went down to the pay office to pay my monthly bills. I waited for a few minutes as Dave and Wes were balancing the books after paying out the pensions the previous week. Dave called out to Wes, "I've got a final figure, mine is 5, what did you get?"

To which Wes replied, "Oh dear, mine is 8!" They were talking about the difference between 8 million and 5 million RUPEES! A few minutes of panic ensued, after which Wes called out that he had found the problem and the final figures matched.

The boys had been away for seven weeks and it was time to arrange for flights and permits to get them back to Dharan for the Christmas holiday which would soon be upon us. Mo and Pushpa Rai would be going to Calcutta to escort them back as I had quite a lot of work to do in the medical stores. We hadn't had a supply from the UK for some time, and although we were reasonably well stocked, I had a signal sent to DMED asking for my previous requests to be expedited as soon as possible. I included a list of the stock I considered to be outstanding—it was a long list. It would be early in the new year when matters would come to a head.

The boys arrived in Dharan for the Christmas break; it was great to have them with us again. Both of them were happy at school and appeared to be doing well. Jason had quite a few of his friends from the Blue Coat School. Mo came back from picking up the boys and had picked up a stomach bug which she attributed to some spinach she had eaten that had not been thoroughly washed.

She was not unwell with it, but after a couple of day of anti-diarrheal medicines and not straying too far away from a loo, she was fit once more.

The butcher had returned from Calcutta with the Freezer King full of meat from the abattoir, where he chose the steers for slaughter. He also had good quantity of snake anti-venom and rabies vaccine from the Institute in Calcutta. Our freezer was well stocked with supplies, including a turkey from Hong Kong. Our Christmas dinner would be the last we would spend in Dharan.

Jason announced that he had asked the butcher if he could watch him slaughter a pig from the cantonment farm, and would Martha get him up at 4 o'clock the next morning. I didn't see him until later the next morning, while I was having my breakfast. He regaled me with all the gory details of Bill stunning the pig, hanging it up to allow the blood to drain in order to make his famous black pudding. He was obviously quite enthralled of the process by which we get our pork chops. Not the ideal topic of conversation to have over breakfast.

The boys returned to school in mid-January, Wes and I along with one or two others made up the escort party as there were quite a few children returning to UK.

Shortly after the boys went back to school, the cantonment was honoured with the visit of the Princess Royal, Princess Anne. The Sgts Mess was designated as the place where the senior non-commissioned ranks, along with their wives, were to be presented to the princess. We were arranged in a circle, dressed in civilian clothes, and instructed on how we should greet and speak to her. She was first to be addressed as 'Your Royal Highness,' and thereafter as Ma'am. She was also accompanied by a large company of dignitaries—the British Ambassador, her ADC, the military liaison office from Kathmandu and her three ladies-in-waiting. The RSM, along with the commander of the cantonment proceeded around the circle of mess members and their wives.

We were each introduced by the RSM to the Princess, who asked us about our work in the cantonment. She asked Mo if we had children, and when Mo replied that our boys were in school in England. The princess replied that it would be very it hard for us and we must miss them very much. I found it surprisingly easy to talk to her, very down to earth, and not at all what I had expected.

Eventually, we were introduced to her ladies-in-waiting, and as the last of three came and spoke to me, she looked around and could not see her charge.

"Bloody hell!" she exclaimed. "Where has she got to now?"

287

I spotted the princess, and nodded towards her. She had plonked herself on a settee, sitting between the RAOC butcher and his wife, engaging them both in animated conversation.

After the party had left for the officers' mess and dinner, most of us gravitated towards Bill and his wife to ask what they had talked about. Bill gave a knowing wink and said the Princess Royal had told him that her feet were killing her.

The next day she toured the cantonment in an open-top Land Rover. We stood outside our house along with rest of our neighbours and waved as she passed by. Bill the butcher lived opposite us, and as she passed and saw him, she leaned over and called out to him, "Excellent curry in the mess last night, Bill!" We all agreed she was lovely and we were happy to have met her.

Trekking the Light Fantastic

Just after my birthday on 21 January, I was playing a round of golf with Major Richard Willis, the Gurkha welfare officer in the cantonment. He was charged with making sure the welfare centres functioned efficiently as regards to pension paying and medical treatment. During the trekking season which ran from October to May, there was always a 'Duty Trekker' who toured around two or three of the centres to make inspections and report his findings to Richard.

During our round of golf, Richard mentioned that one or two of the trekkers had said they had concerns about the medical supplies held by the centres, usually over-stocks of some items and shortages of others. Richard asked me if I could offer him some advice.

I told him that without seeing the problem first hand I would be wary about trying to offer a solution. Richard had baited a trap and I walked right into it!

"I'm pleased you said that," said Richard. "I'm off on two-week trek next Monday and you can come with me."

I suggested I would have to clear it with Maj G, my commanding officer.

"Too late," Richard replied. "I've already spoken to him, and he is happy for you to accompany me."

My next question was, "Can Mo come with us?"

"Of course, she can," said Richard. "She would be most welcome."

Over the next few days, with advice from Richard and Heather, his wife, we gathered together items of clothing we would need to take with us. Shorts and T-shirts mainly, but a couple of warm sweaters and long trousers as we would be up in hills at over 10,000 feet in January where it could get cold in the evenings. We also obtained a few tins of army issue compo rations from the ordnance depot, particularly a couple of tins of boiled sweets, oatmeal biscuits, along with loo paper and a can opener.

The day before we set out, we took all our stuff to Richard's house to meet the six porters who would be coming with us. The head porter, or Sirdar, supervised the loading of the dokos, or carrying baskets, the porters would be using to hold our equipment and supplies during our 12-day trek.

Once he was happy with the loaded baskets, the Sirdar announced we would be ready to go early the next morning. I tried to lift one of the baskets and failed miserably. One of the baskets which would be carried by Ratni Chettri, the Sirdar, contained a length of plastic drainpipe, and I assumed this was for the water supply in one of the centres. I mentioned this to Richard and received a knowing wink, and he said this was a vital piece of trekking equipment.

As dawn was breaking the following morning, we in a left in a Land Rover with a trailer for the start of our trek. We would drive about 30 miles along the main highway before turning off onto a track. The baskets were in the trailer behind the vehicle, and the porters, Richard, Mo and I were crammed into the Land Rover.

After a few miles off-road, we came to the end of the drivable track where we climbed out of our Land Rover after Richard gave our driver instructions to meet us in 12 days' time at Barahakshetra some 60 miles to the east on the other side of the Sun Koshi River. We made our way along a narrow pathway leaving the porters to unload the baskets from the trailer as we three headed north towards Beltar, a village where we could get something to eat before we started the trek proper. We would need to get some food inside us as we had a long day in front of us. The porters soon caught us up and joined us for a curry lunch.

Shortly after leaving Beltar, we started a hard climb, the porters leading the way. We trekked 'Raj Style'—in that we carried very little. Mo had a day sack and water bottle, while I had my camera, water bottle and a knife. The porters carried everything else, unlike holiday trekkers to Nepal who are expected to take a full pack with most of their belongings.

We soon reached the top of the ridge and were greeted with a magnificent view of the wide Sun Koshi River about a thousand feet below. On the far bank, we could make out crowds of people waiting to cross to our side of the river. The

Sun Koshi has its source high up on the Tibetan plateau and flows eastwards through Nepal, and eventually into the Ganges in India.

We made our way down a precipitous pathway, making way for those coming up. At one point, Richard met a retired Gurkha who had a wooden leg, and a heated conversation in Nepali took place.

I asked Richard as we continued down the hill about the conversation he had had with the man. Richard told me the fellow was on his way to Dharan to remonstrate with one of the British Gurkha officers in charge of recruiting, to find out why he had failed his son's assessment to join the brigade. When we met on the slope, the man had walked for five days and had possibly another two before reaching Dharan. At least, he could probably get a bus to the cantonment once he reached the main road.

Having made our way down to the river's edge, we waited our turn to climb into one of several dug-out canoes which was to be our transport across the rapidly flowing water. Six people at a time were ferried across, and we held tightly onto the sides of the boat as we were propelled upstream into the current by the boatman wielding a rough wooden paddle. When we reached the middle of the river, the paddle was shipped and the current took us to the other side. Mo and I clambered out, thankful that we had only got slightly damp during the hair-raising trip.

The crowds on the bank turned out to be hundreds of porters with baskets full of oranges and tomatoes on their way to the markets. We lightened the load of one of them by buying some of his stock. With just half a dozen ferries, some of the porters would be waiting hours before they could cross.

Our first stop on the trek would be on the banks of the Bhor Khola, a tributary of the Sun Koshi and about two hours steady walking from our crossing point. The porters went on ahead of us and we arrived in late afternoon.

The porters had set up the camp site and had water on the boil ready to provide a welcome mug of tea. Mo and I sat on camp chairs next to Richard who was smoking a cigarette, I wasn't aware that Richard smoked and believed my being away from tobacco for a fortnight would help me kick the habit. I mentioned to Richard that I wasn't aware that he smoked, and he told me he only did while away on trek, as his wife thought he didn't smoke.

He had the drain pipe across his knees. He carefully removed the wooden plug from the end, and the secret of the pipe was revealed. Inside was a spinning rod in four sections. The rod was quickly assembled and, attaching a spinning spoon, handed the rod to Mokka, one of the porters, and they made their way to the water's edge, some hundred yards away.

I followed quietly behind, and when Richard had found a suitable spot to stand, he held out his hand to Mokka who placed the rod in his hand. Within five minutes the line went taut and the rod bent fiercely. A flash of gold broke the surface of the water some 50 yards downstream. More disturbance of the water was followed by a large bright golden fish leaping on the end of the line. After a ten-minute tussle, Richard finally landed his catch, a ten-pound Mahseer. Mokka was delighted when Richard handed him the fish, asking him to prepare it for our evening meal.

He quickly gutted and cleaned the fish and raced back to camp, returning a few minutes later with mugs of steaming tea which we drank while Richard continued his fishing.

Despite the Mahseer being common in the local rivers, Richard caught just that one fish during all his other attempts on the trek. He had landed a couple of 50 pounders a couple of years previously and had a photograph of his catch on the wall of his home. The current record for this fish is around 130 pounds, taken from Cauvery River in Bangalore. I managed to take half a dozen tiddlers weighing in at 7 or 8 pounds from the Arun River later in the year. I also lost one which broke the 40-pound line I was using at the time. Whether this was a very big fish or my inexperience as an angler, I shall never know.

As the evening drew on, it became chilly as mist started to rise above the river. We returned to the camp site, sat around a blazing fire, and tucked into our evening meal of curried fish and vegetables. Our porters had prodigious appetites, their plates piled high with curry, rice and dhal. The dinner was delicious and all went back for seconds. Richard's choice of Ratni as Sirdar and cook was obviously a good one.

It was still early evening when dinner was finished, but Mo and I were very tired from the early start and our first day of trekking. We retired to our tent after thanking Richard and the porters for dinner, got into our sleeping bags and were asleep within minutes.

I was awakened the next morning to a voice outside our tent calling, "Sahib, Memsahib, chai." It was Mokka with our morning tea. I took the steaming mugs and we enjoyed our first cuppa in bed for many years.

Poking my head out of the tent, I saw mist filling the valley and the air was cold. Sunrise would be another hour but the porters were already up and about, getting breakfast ready and tidying up the campsite. Through the mist, I could just make out the figure of Richard on the river edge trying his luck with the fish, but to no avail.

I was surprised to find myself ravenously hungry. I was normally a member of the coffee and toast brigade, but this morning I was ready for the proverbial horse. Throughout the trek I ate breakfast as if there would be no tomorrow. A plate of rice with last night's leftover curry, baked beans and a fried egg on top was eaten with relish. A couple of mugs of tea and I was ready to tackle Mount Everest.

After breakfast, Richard said we would trek 'Raj Style.' That meant an early start, leaving the porters to strike camp and repack the baskets; they would easily catch up with us, although one of them came with us, walking behind Mo, ready to help her over the many rocks and boulders. The first hour was most difficult as it took us along the rock-strewn meandering river valley. Going was slow as we picked our way through the rocks and wading through the river, which we must have done at least ten times. Mo had started off wearing her trainers, and at the first time she came to the river, she waded through it, ending up with her trainers soaking wet. She stopped and asked her guardian porter to get her walking boots out of one of the baskets. "No, Memsahib," he said. "More pani (water)."

The rest of the porters caught us up as we reached the bottom of a spur up which a narrow path led up and up, and would eventually lead us to our first destination, the welfare centre at Khotang. The baskets of three of the porters had new additions, pairs of socks, underwear, and t-shirts, washed out the previous evening and now drying in the morning sun.

We had both started out well wrapped up in the chilly morning air, but as we climbed the path and the sun rose higher, we became warmer from our efforts. Starting off in jeans, anorak, sweat shirt, our efforts had started to resemble a walking strip show. I had gradually stripped off and was now walking in shorts and T-shirt.

We climbed the path steadily over the next two or three hours. The porters ahead were picking up dry sticks and leaves heralding the sign of the morning tea break. A couple of them left the main party and headed up the track at a pace we could not hope to match. We met up with them half an hour later at a well-used spot on the side of the pathway, a fire burnt, camp chairs were out and tea was waiting to be drunk.

We rested for half an hour and added some extra energy with chocolate and some of the oranges we had bought the day before. Suitable refreshed, our water bottles were refilled from a nearby stream and sterilising tablets added to kill off any unseen bacteria that may have been lurking in the apparently crystal-clear water. Then we were off along the track for our evening stop at Chisopani.

We arrived at the small hamlet at dusk. Our camp site was set up on a flat section of dried-out paddy field. One of the porters was sent off to buy a chicken, and another to find a source of water. There was almost certainly a spring in the area as the name Chisopani meant 'cold water.'

We were soon the object of curiosity and were quickly surrounded by a group of local people, not used to seeing many white faces in this part of Nepal. Our tents and camp beds roused much amusement, as did our boots we were wearing, particularly among people used to walking around in bare feet.

Richard was chatting to some of them, asking questions about crops and water supply, when a tall distinguished gentleman strode up to him and engaged him in conversation. He turned out to be a local policeman who had that day walked from his village to Beltar, our lunch stop, and back again. He had taken a day to cover the same distance which would have taken us three. He spoke sharply to the crowd of onlookers who wandered off into the night. By pure coincidence, the field we were on belonged to him and he was only too pleased for us to camp overnight. Meanwhile, a loud squawking from around the camp fire informed us that dinner had arrived and was about to be consigned to the cooking pot.

Our journey from Chisopani to Khotang would take us most of the next day and was a steady climb to the top of the spur we had followed from the Bhor river valley. I had my usual breakfast of last night's curry with all the additions, along with a cup of tea. Mo, on the other hand, did not fancy my idea of breakfast and settled for a couple of boiled eggs and some crackers and cheese.

Within an hour of starting the climb up to Khotang, Mo was paying the price of having such a light breakfast, she said she could not go on and needed to rest. We made her eat a couple of Mars bars and two oranges. The result was within 20 minutes she felt ready to continue. She did not skip breakfast after that, although she gave early morning curry a miss.

We had our first sight of the welfare centre at Khotang at about three in the afternoon when Richard pointed out the corrugated metal roof reflecting in the sun, standing out from the thatched roofs of the houses near to it. We had the centre in view for most of the two hours it took us to reach it, having gone down from the spur into a valley, through a river, and up the other side.

We were greeted by Captain (Retired) Chettri who welcomed us to his centre. It was built in the style of a Swiss chalet with a south facing balcony to which Mo and I made our way up to enjoy the view across the hills and valleys.

It was sobering to recall that everything that made up the centre—every brick, bag of cement, nails and screws, and every other item of building material, along with the medical equipment and furniture, had been bought up from the Terai on the backs of teams of porters. Khotang was just two or three days from the main road and there were another 21 similar centres dotted around the foothills, some of them many days away and high into the Himalayas. The use of helicopters to transport building materials was dismissed as being prohibitively expensive at $2000 an hour.

After a short rest, I ventured downstairs to find the shower. It was in a courtyard but due to the dry winter the water pressure was low, only producing a steady trickle of freezing cold water.

One of the porters said he would fetch me a bucket of water from the stream below, so I stripped off and stood under the thin stream of the shower and soaped myself all over. A shout from outside told me my bucket of water had arrived and I called to the porter to let me have it intending to use it rinse myself off. Instead, the porter opened the door, leaving me standing there in my soapy nakedness and threw the bucket of ice-cold water all over me. I was sure most of the water was ice before it hit me, and my roar of shock must have been heard in the village below.

While our porters and Richard were tucking into a pork curry, Mo and I fancying a change, treated ourselves to a meal of tinned steak and kidney pudding, followed by army issue plum duff. One thing we were not worried about was adding inches to our waist lines, the exertions over the next few days would surely burn off any excess calories.

To show his satisfaction with the porters, Richard treated them to a couple of bottles of Roxi, a Nepalese spirit, distilled from fermented millet. The quality of this throat burning firewater depended on the number of times it had been 'through the pipe'—how many times it had been distilled. Tonight's brew was guaranteed a 'three times' product and was only slightly cloudy with just a hint of kerosene. It was certainly a change from my usual gin and tonic, and anyway, there was no gin, no tonic, and no lemon, although there may have been some ice left over from my earlier shower.

I rose early the next morning, having spent a comfortable night in a real bed with a real mattress. I went down to the medical room to have a look at the supplies of drugs and equipment in order for me to make any recommendations to Richard. The was a good range of items suitable for treating common ailments such as coughs, colds, stomach upsets and cuts and bruises, and the occasional simple fracture. Anything more serious would be a matter of first aid and transporting the patient to nearest hospital. Despite the limitations imposed by a tight budget, and judging by the numbers waiting outside, the centre managed to help quite a few people. I completed my inspection, made a few notes to serve as an aide memoire when I wrote my report for Richard.

We were getting ready to leave and say our goodbyes to Captain Chettri. A watery sun was rising above the ridge over which we would be travelling on to our next destination at Diktel. The captain looking knowingly at the sky suggested it may rain before mid-day. Hoping he wrong we said a final farewells and started out on day five of our trek. There would be two days of hard trekking to get to Diktel. It was intended to make the bottom of the valley below Diktel before nightfall which would allow us to arrive at the welfare centre before it got dark.

Within a couple of hours, it became apparent that the captain's prediction was likely to come true. Gradually, clouds began to form in the valley below the ridge and started to drift up towards us. Soon we were walking in a damp, clinging mist which found its way under our waterproof clothing and we were starting to get chilled. We were at about 8000 feet when a fine drizzle began to fall along with the temperature. The pathway quickly became slippery and after one of the porters fell heavily, Richard decided it was time to call a halt and quickly.

The pathway led down towards the river below and there was a cluster of houses on the ridge. We made our way towards these, Richard calling out to the occupants of one of the buildings who were inside keeping themselves warm beside their fire.

The farmer stepped out onto his veranda and Richard asked him if he could accommodate us for the night. The farmer replied that he was sorry but his house was full and the roof of his barn was being rethatched and would not be suitable for us. However, he suggested one of his neighbours, about half a mile up the ridge may be able to help.

Ratni was sent up to the other house pointed out to us, while we stood and shivered with the cold on the veranda. Mo needed to quickly get out of her wet clothes if she was not to get too chilled. The porters found her some dry clothes and a thick jumper from the baskets. Four of the porters held up a screen of blankets while she changed out of her damp skirt and top. The porters were careful to hold the blankets above their eye level so Mo's modesty was preserved as she struggled into the warmer clothes.

Ratni returned with the good news that he had found us board and lodging for the night and we made our way up to the farm house. Richard greeted the farmer, apologising for the inconvenience to him and his family. The apologies were waved away and we were invited in. There was just one large, gloomy smoke-filled room on the ground floor of the house. The upper floor was the sleeping accommodation for the farmer and his large family.

Chickens and goats wandered in and out with no concern for anyone. Two of the chickens were selected to be guests of honour at our evening meal and we settled down on the less crowded veranda to while away the rest of the day as the cold rain continued to fall. There was little likelihood of the weather clearing before nightfall so we made the best of our situation.

The original intention had been to arrive in Diktel the following afternoon. There was a market in the town which was open on this one particular day. Here we would be able to replenish our food supplies with more rice, vegetables, and other food stocks until we reached the bigger town of Bhojpur. Richard called for a volunteer to brave the weather and make his way to Diktel before nightfall, and make the necessary purchases at the market the next day.

Shyamm Tamang offered to make the trip, braving the weather and the treacherous downward pathway, and, after Richard handed over some cash and words of instruction, he disappeared into the mist and rain. On his own, and with no load in his basket he would surely make good time. Despite the slippery pathway, he arrived in Diktel before nightfall, found a bed for the night and went to the market the next day.

While Shyamm was heading off down the hill, we tacked up a few blankets across the open front of the veranda to keep out the wind. We also wrapped ourselves in spare blankets and tried to get warm again. Then we decided it was time to break out the medicinal whiskey. We had picked up a few lemons from a wayside shop to make hot toddies to keep out the cold. Three of our porters joined us, although they preferred Roxi to fine Scotch whiskey. Pretty soon though, with a combination of Scotch, hot water and blankets we were soon all glowing with warmth on the windswept veranda.

Ratni and Raj Kumar were inside preparing a chicken curry and I asked Richard why our other three porters were not with them, at least it would be warmer by the fire in the house. I was somewhat surprised by Richard's answer. The farmer was a Chettri, a fairly high caste in the hierarchy of Nepal, while the three porters were Limbu, Tamang and Moktan, much lower castes, and as a consequence were not allowed to be present while food was prepared. They would be allowed into the house to eat, but would be served last. Fortunately, Ratni, our Sirdar/cook, was also a Chettri, so he was welcome at the fireside. All this, 25 years after the caste system had been outlawed in Nepal and India.

After dinner, Mo and I retired to the hay loft and spent the coldest night of our lives, despite being wrapped in heavy feather and down sleeping bags. We both dozed fitfully through the long, cold night, wishing for the dawn.

The night finally fled, taking the rain with it. The morning brought clear skies above, and clouds rapidly disappearing into the valley below. A warmer day was forecast and the prospect dissipated the memories of the previous cold night.

By the time we were fully awake after a quick breakfast and a mug of tea, the porters had loaded their baskets, evenly dividing Shyamm's load between them. Two of them went on ahead to the bottom of the valley and the river side. There they would meet us and have a meal ready for us when we arrived.

Meanwhile, Richard was settling up with the farmer for our accommodation for the night. Altogether, eight of us had slept in and around his house, used a lot of his precious wood and water, and prepared our dinner from two of his chickens.

The asking price for this was about £4.00 and a small favour. Pointing to my camera, the farmer asked if I would take a picture of him and his wife. I immediately agreed and he dashed off to his house to re-emerge a few minutes later dressed in his best suit, his wife beside him in her Sunday Sari. I took a few pictures, including a few of him and his family, promising to send him copies as soon as I could.

When we returned to the cantonment, and after I had got prints of the pictures back from processing, I went to the Gurkha welfare office and asked them to let me know when there would be trekkers in the area again. Two months later a consignment of supplies was destined for Diktel, and one of the porters on the trip was requested to deliver the photographs. I have every reason to believe the pictures arrived safely and they are hanging on the wall of a wind-swept farmhouse, 8000 feet up in the foothills of the Himalayas.

We bade the farmer and his family a fond farewell and, accompanied by several of the villagers made our way downhill on the still slippery path to meet up with our two porters at the river. One of the porters stayed with Mo all the way down the track, lending her his strong arm over the most difficult part to prevent her from slipping.

Half way down we rested in the shade of a wayside Peepal tree. And Richard pointed out the village of Diktel resting in the saddle of a ridge in the distance. We finally got to the bottom of the valley at mid-day, and after negotiating a couple of very suspect bridges across the rivers, met up with our porters who had set up a temporary camp site and had lunch ready to eat. Mo joined us with her trusty porter 20 minutes after Richard and I had arrived.

We had made good time on our way down so we could take a leisurely lunch break before striking upwards towards Diktel. We followed a party of school children out for a picnic further on up the track and Richard walked a little way behind one of them who was carrying a portable radio. After a short while, Richard dropped back looking a little exasperated. He said he had been enjoying a play on the radio when its owner had changed the channel just as things were getting interesting.

We reached the western edge of the ridge which marked the start of the small hamlet of Diktel and made our way along its single main street. The welfare centre was at the other end of the village. Here we met up with Shyamm. The porter who had made the trip the previous day to get supplies from the market. He had been successful in buying food and enough rice to see us through the remainder of the trek. Richard decided that a further ration of Roxi was the order of the day.

We met the welfare officer who welcomed us to his centre. Fortunately, water here was plentiful, although very cold. I had not had a decent wash and shave for two days, but I was given a bowl of warm water for a shave before braving the freezing shower. Despite the cold water, I emerged clean and invigorated, urging Mo to take the plunge, her shouts as the water poured over her could have been heard all over Diktel.

Richard and I made our inspections the next morning. Both the medical consulting room and the small dispensary were clean and tidy, and reasonably well stocked. I made a number of notes and recommendations for my report to Richard when we returned to the cantonment.

Once we had finished our inspections, a small crowd had appeared, many of them, I was told, were here to collect their pensions. One by one they came forward, signed, or made his or her mark in the ledger, and received their pension.

Just before we left around 11 o'clock, Mo thought one of the porters had caught a chill as he was shivering, and she dug into one of the baskets and found one of her spare sweaters which she handed to him. I gave him a couple of aspirins to reduce his fever, telling him to see me if matters got worse during the day. We had a choice of route to take for our trek into Bhojpur—a shorter higher pathway which would take us up to 11,000 feet and save us a day, or a lower path which would still mean a climb up and over a ridge at 10,00 feet but would take three full days to complete.

The decision was taken for us when a visitor to the centre told us that heavy snow had fallen during the night and there was a meter of snow on the higher route. The prospect of being hit with bad weather a second time in three days was not appealing. The longer lower route was chosen and we started the final third of our trek.

We were given a fond farewell by the welfare officer who garlanded us with the traditional marigolds, wishing us a safe journey. We thanked him for his hospitality and began our walk to the bottom of the valley.

Here we encountered the first of many suspension bridges across a river flowing through a rocky gorge. I hung back up the path to take a photograph of our band of travellers. Having got the picture, I bounded off down the track to meet up with the rest. I made the mistake of running across the bridge which started bouncing and swaying under my feet. I had to grab hold of the supporting cables of the bridge to steady myself while the bridge stopped its oscillations. Looking up I could see the porters in fits of laughter as I wobbled around on the swaying bridge. I was careful not to be so enthusiastic on the bridges we crossed later.

Just up from the bridge we came to a wayside tea house and stopped for some refreshment. While we were drinking our tea, we could hear the sound of a group of men playing cards inside. Although we were unable to see inside, it was obvious the game was proceeding with excitement. Richard was speaking to the owner of the tea house when the noise from inside suddenly fell silent and one of the players poked his head outside.

On seeing Richard, his face broke into a broad smile and rushed forward and seized him by the hand, greeting Richard like a long-lost brother. After a few minutes, Richard realised this was a retired Gurkha soldier who had served with him over ten years previously in Hong Kong. The sound of Richard's voice had brought instant recognition to this man, and he and Richard spent the next half hour reminiscing about old times and mutual friends. The conversation took place in Nepali, and I understood not a word of it, except to say I recognised it as a happy reunion.

We left the tea house and climbed up the side of the river valley and eventually reached a dry paddy field where we pitched our tents. We could hear the sound of the river tumbling over the rocks far below. We both slept like logs after our evening meal, and the next day continued our on our way to Bhojpur. We finally crossed the ridge at 10,500 feet, just 500 feet below the snow-covered summit of Tembe. There was a cold wind against us as we made our way down towards our camp site near Dilpa for that night. We were hoping to have the tents up before the weather changed for the worst.

As usual, the porters were busy getting everything ready, and Raj Kumar had gone off to a nearby house to ask if they would sell him some firewood. He returned empty handed and told Richard they had no firewood. Richard laughed at this, saying that a house with no firewood in Nepal was like a house in Surrey with no bathroom. We all went foraging for fuel and soon had a large stockpile. There would be enough to prepare our dinner along with breakfast the next morning. There would also be enough left over for the people in the house.

The next morning dawned with ominous grey clouds shrouding the high ridge to the north. This would have been the track we would have travelled had we decided on the shorter route. Fortunately, the wind was blowing better weather towards us and soon the skies became clear and bright. The wind had dropped and the temperature rose. The clouds rose high over the ridge above to reveal a white covering of snow, the view through binoculars suggested a depth of about three feet. The choice of the longer, lower route was fortuitous. The thought being forced to spending another freezing night, this time in thigh deep snow did not bear thinking about.

From our vantage point high on the side of the ridge, we just make out the Pikhwa Kola river valley through the faint haze. We would be heading down this valley in two days' time on the final leg of our trip. Bhojpur was not visible to us except for the tell-tale wisps of wood smoke from cooking fires on the spine of the spur above the valley.

The walk to Bhojpur was a lot easier now we had passed over the high point of our journey. We still had a couple of high ridges to cross on our way, but for the most part we were slowly descending, and travelling along level pathways for the first time in a week.

We arrived at the welfare centre by mid-afternoon and were just in time to witness pension and allowances being paid to a large group of people waiting patiently in line to the welfare officer. He was seated at a table with piles of papers, ledgers and a large stack of Nepalese rupees. Each person produced an identity card, and, after signing or making a mark, made a thumb print in one of the ledgers, before being given their payment.

One old lady, wrapped in a blanket against the chill, sat propped up against the wall chatting tour porters and taking a well earn break. Meanwhile a young man was engaged in an animated conversation with the welfare officer. Richard joined in, and after a few moments the young man smiled and grasped Richard by the hand and went over to the old lady. Apparently, he had carried his grandmother in a doka for three days for her to collect her widow's pension. The journey was difficult at the best of times and, during the monsoon, well-nigh impossible.

He had asked for permission to collect his grandmother's pension on her behalf to spare her the long and uncomfortable trip to Bhojpur. This request could only be granted, usually after long and protracted correspondence by the welfare organisation back in the cantonment. In a country with poor communications, this might take months. It was fortunate that we arrived when we did. Richard was able to make the decision to allow the young man to collect his grandmother's pension and so eased the burden on both of them at pension time.

The centre overlooked the town of Bhojpur and Mo and I sat and watched the bustle of this important market town below. Its proximity to the larger towns on the Terai, about two or three days walk to the south, was indicated by the use of corrugated metal roofing in place of the thatch common in the villages to the north.

We could see down the length of the main street of the town with its busy open-air market and shops. All manner of goods were available for sale, brass and aluminium pots were piled high reflecting the early evening sun. Bolts of cloth splashed their bright colours along the street and occasionally we caught the piping sound of a flute played by a street musician.

As we had arrived in the afternoon Richard and I were able to complete our inspections and write up our reports in the evening, allowing us to make an early start the next morning. We had managed to make up the time we had lost on our way to Diktel, and, with our respective tasks for this trek complete, Richard was keen to get in some more fishing at Tribeni, which was day and a half away. We made our way along the main street, pausing to buy some fresh fruit and vegetables, along with few trinkets, and headed down towards the Pikhwa River.

The path downwards was well trodden with many porters on their way up and down the finger of the spur to and from the market in the town. Both sides of the track were covered in bushes, their bright pink and red blossoms heralding the coming of spring. There was a noticeable change tin the air as we descended; it was becoming noticeably warmer and more humid and we dropped below 2500 feet. Our two remaining nights in the open would not be interrupted by the cold.

On the way down, we passed through a village which had been destroyed by fire. With its distance from the river far below, it would have been impossible to fetch enough water to put out the fire, and every house was in ruins, which were blackened with soot. Richard made a note for enquiries to be made of the fate of the villagers.

The clucking of chickens as we passed through another small village of Harsa immediately bought to mind the menu for the evening meal. Having found the owner of the chickens, a bargain was struck for a couple of the best ones, and the business of rounding them up began. Two of the porters, Shyamm and Raj Kumar chased our dinner along the village street and into several houses and gardens, much to the amusement of the local population. They finally cornered and caught their quarry and tied them securely on to their baskets.

We turned off the main track and headed down a narrow twisting pathway which ended in the wide, flat Pikhwa River valley. The soft sandy floor of the river bed was bounded on either side by steep sided ridges, and being the dry season, the river was shallow, no more than 50 yards wide as it meandered along its sandy course. Its twists and turns took it tight against the valley walls and we were forced to ford the river many times before we reached the point where it joined the Arun.

A high-water mark on the rocks above our heads indicated the depth of this river during the monsoon. It was difficult to imagine the surface of this gently flowing river as we plodded through the soft sand being thirty feet above our heads in six months hence. We waded through the Pikhwa over twenty times before we finally reached the trail along the Arun River on the way to Tribeni.

We made our camp side on a sandy spot near the bank of the Arun, Richard trying his hand at catching a fish, but to no avail. Later in the evening once our two reluctant chickens became our dinner, a curry cooked to perfection by Ratni. Mo and I lay on our backs replete from our meal. There was no moon, the fire had died down and the night had a sharp, crystal clarity. I had never seen so many stars. The sky had an inky blackness of the kind one gets in the absence of light from towns and cities.

The dark and frosty night sky in England would be lit by just a few bright stars, but this paled into insignificance in the presence of this magnificent display. Scattered all over like salt crystals sprinkled over black velvet, the heavens above were full of thousands of twinkling pinpoints of starlight, ranging from the barely visible to the burning brightness of Jupiter.

Occasionally we spotted fiery trail of a shooting star and the track of a man-made satellite making its unwavering progress across the vault of the sky. Gazing up at the stars we could see some of the constellations and tried to remember the names of some of the millions of brighter stars arrayed above our heads. It was a sight to savour and one we were unlikely to see again in the short time we had left in Nepal.

The next day saw us trekking along a pathway high above the Arun and on our way to our final overnight camp at Tribeni. We were on the northern side of the river and we would have to cross the deep and swirling waters at some point. A couple of hours later we came to the crossing point to find a large boat tethered across the river by a stout rope hawser. This seemed to be a far safer prospect than the dug-out canoe we had used to cross the Sun Koshi some days ago.

We were joined by a number of porters, their baskets loaded with fresh produce bound for market. Most of rivers in Nepal rise by many feet in the monsoon season and I asked one of the porters how they managed during this period. He pointed to a steel cable high above the waters. A flimsy seat hung from the cable on thin wire and twisted slowly in the breeze. The whole contraption did not look strong enough to support a child, let alone a porter with a 40-kilogram load.

Once we were over the river, Richard was impatient for one last chance to continue his hunt for the elusive Mahseer and asked if we minded if he and Ratni made a dash for the camp site. We readily agreed and Ratni's load was distributed amongst the remaining five porters. Armed with only the drainpipe containing the fishing rod, a box of tackle and some cooking pots, the pair rapidly disappeared along the track. Richard was sure he would be at Tribeni at least two hours before the rest of us and he would get in half a day's fishing before we arrived. We all hoped he would be successful and looked forward to another dish of fried Mahseer later that evening.

We continued on our steady way, following the Arun, and stopping frequently at most of the tea stalls that were now becoming more numerous. I wasn't too concerned about our slow progress; the porters knew the way and they would not want to arrive at Tribeni in darkness. They would get us there in good time.

There was only one way of making tea in Nepal, and that was by tossing all the ingredients, tea, sugar, milk and water into a battered blackened kettle and bringing it to boil over an open wood fire. Despite using a method that would bring tears to the eyes of tea aficionados, the resulting brew was always welcome and refreshing.

Often spices such as nutmeg and pepper were sprinkled on top which certainly added to the flavour. We had encountered tea stalls in some very remote place on our travels, some of them visible in the distance before we got to them. The thought of a glass of tea a few miles along the track tended to add a spring to the step. The porters always knew where the tea stalls were to be found.

The sight of the towers of the suspension bridge across the Arun heralded our arrival at Tribeni. Our camp site was on the other side of the river on a triangular spit of land. On one side of this point ran the brown water of the Arun and on the other, the pea green Sun Koshi. Once across the bridge we climbed up to a knife edged ridge some 300 feet above the swirling waters on the rivers on either side. In some places, the pathway along the ridge was just a yard wide, and dropped off sheer cliffs on both sides into the waters below. Far below we could make out the tiny figure of Richard standing at the end of the spit and casting out for the Mahseer.

The two mighty rivers met at this point, but the power of their currents prevented them from intermixing completely until they tumbled over the rapids some 500 yards downstream and became the Sapt Koshi. Further down they were met by the Tamur, thus the three rivers gave the name of the place we were in—Tribeni.

Richard was casting into 'the seam' between the two rivers were the Mahseer hunts. He sent the lure some 75 yards into mid-stream to have the current bringing the line and lure back into the line where the two rivers met.

Richard was not successful and as time was pressing towards meal time one of the porters was despatched back to the village across the river to get some pork. He returned half an hour later with the pork and a few bottles of beer.

Mo and I decided to finish off the remains of the tins of compo rations, thus lightening the loads of the porters by a couple of tins of goulash, new potatoes and apple pudding, followed by the last of the cheese and oatmeal biscuits. Our final meal was almost a gourmet affair, all we needed to finish off our last meal on trek was a bottle of vintage port, but a bottle of Star beer would do nicely.

Rising early the next morning, I decided to treat myself to the first decent bath I had had in a week. The Sun Koshi had cut its way into the bank and created a deep pool, known as the 'sheep dip' away from the pull of the strong current. I plunged into the water, gasping at the chill. Cold as it was, the temperature was higher than that of the Arun a few yards across from me. The Sun Koshi originated from the glaciers of the distant mountains to the west and gained some heat from the sun on its way southwards. The track of the Arun was shorter and its cold glacial waters did not have the benefit of a warming from the sun.

I spent about ten minutes splashing around and singing bathroom songs, soaping myself all over to remove the dust and grime of a week travelling along dusty pathways. Standing on the river bank, I towelled myself off to a rosy glow. It was not until I turned to make my way back to camp that I realised my ablutions had been witnessed from the far bank by a group of children who were now beside themselves with laughter at the sight of the antics of a naked mad white man at 6 o'clock in the morning.

By the time I returned, the camp was packed away ready for the last leg of our trek. Finishing off a quick breakfast we made our way back up along the ridge and down to the suspension bridge across the Tamur River. This was a well-constructed bridge, its footway being 100 feet above the dry season level of the river. Below us on both banks of the river were stumps of brick and concrete, standing out like broken teeth.

Some years previously, American engineers had decided to build a bridge at this point, and in order not to get caught out by a rise in the water level during the rainy season, had carefully inspected the records of the depth of water in the gorge over the past forty years.

It was decided that whoever had taken the level in one previous year had imbibed too much Roxi the night before. Adding a few feet to allow for error the bridge was built 70 feet above the dry season bed of the river. In 1968, the river rose 80 feet in one night and swept the bridge away!

The new bridge, built by British engineers is 100 feet high and bounces and sways as the wind whistles through the gorge. The area along the course of the river until it joins the Sapt Koshi was still littered with the rubble left by the momentous cataract. Looking down to the waters far below it was impossible to imagine the volume and power of the waters contained within the bottleneck of the gorge 15 years previously.

Apart from the knife edge, the pathway had been relatively safe and presented little danger from falling down the ridges or off a cliff. The final part of the walk Barahakshetra was altogether a different matter. The track had been hacked out the cliff high above the river and in several places the cliff overhung the path forming a low archway under which we were forced to duck down. A number of times we had to press tightly against the cliff face as people coming the other way approached with loads that scraped along the sides. Most frightening was meeting the occasional farmers driving their herds of cattle or goats along the narrow track. We stayed flat against the wall until they had passed by, dislodging stones off the path into the water below.

Twice we negotiated small landslides, rocks and stones cascading down from above. In a number of places, the path was broken away, leaving a gap just narrow enough to cross with a long stretch. It was difficult to imagine how the local people managed, so easily it seemed, with their heavy loads or driving animals along. We had heard reports of porters falling to their deaths from this stretch and we picked our way carefully along it. This particular path is one of the oldest in Nepal, being an ancient salt trail, winding its way into the far north, across the mountains and into Tibet.

Away in the hazy distance we could make out wide expanse of water as the Sapt Koshi had built up into a lake behind the Koshi Barrage. Here the strong currents and the great weight of water tumbling down from the Himalayas would be put to use generating electricity for this part of Nepal. The lake also served as a resting place for many thousands of water birds during migration season when the surface of the waters would be covered by up to a quarter of a million birds. We could also hear the muffled sound of blasting echoing around the surrounding hills.

Soon the track became wider and rounding a bend the temples of Barahakshetra came into view. The name of the village means twelve temples, and domes and spires dominated the view. We crossed over the final suspension bridge of our trek, swaying over the dry bed of the Khoka Kola (really!), and entered the village. As usual we collected an entourage of chattering and laughing children who stayed with us for a mile or so along the track out of the village.

We now discovered the reason for the blasting we had heard earlier. A new road was being built allowing vehicles up to and through the village. And for the next few miles we had the treat of walking along a flat, graded surface. Occasionally the road bent around a rocky outcrop or followed the contour around a re-entrant formed by two spurs. It was here a gang of labourers toiled away to drive the road through this most unyielding terrain.

Crowds of workers high on the hillside wielded pickaxes and crowbars and a pall of red dust overhung the area. Now and then a large boulder would be grudgingly dislodged and levered over the edge, throwing up great clouds of dust as it crashed down the hillside into the undergrowth below.

The sight of the Land Rover waiting on the road just above Chhatra signalled the end of our trek in the hills. I was both glad at the prospect of not having to walk anymore, and sorry that the wonderful experience of the previous twelve days was over.

Despite the cold, the rain, the long, hard days of continual uphill walking, Mo and I had enjoyed the trek. The memory of these days will stay with me forever, the amazing people we met on the way and the beautiful scenery will never leave me. I had shot a dozen rolls of transparency film and I never tire of watching the slides produced from them.

Our porters had done us proud and not one of them had made the least complaint as they toiled away on the trek, often singing as they went along. The slow pace and the lightness of their loads may well have made the trip one of the easiest they had done for a while. Nevertheless, they had looked after us well, particularly towards Mo, helping her along the way when she found the going difficult. They had earned their bonusses in addition to their agreed wages.

Martha, Tika and Raj were pleased to see us when we arrived back home in the afternoon. The first thing Martha asked us was what we would like to eat. Having got through a fair amount of curry and chicken during the trek, Mo and I both asked if there was any fish in the freezer. Of course, there was, and Martha had pre-empted us and had a fish pie in the refrigerator.

We both needed a good wash before dinner, and I let Mo go first, before I enjoyed a long, hot soak in the warm shower. When I had finished, there was a trail of sand and mica in the bottom of the bath. Over the next few days, I was continually finding grains of sand in the bath after my shower, left over from the sediments in the rivers we had washed in during our travels.

I returned to work to find my two Nepali staff looking down in the mouth. Before I could ask what was troubling them, MB said that Ranjit wanted to see me as soon as I came in. I went round to his office, and as I wished him a cheery good morning, he handed me a signal from the embassy in Kathmandu.

I had to read it twice, as I did not believe what I had read the first time. Once I understood the message, the air in Ranjit's office turned blue. The Nepalese government had impounded the all the medical supplies for Dharan unloaded from two flights from the UK. We had inadvertently overspent our budget for supplies into Dharan.

The vagaries of the Nepalese financial system meant that their financial year started in August. The volume of supplies arriving in February was more than our budget allowed. We had received few supplies from UK in the previous year to the end of August and up to that point although our budget was well under spent, we were not allowed to carry any surplus underspend forward. I had not been made aware that we had budgetary constraints, and as far as I was concerned this was a matter for DMED to keep under control.

I went to see Maj G, my commanding Officer. He said he had seen the signal and he suggested that we may have to shut the hospital down until the problem was resolved. I explained that we had minimal supplies in the stores and we would have to cope until things became untenable. Meanwhile, the signal did state the Ambassador and the military liaison officer at the embassy were in negotiations to try and bring the situation to a satisfactory conclusion, especially as over ninety percent of the drugs and medical equipment were used to treat Nepalese nationals.

A signal to the embassy suggesting the release of urgent antibiotics and medicines, particularly for tuberculosis, along with pain killers and antiseptics could somehow be allowed. I was particularly concerned as to how some of the items that were subject to temperature control were being stored. I received reassurance that the warehouse holding our stock was air-conditioned and temperature sensitive items were kept in refrigerators.

Over the next two or three weeks we received a dribble of items which managed to keep us ticking over. I also received a package containing the vouchers supporting the stock being held. Going through this large amount of paperwork it became clear that my original order for stock back in March and April the previous year was on board the flight. My signal later in the year requesting the orders be expedited had also been fulfilled. Therefore, the flight contained a doubling of the orders for all the stock requested over the previous nine months, that duplication overspent the budget.

I later found discovered what had caused the chaos. My original orders had been processed, picked, packed, and sent for despatch. The equipment was loaded on to an aircraft ready to be shipped out to us. Then the war in the Falklands started, and all available aircraft were needed to head for the South Atlantic. My stores were unloaded and stored in a warehouse on the RAF base. My later signal itemising all the stock I had requested and not yet received and I asked for it to be sent as soon as possible.

Following the end of hostilities in the Falklands, matters started to return to normal. My indent for supplies was picked, packed, and sent off for despatch by RAF transport, to the same airbase as the first shipment. Here someone discovered the original consignment and this was loaded onto another flight.

One of my staff in the stores was MB who turned up for work one morning with a bruised face. Before I could ask him what had happened, the telephone rang. It was Ranjit asking MB and myself to come to his office.

It transpired that MB had overheard a conversation by one of the hospital's Nepalese assistants suggesting that the shortage of drugs was all my fault. At this MB had intervened to defend my honour and a minor fracas had started. As a result, the assistant had been floored, but not before he had landed a punch on MB's face. Ranjit was prepared to fire MB, but I asked him to reconsider and told him I would deal with the matter.

I took MB into the stores and proceeded to give him a severe dressing down, telling him to go home for the day and lose a day's pay. He was very contrite and turned to leave, but not before I shook his hand and thanked him for his loyalty to me. Returning to Ranjit, I told him what I had done and he was placated. I had kept MB who was an invaluable member of my staff and I would not have been happy to lose him.

It took six weeks for the embassy staff to gradually convince the Nepalese government to release all the stores being held in Kathmandu and I was advised by signal to expect a delivery within a couple of days. It duly arrived on four truckloads, piled high with boxes. It took most of the day to unload and isolate the boxes containing the most needed items, which were unpacked quickly and placed into stock. I had asked the various departments in the hospital to give me a list of what they were most in need of, these lists were passed onto the dispensary staff and they were told to give them the highest priority.

Everyone was happy, most of all my boss, Major G, who could now get on with running his hospital, as we now had an abundance of supplies.

Two or three days later I received my dozen rolls of film back from processing in UK. I went through them carefully, discarding duplicates, and under and over exposed results. I eventually ended up with about 120 transparencies which would do as a pictorial record of our adventure.

Heather, Richard's wife, had gone to Kathmandu for a few days, and while she would be away, I invited Richard to come over to our house in the evening to see the slides. Over a supper of drinks and sandwiches I showed the slides, Richard saying how much he was enjoying the photographic record of our trek.

I had just passed the point where the pictures showed our night and the following morning at the farmer's house when he asked me to go back a couple of slides. I came to the one where we were standing with the farmer and his wife, thanking them for their hospitality. In the photograph, Richard was plainly to be seen holding a cigarette.

He asked me to remove this particular slide in case Heather should see them. I had arranged to show the slides to the children and adults at the school, and Heather would be back from Kathmandu by then. Richard was convinced his wife was not aware that he smoked. Indeed, he stopped smoking completely a couple of days before our trek ended, and didn't start up again until he was away from the cantonment on another trek.

The boys and some of the other children came to Dharan for the Easter holiday, Mo went to Calcutta with Pat and a couple of the other wives to escort them to Dharan.

Shortly before the holiday an expedition to the mountains had been arranged with the purpose of trying to climb Kala Patthar. This was mountain was just 18,500 feet and therefore a licence to climb was not required. The trek up it is not particularly long, but it is uphill and at altitude. The group included Wes and his son Mark, John W the QM, his wife, and a couple of others.

They flew into Lukla, known as the most dangerous airport in the world. The building of which was supervised by Sir Edmund Hilary in 1964 who bought the land from local farmers. Originally a grass strip, it was flattened by the local population who stomped on it for a few days to compact the soil, it was eventually paved in 2001.

The group spent two days walking to the Everest base camp at Namche Bazaar. The distance was just eight and a half miles, but because of the altitude going was slow. The cantonment received a signal from Namche to tell us they had arrived safely and had set up camp for the night. That was the only message we received for several days; we were getting quite worried as we had had news of heavy snow in the area.

We learnt later that communications from Namche were lost for 5 days, meanwhile the party had left for Kala Patthar.

They reached their objective in 2 days, spending a night in Dingboche. Three of the party got to the summit of Kala Patthar, the others beaten by the altitude. They then returned to Namche where they found communications had been restored and they were able to contact the cantonment. We were all relieved that they were safe and sound.

Towards the end of the Easter break Wes had arranged to take a few of the Children to Tribeni for a weekend. He did most of the arrangements, borrowing tents and cooking utensils from the ordnance depot, along with a good supply of compo rations. Apart from Jason and Justin in Cyprus, I do not think many of the children had ever eaten compo. Wesley also organised the porters; Ratni, our Sirdar from our trek, was amongst them, and would be the head porter. Our gardener, Raj, asked if he could come along as well as a porter and general handy man. Wes and I were glad to have him along.

We took about eight children and one or two other adults to Tribeni, using two Land Rovers to fit everyone in. We drove to Barahakshetra where we were dropped off, walked across the bridges and up to and along the knife edge. The porters had gone ahead the day before to set up the camp site, and take the supplies for the weekend.

Everything was ready for us, as usual the porters had done a good job, selecting the best spot in the shade for our camp site. Wesley called all the children together and warned them about some of the dangers of Tribeni, not least of which was the swirling currents of the rivers, telling them the only safe place to bathe was the 'sheep dip,' the pool worn away on the bank of the Sun Koshi.

By the time, we had everyone settled, it was time for lunch. Wes decided he needed a siesta in the afternoon and I helped him rig up a hammock between two sturdy trees. He heaved himself into the hammock, saying how comfortable it was. Just then, one of the ropes broke and Wes hit the ground and yelled in pain. Directly below the hammock was a sharp rock and Wes had landed on it, the small of his back took the full force of the fall.

Fortunately, Wes had a fair amount of muscle around the area which had absorbed most of the impact, although a large bruise was beginning to appear. I gave him some paracetamol to ease his pain and he hobbled off to his tent to lie down. Over the next couple of days, Wes's discomfort eased with the help of pain killers, although he was quite bruised around the small of his back. An X-ray when we returned to Dharan showed no broken bones or internal damage, and he was fully recovered by the end of the week.

Wes and I went fishing, hunting for the big prize, a large Mahseer. Over the weekend we took about ten fish from the rivers, none of them being big enough for us to get excited over. One or two went back as being too small, but a good few were big enough to make fish curry for the porters and those of us who were happy to have a plateful or two. I believe I hooked a big one which broke the forty-pound line I was using, maybe it was my inexperience as an angler but I like to think it was the one that got away.

There were no Easter eggs for the kids, shipping them in from home or from Hong Kong was far too expensive. We had taken the precaution of bringing a couple of tins of chocolate bars from the compo ration packs. Each tin contained ten bars of Cadbury's dairy milk chocolate, so there was plenty to go around. There was also a plentiful supply of boiled sweets.

Raj surprised the adults by going to a nearby village and bringing back a dozen bottle of the local brew—Star Beer. We were happy to repay him, although he first refused to take our money. The purchase of the beer was, for him, the equivalent of a week's pay.

We played cricket and football, bathed in the sheep dip, and generally had a good time with plenty of fun over that weekend. We were all sorry it had to end. The porters struck camp, tidied up and burnt the rubbish, while we made our way back to Barahakshetra and the waiting Land Rovers to take us back to Dharan.

The boys returned to their usual holiday activities in the cantonment, exploring around on their bikes, swimming and playing golf. Jason entered the weekend competitions on the golf course and won a junior match play against one of the other children and got his name on the competition board in the club house before I did.

All too soon it was time for them to return to school. Mo went to Calcutta with Pat Higginson to escort them on their way. On the way back from Bagdogra, after seeing the children onto their flight to UK, Pat asked Mo if we would like to accompany them on a holiday to Sri Lanka in May. They would be going with their youngest daughter, Pippa, and one of the nursing sisters, Anne, from the hospital.

When Mo asked me, I readily agreed. Pat and Wes had already arranged for a driver to pick us up and take us around the island, others from the cantonment had already used the man and he came highly recommended. We were intending to use government rest houses for our accommodation and a couple of these had been provisionally booked. I applied for leave and bought tickets for the flight, which had us flying from Biratnagar to Kathmandu, and from there by Royal Nepalese Airlines to Colombo in Sri Lanka.

We arrived in Kathmandu in good time for the afternoon flight to Sri Lanka. We boarded the Boeing 737, after minimal security checks and waited for take-off. We were all seated and belted in, when a couple of men, one carrying a tool kit, entered and made their way onto the flight deck.

There followed a lot of hammering and banging from the cockpit, and after half an hour the two men emerged carrying a flight chair. Half an hour later, the two men returned with what appeared to be a replacement chair. A further chorus of hammering and banging followed and the two men left. The cabin doors were closed and we took off on our flight to Sri Lanka.

Once we were airborne, I stopped one of the cain staff to ask what all the noise was about. She told me the flight engineer wasn't happy with his seat and demanded it be changed. Only on Nepalese Airlines would make repairs to a loaded aircraft take place on the runway prior to take-off, any other airline would have delayed the flight for an hour while the problem was fixed. At least, it was only a chair, and not a nose wheel, which had been the problem 18 months previously on our flight in the Avro from Kathmandu to Biratnagar when we first arrived in Nepal.

We were met at the airport in Colombo by our driver Edwin, who took us to our hotel in a comfortable air-conditioned minibus, telling us he would be ready and waiting for us at 8.30 the next morning.

Our first stop was the Galle Face hotel, one of the finest hotels in Sri Lanka. We visited the shops in the arcade, ending up in a jeweller. Edwin probably had an arrangement with the owner as trays of precious and semi-precious stones were placed before us. Sri Lanka is famous for sapphires and topaz, and Mo was particularly taken with a large heart-shaped orange-yellow stone.

The jeweller suggested he could make Mo a pendant with the stone and asked how long we would be staying in Sri Lanka. Telling him we were touring and would be back in Colombo in two weeks, the jeweller said he would have the topaz pendant ready on our return. He did not want any money, and we could pay if and when we returned to his shop. The price he was asking for the finished item was ridiculously cheap, and I agreed we would come back in a fortnight.

We continued on our tour around the south of the island, staying overnight in a couple of government rest houses. These were basic and cheap, but comfortable, close to shops and restaurants. We had taken a supply of drinks, and for the most part ate our meals in local restaurants.

At one of the places, where we were to spend the night, Edwin took us to the rest house, and we were not too impressed with it. At this point, he suggested we stay at the local 5-star hotel. Wes had a guide book with him and, looking up the details of the suggested hotel, said it was far too expensive.

However, Edwin was insistent, and to appease him decided to go and have a look at it. Unknown to us, this side of the island was out of season and hotel prices were rock-bottom. The hotel was cheaper than the rest house, and almost empty. It was built into a cliff and from our balcony overlooked the sea and the beach below.

Wes and I went down to the beach for a swim, despite the sea looking a little rough. There was strong wind blowing but the waters of the Indian Ocean were warm, though neither of us ventured out too far, as the waves were getting strong. I was just heading back to shore when I heard Wes shout. I looked round and saw and enormous wave breaking. The next thing I knew was lying a hundred yards up the beach having been deposited like a piece of drift wood by the breaker. Wes was a few feet further up the beach, and it was then we noticed the red flags, and the notice advising that swimming in the sea was not advisable!

We stayed two nights at the hotel, gave the sea a miss before we made our way up the east coast to Batticaloa. On the way, we stopped off to watch a most unusual way of fishing. These were the stilt fishermen who stood on small precarious crucifixes held together with string and wire and standing in the sea while they angled in the shoals of fish as they swam by in the shallows. It looked to be a decidedly dangerous occupation which started during the second World War and its consequential food shortages.

We continued on to Batticaloa where were offered a choice of cabanas on the beach, some with a tiled roof or some with a thatched roof, the latter being half the price of the former. When asked why the difference in price, the manager told us the thatched cabanas were cheaper because they leaked in the rain! We took our chances with the thatched roof.

From there, we headed up to Trincomalee, where we would spend our final week before heading back to Colombo by train. We said our goodbyes to Edwin who promised to meet us at Colombo station.

It was during our week in Trincomalee that we realised we had a cash flow problem. Wes had been down to the bank to get some cash against his credit card only to find the bank was unable to help, it was only the main banks in Colombo that were able to make a credit card transaction. I had sufficient cash to pay the hotel bill and enough to pay for the occasional meals at the local restaurants. I also had about £250 in Nepalese and Indian rupees, but these were not exchangeable in Sri Lanka.

I was taking a dip in the ocean, when another guest staying at the hotel came up to say hello. We got into conversation while standing knee deep in the warm waters and he told me he and his wife were on honeymoon. I congratulated him and introduced myself. He told me his name was Ralph and they were from Rhodesia, but as that country was rapidly becoming unstable, they had decided to leave and travel for a few months before eventually settling in Australia. Their next port of call was Nepal!

Asking him when they were going to be there, he said they were flying out to Kathmandu the coming Saturday. I told him all our party lived in Dharan and we were probably on the same flight. During the course of our conversation, he asked me if I had any plans to see a bit more of Sri Lanka. I mentioned that a serious shortage of cash meant we were not going to be able to get away before we left for Colombo. I told him I had plenty of Nepalese currency but it was of no use.

He suggested that as were going to on the same flight, he could cash some traveller's cheques at the bank and exchange my Nepalese currency I had with me for Sri Lankan Rupees. I was completely taken by surprise. Here was a chap I had only met half an hour ago, we were standing up to our knees in the Indian Ocean, and he was prepared to help me out to the tune of around £200! I asked him if he was absolutely sure about it, and he said he was only too pleased to do the exchange, and he would go to the bank that afternoon.

We had just returned from our evening meal and we were in our room at the hotel when there was a knock at the door. I opened it to find Ralph telling me he had some good news for me. I asked him in and invited him to take a seat. He handed over about £250 in Sri Lankan Rupees.

I had an idea of the current exchange rate at the banks, which was not as good as the Forces Fixed Rate which was what we were paid in Dharan. I told him this and said I would pay him the better rate, and proceeded to count out the Nepalese rupees for him. We were both happy with the transactions, and so was Mo as I had told her if everything worked out with Ralph, we could take a trip to Kandy the following day.

We went out for a drink with Ralph and his wife, along with Wes and his family. I told Wes we were going off to Kandy the next day and would be away overnight. I had hired a driver to take us for a few rupees, wait and bring us back. With an overnight stay, and the driver, I reckoned the trip would cost about £40, leaving us with enough money to see us out until we got back to Nepal.

We left for Kandy early the next morning, stopping off at the Dambulla Cave Temple where we spent an hour wandering around looking at the paintings and statuary. There were over 150 statues of Buddha and around 80 caves to the complex, although only five were in use and we would not have enough time to explore more. The complex would become a world heritage site in 1991.

A couple of hours drive from Dambulla saw us on the outskirts of Kandy. Our driver took us to what he assured us was a reasonably priced hotel where we got a room for the night. The hotel was clean and comfortable, and true to the driver's word it reasonably priced.

The first place we visited early the next morning was the famous 'Temple of the Tooth.' Here, we joined the throng of visitors, both Buddhist devotees and tourists like ourselves, waiting to see the ancient the tooth of Buddha. Mo bought a spray of fragrant flowers as an offering, not because she was religious, but she thought it was the right thing to do. We finally got to see the gold container housing the tooth. The container is in the shape of a Buddhist stupa, kept in a glass case, the tooth itself not being visible.

The temple had become a world heritage site in 1982. Legend has it that whoever holds the tooth had governance of Sri Lanka. The temple has been attacked with bombs twice in an attempt to take possession of the tooth—in 1989 by the militant JVP and again in 1998 by the Tamil Tigers during the civil war. Neither attack gained possession of the tooth, and the temple was restored very quickly after the bombings.

We left the temple after an hour and wandered around the sights of Kandy, making our way up a hill looking over the lake and the temples. The view from this point was spectacular. The temple is surrounded by a number of buildings of historical significance, including the Queen's bathing pavilion on the edge of the lake.

After having a quick lunch, it was time to meet up with our driver at the hotel, and make our way back to Trincomalee. Apart for a brief stop for refreshments we made it back to our hotel in Trincomalee in about four and a half hours, just in time for dinner. Wes had got a bottle of Arrack, the local spirit distilled from the sap of the coconut flower. It was pretty powerful stuff, but diluted with Coca Cola it was eminently drinkable.

The next day was our last in this part of Sri Lanka, and we were leaving in the evening on the night mail train to Colombo. We spent most of the day on the beach and in the sea, watching local fishermen row out quite a way and deploy their net. They then came back, waited on the beach for an hour or so, then two teams began hauling the net back to shore. We had watched them a few times over the past week, sometimes the catch was plentiful, more often than not there was very little in the net to show for their exertions.

We caught the night mail train from Trincomalee to Colombo just before midnight, the train was quite empty and the vacant seats allowed us to doze away the eight-hour journey. Edwin was waiting for us at the station and took us to the Galle Face hotel where we picked up the topaz pendant the jeweller had made for Mo. It was quite beautiful, in a gold heart-shaped setting and a fine gold chain. The cost was a little over £20.

Wes, meanwhile, had gone over to the hotel reception and managed to get them to advance him some money on his credit card and he returned with a broad grin on his face now that he was solvent once more. It was hard to believe he was the Paymaster in Dharan and handled huge amounts of money!

Once we had freshened up in the hotel toilets, Edwin took us to the airport for our flight back to Kathmandu. We would stay overnight at the Nook as our flight to Biratnagar was mid-morning the next day. We met up with Ralph and his wife and I told them to stay close to us when we arrived in Kathmandu as we may be able to speed their way through customs and immigration.

This time there were no delays with our flight and we arrived in Kathmandu on time. Major Ganesh was still there and was waiting for us. I mentioned to him that the Rhodesian couple were with us. The Major accompanied all seven of us to immigration and passports where an exchange in Nepali took place. Our passports were stamped without comment and we headed to baggage retrieval.

The Major pointed the customs official to all our cases which were duly marked with a cross and released without being examined. We thanked the Major and exited the airport 45 minutes after getting off the aircraft.

The next day we boarded our flight to Biratnagar and home, all of us agreeing that we had had a great holiday, despite the problems with the shortage of cash, although Ralph had solved mine.

Five weeks after we returned to Dharan Sri Lanka erupted into civil war which was to last for over a quarter of a century. The number of casualties of this bloody period has never been calculated, although some estimates put the number of dead and injured at over 200,000.

A few weeks before we went to Sri Lanka, my CO called me to his office. Here we discussed the matter of my annual confidential report which he was preparing to write. He asked me how many points I thought I would need in order to get promoted to warrant officer. I suggested I would need in excess of 105. Confidential reports at the time were far from confidential. We all rang around our contemporaries to ask them what they had scored. Out here in Nepal I would be unable to do this, so it was just a case of keeping my fingers crossed.

In the event, my CO wrote a gold-plated report on my performance, along with a very high score. I was convinced that report resulted in a posting order arriving while we were away posting me to BMH Hannover with the substantive rank of WO2. The date of the posting was to be confirmed.

Towards the end of June, Mo began to feel unwell, she complained of nausea and diarrhoea. Over the next couple of days, she gradually got worse and, on the Saturday, she collapsed in intense pain. As she was unable to walk the short distance to the hospital, I called the BMH and asked for an ambulance to come and pick her up to see the physician. The ambulance arrived within minutes and Mo was taken up the road where she was quickly diagnosed with amoebic dysentery.

She was put to bed and given an intravenous drip of dextrose and saline to combat her loss of fluids. She was also treated with a drug to kill the amoeba infection. After two doses, Mo was suffering from the side-effects of the drugs and hid the third dose under her pillow.

Unfortunately for Mo, one of the nursing sisters found them, and after that, stood over her to make sure she took them. Mo was feeling a lot better after a couple of days having been given other medication to ease the side-effects of the drug. She was discharged on the evening of the third day. She rested at home for a few days before getting back to her normal life.

It would soon be time for the boys to come out for the summer holidays, and this would be their last trip out to us before we left Dharan for the UK and eventually to Hannover. There was a slight problem this time because the end of term times were different; Justin would be travelling first, followed by Jason a week later.

Mo and I had written to both of them and received replies telling us they were completely unfazed at travelling alone, they had both made the journey half a dozen times together and knew what they had to do.

With Mo and I were both confident that the boys would be alright and well looked after by airline staff, we made the necessary arrangements to go down to Calcutta to pick them up. I would go first with Wes to pick up Mark and Pippa, and I would meet Justin.

We were up early to meet the plane when it arrived. Standing on the balcony of the observation deck we watched the aircraft land and taxi to the terminal. We could see the children coming down the steps, first was Mark and Pippa who spotted Wes and waved, but where was Justin?

About five minutes after everyone was off the aircraft, I heard an announcement asking me to go to the BA information desk. I hurried over, expecting the worst. A member of BA staff invited me into the office where I was told that Justin had been taken off the flight from Birmingham at Heathrow with a suspected severe ear infection, and kept overnight in the medical centre. Because of this it was felt he should not be allowed to make the trip to India.

He had been examined by a doctor the following morning who found no evidence of an ear infection. He was then put on a flight back to Birmingham to be met by my mother who took him home to her flat.

Still somewhat perplexed I returned to Dharan with Wes and his children. I told Mo what had happened and went across to the movements office. They assured me that Justin was with his grandmother and arrangements had been made for him to come out to us with his brother the coming week.

Mo went down to Calcutta with Pushpa Rai. This time both our boys arrived safely, Justin looking fit and healthy. They all returned to Dharan where we found out what had happened on the original flight from Birmingham to Heathrow.

Justin's plane had flown through a heavy thunderstorm, and in the process was struck by lightning. Although the aircraft and passengers were never in any danger. Justin ended up with a headache and ringing in his ears, which gave rise to the initial diagnosis of an ear infection.

As this was the last time the boys were going to travel to Nepal we decided on a celebration. It would be Justin's birthday in August when he would be 12 years old and Mo and I planned a party in our garden. I made enquiries with various departments on the cantonment with a view to having a marquee erected, refrigerators for cold drinks, and asking Bill, our butcher, to get sufficient barbeque supplies for around 50 people, he was due to go to Calcutta in the next couple of weeks and I gave him our shopping list. I asked the chefs in the Sgts Mess to make us burger buns on the day.

We had a barbeque stand in the garden and I told Martha what we were planning and asked her if she would be able to manage doing the cooking for around 50. She said she would get her husband, Michael, to help out, and she was confident that between them they would supervise the cooking. Raj and Tika would also be on hand to help out.

To keep the children amused and occupied while Martha and Michael prepared the food for the barbeque, I organised a bicycle orienteering competition around the cantonment. I had obtained a map of the cantonment and I secreted 20 numbered markers around with a question on the back. The markers were all over the place, some in the rough on the golf course, some in the farthest parts of the cantonment, under bridges over the monsoon drains, all would take about two hours of hunting to find them. With a map to guide them, the children would have to find all the markers, answer the questions, and return to our house. Whoever got most questions right would get a prize.

The day before the party a large refrigerator was delivered and plugged in on the veranda and once the temperature had dropped most of the beer and soft drinks delivered from the shop were loaded into it. There were quite a few bottles of drinks which would need to be cooled, but we would solve that problem with a couple of large unglazed terracotta pots bought from the market a few months ago. Filled with cold water which evaporated from the surface from the porous surface of the pots, they would be quite efficient in keeping the contents cool.

Early on the morning of Justin's birthday, half a dozen Gurkha soldiers arrived in a Land Rover. In a trailer on the back was a marquee. The Gurkhas proceeded to erect the tent and its panel in the centre of the garden. They had obviously done this before as within a couple of hours they had it up. I gave them all a beer apiece and they left with smiles and waves all round.

We had plenty of chairs, crockery and cutlery, all borrowed from our neighbours. Tables came from the ordnance depot, as did the refrigerator. We were expecting around forty people, mostly children and a few adults who would help out with the drinks and serving the food.

We were all set for the party, all we now needed was for our guests to arrive.

Gradually all the children had arrived and I got them together and told them about the competition, gave them each a map of the cantonment and sent them on their way. I reckoned it would take at least an hour and a half for the kids to complete the competition, so we had planned for a little after 1.30 to have lunch ready.

Martha and Michael had part-cooked a lot of the barbeque meat in the oven in the kitchen and all would be ready when the orienteering was over, the burgers and sausages would be re-heated on the barbeque and everyone could sit and enjoy lunch. We had a couple of gallons of rum punch for the adults along with plenty of soft drinks for the children. There were also a couple of neighbours' household staff who turned up to help out with the serving and washing up.

The food was perfect and every one enjoyed their lunch. Wes and I checked the answers to the orienteering quiz and ended up with a tie. A boy and a girl had come up with an equal number of correct answers and we had to devise a tie breaker. One of the guests came over and suggested a question—"Who in the cantonment is nicknamed the GREEN INK?" The girl answered straight away and we had a winner, but each got a prize anyway. Fortunately, the nicknamed person in question was not on the guest list.

The party was a great success, most of the food was eaten and there was very little waste. Nearly all the children went home once it got dark, most of them looking very tired after the party. All of them thanked us before they left. Quite a few of the adults stayed until late evening which was warm. By midnight, Mo and I were left sitting alone in the balmy evening air listening to the chirping of the crickets, the monsoon had been kind and the day had been bright and sunny.

We all slept late the next morning, and I awoke believing we had a lot of tidying up to do. Once I had washed and dressed, I went into the kitchen where I could hear Martha moving around. She wished me a cheery 'Good morning, Sahib' and asked what I wanted for breakfast. I asked for coffee and toast and went into the garden expecting to survey the wreckage of the previous day's party.

To my amazement, the only evidence that the party had taken place was the marquee standing in the middle of the lawn. All the borrowed furniture, crockery and cutlery had been returned to their rightful owners, and the barbeque had been cleaned.

The Gurkha soldiers turned up as I wandered around the garden, the marquee was struck and loaded into a waiting Land Rover. Before they left, I gave them a case of beers to take with them.

After breakfast and when Mo and the boys had surfaced, I called to Martha to come into the living room where Mo and I thanked her for helping to make the party such a success. I handed her a bonus of a few hundred rupees to share with Tika, Raj and Michael.

Mo had been working at the cantonment welfare centre for some time. Along with the matron or a midwife from the hospital, she went out into the villages around the area to check up on the mothers and babies which had been delivered in the BMH or in their houses.

While working at the centre, she had become friends with quite a few members of the Britain Nepal Medical Trust in Biratnagar and Kathmandu who visited from time to time and had stayed with us. As we were soon to leave Nepal, Mo said she would like to go to Kathmandu to say goodbye to her friends from BNMT.

I had arranged with the movements staff to fly the boys out from Delhi. Mo would stay in Kathmandu for 5 days and I would fly with the boys to Delhi on the Thursday to see Jason and Justin on to their flight back home on Friday morning, then return to Kathmandu the same day.

We flew to Kathmandu in a Twin Otter on the Sunday and stayed at the Nook Hotel. The next few days would be a round of sightseeing and meals with friends at the various restaurants in Kathmandu.

We met up with Deanna from BNMT who took us to the banks of the Bagmati River where a female Hindu celebration was taking place. This was a fertility puja, and the women were all dressed in their best red saris. They came to anoint a lingam (a phallic symbol) with milk as an offering to the god Shiva. From there, we headed off for a meal at the hotel Vanya on the Pilgrim Road near the Swayambunath which was bathed in the golden light of the evening sunset.

We went off to visit a few of the main temples in Kathmandu including Swayambunath and Boudhanath, where we turned the prayer wheels. Both temples were severely damaged in the 2015 earthquake. Fortunately, they have since been repaired and restored, although a number of important temples were completely destroyed. In the evening, we met up with Major K, the physician from Dharan with his wife and we all went to dinner at a pleasant restaurant called 'My Fair Lady.'

Our last meeting was with a lady from BNMT who I can only remember as Mrs Cowen. We took her for a Chinese dinner at the Mallon Hotel. The barman was called Fred and had lived and worked in Kathmandu for 25 years. He also wrote poetry.

We met many friends and acquaintances in Kathmandu and it was sad for Mo in some respects as most of them she would never meet again. She had made many friends in Nepal and was well regarded by those with whom she had worked.

The next day would be the last the boys would see of Kathmandu. I had an early flight to Delhi with them, and after saying their goodbyes and with tearful hugs with Mo, we made our way to the airport. We would stay overnight in Delhi, after which I would see Jason and Justin onto their final homeward bound flight from the sub-continent for many years. I would see Kathmandu for the penultimate time the next day when I returned to Mo.

As a final treat for the boys, I had got us a room in Claridge's Hotel in Delhi. I had managed to get a substantial discount on the price, mainly due to there being only one restaurant of the five available. The other four being reserved for three weddings and a birthday party taking place in the hotel at the same time.

The hotel was packed with partygoers all dressed in their finery. It was an opportunity to see such great wealth in a country abounding in poverty. Nearly all the women were dressed in their red saris, and adorned with gold bangles and jewellery. The men in fine suits, silk shirts and ties, their gold cufflinks and Rolex watches glinting in the hotel lights.

Having checked in, we left the opulence of the crowd in the lobby, and made our way to our room. We had a table in the one open restaurant and went to get dinner. As it was a special night, I told the boys they could have what they wanted from the menu. Justin decided on Lobster Thermidor and I had the other half with him. It would be the first time I had had this dish since our night on the Singapore Lady with Mike and Midge in Singapore back in 1970. Jason, ever the conservative, ordered a cheeseburger and chips (in Claridge's!).

While Justin and I enjoyed our lobster, Jason was clearly not liking his choice. Unlike a cheeseburger in UK, this one was spicy and not to his taste. At the time, he was not keen on spicy food. How times change, both our sons are excellent cooks, Jason produces some of the best curries I have ever eaten, and Justin will turn his hand to anything culinary, all with first-class results.

I had booked an early call for the next morning ahead of our taxi to the airport. There were still some celebrations going on despite the dawn starting to break over Delhi. Traffic was light and we got to the terminal in good time to check in and get the boys settled for their long non-stop flight to London. They were travelling in Club class and a BA stewardess came to meet us to take the boys to the departure lounge.

As we said our goodbyes, I fought back the tears as this would be the end of an era for the three of us. I would see them in just two months when Mo and I returned to the UK.

I had already checked into my flight back to Kathmandu and headed off to the departure lounge where I had an hour to wait. I was just in time to see the BA aircraft leave for London with our boys on board. My Royal Nepal Airlines 737 to Kathmandu with me on board flew off in the opposite direction.

It had been a tiring 24 hours with the travelling, the early call for our journey to the airport, and my return to Kathmandu and Mo. Mo's friend, Deanna, had called and asked us if we would care to go shopping in the city. I reluctantly agreed, like most men, I was not keen on being dragged around shops with my good lady, let alone with another woman along as well.

We browsed the shops in New Road, me taking more photographs while the ladies haggled over souvenirs and trinkets. Mo bought some knitting wool, probably for her mother as I had never seen Mo knitting. After a couple of hours, we repaired to Deanna's house for a drink or two, before heading back to the Nook for an afternoon nap.

Deanna called us around six o'clock in the evening and told us she was taking us out to dinner. This would be our last but one time in Kathmandu, and she was preparing for us to go out in style. We went to the Annapurna Hotel, at the time owned by the Queen of Nepal. After and excellent meal with corresponding service, we sat back and chatted the evening away before saying our last goodbyes and returning to the Nook.

We returned to Dharan and started to pack up our belongings in earnest. I was able to assemble the boxes on the veranda and gradually started filling them. I sold the boys' bicycles, promising them new ones when we returned. I had also sold our golf clubs, and my Mamiya camera as I wasn't using it.

The most difficult items to pack were the two terracotta pots we had bought in the market. They were bought for pennies but we were keen to keep them. They just fitted into two boxes and filled with assorted clothes, with more packed around them. The carpets were wrapped in plastic sheeting and sewn into hessian using a curved needle and heavy thread.

The boxes were almost filled and ready to be shipped off when I heard a rustling in one of them. I lifted the lid and saw something burrowing into the packing material. I had to find whatever it was and started to unpack the contents of the box. I had almost emptied the box when I found what I was looking for. It was strange shrew-like creature but larger than any shrew I had seen before. An odd looking light grey animal with a long, pointed nose with an equally long tail. From nose to tail, it was about nine inches in length. I moved to try and catch it but it was too quick, ran up my arm, out of the box and on to the veranda.

A few frantic minutes followed as Martha, who was nearby with a broom in her hand proceeded to chase the animal around the garden, flailing at it with the broom. It dodged and weaved its way around her and eventually it found its way into a gully and disappeared. I still have no idea what it was, but it had possibly been living in one of the wardrobes as I later found a tablet of soap that had been nibbled by something. After that, I made sure the boxes had lids fixed, those that weren't ready were covered to stop any more wild life getting in.

Towards the end of September my relief, Mike G and his wife arrived. Martha and Tika had been across the road to their quarter to have it clean and ready for them to move into. Mo and I went down to Biratnagar to welcome them and see them safely to Dharan and their new home. We left them to settle into their house and we were going back to ours when we heard a high-pitched scream coming from their house. We ran back thinking they had a snake as an unwanted guest. I made my way in cautiously to find the Mike's wife pointing up to a corner of the ceiling.

There, firmly attached to the wall, was a lizard. Not a large one but a gecko about 6 inches long. I said there was absolutely no need to be alarmed as they were completely harmless, did not bite and carried no nasty diseases. I guessed they had not been out to the Far East before, and that 'chitchats,' as we called them, were common in houses out here and would help keep them free of mosquitoes, which were far more dangerous.

The next day, I took Mike to the dispensary and stores office and introduced him to the staff. Showed him the stores and the accounts. From there, we went to our escape room in the operating theatre block for a mid-morning cuppa. After this, we toured around the hospital and the cantonment, ending up at the Sgts Mess. Meanwhile, Mo had taken Mike's wife to the stores after introducing her to Martha, Tika and Raj, who they would inherit from us when we would finally leave Dharan in a couple of weeks' time.

Those two weeks passed quickly. Our boxes were gone and were on their way to Hannover. Our freezer was almost empty, most of the contents being divided between Mike and his family, and Martha to share with Tika and Raj.

The day came for us to leave and say our final goodbyes. Martha and Tika were given presents of cloth to make saris for each of them. To Raj we gave a watch—we also gave him some salt and soap to take to his family in the hills. When the Land Rover arrived, most of the families in the cantonment turned out to wish us a safe journey. We were festooned with garlands and scarfs as we got into the vehicle which would take us to Biratnagar.

As we drove out of the gate for the last time, the sentry came to attention and gave us a smart salute as we passed. I returned his salute and, as we turned a corner and out of sight of the cantonment, I brushed a tear from my eye. I noticed Mo was in floods of tears as well, and I put my arm around her, telling her we would never see the like of Dharan again, but we were off to a new beginning in Germany.

A few miles down the road we came to a bridge over a river. I asked the driver to stop and we alighted from the Land Rover. From the parapet of the bridge, we divested ourselves of the garland and scarfs and let them fall into the swirling water below, as was the tradition of those leaving Nepal, in the hope of return.

From Biratnagar, we took a flight to Kathmandu, the last time we would be in this fabled city, and from there on to Delhi for a couple days, before leaving the Sub-continent for the UK and home.

We stayed at a guest house in the city and the next day hired a driver to take us on a tour of both old and New Delhi. We were impressed with Lutyens architectural vision of New Delhi as we wandered around the many buildings he had designed.

From the new city, we toured around the old town of Delhi and inevitably ended up in a jeweller's shop. We weren't too keen on shopping, but Mo spotted a ring she liked. She was also wearing the topaz pendant bought in Sri Lanka. The item that had taken her fancy was a silver ring set with her birthstone, a peridot. I asked the price and was told it was a just a few rupees. I asked if he had a topaz ring to match the on in the pendant, and, of course he had one. I bought them both after a little haggling, and the jeweller adjusted them to fit Mo's slender fingers.

Given the price I had paid I presumed they were cheap stones, but Mo liked them so I was happy. A few years later a friend in the Birmingham Jewellery Quarter remounted the stones onto gold rings. My friend told me the stones were of first-class quality.

We left Delhi on a non-stop flight to Heathrow, and from there by train to Paddington Station. We had decided to stop off in London for a couple of days and stayed at the Victory Services Club. It was cheap and cheerful and a few minutes' walk to the shopping areas of Oxford and Regent Streets. Mo needed some retail therapy.

After a good night's sleep, we were well rested and almost free of jet lag, so after breakfast we headed for the shops—in reality, Mo headed for the shops and I just trailed along with her to carry the bags and provide the funds.

The first stop had to be Marks and Spencer in Oxford Street where we spent ages browsing. When she had got the things, she wanted we headed over to pay, and I received an odd coin in the change. Looking for a pound note, I thought the cashier had made a mistake and queried my change. She pointed out the new one-pound coin which had come into circulation earlier that year, its issue had completely passed us by. After a few more shops, Mo was retailed out and we were ready for lunch. I felt the need for a beefburger and found a nearby McDonalds, where we had a burger free of Indian spices for the first time for ages.

After two three days in the capital, we headed back to Birmingham and our families. I remember seeing an advertising hoarding outside New Street Station when we arrived. It extolled the virtues of the new BBC Microcomputer. The telling strap line of the advertisement read 'Get the new BBC Micro, your kids will show you how to use it.' Computers were beginning to come to the fore in the early 80s and would play a not insignificant part of my life over the next few years.

My mother, now 69, was looking well and had clearly enjoyed looking after the boys during the half-term breaks. We stayed with Mo's family in Kingshurst and spent a few days visiting friends and family in and around Birmingham, all of whom we hadn't seen for over two years.

All too soon, it was time to leave for Hannover. We took the boys out to Birmingham and had a pizza at Gino's in the town before returning them to their schools, and then taking the train to Luton and the flight to Germany.

We were met at the airport by Dave, as my predecessor had already left a few days previously for his posting to UK. Dave told us he was still working in the stores and dispensary, and continued to live in the attic of the hospital. He drove us to the flat we would be living in for the next two years.

Chapter 21
Seelhorststraße, Hannover, West Germany

Our new home was a spacious first floor flat in the suburbs of Hannover. It had three bedrooms, a large living room which gave access to a balcony. It had been recently decorated and was clean and tidy.

While we had been away in Nepal, a new system of stocking quarters had been introduced, and much of the bits and pieces we had come to expect in a quarter were absent. Items which we had taken for granted in the past, such as an ironing board, vegetable rack, a laundry basket etc, were not available. I would be able to obtain these items which would be added to the flat's inventory from the BIA stores. The system, known as 'wharfing,' had been introduced as many soldiers and their families were bringing most of their household belongings with them on posting, and a fair number of everyday items had been removed from quarters' inventories. We made a list of things we needed and I passed it on to the BIA. We could always send some of it back when our boxes arrived from Nepal, along with our items in storage in UK being delivered.

Seelhorststraße was conveniently situated for local shops and the tram service into Hannover City. It was close to the zoo and the Eilenriede City Park. It was also just a couple of miles from the hospital.

Once we had settled in, it was time for me to go to work and meet the people with whom I would be working. Dave picked me up and drove me to the hospital where I went through the usual administration of arrival at a new unit. The RSM escorted me to meet the commanding officer who welcomed me to his hospital. From there, I went down to the medical stores to meet my staff.

My predecessor had left a few days before my arrival, but the medical stores looked clean and tidy. Debbie was still my clerk, Dave H and Dave Y were still in place, and Joe G was the Sgt dispenser who worked in the pharmacy on the ground floor. Sgt Joe C was the medical storeman. There was also a couple of Portuguese general labourers to help out in the stores.

Over the few next days, I counted the stocks of the controlled drugs and dental gold in the safe in the stores, and the pharmacy. I stock-checked the non-expendable stocks such as surgical instruments, and laboratory equipment. The checks threw up one or two anomalies in the accounts. I also found that the departmental inventories were out of date and set about checking the wards and departments holdings along with Joe C, the storeman. Debbie re-wrote the inventories in accordance with what we had found.

It was a time-consuming job taking the best part of two months, these were the days before computer assistance and Debbie typed up the inventories on our battered typewriter. In the end, the inventories of equipment held by the wards and departments, along with the stock in the medical stores were reconciled just after Christmas.

Apart from one seriously expensive item. Somewhere we were missing an operating table! A new one had been received a couple of years previously, but its predecessor was unaccounted for. It was eventually found under a pile of boxes in the recesses of the cellar below the hospital. I asked the REME medical technicians to examine it, and they pronounced it as beyond economical repair (BER). I spoke to the quartermaster, who was my immediate boss and he authorised me to scrap it.

Our boxes had arrived a few days before the Christmas holiday and after the boys had arrived from school. Fortunately, this time there were no problems with end of term breaks as they both arrived together.

I had a few days off and we took the boys to the Christmas market in Hannover, wrapped up warm against the December cold. We wandered around the stalls, bought a few decorations for our Christmas tree, Mo and I enjoying a glass or two of glühwein, all of us walking along munching a bratwurst. We also travelled to the Hartz Mountains to enjoy the snow and sledges.

As usual, we all enjoyed Christmas in Germany, along with all the trimmings, but soon it was all over and the boys returned to school. Holidays with our boys just seemed to get ever shorter, and we missed them badly when they were away from us, but we took comfort in that they were happy at school.

The first priority we had was to buy a car. I had made a few enquiries as to what was available and decided on a 2 litre Opel Ascona, the German equivalent to the Vauxhall Cavalier Sri. I would have to collect it from Osnabruck, a hundred miles down the autobahn from Hannover, which meant begging a ride from Dave H.

Dave took me to collect my new car on the Saturday morning. It was all new and gleaming, ready for me when I arrived. I was a little wary, not having driven for the two years in Nepal, and I had a long trip back to Hannover. I spoke to the salesman, asking him about running the car in. He told me it was not necessary these days, but to keep it below four thousand RPM through the gears for a couple of weeks. The car also had a five-speed gearbox, again something with which I was not was not familiar. The salesman also pointed out to me the various switches and buttons. The only thing I was immediately used to was the car being right-hand drive, and built in Germany to UK specifications, suitable for driving in the Britain when we eventually returned home.

I followed Dave from the dealership to head back to Hannover, filling the fuel tank at the first petrol station on the way to the autobahn. I drove steadily at first letting Dave go on ahead, as now I was on the autobahn, I knew the way home. I carefully kept my eye on the tachometer, gradually increasing my speed as I grew more confident, finally engaging fifth gear. The car cruised quietly and beautifully and I held it at just under 4000 RPM as the salesman had advised me. I glanced over to the speedometer and was amazed to see that I was travelling at 108 miles an hour! I was really enjoying this car as it ate up the miles.

We had a new arrival in early 1984 when L/Cpl Ailee McGregor was posted to us. I cannot remember her arriving, but when I met up with her many years later, long after I had left the RAMC, she reminded me that Mo and I had picked her up from the airport.

At the time of Ailee's arrival, the dispensing service had been moved downstairs to the medical stores while the main pharmacy was having a facelift. Fortunately, the inconvenience would only last a few days before the service reverted to normal.

After a few weeks Ailee came to us, we had another addition to the pharmacy and medical supply department. This was 2nd Lt Liz I, a newly commissioned pharmacist. I picked her up from the airport and took her along to our flat for a coffee and to meet Mo. She seemed very pleasant, very young and keen to start work. I took her to the hospital and dropped her off at the Officers Mess.

Despite first impressions, this woman later, over the next few months, came to almost destroy what had been up until then, a relatively successful and happy career in the RAMC.

A few weeks after Liz arrived, I went to the MOD in London where I took an aptitude test. The test was intended to assess my capability for work on computers. The tests took the form of mathematical and logic problems. In the two years, we had been away in Nepal, computers had become more and more common in the workplace. I was given the results before I left to return to Hannover, and was pleased to hear that I had passed and would be considered for training on computers at a later date.

When I returned from London a couple of days later, Mo told me she had got a job with SSAFA (SOLDIERS, SAILORS, AIRFORCE FAMILIES ASSOCIATION). SSAFA, the armed forces charity, well-regarded and trusted source of support for serving personnel, veterans, and their families in their time of need. She would be working as a receptionist for the SSAFA consultant in the office on the ground floor of the hospital, a short way from the dispensary. Mo worked there until we left Hannover and thoroughly enjoyed the work.

I had been away in London from Hannover for just three days. I that short time I arrived in the stores to find a major rearrangement had taken place. A desk had been taken into the stores and racking had been moved. When I asked what was going on, I was told that Lt I. had decided she wanted to have her office in the stores, and my desk was to be in what used to be the original office.

I was furious that I had not been consulted about the move and suggested that there was no useful purpose to be served. I immediately ordered everything to be put back to where it had been.

Just then, Lt I arrived and demanded to know what I was doing. I told her I did not approve of the move, especially as I was not consulted before I went to London. Also, the rearrangement had taken place while I was away and was certainly underhanded and a completely unnecessary attempt to undermine my authority within the department. She then informed we that she was in charge of the medical supply department and I had no authority. Her office would be in the stores and I would be in the original office with the clerk.

I was outraged at being effectively reprimanded by this junior officer in front of the entire staff of the department. It was patently obvious that man management was not part of the curriculum during her officer training in Sandhurst. My antipathy towards the recruitment of pharmacists into the RAMC was well known, whether her attitude towards me was as a result, I did not know. However, worse was to come.

I retired to my desk, still fuming, and told Debbie I was going for a walk around the hospital grounds to cool off, and she knew where I would be should I be needed. I was confident I would not be. I returned after an hour, sufficiently calm and went through the expendables accounts and preparing indents for replacement stock. These were finished just before lunch; I left the paperwork for the indents on Lt. I's desk for her to sign, and walked over to the Sgts Club for a sandwich and a drink.

Joe C. was at the bar and I joined him, the barman poured him a large vodka and I had a coke. While I ate my sandwich, we chatted together over the next half hour. I noticed that Joe must have drunk at least four large vodkas. I was aware about Joe liking a drink, but considered the amount he had imbibed in such a short time caused me not a little concern. I returned to work and resolved to make some enquiries the next day.

I made an appointment to see the physician the following morning. When I saw her, she asked me what problem I had. Telling her it was not me but a member of my staff about whom I had concerns. I said she could tell me that another person's medical history was confidential, and I replied that what I was to ask was also confidential. I told her that I was aware that Joe C. probably had a drink problem. She assured me that she knew about it but Joe had told her that he had it under control.

My suggestion that four large vodkas in half an hour could hardly be seen as being in control, immediately changed the physician's demeanour. She said she would speak to Joe and see what should be done. She thanked me for my concern and promised that our discussion would remain confidential.

Two days later Joe did not arrive at work. Lt I. asked me if I knew where he might be and I told her I had no idea, but perhaps he had overslept. When Joe had not turned up, she said she was going to see the personnel officer, I presumed she was going to report Joe as being absent.

She returned with half an hour, telling me that Joe had been moved to a facility in BMH Munster to be dried out from his alcoholism. She also said that she would love to know who blew the whistle on him without consulting her. I believed she was fairly certain it was me. But I replied that I neither knew nor cared who had given information about Joe, but his removal from here was blessing to both parties, Joe especially, as he would have been a liability, both to himself and the department.

A few weeks after Joe had left for Munster his replacement, Sgt Barry C arrived to take over as medical storeman. Joe, the dispenser, had gone on leave which left Ailee on her own in the dispensary. As I was feeling somewhat superfluous down stairs, I suggested I went up to assist her. We had a busy morning when the Lt. came up to check up that all was in order.

We were having a welcome coffee break when there was a knock on the door, which opened to reveal Colonel Mike Templar whom I had last met in Nepal a year or so previously.

"Hello Trevor," he said, "congratulations on getting your warrant."

"Hello Colonel," I replied. "I haven't seen you about. How long have you been here?" I asked.

"Just a couple of weeks, I have been in the Falklands for a short while and been very busy since I got in. Everything all right with you and your family?"

"Very well, Colonel, thank you. How is your good lady?"

I noticed a disapproving look on the face of the Lieutenant. She was obviously none too pleased at being ignored by the Colonel and his use of my first name when we spoke.

"Apart from having to put up with me, she's in fine fettle," he replied. "By the way, they're all mad in Fallingbostel!"

He then went on to explain that the military had recently introduced a heights and weights criterion, and one of the men at the unit was 6 feet 5 inches tall and weighed in at a little over 20 stones. The man was given three months to get his weight down, and when he failed, the medical officer had sent him to the Colonel with a view to discharging him from the army as unfit for service.

"What they missed at Fallingbostel, was that this man plays right prop for the army, and is probably fitter than most of the members of his unit. I sent him back to the unit and told them to leave him be."

With that, he turned to leave, saying that he was pleased to see me, telling the Lieutenant that he should mention his being the dispenser's friend as he only knew the name of half a dozen drugs, and three of them were insulin.

After he had left, I told the Lieutenant I had known the Colonel for many years having first met him in Hong Kong in the late 60s when he was a mere Major. Our paths had crossed several times since then.

I was duty dispenser one evening when I was called out to the hospital at around midnight. The caller told me I was required urgently by the on-call medical officer. I jumped into my car and headed off to the hospital. Once over the cross roads I accelerated up the road through the woods.

I was nudging 80 miles an hour when I spotted the blue light of a police car just off the road in the woods. I continued at speed until I neared the s-bend at the top of the road. Easing off the accelerator I saw a traffic policeman waving his baton and torch, indicating for me to pull into the layby where he and a colleague were waiting.

I duly pulled in and stepped out of the car. The policeman approached and asked in perfect English if I knew the speed limit along this road. I replied that I knew it to be 30 kilometres per hour. He then asked me why I was travelling at close to 130 kph when I passed the police car further down the road.

I explained I had been called out in an emergency to the hospital, and he should contact the hospital reception to confirm. I also advised him I had no documents in the car (a legal requirement in Germany), as I had cleaned the car earlier that day and removed the documents while I did the cleaning. All I had with me was my army identification card which he inspected and made notes.

He told me to go to the hospital, but his colleague would follow me to confirm my story of being called out. He questioned the NCO on reception who acknowledged who I was and told the policeman that I had indeed been summoned to the hospital in an emergency. He left to re-join his fellow policeman before telling me to stop at the layby before I went home.

The medical officer who had called me out was waiting in reception for me and told me what he needed. He had a very sick patient in the emergency room and the drugs he required were not available in the out patients department. I opened up the pharmacy and found what he needed, I reminded him he should write a prescription for me when he was done with his patient and leave it in reception for me to pick up in the morning.

I returned to the policeman in the layby who told me he would need to see my car's documents within half an hour. I said I would go home and fetch them. I left driving carefully, observing the speed limit, and went to retrieve all the necessary bits of paper and return.

Stopping in the layby for the third time, I approached the policeman with my documents, along with my spare glasses (another legal requirement in Germany). I also lifted the boot to show him my emergency triangle and first aid kit (more legal stuff). After inspecting the paperwork and walking around the car checking my tyres were legal, he handed my certificates back to me.

"Alles in ordnung," he said (all in order). I was still convinced I was going to get a ticket for speeding, and possibly another for lack of documents. However, he told me he was not going to pursue the matter because of the extenuating circumstances. He bade me good night, telling me to drive carefully and advising me to obey the speed limits in future. That was the one and only time I have ever got away with speeding.

Jason and Justin came out to us for the Easter holiday and wanted set up a car wash on the hospital site. There was a place behind the Sgts club with a water supply and an inspection pit which I had used when we were in Hanover before. It was particularly useful when I need to make running repairs to the exhaust on my previous Chrysler Alpine. I spoke to the QM to ensure it was OK for them to do it and he said it would be alright. I bought them car shampoo and chamois leathers, and within a few days had a small but thriving business. Their customers were pleased with the results paying the boys 10 marks for the work.

Unfortunately, the enterprise came to an end when the QM received the bill for the hospital water supply and saw a spike in usage. It was only a few days before the end of the Easter break and the boys returned to England and school. They left with a sizeable wad of Deutsch Marks for their labours, which I changed for sterling for them to take home with them.

Shortly after the boys left for school, I received a letter bearing Nepalese postage stamps. Opening the envelope I found a letter from Ranjit Singh Rai, the admin officer at BMH Dharan. He wrote to tell me our beloved Raj Kumar had died of meningitis while visiting his family in the hills, he was just 22 years old. Mo and I were devastated at the news, Raj had been a trusted and reliable member of our household staff for two years and his death hit us hard. I wrote back to Ranjit and asked him to convey our sympathies to his family.

I booked two weeks off in July and August for when the boys came back to us for the summer. A minor problem was that I could only get one week at a resort in Heiligenhafen in northern Germany, so we decided on a second week in Füssen in Bavaria. It would mean a drive of nearly 600 miles between the two, but I thought we could do it as it we would be driving on the autobahn almost all the way.

We received a letter from my mother in late June asking if she could come out to visit us. Mo and I agreed that it would be a good idea that she could come on holiday with us, so I wrote back suggesting she come to Hannover a couple of days before we left for Heiligenhafen, telling her of our plans for the summer break.

Everything was set for the holiday, rooms were booked both in Heiligenhafen and Füssen, all that was needed were the boys and my mother. The boys arrived the day before my mum. It was not possible to get them on the same flights as that which the boys were to travel was a chartered military aircraft. We had a few days before we set off on holiday. I was working, so Mo took the boys and Ethel around the sights of Hannover.

The weekend arrived and we set out early for the drive north to the Baltic coast. I assumed the trip would take about 3 hours, but I had not factored in the weather. Just south of Hamburg there was a terrific cloud burst which flooded the road to a couple of inches below the sills of the car. With the windscreen wipers doing their best to clear the screen and failing, there was nothing for it to pull over onto the hard shoulder and wait out the storm. It was impossible to drive any further.

Finally, after half an hour the rain stopped and the skies cleared, but the road was covered in standing water, but at least the traffic was beginning to move, albeit slowly. We continued on our journey, driving through Hamburg and onto a new autobahn, the E1 towards Heiligenhafen. Once clear of Hamburg we picked up speed and finally reached our destination a couple of hours later than planned.

The resort was very nicely equipped. There was an enormous swimming pool, three restaurants, and entertainment in the evenings. There was an extensive beach, but the Baltic Sea which, although looked inviting was very cold even in mid-July. Despite that, the boys ventured in while I stayed and watched from the warmth of the beach. Needless to say, they did not stay in very long.

It was quite fortuitous going on holiday at the time as it was my mother's 69th birthday in July, and I wanted to something special for the occasion. I had suggested trips out to various places reasonably close to the resort, but the boys asked if we could go to Legoland which we had visited a few years previously. The map indicated that the route to Billund was almost directly north once we had made it to the E7 to head north into Denmark, the drive should take about two and a half hours. Mother was taken with the idea, so that was the plan for the next day.

The drive to Billund was easy, and apart from a brief stop at the border, where it was just sufficient to wave our passports out of the passenger side window, we were at our destination in time for lunch.

We had been to Legoland seven years previously, but in that time, much had changed on the site. There were more rides for the boys, and several of the model sites had been expanded, one which was a model in Lego bricks of the Danish Royal Palace, complete with Lego guardsmen. There was a boat ride for the boys which took them past world sites; Abu Simbal in Egypt, the Taj Mahal, and a safari park, all modelled in Lego bricks. The attention to detail in these models served as a tribute to the builders.

We spent some time in the park, the boys enjoying the rides while Mo and I, along with Ethel wandered around looking at the Lego models of towns and cities, and famous buildings, including one of Buckingham Palace.

After 5 hours, it was time to leave, and we made our way back to Heiligenhafen, stopping for dinner on the outskirts of Flensburg, just over the border into Germany. From there, it would take us about 90 minutes to get back to the resort.

My mother had always wanted to go to Copenhagen, so while spending the day at the resort I checked up with the tourist office to determine the best way to get there. The trip could be done in the car and would involve taking a vehicle ferry from Puttgarden in Germany across to Rødby in Denmark. It would take about 3 and a half hours for us to get to Copenhagen, so an early start for us the following morning.

From the resort, we made our way along the A1 Road following the signs to Rødby/Puttgarden, eventually crossing Fehmarnsundbrücke bridge over to the small island of Fehmarn. From there, we drove on to Puttgarden for the ferry to Denmark.

I was surprised at the cost of the ferry; I cannot recall how much I paid for the car and the five of us but it was not expensive. Once we had set sail we ventured around the boat and found ourselves in the duty-free area. I bought a bottle of spirits and a carton of cigarettes, but the majority of the German passengers were stocking up on cheese and butter, dairy products being expensive in Germany.

The voyage to Denmark was a little under an hour. We disembarked and once through customs and immigration, and we were on our way to Copenhagen passing through a tunnel and over another long bridge. Once we had crossed the bridge it was just under an hour before we reached the outskirts of Copenhagen.

The first thing we wanted to see was the famous Mermaid. We found a parking space a few minutes' walk from the statue. It was good to get out of the car and stretch our legs after the long drive from the ferry terminal at Rødby, and we were soon at the iconic statue of the mermaid.

We all agreed it was a lot smaller than we had imagined, having seen innumerable photographs of the statue. Despite that, it was still very beautiful. I took quite a few pictures of my own, taking pains to avoid getting the docks across the water behind the mermaid in the picture.

Leaving the mermaid, we found a café and spent some time over pastries and coffee, before going on into Copenhagen city. Our next stop was the Tivoli Gardens, essentially a theme park, and reportedly the most visited site in Scandinavia. The boys were more interested in the various rides than wandering around the beautifully landscaped gardens. I stayed with them while they went and enjoyed the roller coaster and the carousel. After much nagging, I finally succumbed and joined them on the 'Flying Carpet' ride. While Jason and Justin loved it, and screamed and laughed as the ride did its stuff, I absolutely hated it, convinced I was going to lose my pastries and coffee at any minute.

I was so pleased when we finally stopped, just in time for Mo and my mother to return from their stroll around the gardens. Mo asked the boys if they had had a good time, and, turning to me, mentioned I was looking a little green around the gills.

We left the gardens and found an Italian restaurant to get some dinner before we left Copenhagen to return to Heiligenhafen. The three adults enjoyed a beer— Carlsberg Pilsner—what else should one drink in Copenhagen?

We left on our return journey to Heiligenhafen around six in the evening. The trip would take a little over 3 hours providing there were no hold-ups. In the event, we made the ferry in good time and settled in the dining room for a little light supper, before our boat docked and we were on our way back to the resort.

We had a day and a half in Heiligenhafen before leaving for the drive to Füssen, 650 miles to the south in Bavaria. The boys spent most of the last day around the resort, most of the time in the swimming pool, while we packed up ready to leave early the next morning.

Shortly after settling our final bill at the resort, we set off on the E1 autobahn which took us around Hamburg eventually linking with the E7 for the journey south to Füssen.

The Opel ran well, cruising steadily at 80 to 90 mph, despite being loaded with the five of us and our luggage. The radio was tuned to the German traffic information service, and a few miles north of Hannover we were warned of delays on the autobahn around the city, just as we were approaching slow moving traffic.

I took the decision to pull off the autobahn at the first slip road to Hannover, and make our way to our flat, get a bite to eat, unload any dirty washing and repack our cases.

We were soon at our flat, just two and a half hours after leaving Heiligenhafen. We spent an hour there before resuming our journey by 11 o'clock, picking up the E7 south of Hildesheim. The road was clear and the traffic was quite light, but there was a little light rain starting. Given the average German's propensity for driving at high speed whatever the weather, we soon passed a few shunts in the outside lane of the autobahn.

With the light traffic, and the rain clearing I was able to pick up speed. The Opel cruised easily at 100 mph and it ate up the miles. We stopped at a service area to stretch our legs and for drinks and pastries before continuing our journey to Füssen. When we passed the slip road towards Munich, we knew we would not have far to go and we would reach our destination before nightfall.

We found our bed and breakfast accommodation in Füssen quite easily as the owner had sent us detailed directions on how to get there. We checked in just as the sun was setting, having made good time on the journey south. Showing us to our rooms the manager told us about breakfast times and he gave us a number of guides to Neuschwanstein Castle and the viewpoint, along with other interesting places to visit. There was also a useful pamphlet giving details of various restaurants close by.

Once we had got our luggage from the car, we went to find a restaurant for a little light supper before retiring for an early night. We were all very tired after the long journey and fortunately there was a very good place to eat five minutes' walk away from our pension.

After a good night's sleep and breakfast, we were all refreshed and ready to visit the famous Neuschwanstein Castle, the fairy tale home of King Ludwig II. Work started in 1869 on a hill outside Füssen. Ludwig paid for the construction out of his own personal fortune. It was to be his retreat and in honour of Richard Wagner whose work he admired. Ludwig died in 1886 and the castle was opened to the public just six short weeks after, despite the work not being completed.

We joined the queue of tourists waiting to get into the castle, and were soon ushered in and a small group of us were shepherded around with an English-speaking guide. A few of the rooms were complete and furnished and impressive, but many of them appeared to have been abandoned after being partly constructed.

We spent a couple of hours in the castle before making our way to the viewpoint above the castle, where a panoramic vista placed the castle in the glory to which it had been originally intended. It does indeed have a fairy tale look about it with its spires and turrets.

Below the palace is the Hohenschwangau Castle, much older than Neuschwanstein and the childhood home of King Ludwig. I parked the car and took the 20-minute uphill walk, joining another queue of tourist waiting to be shown around the castle which was the official summer and hunting residence of Maximilian, who began reconstruction of the dilapidated building in 1832. Maximillian died in 1864 and was succeeded by his son who became King Ludwig II. We spent an hour or so touring the castle, admiring the many rooms with their sumptuous furnishings, before making our way back to Füssen.

We made a trip to Oberammergau taking the scenic route through Ettaler Forest, which meant a brief drive through Austria. Our friend, Eileen had been to Oberammergau in 1960 to see the Passion Play for which the town is famous. She had told us before we left for our holiday that the town was worth a visit and it was only an hour away from Füssen.

The journey was worth it as the town was most picturesque, with many of the typical Bavarian houses adorned with hanging baskets and window boxes filled to overflowing with colourful flowers. We stopped at one of the many pavement cafes for a coffee and sandwiches, after which we continued sightseeing around the town.

The Passion Play takes place every 10 years in those that end in a zero. As many as 2000 of the local townspeople take part, either as actors in the play, musicians, technicians, or assisting in the production. Actors are required to grow their hair and beards, as no wigs and false beards are allowed.

The play was first performed in 1634, and according to local legend, is performed every ten years because of a vow made by the inhabitants of the village that if God spared them from the effects of the bubonic plague, then sweeping the region, they would perform a Passion Play every ten years. Apart from a break due to the second world war, it has been performed every ten years since, the one exception being the enactment in 1934 to mark the 300th anniversary of the first Passion Play along with its 350th performance.

We returned to Füssen in time to get an evening meal before retiring back to our pension for an early night. Over the next few days, we explored the area around the town. There were many scenic walks, and one of the days we were high in the hills above the town when we heard the sound of jet engines. Suddenly, about 100 feet below us and following the line of the valley, came two Starfighter F-104 jets of the German Air Force.

This aircraft, built by Lockheed in the United States, was known as the 'Widowmaker' because there had been many crashes during its time with the Luftwaffe. Germany had bought over 900 of these jets of which nearly 300 had crashed, killing over 100 pilots.

On the last day of our time in Füssen, I spotted a poster advertising a Bavarian Entertainment Evening and the cost of the tickets included food. We all decided we should go and make it an enjoyable finale to our holiday.

The evening was a tremendous success. Buxom waitresses bought beer in steins, carrying as many as a dozen around the tables. Food was plentiful and tasty, and the entertainment very much enjoyed by the crowd. A German 'Oompah' band played, later to accompany a 'Schuhplattler'—a traditional dance with men in lederhosen and the ladies in colourful dresses. None of us understood the meaning of the dances or the songs, although the many Germans in the audience laughed or sang along. The evening ended with a standing ovation and much cheering.

We left for home early the next morning after thanking our host for a comfortable and enjoyable stay. The drive would be autobahn almost all of the way back to Hannover and the road was light of traffic and there was little in the way of road works.

The drive home was easy, the Opel cruising along effortlessly at 100mph most of the way. With a break half way to refuel the car, and for a stretch and a coffee, we were in Hannover in a little over 5 hours. My mother flew back to Birmingham the following day. She told us she had enjoyed the holiday and hoped to see us again soon.

A week after we returned from holiday the Sgts mess organised a trip to an amusement park near Hamburg. We all decided to go, although it meant retracing our journey north, the same way we had travelled on our holiday. This time the weather was good and we arrived in good time.

The first ride I spotted as we entered the park was a cork screw roller coaster and the boys made a beeline for it, dragging me along with them. It was over 25 years since I had put aside my dread of roller coasters and win Mo; and here I was again, not wanting to lose face, this time in front of our boys.

I gritted my teeth and followed Mo and the boys to the ticket office. We boarded to ride where I sat holding on to the safety rail with a vice-like grip, convinced I would not survive the ride. As usual the first drop after the climb was the part that frightened me, then the car accelerated into the three corkscrew turns, we were upside down, me still gripping the bar. The boys and Mo were screaming with the exhilaration of it all, while I gritted my teeth, hoping for the ride to end.

We eventually stopped and to my amazement I was quite pleased with myself, realising, despite my initial dread, I had quite enjoyed the ride. So much so we went twice more. The first drop still terrified me, but once that was over, I began to enjoy the experience.

The following week it was time for the boys to return to school. Justin had got a place at Old Swinford Hospital and I drove the boys back to Birmingham via the ferry to Dover from Zeebrugge. We stayed at Mo's mother's home and visited my mother. We went to Stourbridge, first stopping off at Gino's Italian restaurant in Birmingham, where for once my mother joined us for pizza, she had developed a taste for it while we were on holiday. From there, we headed off to Old Swinford school to see Justin settled in to his new surroundings.

After leaving Stourbridge and the boys, I returned my mother home, after which I called round to Mo's family to say goodbye before driving back to Hannover and Mo.

I returned to work, spending most of my time on my own in the pharmacy, filling prescriptions and ward supplies. Ailee had been posted to the Falklands, so I was happy to leave the Lt. running the medical stores with Joe, Barry, and the civvies. If things got busy, I would ring down and Joe or Dave H would come up to help out. For the most part, I only ventured into the store when the Lt. was on leave or on a course.

There was an evening in the community centre with singer/songwriter Harvey Andrews between the summer and Christmas holiday. Harvey was a 'Brummie' like me and born in Stechford, only a few miles from where I had lived in Birmingham. He sang some of his many songs and, in between, regaled us with stories of his early life as a student at Coventry University where he was a member of the entertainments committee.

He told us one of his main duties was to book and get the venue for various groups and bands ready for Saturday night entertainment. He would make sure the lighting and sound systems were working properly before the bash started.

One day he had a call from a promoter saying he had a really good group which Harvey may be interested in. He also told him they would be more expensive than usual—£15.00 for the night. Harvey agreed and went about his business of getting the venue ready, and then went to the pub for the evening. The upshot of the story was that Harvey Andrews had booked 'The Beatles,' and never heard them play!

I joined HATS, the Hannover Amateur Theatrical Society. They were putting on Aladdin, a pantomime for Christmas and I went along to help out, and not with any intention of taking to the stage. The Lt. had also joined and was reading the part of the princess. During rehearsals I read the parts of actors who were unable to attend, and over a few weeks I had read most of the parts, including that of the Peri of the Ring. The play had been written in the late 1920s, and the part of the Peri had been intended as a serious role. It was also written in verse.

A couple of weeks before the show would go on, the original actor who was to play the Peri had to drop out, and I was asked if I would step into the part. I knew the lines, but suggested it should be played for laughs and not seriously as originally intended back in the 20s. The director tentatively agreed and I should play the part as I suggested at the next full rehearsal.

For the dress rehearsal, I borrowed a red silk top and red tights from Mo. I also had my Tibetan boots from Nepal, and one of the ladies in the cast lent me a red felt hat. I made a wand of floppy rubber tubing with a star on the end. Once my make-up was applied, I waited in the wings at the back of the stage ready to make my entrance.

My cue was a pyrotechnic which flashed red and gave off a cloud of smoke through which I appeared as if by magic. I flounced through the smoke and made my way to the front of the stage, tossing silver and gold coloured dust as I went. I had modelled my mannerisms on the then famous star of television, Larry

Grayson, playing the part of the Peri as camp as I could, picking bits of non-existent lint of my clothes as I delivered my lines, while waving my floppy wand. The director was delighted and was keen for me to play the part of the Peri as I had.

I had four appearances during the pantomime, which had six performances, four evenings and two matinees. We played to a packed audience every time. My performance was greeted by raucous laughter every time I appeared. Even when I forgot my lines and had to revert to the off-stage prompt. The pantomime was a great success and the entire cast was met with standing ovations at the end of the play.

Despite the Lt. and I working close together as two of the characters in the pantomime, the coolness between us continued in the working environment after the play. I was considering myself to be surplus to requirements, my role as a warrant officer was superfluous and I had little if no input into the running of the medical supply department, except when the Lt. was away.

Here I was, having worked alongside some of the most experienced pharmacy technicians and medical supply senior NCOs and Warrant officers during my 20 years in the RAMC, reduced to keeping my head down in the hospital pharmacy, filling prescriptions. It was becoming apparent that the officers in the administration of the hospital from the commanding officer downwards were closing ranks around the Lt. and protecting her for what they saw as a supposed threat from me.

My problem with that was, protecting her from what? My ambivalence towards commissioned pharmacists within the RAMC was well known. I was happy to work with them provided they stuck with what they knew, pharmacy—advising doctors and surgeons on the best courses of drugs in their treatment of their patients. I was satisfied to endorse that their knowledge of pharmaceutics, pharmacology and forensic pharmacy was much superior to mine.

The newly commissioned Lt. had absolutely no knowledge of running a medical supply department apart from a brief introduction at DMED prior to coming to BMH Hannover. I would have been perfectly happy to beaver away in the basement, maintaining stocks and managing the accounts and inventories. However, she was in charge and I really had no job worthy of my service and experience.

I was completely dissatisfied in the position in which I found myself. I requested a posting away from Hannover at least once a month but to no avail.

The only light in my life at the time was Mo, and when the boys came out to us when we took some leave to visit places in Germany with them and Mo.

I continued with the Theatrical society and took the lead in a Tom Stoppard play, "The Real Inspector Hound." I have seen the play a couple of times since, both on stage and television and I still do not understand it, apart from it being a play within a play.

I kept the Lt. at arm's length, although always being civil to her and referred to her a Ma'am whenever we had cause to meet. I managed the medical supply department whenever she was away and was always on good terms with the staff in there.

However, matters came to a head in August 1985. The Lt had been selected to attend a computer course at the Royal Signals Headquarters in Blandford Forum. She would be away for three weeks. Two days after she left for her course, I received a notification that I had also been selected to attend the course at Blandford a week after the Lt returned from hers.

The following day I was informed that a Board of Officers was to take place within a month as a result of a change in commanding officer. The Board was effectively an audit of accounts within the unit, those of the medical supply department being one of those to be scrutinised. Looking at the dates, I would be away on the course while the board was to take place.

I had a little under three weeks to get everything ready for the audit, plenty of time. I had Joe and Barry, the medical stores Sgt, out in the wards and departments checking various inventories around the hospital, while I did a stock take of all the expendable items, including the controlled drugs and the dental gold, marking up the account for items to be ordered on DMED. Ailee, back from the Falklands, looked after the dispensary with strict instruction to call me if matters got too busy for her to cope.

I then started on the non-expendables, such as surgical instruments and expensive laboratory equipment held in stock in the stores. Once I was satisfied that the accounts would stand up to the Board inspection, I ruled off the Kardex system initialled and dated it. Any items of non-expendable equipment leaving the stores before the inspection would have to be supported by a signature from the recipient.

With a couple of days to go before the Lt. returned from the UK, and myself to disappear to Blandford Forum for three weeks, the medical stores account was ready for inspection, so we sat back and breathed a collective sigh of relief. Then

Joe, Barry and myself retired to the Sgt's Club for a bite of lunch and a welcome drink.

The Lt. returned from the UK on Friday, so I had just one week to apprise her of the Board of Officer due in 10 days' time while I was away. I detailed to her that the accounts of expendable and non-expendable items were in good order, and a number of inventories had been checked and found to be correct.

I was satisfied I was leaving her with as much information she would need when the inspecting personnel came to visit the medical supply department. As far as I was concerned, we had done everything to ensure the inspection would proceed without any problems, and I could leave the department in her capable hands. How mistaken I was.

I left for Blandford Forum on Saturday afternoon, driving to Zeebrugge to take the overnight ferry to Dover. I managed to get a cabin and settled in for the 7-hour cruise to Dover. At least, I would be reasonably refreshed for the long drive to Blandford the next day.

I arrived at the Royal Signals HQ just before lunchtime and was shown to the Sgts Mess where I was allocated a room. After lunch, I returned to my room in the mess and read through the joining instructions for the course. Along with the details of meal times and the various services in the camp was a memorandum saying that once the course had started none of the students would be able to leave the course and that no one would be failed.

One of the most bizarre items included in the pack was a copy of the 'Ladybird Book of Computers.' I had spoken to my friend Dave, who was in München Gladbeck at the time and he told me the book was intended as a foundation on which a multi-storey building would be erected. I took his word for it as bemused as I was at receiving the book. He also mentioned that he was leaving Germany for DMED shortly, and he would be in Andover while I was at Blandford.

The course started on the Monday morning. I and a dozen others were seated in front of a computer monitor. We were instructed to insert a password to allow us to access our monitors, in order that only its allocated individual would only be able to access it. All the other students, from various parts of the military were younger than I, and from the start it was obvious they we far more conversant with the machinations of the computer world than I was.

Over the next few days, we were introduced to the current computer languages—Cobol and Fortran, which had their own syntax, and to various mathematical languages such as binary and hexadecimal. By the end of the first week, I came to realise I was hopelessly out of my depth. I struggled on through most of the second week, convinced that the phrase 'no one fails this course' did not apply to me.

The bombshell arrived on Thursday in the form of a signal arriving from Hannover requesting my immediate return to the hospital. I had mixed feeling about this, relief at getting off the course, and, at the same time perplexed as to the reason why I should have to return to Germany. The officer in charge of the school said he already replied to the signal denying the request for me to return, telling me it was necessary for me to complete the course.

A second signal arrived the following day alleging anomalies in the medical supply accounts which warranted investigation by the Miliary Police, and I was required to answer to the allegations. I was stunned by this signal; the staff of the medical stores and I had done everything to make sure the account would stand up to scrutiny by the board. The officer asked if there was any truth in the suggestion posed by the signal. I assured him there was not a shred of wrong doing on my part and I asked for a copy of the signal.

I left Blandford on Saturday morning for the drive to Dover. I stopped off to meet with Dave in Andover. Dave was now a Major, heading up a group in DMED who were bringing the depot into the 20th century by computerising its systems. Over coffee I showed Dave the signal, he also asked if there was any possibility there could be a problem with the medical store's accounts in Hannover. I told him of the work we had done while the Lt. was away, and that as far as I was concerned the accounts were perfect, suggesting any difficulty at the hospital would lie at the feet of the Lieutenant who was supposedly in charge of the department.

I left Dave's house and continued on my journey to Dover, making it in good time to board the ferry to Zeebrugge. From there, apart for a stop in Venlo to fill my petrol tank, I drove to non-stop to Hannover and to Mo. She knew I was returning early but I had not told her of the reason I had had to leave Blandford. The following day was Sunday, time to get myself together, ready to meet the Board of Officers on Monday morning. Given the contents of the signal I was extremely worried about what I was about to face.

I contacted Joe and Barry asking if they would meet me in the Garrison Sgts Mess to discuss what was going on. Over a lunch time drink all they could tell me was that the inspecting officers had arrived in the stores to check the accounts. The first thing they looked at was the contents of the safe and counted the controlled drugs and the dental gold. All appeared to be in order, then selecting a tray of Kardex accompanied the Lt. into the stores. They returned to the office within five minutes to announce they would be unable to continue and left.

On Monday morning, I returned to the hospital and knocked on the door of the personnel officer, Captain M. I entered, stood before his desk, and saluted him. I produced the copy of the signal and asked the meaning of it, saying it was defamatory and possibly libellous. I also said once the matter was resolved I intended to ask for a redress of grievance against the administration officer.

I asked why I was made to return to Hannover. He told me there was a problem with the accounts in the medical stores, particularly with an operating table unaccounted for. The board would reconvene in the department that afternoon and I was required to answer their questions.

I duly returned to the stores office and waited for the auditors to arrive. The Lt was there and I gave her a perfunctory good afternoon and turned my attention to the account. The three officers on the board came to the office and taking a couple of trays of Kardex asked for me to accompany them, along with the Lt., into the stores.

As we walked in, one of the members asked me to show them a dozen pairs of Spencer Wells artery forceps. All twelve were at the front of one of the shelves. I pointed them out and we moved on to the next item, a case containing a sigmoidoscope, an expensive piece of equipment. This was taken from the shelf and examined by one of the medical officers, who pronounced it in order.

We then returned to the office where one of the board asked me about the missing operating table. I replied that it was in the cellar and this was noted by a certificate at the back of the distribution card which showed the location of the table. Apparently no one had looked. I was asked why it was there, in reply I told him we were waiting to get it scrapped as the table had been declared beyond economical repair (BER) by the REME medical technicians. The quartermaster was aware and had a copy of the BER certificate.

I found the account card for the table and showed a copy of the certificate which had been placed behind the card to support the account. We then went down into the cellar where I pointed out to the board the table covered in dust, along with a further copy of the certificate Sellotaped to it. Explaining that I did not have the authority to scrap the table, and I was waiting for the QM to sign it off for disposal. I suggested the scrap value would not amount to a great deal, it was out of the way and there was no rush to get rid of it.

We returned to the office where the board pronounced themselves satisfied and would leave us to get on with our work. The Lt. left the office as a collective sigh of relief went around. I asked Joe and Barry what that was all about, the board had been with us for less than half an hour and declared themselves satisfied that all was in order.

Barry told me that when the board went into the stores and asked Lt. I. to show them a couple of items, she was unable to identify them or even where to look for them. The board had called a halt to proceedings and left the office. He had heard this from one of the operating theatre technicians who in turn had heard a member of the board discussing it in theatre. As for the operating table, she was completely in the dark (as was the table in the cellar).

I felt totally vindicated of the whole affair, feeling I was right in my belief that our pharmacist was in no way qualified to run a medical supply department and she should stick to what she knew and leave medical supply to those who knew what they were doing.

I proceeded with my redress of grievance against the admin officer which I duly won along with an apology from the officer concerned. With that out of the way, I thought all was over and done with and my life could return to semblance of normality.

My hopes of matters returning to normal were dashed a couple of days later when I was summoned to the RSM's office. I knew the RSM from years ago when he was on the same dispensers course as me. Unfortunately for him, he did not make it past the first month but that had not made a great difference to his career as he had risen to the rank of RSM of a major military hospital.

I was on good terms with the RSM, but that changed significantly over the next hour. The summons to his office was to tell me I was warned for CO's orders, which meant I was being charged with something. I was at a loss to understand the meaning of this as I could not recall anything I had done wrong since returning from Blandford Forum.

I was marched into the CO's office in the afternoon, flanked on one side by the RSM and on the other by a senior warrant officer. The CO informed me I was to be charged under Section 69 of the Army Act 1955: "Conduct Prejudice to Good Order and Military Discipline." A catch-all section which covered everything from having a button undone on parade, to murder.

I was asked if I understood the charge. I replied that I understood Section 69, but not why I was being charged. I was then asked if I pleaded guilty or not guilty, I replied, "Not guilty."

The CO then went on to say that he was displeased with how the Board of Officers had proceeded, and that it was my responsibility. I replied that I had prepared the account and advised the Lt., who was the officer in charge of the medical supply department, and therefore the responsibility was not mine, but hers. The failure of the Lt. to identify items to the Board was the reason for the audit to be stopped, and my immediate return to Hannover requested.

The CO condemned my attitude towards the Lt. and from that moment on I knew I was to be thrown under the bus. I was incandescent. The officer cadre of the hospital had circled the wagons around the Lt. and were protecting her from what they perceived as a threat from me. I knew was going to leave this office with a blot on my career.

At the end of the proceedings, the CO pronounced me guilty as charged and awarded me a three-month warning. This meant any further transgressions on my part would almost certainly result in a reduction in rank and further damage to my remaining time in the army. The only saving grace was that I had only two months left in Hannover before I left to spend my last six months in another unit in the UK. I had already requested my final months in the army should be spent at DMED in Ludgershall.

My first stop after leaving the CO's office was to that of the RSM. I launched into a diatribe, accusing him of not supporting me. He may have been my superior but in fact that he sat and listened to me sounding off, and him not saying a word, signalled to me he agreed I had been unjustly treated. In the end, he suggested I went home, and to keep my head down for the next couple of months before I left for my posting in October.

I called into the SSAFA office to tell Mo of the outcome of the afternoon, and to say that a posting could not come soon enough. Mo was extremely sympathetic, as was the SSAFA sister who had overheard our conversation. Fortunately, the boys had left for school some days earlier and were not aware of the situation in which I found myself.

The posting to DMED came through the next week. We had six weeks to get organised for the move; having done this a few times over the years, packing up presented no major problem, Mo and I would be ready to go, the sooner the better. Mo would be sorry to leave SSAFA, she enjoyed the work and the sister with whom she worked.

I got a week's leave when the boxes arrived, Mo could stay at work at the hospital while I started the packing. We had already set aside quite a few items which could be listed as 'not wanted on voyage,' and I had half a dozen boxes packed and screwed down by the end of the week.

Back at work, I spent as much time as possible away from the medical stores and the Lt. I was happy to work in the dispensary on my own, or with Ailee. Away from those I considered to be my 'enemies' (paranoid or what?). I only ventured into the medical stores if and when the Lt. was either on a course or on leave. I knew Joe and Barry could run the place and would only call me if there was a problem.

The other place I avoided was the Sgts Club at the hospital. I used the Garrison Sgts Mess for socialising and meetings. I got on well with the Garrison RSM, Peter D. He was Royal Corps of Transport, along with being a driving instructor and examiner. He was also teaching Mo to drive, albeit in his brand-new Audi. His wife, June, had worked with me in the stores when Debbie left as my clerk until she found another job.

The RSM asked me what I wanted as a gift from the hospital Sgts Club, as I would be leaving in a few days' time and he would need to arrange a collection. I told him straight out that I would not be attending a leaving party and I did not require anything which would remind me of the awful time I had spent on my second tour of BMH Hannover. I had my Hannover horse from my first trip in 1977–79, and I would receive a plaque from the Garrison Sgts Mess, which I would be pleased to accept. With that, I turned and left the RSM's office.

Mo would fly back to UK and stay with her parents in Kingshurst, before I collected her to bring her to Tidworth where we had been allocated a quarter. I would travel back to UK in the car. I was also pleased that by the time I joined DMED my three-month warning would have expired, and I would start in a new unit with a clean sheet.

I took Mo to Hannover Airport and waved her goodbye. I would see her at her mother's house in two days' time.

When I returned to the flat, I tidied up and stacked the items I was going to take in the car in the corridor. The march out was scheduled for the next morning and I was happy that it should proceed without any major problems. All the inventory items were laid out in the various rooms to make the job of the BIA easier and hopefully quick, as I was keen to get away.

Before the march out was due, I started loading up the car with my audio equipment, a few cases of wine, along with the contents of our cocktail cabinet. Most of the bottles of spirits had only one or two tots out of them and I was loath to leave them behind considering they were duty-free, and the high price of spirits in UK.

My clothes and uniforms also went in the car which was now full apart from the driving seat. I had packed all the items I would have to declare to the customs at Dover in the boot for easy access. As soon as the march out was completed, I could jump into the car and head for Zeebrugge and the ferry to Dover.

The march out went well, and apart from a few charges for missing and slightly damaged items, was completed in a half hour. I signed off the certificate, thanked the BIA, handed him the keys, and went to my car. I sat there for a few minutes, with a feeling of great relief—the nightmare of my last eighteen months at BMH Hannover was finally over.

I drove non-stop to Zeebrugge, getting to the port with half an hour to wait in the queue for the ferry. Once boarded I made my way up to the cafeteria for a welcome cup of coffee and a light lunch. The English Channel was as calm as a mill pond, and the air not too cold as I wandered around the upper deck, looking forward to the drive from Dover to Kingshurst and Mo.

When we docked at Dover, I stopped at the customs post to declare the assorted bottles of spirits and wine. I also had a couple of hundred duty-free cigarettes, but they were within my allowance, so I did not need to declare them.

I opened to boot and loaded the cartons onto containing the drinks on to the counter as the customs officer checked them over, making notes on his clipboard. Finally, he turned to me and said, "As most of the bottles are opened, I reckon you're 3 litres over the duty-free limit, that works out at ten pounds to pay." I thought that was reasonable and handed over a ten-pound note. As I loaded my booze back into the car, he asked if I had anything else to declare. I told him I had some cigarettes, but they were within the allowable limit.

I slammed down the boot lid and went to get back into my car. As I opened the door to get in, his next question made me take a step back. "What about your car, Sir?" My number plates and model indicated that the car had been purchased in Germany and was VAT and car tax free.

The rules for importing a car bought in Europe were quite strict. The vehicle had to have been driven in Germany for 365 days or more before it could be bought back to UK free of any charges. Any leave taken in UK was deducted from the time out of Europe.

Fortunately, I had all the details of the car in the glove box. I had to take out some of my belongings from the passenger seat before I could get to them. I removed the wallet containing the log book, registration documents and purchase details along with receipts. I handed the documents to the customs officer who nodded and handed me back the wallet, saying, "That appears to be all in order, Sir. Have a safe journey." With that, I replaced the items I had removed, got back into the car and, with a wave of thanks to the officer, drove out of the port and on my way to Kingshurst and Mo.

We spent a week at Mo's parents' home and visited my mother who lived nearby. We had the boys with us for the weekend, taking them back to their school on Sunday. We carried on the tradition of going to Gino's Italian restaurant for lunch before continuing on to their school. They would be with us again soon.

I telephoned DMED who told me our quarter was ready to take over and asked when we were intending to arrive in Ludgershall. I advised the chief clerk we would be there on Monday. He told me he would speak to the BIA to arrange a march in, and he would call me back with a date and time.

We were given an appointment with the BIA to take over quarter in Tidworth at mid-day on the coming Monday. We left a few items at Kingshurst to free up the passenger seat for Mo and drove down to meet the BIA to march into our new home.

Chapter 22
Tidworth Garrison Married Quarters

The quarter was alright, but not what we had been used to either in Hannover or Nepal. It was a bit of a come-down. Its only redeeming feature was that it was clean and well furnished. The lay out was strange. Just in front of the entrance door was what was a utility room, but its position made getting large items into the house awkward.

Within a few days, I suggested to Mo that we would not be staying here very long and we should start looking for a house in Stourbridge. The next day I left Mo to find her way around and to meet some of our neighbours while I went off to DMED to find out what my job was to be.

I met the RSM and the chief clerk before being taken to meet the Commandant of the depot. He greeted me and told me I was to be the warrant officer in charge of the detail section. This was the area of controlled and scheduled drugs, along with small items of dental and surgical equipment. My office would be in the controlled drug safe!

One of the questions the Commandant asked me was did I intend to sign on for a further two years. I advised him that I did not, and I would be taking my pension and retiring in May of the following year.

From there, I was taken down to meet the person I would be replacing. It turned out to be Tony B with whom I had worked in Cyprus and replaced in Nepal. I was pleased to see him again and surprised to see he had been commissioned, and was now a Lieutenant. Tony walked me around the 'Detail' area, where small items such as dental drills, surgical screws were picked and packed. This was to be my 'domain' and introduced me to Cora, a civilian, who was the supervisor of ten other young civilian women who picked the items for indents. Cora was the wife of Tom, also a civilian and the warehouse manager. Both had been at DMED for years.

I would also be responsible for Schedule 4 items (drugs such as benzodiazepines and others attractive to addicts), and controlled drugs such as morphine and cocaine.

From the detail area, Tony took me around the rest of the depot. There were many people, both military and civilian that I knew or knew of. Many greeted me, welcoming me to DMED, and I knew my short stay here would be a lot less stressful than my previous time in Hannover.

We ventured outside to the main gate and the guardroom. Here Tony told me where the keys to the safe were to be kept when I left the depot. They were never to leave the site and I had to keep them with me when I was in DMED. In the guardroom was a safe with the coded dial combination lock which Tony showed me how to change for myself. Once I had done this, I had a couple of practice goes to make sure I would be able to re-open it. Tony handed me the keys which were on the end of a long chain and I attached it to my belt and slipped the keys into my pocket.

From the guardroom our last stop before going back to which was now my department, we called in the office of Dave Y. Here I met up with another old friend, Chris W, who I had known on my dispenser's course in Colchester and was now a captain. Our paths had not crossed since 1968, although we had spoken on the phone a few times. Dave and Chris were busy building the computer network that would eventually form the heart of DMED.

Tony and I finally arrived back at the door of the safe. I took out my keys and opened up. The safe was a large room filled with racking and containing huge amounts of controlled drugs and dental gold. A quick glance suggested at least 10,000 'syrettes' of morphine, these being part of a soldier's personal first aid kit which were issued to those on active service. There were also 10 kilos of pure cocaine, along with boxes of pethidine and diamorphine (heroin). My 'office' in the safe consisted of a desk and chair, telephone, and a filing cabinet.

We spent an hour or so checking the controlled drug register and the account of the gold. Tony told me the accounts were checked at random, at any time without warning. I also had keys to locked and covered racking which held, what was then known as Schedule 4 drugs, and other attractive drugs known to be used by addicts. These items, including the controlled drugs were only to be picked by myself, Cora and her ladies had no access to them.

Tony would still be at DMED, he was the officer in charge of the mobilisation stores. Should I ever be off site, I would be able to hand the keys over to him to make any issues that were needed. During my time at DMED there were only a couple of times when this was necessary.

I spent the next couple of weeks getting to know my way around DMED and meeting up with friends around the depot. I issued a few drugs and watched Cora and her 'chickens,' as I came to refer to them, as they busied themselves around the picking area.

Mo and I had decided we would go house hunting in Stourbridge and the surrounding area. We would also go and get the boys from school for the weekend, easier now that they were both at Old Swinford; and we would be staying in Kingshurst. We took a long weekend off and travelled up to the Midlands, it was an easy drive of just under two hours.

I had a local paper and circled a few houses in our price range and made some phone calls when we were with Mo's mum, but most of those advertised were gone. So, we decided to go to Stourbridge, taking the boys with us and have a hunt around the local estate agents.

None that we approached had anything to offer, and we were leaving the last one when Mo spotted and advertisement on the door which was in our price range. We went back inside and spoke to the women at the desk, asking if that particular house was still for sale. She looked in her files and told us it was, and would we be interested in viewing it. We told her we would be and she made a call to the vendor.

After a few minutes, she said the owner was just going off to get her hair done and would be back home in an hour and would be happy to see us. We said we could go and get some lunch and see the house afterwards.

We settled on fish and chips in a restaurant in Stourbridge High Street, after which we got in the car and went to find the house. The first thing Mo said as we turned into the cul-de-sac was, "Oh dear, it's next to a pub!" I suggested we have a look anyway.

I rang the doorbell and after a few minutes an elderly lady who we came to know as Fran, answered the door and invited us into an open hallway. Our first impressions were that the house was light and airy and appeared to be spotless. It had also been recently decorated. The boys were immediately enthusiastic.

Fran showed us into the living room which was at least 20 feet long with a view out to a fair-sized garden. Fran disappeared into the kitchen and returned with a tray of tea which we drank while she told us about the house and herself.

She was a widow and had a house ready to move into once this one was sold. Great! there was no chain. After tea, she showed us the rest of the house. There were three good-sized bedrooms and a bathroom. Downstairs, the kitchen was large, there was utility room with the central heating boiler, a toilet, and a door into an empty garage. Best of all, the house was detached.

Mo was also keen, but perturbed about the proximity of the pub. Fran assured her that it was quiet and she had never had to complain about noise, or vehicles leaving at night. The house had been on the market for two years, the price being reduced a couple of times during that period. Fran gave us the telephone number for her son-in-law who was handling her affairs and told us that we should contact him if we decided to buy her house.

We sat in the car on the drive after we left and discussed the pros and cons. The house was half a mile from the boys' school, a bus into Stourbridge stopped opposite, there were just 24 houses in the street and all looked to be in a good state of repair. I had noted there were one or two things that need to be done, such as repairing the fence, replacing the French windows, and possibly up-grading the central heating. We also went next door and asked about the pub. The next-door neighbour assured us he had no complaints and had lived there for several years, having moved from a house just across the road.

In the end, we returned to the estate agent to tell them we were interested and would make a few more enquiries with Fran's son-in-law with a view to making an offer. Meanwhile the estate agent recommended a solicitor in Birmingham to manage the conveyancing.

I contacted Graham, Fran's son-in-law, to tell him we were preparing to make an offer on the house. He invited us to visit him at Fran's to discuss matters further and to assure ourselves that the pub was no problem.

In the event, it was a most convivial meeting and there was not a peep from the pub. Graham told us all the residents up the street were all very pleasant, and also agreed to meet us half way with repairs on the porch and garage flat roof should we go ahead with the purchase of the house. The house was a leasehold property, and Graham also suggested that he purchase the lease on Fran's behalf and we should then buy it off her. We also agreed a price for various fixtures and fittings. The next day we made a firm offer on the house, which was accepted.

Chapter 23
1 Gigmill Way, Stourbridge, West Midlands

I do not believe any house purchase went through without problems. We organised a surveyor's report which went reasonably well, apart from him picking up a crack in the outside wall of the kitchen. This called for the services of structural engineer who diagnosed a broken gulley pot in the drainage system. I called Graham to recommend a builder, he said he would send a couple of guys from his work force to make repairs. They did a good job, fixed the problem, repointed the kitchen wall, and re-levelled the patio. The surveyor's report also told us a complete rewire would be necessary, so I got a few estimates in and engaged a local electrician to do the work.

Once all the recommendations from the surveyor's report had been completed, we were provisionally granted a mortgage from the building society, dependant on a deposit of £5,000.00. Of this there was slight problem. I had applied for this sum to be paid in advance of pension and gratuities. The form had been duly signed and sent to DMED for signature, the money could only be used as part of the purchase of a house. A week later, the solicitor called to tell me the forms had been returned, but the advance had not been approved. I spoke to the chief clerk who told me the original request had been signed by the administration officer—a Major. The forms had to be signed by a Colonel, or above. New forms had been submitted, correctly endorsed by the Commandant of the depot, and should be approved within a matter of days.

We had also purchased the lease from Fran and the property was freehold. I received a letter from the solicitor advising us that all that was needed was for contracts to be signed and when would we be available to complete.

We had no telephone in the quarter and I decided to call the solicitors office as soon as possible to arrange a mutually convenient date. I drove out to find the nearest working phone box as snow began to fall, becoming heavier as I went. Eventually, I found a box, by now the snow was turning into a blizzard. Feeding pound coins into the box I eventually got through to the office and fixed a date. I do not believe many people have sealed the deal on a house from a telephone box on Salisbury plain in a blizzard!

We signed contracts at our solicitor's office just before Christmas and the house was ours. All we had to do now was to move from Tidworth to our new home in Stourbridge.

School broke up for the Christmas break within a couple of days after signing the contracts, so we picked up the boys and headed off to Tidworth. The holiday was a happy affair, turkey with all the trimmings along with thoughts of moving to Stourbridge in a few days.

I received a call from Graham while at work on the Monday after Christmas. The news was a little disappointing. Fran had gone to stay with Graham and his wife Annette over the holiday. When she left her house, she had switched off the central heating. A cold snap had led to frozen pipes and a radiator in the main bedroom had burst, flooding the room. Fran had returned home to find water running down the drive.

The bedroom carpet was a write-off, and a new radiator would be required. Graham assured me all the damage would be repaired within the week, but that would delay my collecting the keys. I asked him to call me when everything would be fixed, and when I would be able come and pick up the keys.

As matters turned out, I had to go up to Birmingham the following week. I Called Graham telling him I would collect the keys on the day and he gave me directions to his house. His house was just after junction 4 of the M5, on Hollies Hill, in Belbroughton, which I had to pass on my way to Stourbridge.

Graham hadn't given me the number of his house, but I knew he drove an expensive Mercedes saloon. Turning into Hollies Hill I drove down a lane of about a dozen houses looking for his car parked in a drive. It was nowhere to be seen and I turned back and stopped at the gates of a large mock Tudor house. There was a man painting the gates and I stopped to ask if he knew where Graham lived.

"Yes," he said, "he lives here." With that, he opened the gates and I drove through. The reason I could not spot the Mercedes was because a Range Rover and his and hers Jaguar coupes were parked in front of it. I rang the doorbell and

Annette came and invited me in. The house was beautiful with a highly polished hall floor. A 20-foot, decorated Christmas tree rose up into the stair well.

When I had first met Graham, I asked him what he did for a living. Knowing I was in the army he jokingly replied that he turned out-of-date NAAFI pies into pig food. I was later to find out his business did not revolve around a few expired foodstuffs, but in tonnes of out-of-date food items and quality control failures such as Mars bars, Easter eggs and boxes of chocolates.

Annette showed me into a sitting room and went off to make tea for us and to fetch the keys. Over tea she told me Fran had moved into her new bungalow about 500 yards up the road from Gigmill Way. I complimented Annette her on her lovely home, and left with the keys to our home in my pocket.

A couple of weeks earlier I had asked Derek, Eileen's brother, who had an HGV licence if he could hire a 7-tonne truck with a tail lift and help us move. Once I had got a date for collecting the keys, I contacted Derek and asked him to hire the truck and meet me at the house where I could leave my car and travel down to Tidworth with him in the 7-tonner.

When we got to our quarter in Tidworth and we parked on the grass outside the house. Mo had packed most of our belongings. Determined as we were to find a house, we had only opened a couple of our boxes. We now had to move the heavier items onto the truck. The tail lift was a godsend. Once Derek and I had manoeuvred the larger items out of the front door and onto the tail lift, sliding them into the back of the truck was easy.

By the time we had finished loading the truck, it was getting dark. Time to call it a day, get some food inside us, and head off to Stourbridge in the morning. It had also started sleeting and we hoped it would not turn to snow overnight.

The next morning it was wet, with damp snow on the grass. To our dismay the one of rear wheels of the truck had sunk into the grass and we could not get enough traction to drive the vehicle off the grass and onto the tarmac. The neighbours rallied to help us with their door mats which were placed under the stuck rear wheel. With a little coaching, Derek finally got the truck out of the grass on onto a more stable footing. The grass verge was a mess, and I was expecting a bill for it when I did the march-out the coming week. Thanking the neighbours profusely for their help we made our way to our new home in Stourbridge.

We unloaded the truck of our possessions and started the job of unpacking the boxes of essential items such as pot and pans, and crockery and cutlery. I still had five months left to serve in the army and returned to Ludgershall. Mo was happy for me to leave after the weekend and for her to carry on unpacking until I could get time to travel up to Stourbridge to help.

We had finished unloaded the truck and had settled down for a cup of coffee and a sandwich when the doorbell rang. I opened the front door to be greeted by one of our neighbours and his wife. I asked them to come in, apologising for the collection of boxes in the kitchen and hallway and showed them into the living room. I introduced Mo and Derek, whereupon they produced a bouquet of flowers and a card welcoming us to the neighbourhood.

I completed the march out of our last quarter on the Tuesday after I returned to DMED. Despite the damage to the grass verge, I got away with not having to pay any charges.

I had watched the Superbowl between the Chicago Bears and the New England Patriots on my portable television the night before. The game was famous for the touchdown scored by William 'the Refrigerator' Perry. The Bears won 36 points to 10.

I moved into the Garrison Sgts Mess in Tidworth and became a 'Bean Stealer,' a derogatory term applied to those of us whose family were living away, and were not subject to having to pay for accommodation and meals, unlike the single guys who had to pay living expenses in the mess.

I had applied for a resettlement course; an entitlement military personnel could apply for in their final six months service. I had opted for 'An introduction to the Building Trades,' essentially a three-week DIY course, affectionately known as 'Bricks and Sticks.'

I started the course in March in Aldershot, and Mike, who had left the army, offered to put me up at his house in Farnborough during the weekdays. There were about twenty others with me on the course who were to be taught basic building techniques, such as brick laying, plastering, electrics, carpentry, and plumbing. The latter instruction was very useful as, when I returned home, Mo told me one of the radiators in the bedroom was leaking. With the knowledge gained on the course, I was able to drain the system, resolder the leaking joint and get the central heating working, leak free, again.

Working in DMED was quite easy, I was given time off to attend job interviews, usually I managed to arrange these for a Monday or a Friday which gave me a long weekend off. As I still had time to serve, interviews were a foregone conclusion, as none of the companies were prepared to wait several weeks for me to start. At least, they were good practice in interview techniques.

With Mo now permanently ensconced in Gigmill Way, and me with a few months to go before I left the army, Jason and Justin became weekly boarders at Old Swinford. I would be able to see them altogether when I travelled up to Stourbridge at weekends.

Apart from our two boys we frequently had their schoolfriends staying with us over the weekend. Sometimes as many as four or five other boys shared our meal table. A consequence of this prompted one of our neighbours to ask Mo how many children we actually had!

Mo continued to explore the surrounding area of Wollaston and Stourbridge, frequently with Eileen who often came to stay. My mother and Mo's mother also visited. Mo met all of our neighbours and found them very friendly and helpful, which was a comfort to me knowing she would have someone to turn to while I was away in Ludgershall.

I wrote to Mr Potter at Old Swinford requesting that Justin and Jason should become day boys after the Easter holiday. I received a reply asking me to come and see him. I went up to the school where the headmaster said that it would not be a good idea for the boys to stop being boarders. Jason was in his last year of 'A' levels and had his own study, Justin was in his last year of 'O" levels.

I explained I was shortly due to leave the army and could become potentially unemployed, thus unable to afford the school fees. Mr Potter suggested I applied for a bursary to mitigate the fees, and had the forms ready and signed by himself.

I was duly awarded the bursary a few weeks after I left DMED, it came in the same post as a letter offering me a position with Bayer, the chemical and pharmaceutical company. Contacting Mr Potter, thinking I would have to forgo the bursary now I had a job; I was told the bursary was approved and I should not worry about it.

Soon the day came for me to leave the army, 19 May 1986, after 22 years. Apart from the unpleasantness in Hannover, Mo and I had had a great time travelling around the world.

Other than the troubles in Cyprus, I had never had a shot fired at me in anger. Memories of our time in Nepal will stay with me for ever. I believed I had served my country and my corps well, living up to the RAMC motto, "In Arduis Fidelis" (Faithful in Adversity.)

I had an interview with the Commandant of DMED who wished me well and good luck in civilian life. My successor had not yet arrived and I handed the keys to the safe over to Tony B.

I made a quick tour of the depot, saying goodbye to many friends, most whom I had known for much of my service. I left the depot to go to my car and make the drive to Stourbridge and Mo. The last person I saw as I approached the main gate was Chris W, now a Captain. As I was still in uniform, I snapped up a farewell salute to him, the last I would ever make. The next time I would be in the area would as a civilian for a final discharge medical in Tidworth in a couple of weeks' time.

Afterword

The light and love of my life died in my arms in New Cross Hospital, Wolverhampton in November 2016. She had been diagnosed with cancer just 12 short weeks previously. The wonderful woman who had been my wife, friend and lover was gone forever and I was devastated. In the 55 years of our life together, she had given me two fine sons and travelled the world with me. During her twenty years with me in the army, we had been separated for only 10 weeks, and she had never complained about packing up and moving to yet another one of our twenty-one houses. Indeed, she looked forward to another adventure. She was fearless, friend to all who crossed her path and I miss her terribly.

Her funeral was attended by over 100 of her friends and family, and donations raised over £1000.00, which was donated to Cancer Research.

On Sunday 26th March 2017, Mother's Day, most of her ashes were scattered high up on Kinver Edge, a nearby National Trust area, where she enjoyed walking with her many friends. I visit her often, chatting to her while gazing out towards the Malvern Hills in the distance. More are scattered in her beloved garden, in Jason's Garden in Portishead, and under a flame tree in Penang in Malaysia. She is as well-travelled in death as she was in life.